At one level, Hunter argues, these changes signify a decline in religious orthodoxy; at another the changing definition of orthodoxy. His provocative analysis of the changing cultural milieu of conservative Protestants is situated in the long-standing debate over the future of religion and of American hegemony in the contemporary "world order." As the form of religious orthodoxy to confront modern life longer and more intensely than any other, the case of Evangelicalism sheds new light on how "traditional" religions survive the constraints of modern life.

*Evangelicalism* offers a much-needed study of a major religious force in America. Its accessible prose and illuminating arguments will make it essential reading for anyone interested in Evangelicalism, in religious traditions, and in the dynamics of cultural change in America.

**James Davison Hunter** is assistant professor of sociology at the University of Virginia and is the author of *American Evangelicalism: Conservative Religion and the Quandary of Modernity*. He is the coauthor of *Cultural Analysis: The Work of Peter Berger, Mary Douglas, Michel Foucault and Jurgen Habermas* and *Making Sense of Modern Times*.

# EVANGELICALISM

# *Evangelicalism*
## THE COMING
## GENERATION

# James Davison Hunter

The University of Chicago Press / Chicago and London

JAMES DAVISON HUNTER is assistant professor of sociology at the University of Virginia and is the author of *American Evangelicalism: Conservative Religion and the Quandary of Modernity*. He is the coauthor of *Cultural Analysis: The Work of Peter Berger, Mary Douglas, Michel Foucault, and Jurgen Habermas* and *Making Sense of Modern Times*.

The University of Chicago Press, Chicago 60637
The University of Chicago Press, Ltd., London

96 95 94 93 92 91 90 89 88 87   5432

Library of Congress Cataloging-in-Publication Data

Hunter, James Davison, 1955–
   Evangelicalism : the coming generation.

   Bibliography: p.
   Includes index.
   1. Evangelicalism.   I. Title.
BR1640.H86   1987        306′.6        86-16022
ISBN   0-226-36082-2

*For my parents*

# Contents

vii

# Preface

Largely because of a superficiality of interest and a narrowness of intellectual concern, a good deal of misunderstanding continues to surround the religiocultural phenomenon of American Evangelicalism. To most, it still represents a cultural dinosaur (or as H. L. Mencken [1924] put it, a "childish theology" for "halfwits," "yokels," the "anthropoid rabble"— the "gaping primates of the upland valleys") that somehow survived into the twentieth century. Unbelievably (from the perspective of many), it not only survives but in many respects even thrives.

In an earlier work (*American Evangelicalism: Conservative Religion and the Quandary of Modernity*, 1983), I took up the "why" question (i.e., what accounts for the survival of an orthodoxy in a highly "secular" society?). In this work I am concerned mainly (though not exclusively) with the "what difference does it make?" question. That is, I am concerned with understanding the cultural costs and consequences of its survival in the modern world. In pursuing this question, this book aspires to make a contribution to a broader, more nuanced understanding of this much neglected and often maligned part of American life. Far from being a religious behemoth, simplistic in its social organization and inflexible in its social and religious conventions, it is a richly diverse cultural tradition whose encounter with the twentieth century (and particularly the late twentieth century) has involved it in a whirl of change—change which is intensely relevant to the larger social order.

A caveat—the language of adaptation and accommodation is periodically used to describe that change. The language is in many ways unfortunate because it implies a certain negative judgment, one that I do not necessarily intend. (In dealing with the phenomenon, I simply do not know of a more useful language.) On this issue, I personally am ambivalent. Given Evangelicalism's aims as an orthodoxy and as a social movement, I am not convinced that all of the changes it has undergone and is still undergoing are all that bad, yet neither am I convinced that they are all that good. I state that, however, as a private citizen and not with the authority of social science. In the end it is up to the guardians and the followers of orthodoxy to decide precisely what is acceptable and what is unacceptable change.

A word on the scholarly nature of this book is in order. This work is not intended primarily as a systematic social history, nor is it intended as a rigorous statistical analysis of quantitative data. It is rather (and above all) a *sociological interpretation*, admittedly speculative at many points, yet rooted in factual considerations and related to theoretical concerns in sociology generally and the sociology of religion particularly. In making this interpretation I hope also to make a contribution to an understanding of the fate of religion in the contemporary world order. I further hope to make a modest contribution to a deeper understanding of modern life—how ordinary individuals (for whom traditional religious and cultural realities still provide meaning, encouragement, and hope) make sense out of their daily lives in the modern world.

It goes without saying that I could not have accomplished this research and writing with my own resources or without the help of others. Financial backing for this research came from grants from the Society for the Scientific Study of Religion, the Lilly Endowment (through the aegis of the Institute for the Study of American Evangelicalism), Westmont College, and the University of Virginia summer grants program. Certainly as important was the generous support I received from a large number of people. Those who helped me administer the two main surveys were Stan Gaede, Brendan Furnish, Robert Suggs, Zondra Lindblade, Daniel Yutzy, Paul Johnson, Michael Allen, Richard Perkins, C. Melvin Foreman, Dean Pedersen, Samuel Logan, Donald Mason, Harold Westing, Glen O'Neal, Jack Balswick, and James Plueddeman. Gaede, Lindblade, O'Neal, Balswick, and Pedersen also helped me set up formal interviews with students at their respective institutions. Several others assisted me generously in the collection, coding, and analysis of other important sources of data: Phillip E. Hammond and Robert Gordon-McCutcheon for the public university survey; David Moberg for making his early 1960s student surveys available to me; and Jeffrey Schloss for working with me on the faculty survey. Along these lines, there are a number of students I would like to acknowledge as well. Marci Studholme and April (Trivonovich) West at Westmont College offered tremendous help in sorting through and organizing materials at the initial stages of this project; Jack Jernigan and Leigh Walter at the University of Virginia provided programming and statistical assistance later on. I owe special appreciation to Curt Whiteman of the Religious

Studies Department at Westmont College. He assisted me in conducting interviews with students at Talbot Theological Seminary, and with his theological acumen, he helped me to sort out many of the subtleties of theological debate that currently occupy professional Evangelical theologians. Ken Myer, John Muether, Joseph Foreman, and Boyd Reese, as well as several of my colleagues at Virginia including Paul Kingston, Martin Jaffee, and Abdulaziz Sachedina, engaged me in lively and informative discussion on the subjects of this book at various times. They were all influential in ways of which they were probably unaware. I also greatly profited from the careful reading of the manuscript given by Martin Marty and Grant Wacker and several anonymous reviewers. Two others deserve special acknowledgment. Stan Gaede not only helped me in the field but also offered invaluable critical expertise and moral support for the duration of my work. Robert Wuthnow, also for the duration, has been generous with his time and with technical advice, methodological sophistication, and theoretical insight. His high professional standards and his intellectual discipline have been sources of inspiration; his friendship has been a source of encouragement. Finally, I am enormously indebted to my wife, Honey (not least for her partnership on chapter 4 and her careful editorial work), and to my two children, Kirsten and Colin. Once again they endured academic eccentricity and tolerated familial inattention with extraordinary character and affection.

# Part One

# Introduction

# Evangelicalism as a Global Phenomenon

For well over a century, the future of all world religions has been in question—at least it has been considered so among the educated classes of the West. Out of this debate have emerged three general perspectives. The first and most important of these has been the view that religion will ultimately disappear as civilization progresses. Religious doctrine will be increasingly recognized by civilized people as superstition and mythology. Thus with the advance of modern technological innovations, people will no longer see the need for the safety and comfort of religious beliefs. A competing view has been that with modernization, religion may steadily disappear in its traditional forms yet reemerge in a secular guise. The need for rite, ritual, symbolism and all encompassing interpretations of life exists regardless of the type of society man creates. The form and substance of religion may change but its presence in society remains constant. The third and final perspective has been that in the long run, economic and political development really bring about no appreciable changes in religion at all. What may appear to be fundamental transformations in the culture of developing societies are, in fact, superficial cultural alterations. Supernaturalist beliefs and practices are just as prevalent today as they ever have been, though they exist in a manner appropriate to the time.

## EVANGELICALISM* AS A GLOBAL PHENOMENON

Theologically conservative Protestantism is just one player in the larger cast of world religions and, of course, its future as well has been in question through the past century. Most of the speculation, however,

---

*"Evangelicalism" here and throughout this book refers to the North American expression of theologically conservative Protestantism. As a term it is a broad umbrella encom-

has been about its demise. Yet until the mid–nineteenth century, one could hardly imagine anything but a bright future, for the presence and influence of theologically conservative Protestantism were widespread not only in the United States, northern Europe, and the United Kingdom but, indeed, throughout the world. Protestants everywhere expressed tremendous optimism, if not confidence, in the millenarian vision of a world completely evangelized, if not Christianized. Western colonial expansion was, of course, intricately linked with the bold initiatives and successes of the Christian missionary movement.[1] Nonetheless, the presence of theologically conservative Protestantism as an expanding global phenomenon continued through the end of the century.

Its greatest presence, as one might expect, was in the Anglo-Saxon countries. In 1900, roughly 41 percent of the North American population and 35 percent of the Oceanic population (Australia, New Zealand, New Caledonia, etc.) were theologically conservative Protestants. Though a major force demographically, what may be more important is that Protestantism remained the dominant cultural force in these settings at this time. The distinctly Protestant ethos of work, morality, leisure, and the like prevailed. This was also true to a great extent in Western Europe though only about 15 percent of its population would be properly considered theologically conservative churchmen (see table 1).[2] Though only very small percentages of the populations of East Asia, South Asia, Africa, Latin America, and what is now the Soviet Union and Eastern Europe were Evangelical Protestants at that time, the influence of Protestant culture also extended far beyond these numbers.

Since the turn of the century, substantial demographic changes have taken place within the ranks of conservative Protestants worldwide. Nineteenth-century confidence was, in many respects, short-lived for in all of the industrial powers of the West there were sharp decreases: in North America the percentage of conservative Protestants has decreased by one-fourth from what it was in 1900; in Oceania there was almost a 50 percent decrease; in the United Kingdom and Western Europe there was a drop of over 4 percent—to 10.2 percent of the population. Only marginal increases were made in Latin America and in the countries of

---

passing a wide variety of religious and denominational traditions—from the Pietistic traditions to the Confessional traditions and from the Baptist traditions to the Anabaptist traditions. As used here, it is synonymous with Protestant orthodoxy and conservative Protestantism and while not always synonymous with Fundamentalism it certainly would include it. That is (and let me be emphatic about this point), Fundamentalism is viewed here as a faction *within* Evangelicalism and not as a movement *distinct from* Evangelicalism. For a further elaboration of the terminological meaning of Evangelicalism, see my book *American Evangelicalism* (1983a, 7–9).

**Table 1**
Evangelical Christianity in the World
(Percentage of Total Population)

| | North America | Western Europe | U.S.S.R. and E. Europe | Oceania | Latin America | East Asia | South Asia | Africa |
|---|---|---|---|---|---|---|---|---|
| 1900 | 41.0 | 14.5 | 2.0 | 34.5 | 1.2 | 0.1 | 0.2 | 1.5 |
| 1980 | 31.7 | 10.2 | 3.3 | 19.1 | 4.3 | 1.4 | 1.1 | 8.0 |

SOURCE: Barrett 1982.

East and South Asia. The only significant growth has been in the less economically developed countries of Africa, where the percentage of conservative Protestants is presently more than five times what it was in 1900. Even so, only 8 percent of the African population is under this religious umbrella. While it is true that much of the speculation about the demise of this expression of Christianity in the world has been based upon wishful thinking, there has been, in brief, some empirical grounding for these pessimistic forecasts. Its future remains justifiably in question.

In attempting to responsibly understand the place of religion in the modern world, the demographic factor is clearly an important factor to consider. As important to this task, however, is an adequate grasp of the *cultural factor*—understanding the changes as well as the continuities in the way the religious is experienced, practiced, and believed by its adherents. Now it is a commonplace that the social context in which religion is placed exerts influence upon its quality and substance of expression. No religion transcends social structure. On earth anyway, the "city of God" is built within the "city of Man." Thus it is fair to presume that the enormous shifts in the social and cultural realms that have accompanied social change in the past two centuries, particularly in the West, would alter the texture if not the substance of religion. As Peter Berger notes, of the world religions, it is Christianity and specifically Protestantism which has had the most intense and enduring encounter with the modern world (1979a, xii). Within Protestant circles, virtually the entire theological enterprise for over a century has been directly or indirectly consumed by the passion to deal with this fact (in biblical hermeneutics and exegesis, in Christian ethics, in missiology, and so on). To be expected, repercussions have been felt among the vast majority of ordinary people. The events culminating in the Fundamentalist-Modernist controversy in the United States, for example, at the beginning of the twentieth century were only the start. Out of this emerged a Protestantism divided into conservative and liberal communities of faith. Most important here is the fact that each faction represented and continues to represent distinct responses to these broader changes associated with contemporary social change: one, an aggresive capitulation to the world of modernity; the other, a combination of reluctant accommodation and defensive reaction to it. In both cases, the substance of each respective world view is different from anything preceding it. In brief, the modern world order has been the chief source of Protestantism's century-long identity crisis. Thus in these cultural terms, the nature and future of conservative Protestantism in the world is also in question.

### EVANGELICALISM AS AN AMERICAN PHENOMENON

The position of theologically conservative Protestantism as a global phenomenon may depend in large part on how it fares in North America. For in spite of an overall shrinking demographic base, it is here, under the name of Evangelicalism, that it has its greatest force and vitality. Consider the following:

While virtually all Protestant denominations show increased membership growth between 1955 and 1965, it has only been the traditionally Evangelical denominations that continued this trend from 1965 to the present. Since 1965, membership in liberal denominations has *declined* at an average five-year rate of 4.6 percent. By contrast, Evangelical denominations have *increased* their membership at an average five-year rate of 8 percent.[3]

Conservative Protestants have increased their per capita annual church donations every five years since the end of World War II as measured in constant 1970 dollars. Since 1965, the average five-year increase has been 3 percent. Liberal Protestants, however, have decreased their per capita annual giving since 1965 at an average five-year rate of 1.6 percent. What is perhaps even more striking is the fact that Evangelicals give the church on average 44 percent more than do liberals. In 1983, for example, each Evangelical church member on average donated $535 per year while mainstream Protestants only donated $301.[4]

Private Evangelical primary and secondary schools have increased in number by 47 percent between 1971 and 1978, with a 95 percent increase in student enrollment (Wuthnow 1987). As of 1985, estimates rate the total number of such schools to be between 17,000 and 18,000, representing roughly two and a half million students.[5] This growth is occurring in a climate of sharply declining educational enrollment—

where between 1970 and 1980, overall enrollment in elementary and high schools of all kinds in the United States dropped by approximately 13.6 percent.[6]

Conservative Protestant publishing has also grown prodigiously in the post–World War II era. In this time, the number of periodicals associated with the Evangelical Press Association has grown to 310 and at present shows a net gain of 20 to 25 new member-periodicals per year. Likewise in Evangelical book publishing, the total number of specifically Evangelical publishing houses presently exceeds 70. Marketing a large share of the books published by these houses are independently owned and operated Christian bookstores, of which there are approximately 6,000. Close to 3,500 of these belong to the Christian Booksellers Association. In 1984 these stores alone accounted for one and a quarter billion dollars in gross sales per year.[7]

As of 1985, the 1,180 members and affiliated stations of the National Religious Broadcasters (an affiliate of the National Association of Evangelicals) handled 85 percent of all Protestant religious broadcasts in the United States and 75 percent of all Protestant religious broadcasts in the world.[8]

As of 1975, North America accounted for 70 percent of the free and subsidized Bible distribution in the world (Barrett 1981, 720). Evangelical organizations dominated this activity.

In 1980, the United States sent abroad thirty thousand Evangelical nationals as missionaries, constituting nearly eleven times the number of American liberal Protestant missionaries and twice as many as the combined number of Protestant nationals sent abroad from all of the countries of the world (Barrett 1981, 803; Ostling 1982, 52–56).

Together these facts point to a movement that is far from pale and lifeless. Its hale and hearty complexion relative to its counterpart on other continents, is nothing shy of remarkable. At the same time one can see that the Evangelical infrastructure does extend beyond American political boundaries.

Why conservative Protestantism is so vigorous in North America and the United States in particular is another issue. In part it is likely to be related to the general vitality of all religion in America. One perspective sees the intensive denominational plurality as the principal factor. While denominational dissent is a minor motif in England and countries of the European continent, it is institutionalized in America. A church in America is a denomination after all. As David Martin notes, the universalization of this form of religious dissent permits religion to take on as many images as there are social faces (Martin 1978). Therefore, in a word, there is something available for everyone. No one need be left without a religious expression appropriate to his/her unique psychic needs and social and religious tastes. All of American Protestantism before the great disestablishment at the end of the ninteenth century and conservative Protestantism after it (to the present) has been characterized by sectarianism of this sort. For the past century, sectarianism has been Evangelicalism's greatest strength. Parenthetically, it is this intensive denominational plurality which would also account for much of the Evangelical vitality in the African case.

Another view dealing more explicitly with the case of American Evangelicalism roots an explanation in the discussion of the modern world itself. The argument (Berger, Berger, and Kellner 1974; see also Bellah 1976) is simply that the processes of modernization (in the form of technically spawned economic growth, intense sociocultural pluralism, the bureaucratization of all major institutions and human conduct in those settings, the creation of the private sphere isolated from other spheres of human activity, and rapid cultural change, etc.) foster certain discontents for those people living in these social conditions. This experience has been described variously as a sense of "weightlessness" or "homelessness," "anomie," "alienation"—all, in any case, referring to a central problem of meaning for modern man. In other words, modernity creates conditions which complicate the ability of people to sustain a stable and coherent existence in the world. Modern man suffers from a crisis of belief. Those particularly affected may then find attractive any meaning system which promises resolution—world views offering reliable moral and social coordinates by which to live. Most conservative religious traditions would then benefit demographically by this as would the religious experimentation of the innovative but doctrinaire "new religious" movements and cults. Thus, it is argued, theologically conservative Protestantism in all of its diversity is simply carried along by the general but episodic resurgence of religious dogma in advanced industrial societies.

There are other explanations besides these two important ones. None of them is fundamentally incompatible with the others—each is undoubtedly true to a large extent. Regardless of why American Evangelicalism thrives, one is still left with the fact of its vitality. What is more, there are few indications that its vitality will abate in the very near future. But what does this mean for the future of conservative Protestantism generally in the world? The centrality of American Evangelicalism to the infrastructure of conservative Protestantism around the world has already been noted. Arguably, it is largely because of this vitality that one can speak of conservative Protestantism globally in cultural terms as "evangelicalized" as well. The institutional style and cultural ethos of the

American version are exported and reinstitutionalized in a non-American setting. Doubtless this is true to a large extent and it should come as little surprise. It is merely part of a more general phenomenon of cultural exportation of the West. Therefore, to the degree that conservative Protestantism globally depends on the financial, institutional, and personnel support of American Evangelicalism and to the degree that the cultural ethos of American Evangelicalism is exported and adopted elsewhere in the world, the place and future of theologically conservative Protestantism as a global phenomenon may, in fact, hinge on the way it fares in North America. The American movement will minimally play heavily in the course of affairs of global Evangelicalism into the twenty-first century. An understanding of the American case, while important in its own right, may also then be central to the broader query of the nature, place, and future of conservative Protestantism generally in this extraordinary time in human history.

### THE COMING GENERATION OF AMERICAN EVANGELICALS

Accordingly, the present inquiry focuses upon the conservative Protestant movement in America but takes as its special concern the coming generation in American Evangelicalism—those who will be the lay and professional leadership as well as a large portion of the rank and file membership of Evangelicalism in the next generation. It is principally based upon the results of a 1982–1985 attitudinal survey (the Evangelical Academy Project) of students and faculty at sixteen institutions of higher learning across the nation: nine liberal arts colleges (Wheaton College, Gordon College, Westmont College, Taylor University, Messiah College, George Fox College, Bethel College, Seattle-Pacific University, and Houghton College) and seven Evangelical seminaries (Fuller Theological Seminary, Gordon-Conwell Theological Seminary, Westminster Theological Seminary, Asbury Theological Seminary, Talbot Theological Seminary, Wheaton Graduate School, and Conservative Baptist Theological Seminary) (see Appendix). Each of these institutions is committed by charter to maintaining and propagating the core theological and religious tenets of the Evangelical world view. This sample of colleges and seminaries represents higher education at the very heart of mainstream American Evangelicalism.

It has been noted elsewhere that the mainstream is nonetheless far from monolithic but intensely diverse along many dimensions. The institutions sampled, but more importantly the students surveyed, reflect much of that diversity (see table 2). In varied proportions seminarians and collegians are represented in all of the regions of the United States

**Table 2**
Selected Background Characteristics of
Evangelical Academy Project Sample

| | Evangelical College Students (N = 1,980) (%) | Evangelical Seminary Students (N = 847) (%) |
|---|---|---|
| **Race** | | |
| White | 97 | 92 |
| Nonwhite | 3 | 8 |
| **Father's Occupation** | | |
| Professional | 20 | 17 |
| Business (high) | 5 | 3 |
| Business (low) | 26 | 37 |
| Clerk | 10 | 7 |
| Technical professions | 10 | 9 |
| Skilled worker | 12 | 9 |
| Laborer | 4 | 8 |
| Farm related | 4 | 4 |
| Clergy | 10 | 7 |
| **Father's education** | | |
| Grammar school | 2 | 9 |
| Some high school | 6 | 7 |
| Completed high school | 22 | 25 |
| Some college | 15 | 17 |
| College degree (four-year degree) | 24 | 18 |
| Postgraduate or professional school | 31 | 23 |
| **Region** | | |
| New England | 6 | 7 |
| Mid-Atlantic | 25 | 20 |
| East Central | 16 | 16 |
| West Central | 14 | 8 |
| South | 4 | 16 |
| Rocky Mountain | 3 | 5 |
| Pacific | 30 | 23 |
| Foreign | 3 | 6 |
| **City size** | | |
| Metropolis over 1,000,000 | 3 | 10 |
| Suburb of a metropolis | 12 | 14 |
| Large city (250,000–1,000,000) | 6 | 8 |
| Suburb of a large city | 12 | 9 |
| Medium city (50,000–250,000) | 11 | 14 |
| Suburb of a medium city | 7 | 5 |
| Small city (10,000–50,000) | 17 | 15 |
| Town (2,500–10,000) | 18 | 15 |
| Rural (under 2,500) | 15 | 10 |

and in the range of community sizes—cities of over a million inhabitants to small towns and rural areas. So too one may see diversity in their social class composition—from working-class families (little education and blue collar occupations) to lower-middle-class families (moderate education and white collar occupations of lower prestige) to upper-middle-class families (advanced technical and professional education and executive-level business and professional occupations) as well as church-related families (in which the chief wage earner is a professional missionary or clergyman). Curiously only 11 percent of the collegians and 4 percent of the seminarians had attended private Evangelical high schools—most attended public schools.[9] Before attending seminary, roughly one out of three (30%) of the seminarians had attended a private Evangelical liberal arts college, and one in eight (13%) attended a Bible college. Most of the remaining had attended a state university (39%) or a private, nonsectarian college (14%).

While nearly nine out of ten claimed to have had a born again experience, there was still considerable diversity along religious lines. For example, these students maintain affiliation with a range of denominations (fifty-six in all) and denominational traditions, from the most separatistic and sectarian (such as the General Association of Regular Baptists (GARB); Church of God, Anderson, Indiana; the Assemblies of God; the Plymouth Brethren; and various Pentecostal sects) to the mainstream denominations (such as the United Presbyterian Church, the United Methodist Church, the Lutheran Church in America, and the Episcopal Church). In terms of "denominational tradition," that is, the broader religious heritage, the majority of college students (58%) and seminarians (60%) were associated with the Baptist tradition.[10] Also represented in large numbers were the Holiness-Pentecostal (13%, collegian; 11%, seminarian) and the Reformational-Confessional (22%, collegian; 26%, seminarian). Finally, roughly proportionate to their presence in American Evangelicalism are those in the Anabaptist tradition (3%, collegian; 4%, seminarian). Beyond this, a sizable number claimed to be "charismatic," and most of these claimed to have "spoken in tongues."[11]

As has been noted elsewhere, Evangelicals in the United States are typically from the middle to lower echelons of the social class hierarchy—lower than all other major religious groupings. Though Evangelicals are found throughout the range of social positions, typically they are engaged in the lower-prestige occupations—lower-level white collar or blue collar work; they correspondingly exhibit the lowest degrees of educational achievement and have the lowest average annual family incomes. In light of this, it is apparent that the students in this study represent an elite of a sort. To begin, while they represent the range of social class backgrounds, a fairly large percentage (as one can see from table 2) come from families of relative privilege—middle and upper-middle class. In part a function of this fact, these students are and will be among the most highly trained Evangelicals in the country. As such they will have the formal credentials and the symbolic skills to be able to assume positions of leadership in local congregations as parishioners or in the career they pursue. Minimally, their chances of occupational mobility and higher social standing in their churches and communities stand far above those of their noncollege or nonseminary counterparts. Yet this cohort of students is not only distinguished by their middle and upper-middle-class backgrounds. They are also distinguished by other factors.

Like all institutional and formal education, Evangelical education can be differentiated along several continua: academic competitiveness, insularity, standing in the broader field of higher education, and the like. In these terms, Evangelical higher education on the whole has historically been seen as maintaining low standards on everything but the moral quality of its students' lives and as being sharply sectarian in its educational vision (implicitly anti-intellectual and antisocial) and has been held in low esteem by all but those in the subculture. In many respects this describes the present scene. Some diversity does exist, however, and though the continua representing that diversity may be shorter than those found in the broader culture, empirical cases do fall along their lengths. The colleges and seminaries in this sample are representative of the *most* academically competitive in the Evangelical world (see Appendix). They are also, generally, more liberal in their willingness to acknowledge and address competing secular interpretations of the issues of the liberal arts. As a result they are usually more highly regarded by Evangelicals and non-Evangelicals alike. Thus, the students attending these institutions would likely be at least slightly more achievement oriented and intellectually cosmopolitan than perhaps students attending the many Bible colleges in America or a classic Fundamentalist college after the fashion of Bob Jones University in Greenville, South Carolina, or Liberty University in Lynchburg, Virginia.

But these students are more than a cohort of highly educated Evangelicals. They also represent the "coming generation in American Evangelicalism." By generation, I mean more than a group of individuals with biologically determined age as their only common characteristic. It includes that but it is more. A generation is a social unit bound together by virtue of (1) a similar location in the social structure and a similar relation to the historical process; (2) a cultural system (e.g., common attitudes, values, beliefs, and the like predisposing its members to certain experiences and certain historically relevant modes of action and life-style; (3) social interaction and thus a degree of social solidarity among its members; and (4) a measure of self-consciousness as a social unit.[12] Being American, of similar age, relatively privileged among Evangelicals, and committed to the same cosmology are all obvious factors that together lend to the group's status as a generation of Evangelicals. Another factor which should not be overlooked is the kind and quality of education they are receiving. First off, as was mentioned, these institutions, while not enormously different from all Evangelical-related colleges and seminaries, are among the highest quality. Like all such institutions, they are also relatively free of the contaminating influences of the secular world. Their insulation owes to the fact that faculty, administration, and all but the very smallest percentage ($\approx 1\%$) of students are committed to an Evangelical theology. Perhaps most importantly, the networking that naturally takes place for career advancement is facilitated by an elaborate structure of credentialing institutions. The credentials bestowed by these institutions are not only an official recognition of academic achievement but, additionally, an official recognition of religious qualifications. The individual with a formal credential from an Evangelical college or seminary will be deemed "religiously safe" by his peers, by church congregations, and by an elder Evangelical establishment from whom and through whom he or she may seek employment and career mobility. Thus, this sample of college students and seminarians, if not constituting a sizable fraction of the future lay and professional leadership itself, is largely representative if that leadership. By virtue of their location in the Evangelical social structure, they are representative of a generation of elites and quasi elites who will, with all probability, be in positions of power to define the symbolic universe for the Evangelical movement in the future. At the very least, they will prove to be an important bellwether for the Evangelical movement in the coming generation. This contention is supported by the fact that the vast majority of the *current* leadership in the Evangelical movement (in such areas as periodical and book publishing, academia, evangelistic outreach, and social relief) has had formal training in an Evangelical college or seminary—a significant percentage of these have had formal training in at least one of the sixteen institutions included in the present study.[13]

## METHOD AND SCOPE

One may well wonder whether an attempt is going to be made here to predict the future of Evangelicalism. The answer is a qualified no. A good deal of research has made it clear that late adolescence and early adult-hood are crucial years in terms of value formation. Attitudes and opinions coalesce into a relatively distinct world view, a world view that remains essentially intact through old age. The pursuit of higher education through this period of the life cycle adds a peculiar twist to this pattern. Attitudes and opinions change through this period but they change in a particular direction. Higher education tends to liberalize the way in which people view the world and live their lives. For example, people come to tolerate and even appreciate diversity of cultural expressions; they experiment to various degrees with different life-style patterns; they even become more liberal on social, political, and religious issues. But what happens after the college years? Research on this indicates that what happens depends, in large part, on life experience after college—marriage and parenthood, professional (graduate) education, occupational changes, residential moves, etc. In spite of these intervening factors, certain general tendencies are discernible.[14] For one, experimentation becomes less frequent. While this is so, there is certainly little evidence of ideological retrenchment—that is, a return to a way of viewing the world characteristic of the precollege period. Higher education produces large, pervasive, and enduring effects. The knowledge one acquires and the changes which occur in one's value orientation during this formative period in higher education are, in large part, retained. In recent decades this pattern has held in spite of a growing conservativism in American culture. Data indicate that in many instances and value domains (such as religious belief and civil tolerance) the process of liberalization continues. In this way, the cultural ethos created, fashioned, and experienced by a particular generation at one particular (and formative) period in time will be carried with it to some degree into the future. There is, then, a qualified sense in which one can speak of predicting the future of American Evangelicalism.

Prediction, however, is not the central concern here. More important to our goal (though still slightly tangential) will be the effort to establish cultural trends in the Evangelical movement. As is the case for many research initiatives, directly comparable survey data from years past, which would facilitate trend analysis, do not exist. These patterns will thus be documented in a variety of ways, e.g., through the use of a plethora of related survey information, historical data, and archival sources. As such, systematic and anecdotal comparisons will be made of the world view of the coming generation with the views of conservative Protestants of a decade or two earlier, the views of the general population of conservative Protestants on the present scene, and official pronouncements of Evangelicals from the past and the present. Having said this, it bears repeating that while the analysis and precise measurement of cultural change is important, it is not nor could not be (by virtue of the kinds of information available) the central concern of this work.

The central focus of this book, rather, is the examination of the cultural milieu of contemporary American Evangelicalism, especially as embodied in this emerging generation of Evangelicals. In particular, this book concentrates on four general dimensions of the Evangelical cultural system: its theology; its view of work, morality, and the self; its ideal of the family; and its political culture. In the past century the first three of these were the major pillars of a religious and cultural orthodoxy. Most important, of course, is its theology. It is the center point from which the other dimensions are derived and legitimated. Work, morality, and the self on the one hand and its ideal of the family on the other, however, have been distinct spheres of meaning. In themselves they are dimensions of a cultural orthodoxy, demanding an equivalent conformity. The fourth area, Evangelicalism's political culture, has not been a long-standing feature of the Evangelical heritage (at least in its present configuration) though it has become an important part of the Evangelical culture on the contemporary scene. In short, it will be argued that fundamental changes have begun to take shape in all of these areas. These changes are so rudimentary that the world of the coming generation of Evangelicals may bear little resemblance to the Evangelical world of many previous generations.

Beyond this there will be the task of interpreting this present cultural configuration in the broader context of the social and historical realities of advanced industrial society. Culturally, what is the fate of Protestant orthodoxy in these circumstances? What does this suggest for its own role as a cultural force in the present world order? And finally as the form of religious orthodoxy to confront contemporary social change longer and more intensely than any other, might Evangelicalism be paradigmatic for all such orthodoxies? To attempt to answer these questions is to explore once more the general question of the future of religion. The Evangelical case, I maintain, offers an opportunity through which long-standing assumptions concerning religion and modernity can be reevaluated—a means by which the broader issues surrounding religion and the modern world order can be explored afresh.

# Part Two

# The World of American Evangelicalism
# Redrawing the Boundaries of Faith

# Theology: The Shifting Meaning of Faith

Theology has long occupied a central place within Protestant culture, perhaps the central place. The Protestant Reformation was, at the heart, a *theological* protest, which reverberated throughout northern European culture in the sixteenth century and thereafter. The Reformation established a precedent, for since that time the articulation and rearticulation of the substance of Protestant belief (as opposed to defining religious and moral authority [Catholicism], achieving particular spiritual experiences [Hinduism and Buddhism], or maintaining the cohesion of the religious community [Judaism]) has been the paramount task of the Protestant community. Protestantism's emphasis on belief is unusual in this regard. It seeks to distinguish itself—indeed, it achieves its very identity—principally through the substance of its theological tenets.

Evangelicalism shares with the larger Protestant phenomenon a fixation with theology. Yet its concern is far more intense. Not only do Evangelicals distinguish themselves from other religions this way, but they distinguish themselves from liberal Protestantism this way as well. Orthodoxy, strictly speaking, is a theological matter, not a moral or ritual matter as it is for some other faiths. Indeed, the history of conservative Protestantism in twentieth-century America has, in large measure, been the history of the effort to maintain the purity and integrity of its theology. Notably, the pursuit of doctrinal integrity has consumed not only theologians and ministers but the vast number of those ordinary people calling themselves Evangelicals or Fundamentalists.

The issue here (and one common to all orthodoxies) is the issue of boundaries, the theological criteria determining the range and the limits of acceptability. Such criteria provide a test for group membership: those who adhere belong; those who do not adhere entirely or on particular points do not belong. While all ideological systems or world views maintain cognitive, moral, and behavioral boundaries of one sort or another, religious orthodoxies are often distinguished by the narrowness with which these lines are drawn and the strictness with which they are enforced. Conservative Protestantism in the twentieth century is no exception.

Under siege by the dramatic social and cultural changes at the turn of this century, Protestantism split. The "disestablishment" largely followed two distinct strategies for dealing with those changes. Liberalism, of course, opted for the path of aggressive accommodation—adjusting religious and theological truths to account for the new and emerging realities of twentieth-century experience. Among other things, the result was the devaluation of the spiritual bases of Protestant faith, the accentuation of the social/ethical dimensions, and a marked trend toward universalization of spiritual salvation (Cauthen 1962; Hutchinson 1968). Conservative Protestantism, or Fundamentalism as it was then called, sought to resist the cultural pressures of the emerging secular order principally through a deliberate effort to reassert and defend the theological boundaries of the historic faith (Hunter 1983a, chap. 2; Marsden 1980). Out of this effort emerged a variant of the historic faith in which some doctrines became more prominent than others in Fundamentalist culture as measures of an individual's or a church's orthodoxy. Notably, the doctrinal nucleus comprising the "fundamentals" of conservative theology was regarded by liberal Protestants and most of the secular cultural elite as a form of theological obscurantism—ridiculously constricting and intellectually untenable. Yet, as mentioned, the defense of these fundamentals as the cognitive boundaries of Protestant orthodoxy has remained the central task of the conservative Protestant establishment in America for the better part of the twentieth century. What then can be said for its efforts? The focus of this question will be not on formal theology (the discourse of professionals (but on the "working theology" or practical theology by which ordinary Evangelicals operate and derive meaning.

## The Problem of Biblical Inerrancy

At the heart of the defense and maintenance of conservative Protestantism in the past century has been the tenacious insistence on the intrinsic faultlessness of the Bible as the Word of God. In the disestablishment of nineteenth-century Evangelicalism into liberal and Fundamentalist factions, few issues were more important to the Fundamentalist self-identity than the belief in the inerrancy of the biblical literature. Fundamentalists maintained that in the pursuit of the Social Gospel, liberals had abandoned the cornerstone of the faith. Without an unerring Bible as the standard and final authority on spiritual, religious, and moral matters, there would be no test by which to measure the ultimate truth or falsehood of doctrinal or spiritual innovations (Marsden 1980; Sandeen 1970). Christianity, without this authority, could then slip perilously into heresy; the purity of Christian truth could then be compromised. In the mind of the late nineteenth- and early twentieth-century Fundamentalists, this was precisely what was occurring in the development of liberal Christianity and the Social Gospel (Marsden 1980; Sandeen 1968; Handy 1971; Marty 1970; Hunter 1983a).

Inerrancy as a formal doctrine, however, really did not become part of the folk religion of Protestantism until the late 1880s (Marsden 1980, 51). Until that time Protestant culture had, in the main, simply presupposed the ultimate authority and reliability of the Bible. The Reformational principle of *sola Scriptura* was, indeed, the unifying principle behind American Protestantism to that point. The primitive forms of "biblicism" practiced by the Puritans, for example, endured through the early nineteenth century, particularly at the level of common faith.[1] The Bible was factual and it alone should be one's religious, moral, and social guide. In the face of the "modernist apostasy," this popular though intellectually undeveloped orientation toward Scripture was transformed. It *crystallized* into the formal doctrine of inerrancy. The doctrine of inerrancy came to mean that the statements and teachings of the Bible, as the inspired revelation of God written by men, are completely without error of any kind; the Bible is absolutely and exclusively true.[2] Though not a detailed guide to moral and ethical conduct for every conceivable life situation, in its statements and teachings on such principles it is also entirely true and without error. Finally, though not designed as a historical and scientific text, where it makes historical and scientific statements, it is again entirely accurate and true. Indeed, any science or scientific conclusion that does not conform to the factual statements of the Bible is regarded as illegitimate and even unscientific (Marsden 1980, 212, n. 8).[3]

Part and parcel of the doctrine of inerrancy has been a particular hermeneutic, or method of interpreting the biblical literature. The method is essentially literalistic, meaning that the Bible should be interpreted at face value whenever possible. This has not meant, as some have caricatured, that every single statement was to be understood in a literal sense (e.g., when Christ claimed to be the door, Evangelicals do not look for a literal door). The intent of the author is taken into account in interpreting the text. Though this intent would logically always be a point of debate, evidence overwhelmingly substantiates that a simple literalistic interpretation of an unreproachable Bible has been normative within Evangelicalism for the better part of the twentieth century.

It was certainly so at the beginning of the century as the lines of division between Modernists and Fundamentalists were being drawn. Chief among *The Fundamentals* (published between 1910 and 1915), around which conservatives rallied, was the defense of the authority of God in Scripture, particularly against the claims of modern science and a "higher criticism" that undermined, a priori, the supernatural and miraculous elements of Scripture. Up to a third of the essays in the eleven volumes of *The Fundamentals* were devoted to the defense of the integrity of the Bible. A decade later, William Jennings Bryan spoke for all of Fundamentalism in standing for Biblical literalism on such points as a six-day creation, a flood that destroyed the ancient world, a large fish swallowing the prophet Jonah, and the like. About the same time, Robert and Helen Lynd were conducting their rich and detailed study of "Middletown" (Muncie, Indiana). There they noted "a general feeling in Middletown that the book [the Bible] is 'perfect' and free from inconsistencies" (Lynd and Lynd 1929, 318). Even without differentiating between those who came from conservative families and those who came from more liberal families, the Lynds found that approximately two-thirds of the student body in a survey of high school students agreed that "the Bible is a sufficient guide to all the problems of modern life" (Lynd and Lynd 1929, 318). Such an orientation also prevailed in the Fundamentalist churches and sects in Gastonia, North Carolina, in the late 1930s as documented in Liston Pope's (1976) study of social change in that community.

When conservative denominations realigned in the early 1940s, the "fundamentals" of the faith were all publicly and officially reaffirmed. Thus, for example, at the top of the preamble to the constitution of the fundamentalist American Council of Christian Churches was the belief in "the full truthfulness, inerrancy, and authority of the Bible, which is the Word of God" (Gaspar 1963, 23). Moderates who dissented from the separatism of Rev. Carl McIntire and the ACCC, in establishing the National Association of Evangelicals in 1942 and 1943, also held at the top of their common statement of faith that the Bible is the "inspired, the only infallible, authoritarian Word of God" (Gaspar 1963, 28). These public reaffirmations of the centrality of Scripture to orthodox Protestant faith were not somehow detached from the views of the ordinary believer. To the contrary, they continued to have a deep resonance in the everyday faith of the average conservative churchgoer. For example, in an ethnography (conducted in 1948) of "Kent," a mill town in North

Carolina, researchers found that "of the patterns of belief that emerge from observation of and participation in mill-village religious life, none is more striking than faith in the Bible. The Bible is accepted as the ultimate authority in all religious matters, and to some extent in secular matters as well" (Moreland 1958, 131). Moreland, the author, goes on to say that "Literal acceptance of the Bible is the cornerstone of belief in the mill churches, and the Book is taken as a basis for making decisions in political, educational, and scientific, as well as religious areas of life" (1958,131). It was this passion for the total authority and infallibility of the Bible that was at the heart of the proliferation in Bible institutes around the country in the first half of the twentieth century. Before 1900, only nine such institutes had been formed, but between 1900 and 1930, forty-nine more were established. Such growth did not abate either, for between 1930 and 1940, thirty-five additional institutes were founded and in the following decade, sixty more (Gaspar 1963, 93).

By the 1960s, conservative Protestants had not altered their views appreciably. For the vast majority, the Bible was still literally and factually true. This is seen, for example, in a survey conducted in 1963 where church members overwhelmingly affirmed the complete authenticity of the biblical miracles—that "miracles actually happened just as the Bible says they did."[4] They also maintained absolute certainty in the deity of Christ, his virgin birth, his actual return to earth, and a life after death.

From all appearances little altered in the next decade or so. Surveys continued to show nearly universal commitment to the absolute authority and even inerrancy of the Bible. All major Evangelistic organizations, such as colleges, seminaries, youth groups, and events (such as the Lausanne Conference in 1974), also continued to affirm this belief.[5] Given this long-standing tradition one might assume that an Evangelical theology of the Bible is safely institutionalized—that it is no longer a matter of discussion or debate. A closer look, however, suggests less stability than might be supposed.

It is not as though the popular reverence for the Bible traditionally held by Evangelicals has diminished by the present day. It has not. However, early twentieth-century understandings of biblical inerrancy and traditional methodologies for interpreting the biblical literature have minimally softened among contemporary Evangelicals. The results of the Evangelical Academy Project provide an initial indication of a diversity of perspective (see table 3). Roughly 40 percent of all respondents (collegians, 38%; seminarians, 43%) maintain the traditional orthodox position (i.e., that the Bible is the inerrant Word of God). For both groups students were careful to point out that interpreting the

Scriptures "literally, word for word," did not mean that, for example, obvious symbolic language is to be interpreted literally.

> History is to be read as history, metaphor as metaphor, symbol as symbol, parable as parable, and so on. The context of the passage and literary style of the author must be taken into account. (male, third-year master of divinity candidate, Church of Christ)

> The Bible has a lot of figurative language: e.g., the hills leap, the earth has ears, the sun rejoices, knows, rises, and sets. However, when the Bible speaks self-consciously about history, we are to read it literally (e.g., Creation, the Flood, the Exodus). (male, junior, biology major, Baptist)

> The Bible is to be taken literally but it must simultaneously be taken in its literary, cultural, and historical context. (male, second-year master of divinity candidate, Presbyterian)

**Table 3**
Views of the Bible according to Campus Setting

|  | Evangelical College Students ($N$ = 1,980) (% agreeing) | Evangelical Seminary Students ($N$ = 847) (% agreeing) |
|---|---|---|
| 1. The Bible is the inspired Word of God, not mistaken in its statements and teachings, and is to be taken literally, word for word | 38 | 43 |
| 2. The Bible is the inspired Word of God, not mistaken in its teachings, but is not always to be taken literally in its statements concerning matters of science, historical reporting, etc. | 50 | 54 |
| 3. The Bible becomes the Word of God for a person when he reads it in faith | 10 | 3 |
| 4. The Bible is an ancient book of legends, history, and moral precepts recorded by men | — | — |
| 5. Don't know | 2 | — |

NOTE: — = less than 1%.

The majority (collegians, 50%; seminarians, 54%), however, maintained the view that "the Bible is the inspired Word of God, is not mistaken in its teachings, but is not always to be taken literally in its statements concerning matters of science and historical reporting, etc." The difference between this choice and the former is subtle. It does, however, suggest a slightly more critical approach to biblical interpretation. Implied is the recognition that there are some, if only a few, statements in the biblical literature that were intended by the author to be historical or scientific in nature but may in fact be mistaken or contradictory. In this view, the religious, spiritual, and moral integrity of the Bible is in no way impugned. Nonetheless, human error, even if slight, is recognized.

Of those holding this position, it was emphasized by many that one should not attach too much significance to these flaws if only because of the fact that the primary purpose of the Scriptures is not to be a historical or even scientific text. Conversely, it would be inappropriate to impose the canons of modern scientific inquiry upon a document written over nineteen centuries ago. Said one college student, "I don't think it made mistakes in terms of the culture in which it was presented. When our twentieth-century scientific standards are imposed upon it, I'm not sure it can hold up to that but that's unimportant." Another noted: "I don't think historical reporting is the primary purpose of Scripture, but I think there could be human errors within it. I don't think there would be historical errors that would interfere with what it is that God is teaching through Scripture. . . . It does not make errors in what the Bible teaches us." As still another student put it, "some of the Bible is contradictory, but that's not the essence of what the Lord wants us to know." What is at stake here? In simple terms, the traditional response of Evangelicals would have hypothetically been that "the primary purpose of the Bible is not to be a historical or scientific text. Nevertheless, when it makes statements of historical or scientific fact, it does not err." The position taken by a majority surveyed in the Evangelical Academy would be that "the primary purpose of the Bible is not to be a historical or scientific text. Therefore, it might make mistakes of this kind, but that does not compromise its authority as the Word of God."

## The Threat of Neo-Orthodoxy

These differences might appear to be picayune to an outside observer, but within the Evangelical culture, they have been tremendously significant. Yet even more significant to the Evangelical view of the Bible has been the threat of "neo-orthodoxy."[6] As a theological movement, neo-orthodoxy emerged between World Wars as an attempted reversal of liberalizing trends in theology dominant in the period. Under the leadership of such theologians as Karl Barth and Emil Brunner, neo-orthodoxy became a formidable challenge to secular theological currents, attempting to establish itself as a new Reformation. Soon after World War II, however, the movement lost its impetus. Both its size and influence dwindled steadily. Though an infrastructure for neo-orthodoxy still exists today, overall this movement performed little better than most theological movements of this century, being an ephemeral fashion.

Though never a uniform theology, as a mode of theological discourse, it attempted to reestablish an intellectually defensible orthodox theology—faith unconditionally based upon God's revelation. From a distance, neo-orthodoxy would appear to have provided general ideological support for an increasingly beleaguered orthodox Protestant faith. But American Evangelicalism from the beginning, and especially in the postwar period, actively maintained a distance from neo-orthodoxy. More than that, it marked neo-orthodoxy as a bastard orthodoxy, a pale replica of the true faith, and, as such, a dangerous theological deception.[7]

The Evangelical complaint has been multiple. Though neo-orthodoxy advocates the Reformational conviction that the Bible is the sole authority for religious faith and Christian life, Evangelicals have argued that this does not go far enough. Where Evangelicalism argued that the Bible itself in its original form is the unerring Word of God, neo-orthodoxy argues that the Bible "becomes" the Word of God. It is only when the individual reads or hears the Scriptures through the eyes and ears of faith that the text becomes the Word of God. What is more, neo-orthodoxy has devalued the historicity of the biblical account of historical events. The crucial issue from this standpoint is not that these events actually occurred but simply that God is trying to teach us something of spiritual significance by the symbolism in these stories. Thus, for example, the believer does not have to be concerned whether or not the origin of the world occurred precisely in the manner described in the Book of Genesis. What is central is that the believer learns from this that, among other things, God is the source and creator of life. In its logical extreme, this form of theologizing would conclude that it is unimportant whether the Resurrection of Christ actually occurred, but merely that God is teaching the believer something of tremendous importance by this story. But if the Bible does not become the Word of God until it is appropriated by the believer in an act of faith, then the *meaning of a text or a story would necessarily vary for each believer* since everyone would be approaching the Bible from a different life situation. One then cannot speak of ultimate truth per se, only ultimate truth for each believer. In sum, the neo-orthodox position advocates a *subjectivist* approach to biblical interpretation in contrast to the Evangelical's more *objectivist* approach (where, presumably, the ultimate truth and meaning of a text is plain and objectively apprehended).

Though the neo-orthodox movement in theology has played itself out, there are indications that as a mode of theological discourse, it may be gaining intellectual credibility and popular support—yet not from the ranks of disaffected liberals but, rather, from *within* Evangelical quarters. Marginal indications of this can be seen in table 3. At first blush, it appears that the neo-orthodox view of the Bible ("the Bible becomes the Word of God for a person when he reads it in faith") is plausible only to a small minority in the Evangelical Academy (collegians, 10%; seminarians, 3%). There are other signs of support for the neo-orthodox position that are more subtle than this but no less telling. Illustrative of this are the responses to specific points of doctrine.

When asked about their views of the Devil, the majority of collegians (85%) and seminarians (93%) gave the traditional conservative response that the Devil is a personal being who directs evil forces and influences people to do wrong (see table 4). Only 11 percent of all college students and 4 percent of the seminarians held the more neo-orthodox view, that the Devil is an impersonal force influencing people to do wrong. Even more suggestive are the responses to the questions concerning the origin of man. Once again the majority (collegians, 78%; seminarians, 79%) maintained the traditionalist view that human life began with God's creation of Adam and Eve. Nonetheless, a small though significant percentage (14%) held the view that "God began an evolutionary cycle for all living things, including man, but personally intervened at a point in time and transformed man into a human being in his own image." Though conservative in tone, something less than the early twentieth-century literalism is represented by this option.[8] When asked directly about their views of the biblical account of the origin of the world, just under 30 percent affirmed the view that the world was created in six twenty-four hour days. Another one-third believed that the world was created in six days as the biblical account maintains, yet that each day was an age corresponding roughly to a geological age or period. Most importantly, nearly 17 percent of all Evangelical college students and 21 percent of all seminarians opted for the neo-orthodox position: the biblical account of the origin of the world is intended to be symbolic and not literal. It is significant that one-fourth of all Evangelical collegians and one-fifth of all seminarians could not decide where they stood on this issue. For this large number of Evangelicals, the question of interpretation is not clear-cut, implying again that there is a move away from conventional certainties on such matters. A neo-orthodoxy impulse of limited expression then appears, at a closer glance, to be making some inroads in the practical theological thinking of Evangelicals.

When pressed on the problem of interpreting the Bible, the indica-

**Table 4**

Stance on Doctrinal Issues according to Campus Setting

| | Evangelical College Students (N = 1,980) (% agreeing) | Evangelical Seminary Students (N = 847) (% agreeing) |
|---|---|---|
| Views of the Devil | | |
| 1. The Devil is a personal *being* who directs evil forces and influences people to do wrong | 85 | 93 |
| 2. The Devil is an impersonal *force* that influences people to do wrong | 11 | 4 |
| 3. The Devil does not exist, either as a being or as a force | — | — |
| 4. Can't say | 4 | 2 |
| | | |
| Views of the origin of man | | |
| 1. God created Adam and Eve, which was the start of human life | 78 | 79 |
| 2. God began an evolutionary cycle for all living things, including man, but personally intervened at a point in time and transformed man into a human being in his own image | 14 | 14 |
| 3. God began an evolutionary cycle for all living things, including man, but *did not* personally intervene at a point in time and transform man into a human being in his own image | 1 | 1 |
| 4. Man evolved from other animals | — | — |
| 5. Can't say | 7 | 6 |
| | | |
| Views of the biblical account of the origin of the world | | |
| 1. The world was created in six twenty-four hour days | 28 | 29 |
| 2. The world was created in six days, but each day was an age corresponding roughly to a geological age or period | 30 | 31 |
| 3. The Biblical account of the origin of the world is intended to be symbolic and not literal | 17 | 21 |
| 4. Can't say | 25 | 19 |

NOTE: — = less than 1%.

tions became more clear. Even among those who maintained traditional doctrinal positions, more than a trace of reservation was apparent. Concerning the issue of the origin of the world, the following comments were typical:

> When I think of Adam I think of the first man that was created, Eve, the first woman, and I think of a literal garden and the literal trees that were there. I can understand, however, and am open to the idea of the creation story being symbolism—God teaching us something about himself. (male, sophomore, sociology major, Presbyterian)

> I was brought up to believe that the creation story was real, and I guess I would kind of lean toward that, but I would feel comfortable with a symbolic interpretation too. (female, sophomore, music major, Southern Baptist)

> I lean toward the fact that creation probably happened as it is described in the Bible. It makes sense that the human race began not with a herd of people but with the original man and woman. I see the story as a whole, the garden, the trees, Adam and Eve themselves as actual things, but the story as a whole could have been figurative. . . . I probably wouldn't argue strongly either way. (male, junior, elementary education major, Independent Fundamentalist)

Concerning the story of the prophet Jonah being swallowed by a large sea creature, students responded similarly:

> I would tend to say that he was swallowed by a large fish or whatever the Bible says, but I would not rule out the possibility that it is a figurative statement to teach us something about the nature of God, the nature of our calling, and the nature of our expected response to God. It's important that Jonah was swallowed by a whale to the way the story progresses. It is not important to me that it happened historically. (male, junior, elementary education major, Independent Fundamentalist)

> It is not crucial to me that it happened historically, though I have always believed that it was. God's message is far more important. (female, senior, sociology major, nondenominational)

It is important to point out that nearly all of these Evangelicals maintained a strong literalist approach in understanding the life of

Christ, his miracles, his crucifixion, his resurrection, and so on. An implicit distinction, then, was imposed on the biblical events that were important to be read literally and those that were not so important.

So what is really occurring here? There is little doubt that the coming generation holds the Bible in high regard and that they see it as central to their faith. One student expressed it this way:

> If the Bible isn't true, everything in my life would be so tentative. I think there would be no rock to go back to. Why hold so tightly to my faith if it is not even stable? (female, senior, English literature major, nondenominational)

Another remarked similarly:

> If we can't believe the Bible is our authority, then we really don't have much besides an emotional experience or some kind of abstract feeling. (male, sophomore, elementary education major, nondenominational)

In the spectrum of theological opinion, it is clear that the coming generation of Evangelicals remains squarely conservative in its view of the Bible and in its method of interpretation. Thus, on the surface, little has taken place at all. Yet on Evangelical terms, that is, in terms of the way the "doctrine" of inerrancy has historically been defined by Evangelicals themselves, one can see that a dynamic is at play. The essence of this dynamic is a retreat from a position of strict inerrancy celebrated in the early decades of the twentieth century. In a word, the key is that the Bible is the final authority in matters of faith and practice, not that it is inerrant on all technical, historical, or scientific points. In this light, the late nineteenth- and early twentieth-century Evangelical defensiveness—the urgency to uphold or defend a totally unerring Bible—appears to have weakened dramatically. Most students surveyed felt that Christians have spent too much time in the past defending what they themselves considered "unimportant" or "meaningless" or "inconsequential" matters, such as the historical validity of many biblical events (e.g., that time really stood still for a day, that the world really was created in six twenty-four hour days). Such matters, as one seminarian noted, "are not essential." At least now they are not considered essential. Such was the measure of "true faith" a generation or two before. The coming generation, then, is less demanding in its expectations of the Bible. Beyond this, however, there is a marked tendency toward "hermeneutical subjectivism" (the neo-orthodox impulse) on the part of a substantial number of Evangelical students as seen in the willingness of students to view portions of Scripture, traditionally viewed as historical fact, as symbolic representations of some spiritual reality. Biblical literalism as previously understood would then be considered excessive for most in the coming generation. Minimally, these cultural tendencies represent a softening up of culturally galvanized doctrine, and they may foreshadow further shifts in Evangelical theology. This argument gains plausibility when considering the developments in Evangelical intellectual circles and, particularly, theological circles. Here these trends are well established.

## Trends in Formal Theology

The discussion about the Bible is, of course, held at a higher level of sophistication than it is among laymen, but the issue remains the same: what is the nature of the Bible? As an intellectual problem, this question has been pursued at different levels. *Philosophically* it emerges as a dilemma surrounding the humanity of Scripture. Even though all Evangelical theologians maintain the belief that the Bible is the divinely inspired Word of God (98% according to one survey), differences in the actual interpretation of the Bible by Evangelical scholars accentuate, for some Evangelicals, the reality that the Bible was written down by fallible, error-prone, and often foolish human beings who had different biographies, who lived and wrote in different historical periods and different socio-cultural contexts. Given these facts, the meaning of "inerrancy" and "infallibility" becomes a riddle indeed. Concluded one Evangelical theologian, the commonly accepted Evangelical concept of biblical inerrancy is "exegetically improbable, hermeneutically defective, theologically dangerous, and educationally disastrous" (Ramm 1983, 34; see also Dunn 1983, 118).[9] This theologian is not alone, for nearly 40 percent of all Evangelical theologians have abandoned the belief in the inerrancy of Scripture.[10] Nonetheless, whether the above statement is finally true or not, it is clear that there is no universally held working hypothesis for Evangelicals as they confront the human element in Scripture; there is no consensus in the application of principles of inerrancy or infallibility to biblical understanding. The irony, of course, is that Evangelical theologians insist that the Bible is the sole authority in spiritual and religious matters, and yet, as a profession, they are unable to come to any agreement on what the Bible says.

Closely related to this is the *methodological* problem of appropriating the message of a Bible that is at once divine and human in an era of modern biblical criticism: how to maintain integrity with both the doctrinal creed of Scripture as the absolute Word of God and, at the same time, the historical treatment of Scripture as the words of men. At the heart of this is the debate over the use of modern techniques of literary criticism as tools for biblical study. "Redaction criticism" is one such technique, the purpose of which is the analysis of the ways in which the human authors of Scripture edited their materials (through selection, deletion, addition, and embellishment of information) in order to more effectively make a theological point. Robert Gundry's (1982) literary and theological commentary on the Gospel of Matthew was not the only example of the Evangelical use of these techniques in the early 1980s (another key example is Guelich 1982), but it was perhaps the most important one. Gundry argued that large sections of this gospel were, in fact, Matthew's own divinely inspired reflections on the meaning of Jesus's ministry, rather than a historical and factual presentation of the actual words and deeds of Jesus. Thus, for example, Matthew "turns the visit of the local Jewish shepherds [in the Christmas narrative] into the adoration by Gentile magi from foreign parts" in order to develop the theme of Christ's mission to the Gentiles. More than an example, Gundry's *Matthew* became an important symbol: for some, a symbol of the creative potential of Evangelical theology after decades of stagnant theologizing; for others, a symbol of the decline of orthodoxy into modernist heresy. The divisions that have ensued the publication of this book (including Gundry's own "heresy trial" at the 1983 Evangelical Theological Society meeting) betray a theological tradition in disarray.[11]

Corresponding to these developments have been perplexities in the way Evangelicals view themselves theologically—a problem of self-identity expressing itself as the question, theologically, what does it mean to be an Evangelical?[12] While there has always been a measure of imprecision and debate about this among Evangelicals, the imprecision is expanding. For what one finds is a brand of theology that for generations had been considered "modernistic" being advocated by theologians who vigorously defend their right to use the name of evangelical. What is more, some Evangelical theologians are facing up to these developments squarely and rather than rejecting them out of hand (as had long been the practice) are, instead, welcoming the "liberal" (read, neo-orthodox) theologians and their contributions. Evangelical theologian Bernard Ramm's (1983) recommendation that Evangelicals accept Karl Barth's paradigm for coming to terms with both the humanity of Scripture and biblical criticism is one telling illustration of this.[13]

It is difficult to assess just how far these trends have gone or for how many these developments represent the cutting edge for Evangelical theology. The issues are highly sensitive in Evangelical circles and those who hold such positions would not be likely to advertise what they know others consider to be suspect if not heretical. But the extent of this phenomenon is less important than the fact that the phenomenon exists at all. Open debate exists at all levels where there was once little or none at all, only reflexive and defensive reaction. For example, on the question of the origin of the world, 48 percent of all Evangelical theologians in America have abandoned the popular, early twentieth-century view that evolution is a denial of God's creation. Instead they view it as an explanation of how God works in creation. So too on the problem of final matters, there was virtual consensus on the belief in immortal life and even final judgment, yet a sizable minority (18%) were not willing to believe in "a place of eternal torment" for nonbelievers.[14]

Curiously, it is not as though these philosophical and methodological problems did not exist before. They have, of course, perplexed liberal Protestants for more than a century. But it is only now that these issues are relevant to the Evangelical theological experience; for the better part of the 1900s, these issues were simply ignored. These issues are now problematic for Evangelicals because they have defined them as problematic. Lending legitimacy to these "problems" may prove the opened Pandora's box for Evangelical theology in the long run.

Upon reflection, it is not accidental that discontent in these areas is visible in theological circles. The role of intellectuals in undermining established ideologies (albeit, even unintentionally) at least since the Enlightenment is well documented.[15] Indeed, such activity is part of the stock-in-trade of all intellectuals. The irony in the Evangelical case is that the emphasis placed upon gaining intellectual credibility for the Evangelical position (from the late 1940s to the present) may ultimately have the unintended consequence of undermining the Evangelical position. What began as an enterprise to defend orthodoxy openly and with intellectual integrity may result in the weakening or even the demise of orthodoxy as it has been defined for the better part of this century. To come full circle, the weakening of the plausibility of traditionalist approaches to the Bible among Evangelical intellectuals appears to be foreshadowing a similar dynamic among the larger Evangelical population. The pattern is well documented. Philosophical innovations, and ideas generally, originating from an elitist echelon in society have a marked proclivity for filtering down to the rest of the society's population. The experimentations of a cultural elite often become, in time, the canons of the populace. But for now this is idle speculation. Other dimensions of the working theology of Evangelicalism beg to be considered now.

### THE PROBLEM OF SALVATION

Equally central to an Evangelical theology is its particular "soteriological" formulation. Soteriology is simply the theological problem of salvation—how does one enter into the state of eternal rest? There is considerable diversity in the world religions on this matter. As is obvious enough, Evangelicals hold to conventional Christian perspectives. Salvation is only possible through faith in Jesus Christ. The exemplary life is, in itself, insufficient to merit the heavenly reward.

The importance of this belief to orthodox Christianity should not be underplayed. Over nineteen centuries of Christian missionary activity hinged on this belief alone: that those who did not believe in the salvific capabilities of Jesus Christ had no hope of receiving eternal life. It followed that the unevangelized—those who had lived without the knowledge of the claims of Christianity—would also be damned to an eternity in hell. These were the "heathen," who, in the words of one Victorian hymn, were "bound in the darksome prison house of sin, with none to tell them of the Savior's dying, or the life He died for them to win."[16] Regardless of whether they "framed their lives according to the light of nature, and the laws of the religion they professed," to believe otherwise was as the Westminster Confession of Faith put it "very pernicious and to be detested."[17] They were "lost in the ruin of sin" without the saving grace of Jesus Christ. It was, after all, the spiritual status of the heathen in conjunction with the compassion felt by Christian people of conscience which dictated the sense of urgency about missionary work. Missionaries from the Reformation on viewed themselves as those who "went as dying men" (referring to the high mortality rate of missionaries) "to preach to [spiritually] dying men."[18] Thus, it is this exclusivism (Christianity as the one true faith) and the passions it spawned among the faithful that have been at the center of almost as many centuries of Christian expansionism in the West.

The exclusivism and finality of the Christian soteriology is also the single most socially offensive aspect of Christian theology; the single most important source of contention between Christians and non-Christians (Cuddihy 1978). For Evangelicals, all other religious faiths and world views are either misdirected or else patently false and, therefore, potential instruments of satanic delusion. There is only one absolutely true faith. The emotional, not to mention intellectual, hostility this would engender for non-Christians is predictable. Yet without this particularity, there is no orthodoxy (historically understood).

In the face of intense religious and cultural pluralism in the past century, the pressures to deny Christianity's exclusive claims to truth have been fantastic. Intensive cultural pluralism, one of the hallmarks of the modern world order, has, at least in the United States, institutional-ized an ethic of toleration and civility. To be sure, the net effect of theological liberalism in the past century and a half has been the repudia-tion of the exclusivism of the Bible (as the only true religious authority) and of faith in Jesus Christ (as the only means of eternal salvation). Yet by contrast, the heritage of Evangelicalism in the past century has been one of continuity with historic Christianity along these lines—a stout defense of these principles.[19] Along with the defense of the Bible, this posture has largely defined the character of conservative Protestantism in America. Once more, however, shifts in the Evangelical theological view of salva-tion are discernible.

From the survey of the Evangelical Academy Project it appears that most retained traditional convictions about these matters. For example, when asked whether they personally believed that a place of eternal torment exists for those who do not believe in Jesus Christ, 95 percent of all Evangelical seminarians said they did. Yet when asked about their views about life after death, more insight was gained. Approximately two-thirds of those surveyed (collegians, 66%; seminarians, 68%) held the traditional view that "the only hope for Heaven is through personal faith in Jesus Christ" (see table 5). One out of three, however, held the view that "the only hope for Heaven is through personal faith in Jesus Christ *except for those who have not had the opportunity to hear of Jesus Christ.*" The difference between these perspectives is, from the perspec-tive of historical orthodoxy, very important. Those holding to the latter imply that some form of alternative arrangement is provided for those not exposed to the truths of Christianity. God's dealings with the un-evangelized are somehow different from his dealings with those who have heard.

The difference between this generation of Evangelicals and previous generations on this point is noteworthy. In 1948 a researcher examining the religious views of the townspeople of a small, southern mill town (most of whom were conservative Protestants) noted the belief that all non-Christians would go to hell when they died, yet there are "varying degrees of heat." "The hottest [parts of hell] are reserved for those who have had an opportunity to hear about the Savior but have not heeded him. There is less severe punishment for the ones in China and elsewhere who have never had a chance to hear about Jesus" (Moreland 1958, 136). In a survey of midwestern Evangelical students in 1964, a similar sentiment about the fate of all non-Christians was found. Roughly 93 percent agreed that "all men are going to hell unless they receive Christ as their personal Savior," and 98 percent agreed that "those that reject Jesus Christ will *eternally* suffer the torments of hell."[20] Yet even in this

## Table 5
### Views of Life after Death according to Campus Setting

|  | Evangelical College Students ($N = 1,980$) (% agreeing) | Evangelical Seminary Students ($N = 847$) (% agreeing) |
|---|---|---|
| 1. There is no life after death | — | — |
| 2. There is life after death but what a person does in this life has no bearing on it | — | — |
| 3. Heaven is a divine reward for those who earn it by their good life | 1 | — |
| 4. The only hope for Heaven is through personal faith in Jesus Christ *except* for those who have not had the opportunity to hear of Jesus Christ | 32 | 31 |
| 5. The only hope for heaven is through personal faith in Jesus Christ | 66 | 68 |

NOTE: — = less than 1%.

generation there were signs of some difference of opinion over the finer points of this belief. For example, though 97 percent of all Evangelicals (in still another survey conducted in 1963) agreed that "belief in Jesus Christ as Savior was absolutely necessary for salvation," only 79 percent were inclined to accept the view that "being completely ignorant of Jesus, as might be the case for people living in other countries, would prevent salvation."[21] Likewise in a 1962 survey of Baptist (General Conference) youth, 89 percent agreed that "all non-Christians will go to hell," yet only 67 percent agreed that "unless missionaries and others are successful in converting people in non-Christian lands, these people will have no chance for salvation."[22] These surveys show the beginning of a sentiment that is highly representative of the present generation.

The tension this issue (of the fate of the unevangelized) posed for the coming generation was articulated very well by the students themselves:

> That's a question I try to avoid because it's something I can do nothing about. . . . It's hard for me to say. If I had to say yes or no (pause) I guess I would have to say yes, they are in hell. But I don't have full conviction about what God is doing there. (male, second-year master of divinity candidate, Methodist)

In my opinion, I feel it *would* be possible for people who have never heard the gospel to realize that there is a God. The Bible says that people know that there is a God in their hearts. Maybe God [saves them] in a different way, maybe he gives them a second chance after they die depending on how they've lived their lives. (female, sophomore, Bible major, Orthodox Presbyterian)

I'm not clear on this issue. I don't know what God does with people who don't have any chance to know him. In one sense, I could see how it would not be right for them to be in heaven. But in another sense, I don't think that God would be unfair by not allowing them in heaven. I think he would keep the doors of heaven open for anyone to come in who wants to. (male, senior, Bible major, Episcopalian)

I think it would be unfair for those who have not heard of Christ to be sent to hell. What is important in their case is that they have conformed to the law of God as they know it in their hearts. (female, senior, sociology major, Independent Fundamentalist)

I believe that there are "virtuous pagans" who do go to heaven. I believe that everyone has a knowledge of God in their hearts, even those who have never heard of Jesus. God will judge them according to what they do with that knowledge. (female, freshman, business major, Episcopalian)

Interestingly, this kind of reflection is not occurring independently of formal theology but, in fact, gains legitimacy from it. Writes one Evangelical theologian, "though our knowledge about God's dealings with the unevangelized is slight, it is sufficient to dispel the notion that the hopes of untold millions are simply cancelled out *a priori.*" This was put even more strongly: "Of one thing we can be certain, God will not abandon in hell those who have not known and therefore have not declined his offer of grace."[23] Other Evangelical theologians have concurred.[24]

A similar posture of reticence was expressed when asked about the eternal disposition of various types of people who are not Christians but who might be considered special cases: exemplary people whose lives were characterized by extraordinary good will and charity. The obvious and paradigmatic case is Gandhi, the "Great Soul," who provided the inspirational leadership in India's midcentury struggle to become independent of Britain's colonial rule. Mohandas K. Gandhi, regarded as a good man by virtually any human standard, was nonetheless a devout Hindu (and not a Christian by traditional definitions). When asked about Gandhi's fate, some were absolutely certain he was saved, a few were certain he was not, but most were unsure of either:

> The human part of me wants to say that Gandhi would be good enough to get him eternal life, but I think Scripture would indicate that he is not. (male, second-year master of divinity candidate, United Methodist)

> I would tend to say that Gandhi probably is in hell . . . but on the other hand, I do not know God's mind nor his methods of judgment so it's possible that Gandhi's in heaven. If you read the Bible, I think that maybe he had served a God under a different name. (female, senior, English literature major, non-denominational)

> That's a big question. I would say that the Lord would know his heart and somehow would judge him fairly. I hope the Lord would judge his heart and if he was a good man and he knew to live an honest life and he was generous and loving, maybe the Lord would take him. (female, senior, Bible major, Plymouth Brethren)

> For me this is kind of a foggy area and I don't have a hard and firm answer on that. I'd say there is a possibility that a guy like that could be in heaven. The gospel may never have been presented to him in a way that is viable or in such a way that it appears true. I think it makes a difference whether he was presented with true Christianity or with something calling itself Christian but was really something else. (male, sophomore, sociology major, Presbyterian)

The significance of all of this is plain. The introduction of these qualifications tempers the purity of the theological exclusivism traditionally held. Ultimate truth is not at issue here, only what people perceive to be ultimate truth. Thus, the existence of such a sizable minority of Evangelicals maintaining this stance represents a noteworthy shift away from the historical interpretations.

Whatever the specific reason for this, it is clear that there is a measurable degree of uneasiness within this generation of Evangelicals with the notion of an eternal damnation. Asked whether they believed in a place of eternal torment for nonbelievers, most affirmed this, yet not without some equivocation.

> I hope that hell would be like soul sleep—a kind of nothing-ness—but the Bible doesn't say that. I can't imagine a loving God being so cruel forever and ever. It is an awfully long time for someone to be unhappy. I hope it wouldn't be like that but I have a feeling it might be. I'm just glad I am where I am so I don't have to be worried about that. (female, senior, Bible major, Plymouth Brethren)

> I believe there is a hell but I think there are different levels, but not like purgatory. For example, I'm not sure whether people who live in far off lands for whom no one else has ever come and taught them about Jesus Christ are in hell. I hope not, but I think if they are in hell it would not be anything terrible. (female, sophomore, mathematics major, Methodist)

> I don't believe there is a cavern underneath the earth where people burn or where Jesus walked around for three days. When you die your body goes back to the earth and rots in the dust and your spirit goes back to God, who gave it. At Judgment we are judged by our deeds and by the light we have to live by. People who God considers wicked will be cast into the lake of fire right along with the Beast—at which point they go "piff" and they are gone. I don't believe in eternal torment—it may be but it seems to be inconsistent with God's nature. (male, senior, political science major, nondenominational)

> I don't know exactly. I think there is a hell but I don't think it is like Dante's Inferno. I think that hell is just not living forever with God. (male, senior, Bible major, Episcopalian)

The sentiment among the coming generation, then is mixed. It is clear that they know what they "should" believe but with that they struggle. Intellectually grasping the soteriological demands of orthodox Christianity is one matter; emotionally accepting them is quite another.

Yet, at the same time that conventional Evangelical soteriology may be emotionally problematic, there appears to be wide recognition that it is *socially* problematic as well. When hypothetically presented with the not-so-hypothetical situation of trying to persuade someone to become a Christian and then asked what would most likely be the first reason they would give, only one out of ten said it would be to "escape the wrath of

God and eternal damnation."[25] On the most important reason over twice this number (25%) gave that reply.[26] Yet most (67%) claimed that the first reason they would give a nonbeliever would be either the "sense of meaning and purpose in life" coming from being a Christian or the fact that "God has made a difference in my life." Seminarians, likewise, expressed a recognition of the socially offensive nature of their views of the afterworld and of salvation in particular. Virtually half (46%) felt that under most circumstances or even all circumstances, to emphasize to nonbelievers that "they will be eternally damned in hell if they do not repent of their sins" was in "poor taste."[27] As one midwestern coed put it: "When you emphasize hell to a nonbeliever, you will tend to turn him off, and then you may never have another chance to talk to him. It comes off as being really arrogant."

Overall, this cohort of Evangelicals has not, for all practical purposes, repudiated traditional Protestant theology on the matter of salvation. A dynamic is at work nonetheless. As with their view of the Bible, it minimally represents a softening of earlier doctrinal certainties. Of their own salvation, they are confident. It is with regard to the salvation of others that there is ambiguity and doubt. The certainties characteristic of previous generations appear to be giving way to a measure of hesitancy and questioning. More can be said about this for the indications are much more compelling. Yet a final problem must be addressed first.

## THE PROBLEM OF A SOCIAL GOSPEL

As several scholars have noted, the legacy of nineteenth-century Evangelicalism was not only a stalwart commitment to the growth of Christianity (through domestic revivals and evangelization and through foreign missionary activity) but also, within many quarters, a dedication to concretely address the needs of the socially and economically disadvantaged (Dayton 1976; Smith 1976; Moberg 1972; Marsden 1980). Though the chief priority was always "spreading the gospel," the philanthropic dimension of Christianity was in no way ignored. This was true not only among the Presbyterian Calvinists and the Baptists, who connected this with their postmillennial hope of reforming society in preparation for the return of Christ, but also among the Holiness and Pentecostal denominations and sects in their passion for revival (Marsden 1980, chaps. 9 and 10). Social service initiatives such as rescue missions for drunkards and the disreputable urban poor, orphanages, homes for "fallen women," relief programs for immigrants and the needy (which included providing lodging and food as well as finding jobs for these people), and medical missions were commonplace within nineteenth-

and twentieth-century Evangelicalism. Conservatives were also known to have endorsed labor unions, worked for legislation concerning women's and children's labor, and advocated better treatment of immigrants and blacks. Once again, though the practical, benevolent side of Christianity was always secondary to the supreme purpose of evangelism and personal piety, the two objectives were seen as working hand in hand. Uplifting the sinner and saving his soul fused together in an integrated thrust.

The divisions in the Protestant house in the first quarter of the twentieth century had, as one of their chief sources, the problem of the priority of social service in the mission of the Christian church. The events surrounding the rise of "Social Christianity" and its place in Protestant culture have, of course, been treated in depth by others and are unnecessary to elaborate here (Marty 1970; Marsden 1980; Sandeen 1968). Suffice it to say that conservatives and liberals differed, often bitterly.

In brief, liberals became simultaneously sensitized to the appalling social conditions and needs generated by industrial capitalism and aware of the churches' failings in ameliorating those needs. Born in response was the Social Gospel, a theological legitimation of the churches' growing posture of social advocacy. In time, the Social Gospel gained a de facto ascendancy over Protestantism's long-standing emphasis on evangelism. As is well known, many prominent conservatives, in reaction to this "apostasy," accentuated the churches' spiritual message, the need for evangelism and pure doctrine for Christian living. It is not entirely clear whether there was, in practice, any appreciable diminution of social ministry in conservative denominations after the Fundamentalist reaction. Through the first six decades of the twentieth century, conservatives continued to minister socially to the poor much as they had in the nineteenth century, through rescue missions, medical missions abroad, and various charities and "benevolences." The main difference was one of ideology and official polity. In these terms the polarity between these two wings of Protestantism remained fairly strong from the turn of the century to the mid-1960s.[28] In the following decade, much of the tension abated though the fundamental ideological differences remained.

In the broadest view, the present generation of Evangelicals, like its predecessors, continues to hold spiritual concerns preeminent over the material concerns of social and political justice. For example, when asked to choose the most important priority for Christians today, nine out of ten Evangelical seminarians chose priorities of a spiritual nature.[29] The pattern of continuity continues.

While this is so, there are also obvious differences in the Evangelical attitude toward the social factor from that which predominated even as late as 1970. But what are they? Since that time, Evangelicals have neither increased nor decreased the amount of resources given over to "benevolences." In 1980 as in 1970, conservative denominations, on average, channeled roughly 18 percent of their annual budgets to these needs—the *same* percentage as the liberal denominations.[30] What did not remain the same, and in fact represented a significant alteration, was the level of Evangelical rhetoric endorsing social ministry as *an end in itself* and thus its legitimacy in the Evangelical community. Both increased.

Some of the momentum came from an emerging left-wing faction in Evangelicalism—the "young Evangelicals" or "radical Evangelicals" as they have been called. Much of the infrastructure of this movement was a social-action-oriented and often charismatically based communitarian movement. Virtually all of these communities came into being after 1965, and while the longevity of a large number of them was brief, many of them did survive through to the early 1980s. The Community of Communities and the Shalom Communities, for example, in 1983 listed thirty active communities in the United States.[31] Other institutional supports to the social activism of the Evangelical Left were provided by such groups as Evangelicals for Social Action and their related program of Discipleship Workshops, the Association for Public Justice, and the Seminary Consortium on Urban Pastoral Education. Giving ideological momentum to the Evangelical Left as well as media attention were the periodicals that emerged to give voice to their concerns. With one exception (*The Other Side*, which began publishing in the mid-1960s), all of these periodicals (the most visible being *Sojourners*, *Radix*, *Seeds*, and *Inside*) began publishing after 1970.[32] Add to this over thirty books authored by Evangelicals advocating a liberal/radical social and political agenda for Evangelicals. Fitting the pattern, all but a few of these were published after 1970.[33]

But gains in the legitimacy of social action as such in Evangelical Christianity were not confined to a vocal left-liberal minority. Gains were made in the mainstream. As a spokesman for the National Association of Evangelicals noted, "social ministry in Evangelicalism and for the NAE came into its own in the early 1970s."[34] But, once again, it came into its own more at the ideological level, as seen by the fact that most of the member denominations of the NAE have long had social ministries, but they were not formalized in terms of a "commission" or a committee. Since the late 1960s and early 1970s, however, approximately one-third of these denominations did formalize their social welfare activity in this way. Correspondingly, since 1970 at least four major parachurch social relief agencies were established which had evangelism only as a tangential concern.[35] Moreover, when a national sample of Evangelical theologians was surveyed on this issue, most felt that their own denominations placed a substantial amount of emphasis on matters of social justice, yet they felt that they should place more.[36] A final indication is that since the early 1970s, mainstream Evangelical periodicals such as *Christianity Today* have given more attention to social justice issues. Increasingly, articles and editorials have tended to encourage greater participation (Wuthnow 1983b, 167–85).

Though social activism in itself has gained legitimacy in Evangelicalism generally, it appears to be especially true for the coming generation. When asked to rate the relative importance of the pursuit of social, economic, and political justice in the world and "telling the world about the claims of Christ," Evangelical collegians and seminarians held a similar view (see table 6). Over half (54%) of each group claimed that the pursuit of justice was "just as important" or "almost as important" as evangelism. In a comparison of older seminarians (thirty-five and older) with younger seminarians (under thirty-five years) the same percentage held the view that the pursuit of justice was just as important as evangelism, yet 14 percent more of the younger seminarians held the view that the concern for justice was almost as important as the concern for evangelism.[37] These findings were confirmed when the seminarians were pressed on the point. Faced with a forced-choice situation of choosing the "primary focus of missionary efforts overseas," predictably almost nine of ten (88%) Evangelical seminarians chose "bring[ing] people to faith in Jesus" (see table 6). Four percent said that it should be to "improve the material lot of the poor." Most significantly, however, 8 percent absolutely refused to separate the two concerns. Notably, all but one of these were younger seminarians.[38] As one third-year seminarian (Episcopalian) put it: "The question is hypothetical. I cannot imagine in real life when one would have to choose between the two. Both are essential and fundamental tasks for the Christian. I refuse to dichotomize these." Other comments were similar:

> This cannot be an either/or question. Both are necessary for it is through meeting the needs of the poor in Christian love that we bring them to a faith in Jesus Christ. (male, first-year master of religion candidate, Baptist)

> These tasks should be performed simultaneously—the latter representing the incarnational aspect of the Christian witness. (female, third-year master of divinity candidate, nondenominational)

An empty stomach has a hard time deciding on the more "spiritual questions." But then again, a full stomach has a hard time listening because of other preoccupations. I would have to say that both must be carried out simultaneously. I cannot prioritize them. (male, third-year master of divinity candidate, Mennonite)

Of no little consequence was the fact that a large number choosing evangelism as the chief focus of missionary activity were not comfortable with an unqualified choice of evangelism distinct from the social and economic issue.

Social ministry as a distinctly Christian responsibility has then gained prominence and legitimacy since its decline at the turn of the century. Most Evangelicals would agree that it is a crucial dimension of the Christian life and witness. This is particularly true for a large sector of the coming generation of Evangelicals.

Some have argued that within these developments is a return to the nineteenth-century "balance" between evangelistic and social concerns (Dayton 1976). In terms of the public legitimacy of assisting the needy, the argument is partially plausible. Yet alone this masks an important qualifying reality, namely, that the contemporary Evangelical view of social ministry is different from that held by many Evangelicals a century

**Table 6**
The Importance of the Pursuit of Justice relative to Evangelism
according to Campus Setting

|  | Evangelical College Students ($N = 1,980$) (% agreeing) | Evangelical Seminary Students ($N = 847$) (% agreeing) |
|---|---|---|
| The pursuit of justice |  |  |
| 1. More important | 2 | a |
| 2. Just as important | 21 | 22 |
| 3. Almost as important | 32 | 32 |
| 4. Less important | 45 | 45 |
|  |  |  |
| The primary focus of missionary efforts |  |  |
| 1. To bring people to faith in Jesus | b | 88 |
| 2. To improve the material lot of the poor | b | 4 |
| 3. Both together (volunteered response) | b | 8 |

[a]Less than 1%.
[b]Question not asked.

before. At that time, it was understood as a facet of the ideology of "Christian civilization." Religion, it was reasoned, was the basis of true virtue; the purer the religion, the higher the morality. Christianity (read Protestantism) was the purest religion and was, therefore, the obvious source of the superiority of Western civilization (and particularly northern Europe and North America) over all others (Marsden 1980, 12). For this reason, the assumption that Christianity was the only basis for a healthy civilization prevailed: to evangelize or Christianize meant to civilize the "heathen lands and hostile peoples of the world."[39] Even as late as 1910, Robert Speer wrote: "Conditions in Christian lands are not what they should be, but they are infinitely superior to the conditions in other lands, and in proportion as they are Christian, famine, disease, and want are overcome. Are these blessings to be ours alone? The world needs the social message and redemption of Christianity."[40] In a similar vein, Henry Frost noted that "It is certainly true, as men say, that non-Christian nations are in a pitiable state, governmentally, educationally, commercially, socially, and physically; and it is equally true that nothing but Christianity will alter the conditions which are existing."[41] This orientation did not only refer to international missionary activity but was carried over as an approach to the needy "at home." The formula was the same: to save their souls was simultaneously to improve their living conditions and moral standards. The motivating impulse was also the same: to realize the millenarian hope of the Kingdom of God on earth.

It goes without saying that contemporary Evangelicals no longer maintain the antiquated notions that for all practical purposes equated social concern with the effort to export bourgeois civilities. Rather (as has been argued), social ministry has gained autonomy from these millenarian aspirations. It is increasingly viewed as a legitimate activity *in itself*. It has intrinsic worth and humanitarian appeal *apart* from ultimate spiritual concerns. Evangelism can and ideally should accompany it, but if it does not, it is not, therefore, illegitimate. To the contrary, it retains its value as an act of Christian charity. Evangelical parachurch relief organizations principally devoted to social ministry would not have emerged (in number and in size) as legitimate Evangelical organizations without this subtle though fundamental shift in ideological orientation.

Notably, a faction of the coming generation of Evangelicals (principally in the political Left) has taken social concern a step beyond the status of "legitimate in itself" to a position of "exclusively legitimate." Put differently, social and political activism is redefined as the essential Christian act. This is precisely the significance of the Evangelical Left's view that Mahatma Gandhi, in his concern with social justice and pacifism, showed Christians their salvation, their way out of hell.[42] Though representative of an extreme, it is nonetheless merely the culmination of the same sociological process within which the larger Evangelical world participates. In this light, any effort to equate the alleged "balance" between evangelistic and social concerns in the nineteenth century with that which presently prevails is roundly misplaced.

### THE DE-GHETTOIZATION OF EVANGELICAL THEOLOGY

In substantive terms, the continuity in conservative Protestant theology in America is plainly discernible. From a distance, it would appear as though little if any change has occurred in the past century. Evangelicals have, by and large, been successful at maintaining the cognitive boundaries which encompass theological orthodoxy as they have defined it. Yet upon closer scrutiny, one can see that the continuity is far from perfect. Qualitatively there are some noteworthy differences.[43] There is less sharpness, less boldness, and, accordingly, a measure of opaqueness in their theological vision that did not exist in previous generations (at least to their present extent). A dynamic would appear to be operating that strikes at the very heart of the Evangelical self-identity. But what is one to make of it?

It would be superficial simply to say that Evangelical theology as practiced by the coming generation is becoming more liberal. Yet the evidence is suggestive of a common trend, one in which the theological tradition is conforming in its own unique way to the cognitive and normative assumptions of modern culture (Berger 1967b).

In the case of the Evangelical orientation toward the Bible, the trend at one level involves an accommodation of varying degrees to modern epistemology—philosophical rationalism, even shades of positivism. Traditional literalistic renditions of the biblical literature (at least parts of it), for example, are simply not quite so believable because they no longer meet certain modern philosophical or scientific criteria of validity. For those engaged in formal theological discourse, these criteria are formalized and articulated; for those whose theology is less sophisticated, these criteria are nonreflective. Whether on the part of the expert or the ordinary believer, however, there is the recognition of the "need" for a theology and the Scriptures upon which it is based to be internally consistent, historically accurate, and marginally credible at face value. If they cannot be that, then there is a "need" to provide a rational explanation for any stubborn problems. As respondents themselves put it, even if the Bible stories do contradict themselves or defy historical fact, the integrity of Scriptures is "not really undermined." Meeting twentieth-

46

century standards of accuracy "is not what the Bible is all about." This leads to another level of adjustment.

When traditional affirmations of religious reality are, to whatever degree, undermined by modern forms of rationalism, they are simultaneously de-objectified. What was "known" with a taken-for-granted certitude becomes, at best, a "belief." Further along in this process, it becomes a "religious opinion" or a "feeling." Thus when students approach a biblical story which their tradition regarded as an objective historical fact and say that they are "open" to or "comfortable" with the idea that it is just symbolic, or that it is "not really important (to them) that it happened historically," religious truth devolves to religious opinion. The reality has been de-objectified. The other side of de-objectivation, though, is what social scientists call subjectivization. The emphasis shifts from a concern with the proclamation of an objective and universal truth to a concern with the subjective applicability of truth. In different terms, there is a shift from a concern with "what the Bible states" to "what God is telling us." A shift from the former to the latter eases the tension arising from differences of opinion over what, in fact, the Bible does state.

With regard to the problem of salvation, the adjustment simply entails an alignment to the normative codes of civility spawned by the contemporary milieu of pluralism. More accurately, there is a certain affinity between a normative ethic of civility, tolerance, and tolerability and the theological doctrine of universalism. Putting it bluntly, being socially intolerant of others has a soteriological equivalent of being willing to let someone spend an eternity in hell—it is intolerance or social rejection in an ultimate sense. In the Evangelical case, however, the universalism is expressed in a sharply modified form. Everyone will not go to heaven—faith in Jesus Christ is still the only means of salvation. But neither will everyone who does not profess faith in this life go to hell. For a substantial minority of the coming generation, there appears to be a middle ground that did not, for all practical purposes, exist for previous generations. For the unevangelized and for those who reveal exceptional Christian virtue but are not professed Christians, there is hope that they also will receive salvation. The most prominent rationale, sometimes called the "second chance theory," posits that death is the occasion when the unevangelized, those who did not see Christianity fairly presented, are confronted with the truth and thereby are justly able to make a decision about Jesus Christ and their eternal fate. Needless to say, this posture would, and in fact does, lessen substantially the sense of urgency to evangelize the unreached.[44]

Having said this, it is important to recall that the majority still hold the traditional approach to the problem of salvation. Yet as the interviews suggest, even among these there is a pervasive uneasiness both about the nature of hell and about who is relegated to it. It is an uneasiness which may portend a greater cultural accommodation.

Concerning the development of a social gospel among sectors of the Evangelical population, the adaptation comprises a shift in varying degrees from other-worldly interests to inner-worldly interests; from the transcendent to the imminent. Temporal matters are given a heightened importance. Such an orientation is, of course, entirely compatible with the cultural ethos that predominates in advanced industrial society, one in which the other-worldly reality is utterly devalued. The issue of an Evangelical social gospel plainly does not carry nearly the intrinsic significance for theological discourse as do the other dimensions examined here. It is metatheological, as it were. Nonetheless, it does have import for theology. Namely, in practical terms, the elevation of the temporal more often than not involves a devaluation of the spiritual. As was noted, the Evangelical Left currently represents a certain culmination of this tendency such that the social agenda achieves a de facto priority over the spiritual. The mainstream of the coming generation reveals similar inclinations, though to a lesser extent. The significance of this trend, however, is highlighted by the precedent set by liberal Protestant theology in the twentieth century, where the Social Gospel achieved proportions unintended by its original advocates.

This overall course—of tradition conforming to the cognitive and normative assumptions of the modern world view—is relatively new to Evangelicalism but not to the theological enterprise generally. It has gone furthest in liberal theological traditions. And though the Evangelical pattern has not gone as far as theological liberalism, the two share the central process.

As religious traditions and the sociohistorical realities of the modern world order confront each other, there is little question as to which of the two gives way to the other. Almost invariably the former yields to the latter. As the religious tradition conforms to the modern paradigm, it gains a legitimacy and respectability. The response of Protestant orthodoxy to the increasing dominance of these cultural realities (and particularly to their influence within Protestantism) was a retreat to a sociocultural ghetto. Isolated and insulated, it was able to successfully maintain a certain version of theological orthodoxy alive and protected. But in many ways, the history of Evangelicalism in the latter half of the twentieth century has been the history of its passage out of this ghetto. Evangelical theology at all levels of sophistication has been advancing (albeit slowly) out of its ghetto and correspondingly has gained a measure of legitimacy. Serious public discussion about a possible endowment of a professorship for an Evangelical theologian at the Harvard Divinity School in the early 1980s was merely a symbol of this. The ultimate significance of these adaptations is unclear. On the one hand, they can be legitimately viewed as essential to ensure the very survival and vitality of conservative Christianity in the contemporary world. On the other hand, they may signal the begining of the collapse of traditional theological orthodoxy. Certainly, in its move out of its ghetto, it has risked the unintentional contamination by the very reality it has tried to keep out. That this process has begun, there is little doubt. Where it will go from here is an open question. If historical precedent is instructive, it becomes clear that these tendencies will probably escalate.

# Work, Morality, and the Self: Asceticism Revised

Religious truth as embodied in a theology is not merely a matter of the mind, an intellectual exercise for the faithful. Religious truths invariably make claims on other dimensions of the believer's life. They have concrete implications for conduct in all of life's affairs—in the marketplace, in the political sphere, and in interpersonal and familial affairs. The Protestant legacy is no exception and here the pattern follows expectations: orthodoxy spawned an "orthopraxy" after a fashion. In this case it fostered what the sociologist Max Weber originally termed "inner-worldly asceticism."[1] Inner-worldly asceticism was nothing less than a total life ethic, and as such it comprised an entire constellation of values, attitudes, and beliefs about human conduct. At the heart of it, though, was a moral code orienting believers toward austerity, ascetic self-denial, and self-discipline.

At one level this took form as a posture of renunciation toward the "world." Practically this meant a repudiation of any "waste of time" through "sociability," "idle talk," "inactive contemplation," and even "more sleep than is necessary for health" (Weber 1958, 167). More prominently it meant a rejection of any "spontaneous and sinful enjoyment of life" or "living merrily and without care." This naturally included an elaborate structure of prohibitions against every expression of sexual immorality (fornication, adultery, homosexuality, and even excessive marital passion), drunkenness and loose behavior, Sabbath breaking, and so on. Many sectors of Protestantism even nurtured an aversion to sports and games, art, the theater, and the "enjoyment of worldly luxury." All of these practices were considered worthy of absolute moral condemnation. The early Protestant ethic thus embodied the values of sobriety, restraint, frugality, temperateness, and self-mastery. In this, it inspired the second principal thrust of this ethic, an orientation of calculation and rational planning in day-to-day activity. This implied a discipline in the observance of religious duties such as in faithful church attendance, tithing, study of Scriptures, and prayer. It also implied the rigorous attention to the development of moral character for oneself and one's children, moral purity being the goal here. Most importantly, it required a relentless pursuit of excellence and success in one's work. Industriousness, efficiency, and productivity in vocation were supremely valued for it was through one's vocation that the Protestant worked out his faith in God and, ultimately, his salvation. The legacy of Protestant asceticism, then, was one of mastery over the mundane affairs of day-to-day life. As Weber (1958, 121) himself put it, "every Christian had to be a monk all of his life"—but in the world and not in a monastic retreat.

This legacy of asceticism left a deep imprint on Western civilization for centuries after the Protestant Reformation. Its relation to the development of industrial capitalism is well known.[2] But for the present purposes, it is only necessary to note that the further the Reformation receded into the past, the more it became a diffused and secular ethic—separated from the religious impulse that had spawned it and that had given it its ultimate justification. Where it remained strongest as a *religious* ethic was in those Protestant sects that zealously maintained their connections with their religious forebears in the Reformation. But even among these, by the early decades of the twentieth century, the legacy had altered. Insofar as it meant the denial of self in the face of worldly amusements and the rejection of worldly vices, the ethic remained robust in Fundamentalist circles. One of the dominant themes of conservative sermons and tract literature of the day was the condemnation of all "pleasure loving" and all of the "appetites of the flesh," such as card playing, dancing, theater attendance, smoking tobacco, "worldly dress," and, chief among these, alcohol and immoral sexual practices (Marsden 1980, 26, 32, 135, 156). To be saved from a life of sin more often than not meant being saved from these "shameful practices."[3] The Lynds, in their study of Middletown in 1925 and again in 1935 found this preoccupation to prevail in certain quarters, as did Liston Pope in 1938 in his study of Gastonia, North Carolina (Lynd and Lynd 1929, 1937; cf. McLoughlin 1959). According to Pope, "The principal sins, in the eyes of the mill villagers, are such uptown 'worldly amusements' as playing cards, dancing, gambling, drinking, [profanity], and swimming with members of the opposite sex" (Pope 1976, 88).

Where the legacy had changed was in the theological notion of a "calling in one's vocation"; it had been thoroughly secularized even within Fundamentalist culture.[4] Though devoid of spiritual meaning, industriousness remained an important value all the same. For example, Billy Sunday, one of the most celebrated evangelists of the early 1900s, continually expounded a mixture of the "Gospel message with the traditional American moral virtues of decency, patriotism, manliness, thrift, sobriety, piety and hard work"(Marsden 1980, 135). Perhaps because the virtues of industriousness had long been institutionalized as a general cultural feature of industrial societies, the negative side of this ethic (prohibitions against immoral behavior) was given greater prominence in Fundamentalist culture.

Throughout the twentieth century, all the evidence portrays an Evangelical world largely untouched by shifting cultural currents.[5] The ethic of inner-worldly asceticism, though diffused and in part secularized, remains relatively intact within American Evangelicalism. Insofar as this ethic has continued to be a feature of American culture at all, it has remained perhaps most characteristic of this cultural enclave.

For example, moral asceticism is reputed by contemporary scholarship to be more deeply institutionalized in American Evangelicalism than in any other part of American society. From midcentury through the early 1960s, conservative Protestants continued to be far more likely than liberal or mainstream Protestants to adhere to the injunctions against "breaking the Sabbath," "taking the Lord's name in vain," dancing, gambling, smoking, going to the movies, and "drinking liquor" (Moreland 1958, 137–139).[6] They, more than any other religious group, remained adamant about the immorality of homosexuality, premarital and extramarital sexual relations, divorce, and abortion (Hunter 1983a, 85). In short, Evangelicals have maintained their rigid codes of moral discipline, and therefore, they are said to find the experimentations represented by the "new morality" to be self-indulgent, hedonistic, and reprehensible to the life of the community and the values of the American heritage. Likewise, conservative Protestants have tended to value productive or constructive activities in their leisure (e.g., volunteer work, working around the house, taking courses, and gardening) more than other groups, who are more likely to engage in "self-indulgent" activities (e.g., going to the movies, watching television, going to social clubs) (Lenski 1963, 227, 274, 351, 358). This attitude has also been reflected in the child-rearing values of Protestants (conservative and mainstream alike), who have been more likely than Catholics to imbue their children with a future or goal orientation (Lenski 1963, 229–31). More than this, marriage and family life are intensely valued here to the point that individual needs and desires are temporarily suppressed if not denied outright for the sake of the larger group. The rewards sought and the rewards attained are family loyalty and stability and the generational perpetuation of family respectability. Self-sacrifice, hard work, and commitment in this sphere and in the occupational sphere provide much of the foundation for a meaningful life. In the latter case, the rewards have been and continue to be material success and the respect of the community.

Conservative Protestants then, from all appearances, continue to abide by a general cultural ethic of austerity as they face day-to-day life. As Daniel Yankelovich has argued, they are strongly represented among those who make up the last bastion of social support for the "old rules" of American life—the traditional virtues of self-denial and self-sacrifice as they apply to all facets of day-to-day existence (Yankelovich 1981, 5–6, 91). For them, meaning in life and self-fulfillment are not something pursued for their own sake but naturally emerge out of a life committed to these ideals.

At face value, contemporary scholarship is convincing. It corresponds with casual observations of the phenomena and deeply imbedded cultural stereotypes. But at another level, there are grounds to be suspicious of this image. For one, the evidence is too broad to be satisfying. Sweeping generalizations are made on the basis of only a few facts. Furthermore, it proceeds from a base of only vague familiarity with the world as Evangelicals perceive it. Neither is there any appreciation of the historical evolution of the Evangelical subculture in this century. The unsatisfactory nature of contemporary scholarship on this point, then, invites further inquiry. Bearing the inheritance of the Protestant legacy, the Evangelical academy provides an appropriate place for more closely examining what remains of inner-worldly asceticism in contemporary American Evangelicalism.

### Vocational Asceticism

As has been suggested, work had a special place in early Protestant (and specifically, Lutheran) culture. For it was here in one's vocation that the believer worked out his salvation. Martin Luther's theological notion of the "priesthood of all believers" meant, contrary to practices in Catholicism, that priests were no more privileged in the sight of God (having special access to the grace and mercies of God) than anyone else; that the priesthood was no more a spiritually favored vocation than any other. Rather, God's benevolence was "democratic." Whatever the believer did vocationally was important to God's plan and, as such, he had a spiritual duty to be diligent and faithful to his calling—to perform his labor in the biblical formula, as "unto God and not unto men." If one were successful at one's calling, it was understood to be a sign of God's favor and of one's divine "election." As Weber (1958) argued, it was the anxiety of not knowing one's eternal fate and the passion to establish it beyond reasonable doubt that drove early generations of Protestants to extraordinary efforts in realizing their ascetic ideals. Asceticism, then, was indirectly tied to spiritual ends. Mediating between ascetic denial and spiritual goals was the believer's activity in this world and, in particular, his vocation.

It has been pointed out already that the theological significance of "work in one's calling" waned dramatically in Protestant culture in the centuries following the Reformation. It is really not a question, then, of measuring the spiritual meaning of work within the Evangelical world. Yet the examination of the place and value of work for the coming generation of Evangelicals would be highly suggestive for what it would tell us about the present status of the ethic of asceticism.

Among the majority of Evangelical collegians the values of industriousness and productivity appear at first blush to be fairly important in themselves. For example, most (65%) agreed that "being productive in life and making a constant effort in a chosen field are among the most important qualities of life"(see table 7). An even larger number (83%) maintained that "hard work is a good builder of character." Though with considerably less enthusiasm (47%) (still more than a sample of students attending a large public university; see Appendix), they also endorsed

**Table 7**
Attitudes toward Work according to Campus Setting

|  | Evangelical College Students (N = 1,980) (% agreeing) | Evangelical Seminary Students (N = 847) (% agreeing) | Public University Students (N = 426) (% agreeing) |
|---|---|---|---|
| Being productive in life and making a constant effort in a chosen field are among the most important qualities of life | 65[a] | 37 | [b] |
| Hard work is a good builder of character | 83[a] | 75 | [b] |
| Competition encourages excellence | 47 | 33 | 41 |
| Hard work always pays off | 47 | 39 | 51 |
| If someone is poor, it is probably his own fault | 6 | 3 | 9 |
| I get more satisfaction in life from my friends, family, and hobbies than from my work | 59 | 36 | 54 |
| I prefer a more creative life to financial well-being | 60 | 75 | 50 |

[a]EAP college minisurvey; see Appendix.
[b]Question not asked.

the belief that "competition" (implying hard work, calculated effort, efficiency, and the like) "encourages excellence" (presumably in work and leisure alike). Finally, a greater number of the collegians (47%) agreed than disagreed (25% were undecided) (or roughly the same as the public university students, 51%) that "hard work always pays off." This is also roughly equivalent to a national sample of American adults taken in 1976, 43 percent of whom agreed with that statement—down from 58 percent in 1969 (Yankelovich 1981, 94). In brief, most of the coming generation of Evangelicals hold the view that if one is persistent enough, one can attain a measure of success in most endeavors. Even so, they were not strong enough in this conviction to believe that poverty is of one's own doing, that is, a result of negligence, sloth, and apathy or the unwillingness to work hard. Only a very small portion (collegians, 6%; seminarians, 3%; and public university students, 9%) agreed with the coarse capitalistic principle that "if someone is poor, it is probably his own fault."

In sum, the coming generation of Evangelicals do not distinguish themselves from others in their views of the place of work in their overall value system. Like their secular counterparts, they show a positive though not resounding endorsement of the values of productivity, hard work, persistence, and competitiveness. Even among those who have denominational roots in ethnic, northern European Protestantism (the Reformational-Confessional tradition in Evangelicalism: Lutheranism, Orthodox Presbyterianism, etc.), these values are not particularly prominent.[7]

But there is more to this story. The significance of vocation for the contemporary Evangelical is even less than it would appear on the surface. It is qualified by other values. For though most held a belief in the importance of work for building character, the majority (59%) also maintained that they "get *more* satisfaction in life from friends, family, and hobbies than from [their] work." One might wonder about the meaning of this inasmuch as the work they refer to is that of being a student, except that virtually the same percentage (60%) claimed as a matter of general principle to "prefer a more creative life to financial well-being." Thus, work and the financial rewards resulting from a good performance in it are significant and meaningful but not nearly so much as other values associated with the private sphere.

This is still further supported by the way students rated different types of personal needs: (1) "instrumental" needs associated with occupation, (2) "affective" needs oriented toward self-fulfillment, and (3) affective needs oriented toward interpersonal relationships.[8] Both collegians and seminarians collectively rated as least important the instrumental needs, such as the need for financial security and achievement. More important were the affective self-fulfillment needs, that is, needs for such intangibles as a sense of independence and personal freedom, purpose in life, and self-fulfillment. Only slightly more important were the affective interpersonal needs, such as the need for friendship, love and affection, and even marriage. The public university students rated their needs identically except that they ranked affective self-fulfillment needs slightly more important than the affective interpersonal needs.

It bears repeating, the legacy of Protestant asceticism involved a constellation of values, attitudes, and beliefs. In part though, it was a special orientation toward work. What has been seen thus far merely confirms what is already well known about the place and value of work for Evangelicalism—that work has lost any spiritual and eternal significance and that it is important only insofar as it fosters certain qualities of the personality. But there is more. Though the work ethic has long been secularized in American culture, it remained a dominant value all the same, at least through midcentury. The primacy of private sphere activity relative to occupational activity in the overall value and meaning system of the coming generation, then, suggests that this ethic has undergone still further transformations. But all of this is only suggestive and not yet conclusive. The legacy of asceticism has yet a darker side. It is that which is constituted by the seemingly endless number of prohibitions against activities deemed immoral. A look at this dimension of the Protestant legacy will reveal more.

### MORAL ASCETICISM

As with the theological definitions of orthodoxy, the fundamental issue of "orthopraxy" or "right-living" is also one of boundaries—normative boundaries distinguishing the acceptable from the unacceptable, the approved from the disapproved. In this case, of course, the boundaries are behavioral and not cognitive. Yet unlike orthodoxy, which has been defined positively (what one *should* believe), the main thrust of Protestant orthopraxy has been its negative character (what one *should not* do). As seen in Protestant culture, correct living has traditionally been construed fairly narrowly. For generations if not centuries, it demanded the strict observance of injunctions against such activities as working on the Sabbath, enjoying the range of worldly amusements (card playing, the theater, dancing, and the like), and engaging in numerous vices (alcohol, narcotics of any sort, tobacco, and sexual relations outside marriage).

The ultimate justification for these strictures had been that they were biblically inspired. God's word, it would be reasoned, provided clear principles for Christian living which prohibited these types of activities.

As important a justification was the belief that their observance was the principal way of distinguishing "godly living" from "worldliness." Moral character, defined as conformity to these normative standards, was, in other words, significant for the purely practical purpose of distinguishing the faithful from the unfaithful. The premise was simply that there must be some clear correspondence between the quality of the inner life and the quality of moral conduct. If one's soul had truly been transformed in salvation then this would be reflected in one's manner of living. If there were no observable differences in the quality of one's moral character, the depth if not the sincerity of the individual's belief could be rightly questioned. In this light, conduct became an external index by which a person's spiritual state could be distinguished, a yardstick by which a person's spiritual growth could be measured.

It is difficult to overemphasize the importance of these notions to Evangelical faith in the twentieth century. For the better part of the century, the word *worldly* has been a symbol having immediate and universal meaning for conservative Protestants. Anything that was defined as worldly was understood to be tainted by moral impurity. It was the opposite of Christian virtue. This view of course presupposed that a clear and fundamental distinction could be made between Christian conduct and non-Christian, or worldly, conduct. In this dualistic conception of good and evil, there was, for all practical purposes, no middle ground, no ethically dubious territory. But far from being a passive category, worldiness ever imposed itself, ever threatened to contaminate true moral (Christian) goodness. As one turn of the century minister put it, "for once let worldly and lustful thoughts find their place in the heart, and oh! how quick, how strong, how rampant is their growth!"[9] In the face of all this, the believer was compelled to "separate" himself from the world. He was not to be "unequally yoked" with unbelievers and their habits of life. As one of Pope's mill villagers put it, "You got to be different from the World!" (Pope 1976, 88).[10] Indeed, the believer was different and in the particular way that his religious tradition dictated. This was so for several reasons. Conformity to these strictures became an essential means for the believer to document the sincerity of his faith and the depth of his commitment within the Christian community. His claim to salvation, to put it differently, gained validity in the minds of his fellows if it was backed up by strict moral discipline. The obverse of this was simply that by not holding to the legitimacy of those standards or by not conforming to them, one risked exclusion from the fellowship of the community and censure from one of its prevailing institutions. There was, then, moral virtue in maintaining the inviolability of these behavioral norms.

The question of how successful conservative Protestants have been in living up to these standards then is not the critical one for the purposes of this chapter. Much more important is the continuity of the behavioral standards themselves, that is, the historical integrity of the moral boundaries. For the boundaries themselves, not so much the conformance to them, were crucial to the religious identity of conservative Protestantism. It was only by maintaining the legitimacy of strict behavioral standards (which sharply contrasted with the "world's" standards) that the believer and the church community could justify their claim to spiritual superiority in a secular world. It has already been observed that the elaborate structure of behavioral norms of conservative Protestantism remained relatively intact through the first half of the twentieth century. But since the 1960s a dynamic has been at play which has profoundly affected this structure. The moral boundaries separating Christian conduct from worldly conduct have been substantially undermined.

This dynamic is illustrated by comparing different generations of Evangelical students in their attitudes about the moral propriety of specific types of behavior. In virtually each case, there has been a dramatic decrease in the percentage of those who consider that activity to be morally wrong all of the time (see fig. 1).[11] For example, this decrease is seen with regard to "studying on Sunday" (11% decrease), "playing pool" or billiards (22% decrease), "playing cards" (44% decrease), "folk dancing" (28% decrease), and even "social dancing" (30% decrease)—all in the course of a single decade, 1951 to 1961. Comparable survey data for these items do not exist after this. However, when students in 1982 were asked about these activities (in the interview setting), not one felt that participation in them was ever morally wrong unless abused by carrying it to excess. As one coed noted, "These things could be sinful if they become an obsession but they are not intrinsically wrong." This general pattern also held true for "attending 'Hollywood-type' movies." Between 1951 and 1961 those considering that behavior morally wrong all of the time dropped from 46 percent to 14 percent. By 1982, again, no one maintained this view. In fact, only 7 percent in 1982 regarded "attending an 'R-rated' movie" (with its varying dosages of sexual activity, violence, and/or profanity) as being morally wrong all of the time.

An identical pattern of change is observable with regard to illicit personal habits. For instance, those viewing "smoking cigarettes" as an unqualified transgression decreased 42 percent in three decades (and most of the remaining 51% holding this conviction cited violence to physical health as the factor in their belief as opposed to a more spiritual reason). The single most dramatic decrease, however, was seen on the

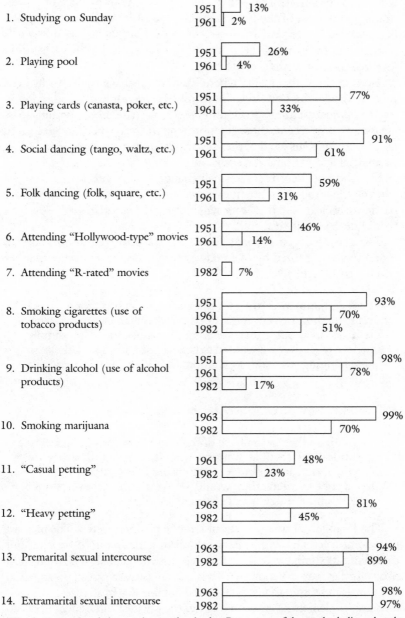

1. Studying on Sunday
   1951  13%
   1961  2%

2. Playing pool
   1951  26%
   1961  4%

3. Playing cards (canasta, poker, etc.)
   1951  77%
   1961  33%

4. Social dancing (tango, waltz, etc.)
   1951  91%
   1961  61%

5. Folk dancing (folk, square, etc.)
   1951  59%
   1961  31%

6. Attending "Hollywood-type" movies
   1951  46%
   1961  14%

7. Attending "R-rated" movies
   1982  7%

8. Smoking cigarettes (use of tobacco products)
   1951  93%
   1961  70%
   1982  51%

9. Drinking alcohol (use of alcohol products)
   1951  98%
   1961  78%
   1982  17%

10. Smoking marijuana
    1963  99%
    1982  70%

11. "Casual petting"
    1961  48%
    1982  23%

12. "Heavy petting"
    1963  81%
    1982  45%

13. Premarital sexual intercourse
    1963  94%
    1982  89%

14. Extramarital sexual intercourse
    1963  98%
    1982  97%

Fig. 1. Generational changes in moral attitudes. Percentage of those who believe that the listed activities are morally wrong all of the time.

issue of drinking alcohol. Where in 1951, 98 percent held this to be morally wrong all of the time, only 17 percent in 1982 believed this, a decrease of 81 percent. Likewise, smoking marijuana was universally condemned by Evangelicals in the early 1960s, but by the early 1980s less than three-fourths felt the same way.

Even in the sexual realm, where Evangelicals have traditionally been most sensitive, this pattern is discernible. For example, those disapproving of "casual petting" (including "necking" and light fondling) decreased by 25 percent; those disapproving of "heavy petting" decreased by 36 percent. Out of all of these activities, only the norms surrounding premarital and extramarital sexual intercourse have not changed appreciably (though there is some small change in this direction). Here, of course, the biblical injunctions against fornication and adultery are particularly clear, and thus, rationalizing any deviation from these norms would be especially difficult.

The sense of generational change in the Evangelical structure of morality was captured by one midwestern coed who, in comparing her parents to herself, remarked:

> I am certainly more tolerant than my parents [on moral issues] yet even they are now more open-minded than they used to be. It is not as though they are "morally stubborn." They simply believe what they were raised to believe. But, like I said, they too are changing. (female, sophomore, music major, Conservative Baptist)

Still another very conservative student noted:

> I would say that, overall, we differ in our positions on morality in subtle ways. I would be more uncertain of things that they are certain about. For example, I am unsure of my views on drinking alcohol, where they would say you should never drink. (male, senior, Bible major, Evangelical Free)

The Evangelical situation should not be misinterpreted. The increasing moral tolerance within Evangelicalism is dramatic to be sure, but qualifying its significance is the fact that students outside the Evangelical orbit are far *more* tolerant. The relative conservativism of Evangelical collegians and seminarians is illustrated in table 8.[12] In all cases, Evangelicals are less lenient. Yet, by and large, the greatest differences between Evangelical and public university students are seen in precisely those norms on which Evangelicals are most intransigent: premarital sexual relations (76% difference), homosexual relations between consenting adults (66% difference), watching an X-rated movie (54% difference), smoking marijuana (53% difference), and heavy petting (46% difference). As a group, public university students are most supportive of traditional norms surrounding extramarital sexual relations (59% say it is morally wrong all of the time), yet even on this there is a 39% difference between themselves and the coming generation of Evangelicals.

It is quite conceivable that the process described here has proceeded further among the coming generation of Evangelicals than it has elsewhere in the Evangelical world. Nevertheless, it is still a reflection of a process of wider proportions—one that, of course, encompasses the broader Evangelical culture.

One telling indication of the recognition and concern shared by the larger Evangelical community about these cultural tendencies is the quantity, distribution, and substance of commentary addressing these subjects produced by popular Evangelical periodicals. An analysis of the editorials and articles of four such periodicals (*Christianity Today*, *Eternity*, *Moody Monthly*, and *His* magazine) in five-year periods from 1950 to 1983 showed that the commentary addressing specific moral problems has increased at a steady rate—to over four times the number of articles.[13] Minimally this implies a heightened awareness of and concern about the changing cultural milieu in which Evangelicals have found themselves.

**Table 8**
Behavioral Norms among Evangelical and Public University Students

| | Percentage Believing the Activity Is Morally Wrong All of the Time | | | Av. % Difference between |
| --- | --- | --- | --- | --- |
| | Evangelical College Students ($N = 1,980$) | Evangelical Seminary Students ($N = 847$) | Public University Students ($N = 426$) | Evangel. and Pub. Univ. Stud. |
| Drinking alcohol | 17 | 12 | 2 | 13 |
| Smoking cigarettes | 51 | 38 | 22 | 23 |
| Smoking marijuana | 70 | 70 | 17 | 53 |
| Casual petting | 23 | 33 | 4 | 24 |
| Heavy petting | 45 | 61 | 7 | 46 |
| Premarital sexual intercourse | 89 | 92 | 15 | 76 |
| Homosexual relations between consenting adults | 94 | 97 | 30 | 66 |
| Extramarital sexual intercourse | 97 | 98 | 59 | 39 |
| Watching an R-rated movie | 7 | 11 | 1 | 8 |
| Watching an X-rated movie | 69 | 64 | 13 | 54 |
| Cheating on your income tax | 86 | 91 | 44 | 45 |

The distribution, however, has been uneven. For instance, the problem of sexual permissiveness (predominantly premarital) has been the most intense and consistent area of concern since 1950; homosexuality has also been a substantial concern though only since the mid-1960s. The moral threat of tobacco use ceased to be a subject of discussion after the early 1960s (and even to that point, it was not very important). Written discourse on the use of alcohol was also prolific in the latter half of the 1950s, only reviving after 1970. In this gap, attention had been diverted to the use of illegal drugs (marijuana, LSD, and the like). Yet for the most part, the number of articles and editorials on drug use dwindled rapidly after 1975. In this light the unevenness of the distribution of commentary provides an implicit indication of certain moral trends and Evangelicalism's response to them.

But what is even more suggestive than this is the changing substance of the commentary in this thirty-year period. The least one can say is that a qualitative change in tone is discernible. Beyond this, though, the substance of these editorials and articles suggests a subtle though fundamental moral reposturing. For instance, commentary on the problem of alcohol use has shifted from a focus in the late 1950s on the virtues of total abstinence and temperance and the moral problems of consumption even in moderation to a more compassionate portrayal in the early 1980s of the social problem of alcoholism in the church and in the broader society and its spiritual and social solutions.[14] Similarly, on the problem of sexual permissiveness, commentary in the early 1950s and 1960s unsympathetically condemned loose morals, the "new morality," and the "sexual revolution" (which included necking and petting) and encouraged their readership to hold fast to biblical standards of sexual propriety. Three decades later, the focus was on appreciating the human vulnerability to sexual temptations (no longer petting but "living together," adultery, etc.) and why yielding to them was wrong as well as how to responsibly deal with those people who have sinned sexually (including unwed mothers).[15] Even on the problem of homosexuality, though the fundamental moral judgment has not altered, the tone has. Commentary in the early years of the 1980s is notably more sympathetic to the "psychological anguish of the homosexual"; the harshness is almost entirely gone.[16]

All of this merely illustrates that the cultural tendency observable within the coming generation is not unique, but occurs in concert with developments active in the larger Evangelical world. The process is one in which "sin" is being redefined. What had once been morally intolerable is now quite acceptable; what had previously been a cause for exclusion from Christian fellowship does not even call attention to itself.[17] Clearly some norms have not changed. Evangelicals still adhere to prohibitions against premarital, extramarital, and homosexual relations. But even here, the attitude toward those prohibitions has noticeably softened. In brief, the symbolic boundaries which previously defined moral propriety for conservative Protestantism have lost a measure of clarity. Many of the distinctions separating Christian conduct from "worldly conduct" have been challenged if not altogether undermined. Even the words *worldly* and *worldliness* have, within a generation, lost most of their traditional meaning. When asked "what does it mean for a Christian to be different from the 'world'?" most did not invoke traditional understandings at all.

> For me this has less to do with external considerations and more to do with our motives—like making a conscious effort to please God in our lives. Ultimately I suppose this would be reflected in our actions, but I am not quite sure how. (male, senior, Bible major, Evangelical Free)

> I don't think being different from the world means just following a long list of do's and don'ts. That would come out but it really starts out with basic values and attitudes. The core of the issue is in the heart, the values, and the mind set of the Christian. The Christian's main desire should be to serve God, to love God, and to obey God. This would come out in loving your neighbor, not killing, not stealing, not committing adultery, and so on. (female, sophomore, Bible major, Orthodox Presbyterian)

> There are behavioral standards we need to follow, but these are not as clearly spelled out as some Evangelicals try to make them or as some circles of Evangelicals have tried in the past to make them. The more important difference is a sense of joy that Christians have. There is joy because there is a purpose in our life and because we do know our creator. This will show up in the way we respond to people and to situations—especially hardships. (male, sophomore, sociology major, Presbyterian)

> When the Bible says, separate yourself from the world, I understand that to mean that we are not to let the world control how we as Christians think. It is a difference in priorities, and for me, God is my first priority. Worldly behavior is mainly being self-serving. (male, sophomore, physics major, Methodist)

The traditional meaning of worldliness has indeed lost its relevance for the coming generation of Evangelicals.

The issue at one level is not whether traditional definitions of worldliness were right or wrong, biblically correct or incorrect, or even whether these changes are, in an ultimate sense, good or bad. The issue is, instead, sociological. In a word, as long as these traditional norms constituting the moral boundaries of conservative Protestantism remained intact (that is, plausible and legitimate for most conservative Protestants), they performed the important sociological function of providing a means of generating social solidarity and cohesiveness for conservative Protestants as a moral community. By opposing worldliness and those who engaged in worldly behavior, they were able to reestablish their moral authority and reaffirm their collective sense of identity as a unique and even "chosen" people—light in a world of darkness; a city set upon a hill. With the erosion of these moral boundaries and no substitutionary norms replacing them, social cohesiveness is much more difficult to attain, as is a collective sense of identity as a distinctive moral and religious community.

What was latent in the Evangelical view of work is then more visible in an examination of Evangelical definitions of moral discipline. The legacy of Protestant asceticism is indeed undergoing a transformation. The full character of that transformation, though, is not yet discernible.

### THE SELF EXAMINED

As much as inner-worldly asceticism is an attitude about work and about moral propriety, it is also an attitude about the self. For implied in both the competitive pursuit of success in one's vocation and the conformance to rigorous moral codes of conduct is a peculiar orientation toward the self—one of harsh self-denial and rigorous self-discipline. The ethic of renunciation then applies not only to things worldly but to the self as well. It could not be otherwise. The investment of extraordinary effort into work and moral discipline would have, in principle if not in fact, left little place for either indolence or self-indulgence. Yet it was more than a logical necessity for a life given over to these goals. This orientation was also infused with a powerful religious motive.

In traditional theology, the self was a curious mixture. Though retaining certain divine qualities (e.g., the capacity to love, to create, to desire), the self was also viewed as being weak and inherently vulnerable to temptation. In its natural state it was predisposed to disobedience to God's divine laws. Yet traditional conceptions were even more pessimistic than this. Since man's fall from grace, the self would forever be tainted with original sin and was, therefore, viewed as a source of rebellion against God. Pride, lust, covetousness, and other "desires of the flesh" all had their origin there. By its very nature it was hostile to spiritual ideals. In this light, it followed that in order to attain any measure of spirituality or holiness, the believer had to "put to death" all innate passions. The self was something to be mastered and disciplined, its desires to be kept subordinate to loftier goals. In practical terms, this meant that emotions and affections were to be kept in tight control, expressed only in moderation. It also meant that service to God would subjugate the human will (as expressed in specific wants and needs).

With the secularization of the work ethic generally, this religious motive naturally lost its significance and its role in fostering an attitude of mastery over the self. But once again, this was no longer important, for self-mastery had become an institutional requirement of industrial economic activity. People, in other words, maintained the moral posture of self-denial and self-discipline simply because their own economic survival (whether as a wage earner in the factory or as a corporate manager) depended upon it. Such a posture was not without its cultural legitimations, however. It remained a dominant value in the broader culture in the United States at least until midcentury.[18] To the degree that this was so, the implication was the same. The self, as the repository of human emotions and of subjectivity, continued to be a latent as well as negatively valued phenomenon.

Both popular and more serious academic scholarship have documented a dramatic turnabout within the larger American culture on this count from the mid-1960s. It was a turnabout entailing an accentuation of subjectivity and the virtual veneration of the self, exhibited in deliberate efforts to achieve self-understanding, self-improvement, and self-fulfillment.[19] Though it might be supposed that Evangelicalism would be most resistant to change along these lines, traditional assumptions about the self appear to have weakened substantially here as well. There are, in fact, strong indications that a total reversal has taken place in the Evangelical conception of the nature and value of the self. As one might expect, this is particularly prominent within the coming generation of Evangelicals. For example, nearly nine out of every ten Evangelical students (roughly paralleling the number of public university students) agreed that "self-improvement is important to me and I work hard at it" (see table 9). Likewise most (collegians, 68%; seminarians, 52%) agreed that they felt a "strong need for new experiences." The relative significance of these responses is highlighted when they are compared to a national survey of adult Americans conducted by Yankelovich in 1979 (Yankelovich 1981, 82–84). The percentage of Evangelical students agreeing with these statements far exceeded the corresponding percentage of the general population on both the importance of self-improvement and the

**Table 9**
Views of the "Self" according to Campus Setting

| | Evangelical College Students (N = 1,980) (% agreeing) | Evangelical Seminary Students (N = 847) (% agreeing) | Public University Students (N = 426) (% agreeing) | General Population[a] (% agreeing) |
|---|---|---|---|---|
| Self-improvement is important to me and I work hard at it | 87 | 82 | 87 | 66 |
| I feel a strong need for new experiences | 68 | 52 | 78 | 46 |
| A good Christian will strive to be a "well-rounded person" | 79 | 80 | 48 | [b] |
| For the Christian, realizing your full potential as a human being is just as important as putting others before you | 62 | 46 | 44 | [b] |

[a]Yankelovich's (1981) "strong-formers."
[b]Question not asked.

need for new experiences. On the former, only 39 percent of the general population agreed; on the latter, only 22 percent agreed. But there is more. In this general population survey, Yankelovich statistically isolated a special minority. This minority (17% of the adult, working population) manifested and was distinguished by a particularly strong orientation toward self-fulfillment, self-expression, and personal freedom. These were the dominant values upon which they shaped their lives. Yet only 66 percent of this group agreed with the statement that "self-improvement is important to me and I work hard at it," and only 46 percent agreed with the statement that they felt a strong personal need for new experiences. Evangelical students, then, more uniformly endorsed these values than did Yankelovich's "strong-formers."

On the surface, one might expect college students generally in their special life circumstances to give even greater priority to matters of the self than those adults who work full-time for pay. After all, most college students are single and have only their own present needs and future interests to contemplate. Nevertheless, one would also expect that within the American student population, the Evangelicals would be the least likely to endorse this orientation. They of all groups should be most out of step with dominant cultural patterns. But such is not the case. There is, instead, a very clear parallel between Evangelicals and non-Evangelicals in their attitudes about the self.

Given this, it should come as little surprise that this general orientation pervades the manner in which the coming generation of Evangelicals understand their Christian identity. For instance, 80 percent agreed that "a good Christian will strive to be a 'well-rounded person.'" Even more interesting, the majority of Evangelicals (collegians, 62%; seminarians, 46%) agreed that "for the Christian, realizing your full-potential as a human being is *just as important* as putting others before you." It is not insignificant that a far smaller number in the public university (only a small fraction of whom had a strong Christian orientation) perceived this to be the nature of the Christian identity.

Make no mistake, the preoccupation with the self (whether it be oriented toward understanding, fulfillment, or improvement) is not unbridled narcissism. As one would expect, it is qualified in part by the symbolic realities of their faith. In other words, self-understanding or self-fulfillment is partially interpreted through the filter of their Evangelical beliefs. Several spoke to this directly.

> I'm beginning to find that meaning in life is more or less defined in relation to God. It's not as though my job or my educational degrees are unimportant to me—they are—it's just that they take on special meaning in light of God's plan for my life. (male, senior, Bible major, Episcopalian)

> To me, self-fulfillment is very important. Getting married and having kids would be a big part of that; so would finding a good job. Ultimately, though, my fulfillment would come through my belief in God. (female, sophomore, mathematics major, Methodist)

> All of this self-fulfillment talk is very new to me. I used to be very wary of it, but now I'm realizing that you need to know who you are in order to do something with your life. You need to know what your values are and what you want to do with your life before you can fulfill your life and adequately minister to people. (female, sophomore, Bible major, Orthodox Presbyterian)

It is not entirely clear whether their faith lessens appreciably their preoccupation with matters of the self. It is clear that the symbolic realities of their faith do legitimate this orientation. As the last student suggested, self-understanding and self-improvement are requisites to a maturing faith.

Once again it is quite likely that the processes implied in these data have gone furthest within this cohort. Students, for example, were quick to acknowledge differences between themselves and their parents on this count.

> For my dad, the most important thing in the world was to provide for his family financially. Until about two years ago, he worked two to three jobs all of the time. Since my basic needs have been taken care of, I can pursue what I find fulfilling, which is different than just financial security. (female, senior, literature major, Fundamentalist Baptist)

> I think success to my father was providing really well for my mother and maybe being recognized as being a very good salesman. That was fulfilling for him. But for me, I am definitely more interested in living a well-rounded life-style. (female, senior, sociology major, Plymouth Brethren)

In spite of generational differences, it should not be imagined that these processes are somehow unique to the younger generation. This is an orientation and a process occurring within the larger Evangelical world. It is supported, on the one hand, by a publishing industry which devotes over 12 percent of all of its titles to understanding or solving the various emotional and psychological complexities of human experience from an Evangelical perspective (Hunter 1983a, 91–99). This literature varies in theoretical sophistication, but most of it has a popular, mass-market appeal. It is further supported by an expansive service industry of "helping" professionals. Since it was founded in 1953, the (Evangelical) National Association of Christians in Social Work has grown steadily to over 1,500 members.[20] Likewise, the Christian Association of Psychological Studies (CAPS; a largely Evangelical organization for clinical, pastoral, and counseling psychologists) has, since 1952, grown to a total membership of 2,350 (85% of that growth has taken place since the early 1970s).[21] These "experts" have specialized and are credentialed in matters of the self. More importantly, they derive their livelihoods from (and thus have a vested interest in) refining and perpetuating this orientation as a legitimate area of spiritual concern. In doing this, these experts have freely adopted the languages of humanistic, behavioristic, and psychoanalytic psychologies. (All of these perspectives, for example, are widely represented among the membership of CAPS.) Indeed, one of the most interesting aspects of this phenomenon is the way traditional theologies are integrated with these highly secular (at least at the assumptive level) models of the person and the human psyche.

Though only illustrative, one can assume that these expanding industries correspond to the expanding "needs" of an Evangelical populace. These industries also provide institutional legitimacy to these processes as well as institutional inertia toward any change away from this orientation. The fascination with the self and with human subjectivity has then become a well-established cultural feature of Evangelicalism generally in the latter part of the twentieth century, not simply an ephemeral fashion among the younger generation.

But what is one to make of all of this? At one level the phenomenon of the self has been brought into cultural relief, achieving a measure of attention previously unknown. It is pursued not for the purpose of putting it under subjection to God's will (in acts of self-mortification) but as an end in itself. The self is a phenomenon to be analyzed, explored, and understood in part out of a posture of naive curiosity.

The practical side of all of this is expressed in the efforts to understand and deal with such problems as guilt, anxiety, depression, stress, and tension (Hunter 1983a, 91–99). These are all problems besetting the self, and the assumption maintained by most (experts and laymen alike) is that if one can probe deeply enough into human subjectivity, one can understand the source of and solution to these problems. In Evangelical parlance, of course, all of these problems indirectly stem from man's spiritual condition as one fallen from God's favor. Aside from specific therapeutic techniques, then, the ultimate solution may be found in a restored and matured faith in Jesus.

But the ideology goes beyond this. The self and human subjectivity have not only gained attention but have gained legitimacy as well. They have attained a positive value in Evangelical culture. Logically, any discussion of self-improvement, self-fulfillment, and "self-actualization" presupposes that the self can be and is worth being improved, fulfilled, and actualized; any discussion of human potentiality and emotional and psychological maturity presupposes these as legitimate and worthwhile goals. Indeed, the self would seem to achieve ultimate significance and ultimate value when these concerns are framed within biblical and Christian symbolism. Not only is there a moral imperative to seek one's full potential as a human being but there is a divine imperative as well. It is God's will for every Christian. This has been suggested by the comments of students, but it is also precisely the message of such books as *Mental Health: A Christian Approach* (Cosgrove and Mallory, 1977), *The Psychology of Jesus and Mental Health* (Cramer, 1980), *The Art of Understanding Yourself* (Osborne, 1968), *The Undivided Self: Bringing Your Whole Life in Line with God's Will* (Wilson, 1983), *You Can Become the Person You Want to Be* (Schuller, 1973), *The Healthy Personality and the*

*Christian Life* (Hooker, 1977), *You Count—You Really Do!* (Miller, 1976), *Christo-Psychology* (Kelsey, 1982), *How to Become Your Own Best Self* (Grimes, 1979), and *Self-Esteem: The New Reformation* (Schuller, 1983).

The last book, by Robert Schuller, is particulary noteworthy if only because of its extraordinary circulation—250,000 copies were distributed free of charge to religious leaders across the country. It is also noteworthy for the boldness with which he addresses this issue. In it Schuller argues that Reformational theology was "imperfect" for it was not a "well-rounded, full-orbed, honestly-interrelated theology system" (pp. 145–46). For nearly 500 years the basic elements of Christian faith have been misunderstood and misapplied. For example, the traditional theological definition of sin (i.e., rebellion against God) "is not incorrect as much as it is shallow and insulting to the human being" (p. 65). "Reformational theology failed to make clear that the core of sin is a lack of self-esteem" p. 98). In this light, salvation "means to be permanently lifted from sin (psychological self-abuse with all of its consequences as seen above) and shame to self-esteem and its God-glorifying human need-meeting, constructive and creative consequences. . . . To be saved is to know that Christ forgives me and now I dare to believe that I am somebody and I can do something for God and my fellow human beings" (p. 99). So, too, hell is redefined as the "loss of pride that naturally follows separation from God—the ultimate and unfailing source of our soul's sense of self-respect" (p. 14). Schuller then goes on to discuss "the deepest need of human beings."

> The church has survived through the centuries by assuming that every person's ultimate need was "salvation from sin." It has held out "hope for forgiveness" as the ultimate answer. (P. 31)
>     What's wrong with this interpretation today? Nothing, and yet, everything, if in the process of interpreting sin and repentance the gospel is presented in substance or spirit in a way that assaults a person's self-esteem. . . . The need for dignity, self-worth, self-respect, and self-esteem is the deepest of all human needs. (P. 62)

Correspondingly, the "basic problem in our world today" is that "many human beings don't realize who they are. And if we don't know who we are and where we have come from, we will never become what we were meant to be" (p. 62). Given this, Schuller calls upon the church to remodel itself around the mission of addressing these problems. For individual Christians, self-denial will no longer "mean the rejection of that positive emotion we call self-esteem—the joy of experiencing my self-worth—" but will mean a "willingness to be involved in the spiritual and social solutions in society" (pp. 115–16). Likewise the "work-ethic" will become "a person's self-worth epic" (p. 94).

Though Schuller has been criticized (and sharply by some) for the extent to which he redefines historical theology and the mission of the church, most Evangelicals do in fact share the assumptions upon which this book is based: namely, that the attention the self is receiving is legitimate and that the self, as the repository of human emotions and subjectivity, has intrinsic and ultimate worth and significance.

The place, value, and meaning of the self have then altered in the culture of American Evangelicalism. And as expected, these cultural innovations are especially prominent in the world of the coming generation. Charmed by it as opposed to being oblivious to it, absorbed in it rather than being (spiritually) repelled by it, modern Evangelicals have accorded the self a level of attention and legitimacy unknown in previous generations. Traditional assumptions about the self have undergone a fundamental assault.

A LEGACY REVISED

The imperative giving form to inner-worldly asceticism was, as Weber (1958) noted, psychological and not philosophical or intellectual. It was simply born out of the Protestant's passion to serve God and to be assured of personal salvation. Whether it was a historical accident or not is a debatable point. What is less debatable is the fact that a life-ethic was established and a legacy was passed on to succeeding generations of Protestants. Inner-worldly asceticism, a disparate and in some ways unlikely cluster of values and sentiments toward work, toward morality and the world, and toward the self, formed both a real and a mythic cultural heritage for Protestantism. By the twentieth century, much of what originally constituted that ethic had been seriously challenged. As important as the values of hard work and industriousness continued to be, they had become secularized even for Fundamentalists. They had lost virtually all spiritual significance. By contrast, the general posture of austerity and renunciation of the world and the endless number of moral prohibitions that that inspired remained firmly institutionalized. This, by and large, described the situation for conservative Protestantism through midcentury. But what has happened since that time? What remains of the legacy of inner-worldly asceticism in contemporary America?

It should be amply clear at this point that whatever remained of that constellation of values and sentiments through midcentury has since lost most of its cohesiveness. The legacy has paled. It comes as little surprise, for example, to find out that industriousness, competitiveness, vocational discipline, and the like continue to carry only marginal moral value and virtually no spiritual meaning for the Evangelical. It is perhaps more surprising to discover that even as secular values, they have become marginal, deferring to values surrounding the private sphere (e.g., the importance of a creative life-style, of friends, family, and hobbies). By itself, however, this provides little cause for wonder. In the broader picture it does presage other developments.

Since mid-century the elaborate structure of prohibitions constituting the moral boundaries of Protestant orthopraxy has also weakened substantially, and parts of the structure have collapsed altogether. The significance of all of this for the legacy of asceticism is plain. As has been pointed out, conformity to traditional moral strictures at one time defined, in large measure, the quality of individual moral character. Inner-worldly asceticism was only possible insofar as it was based on an ethic of renunciation with regard to the passions of the world. But with the general erosion of these traditional behavioral standards, one central ingredient to the ascetic ideal has been lost. It is logical that traditional asceticism need not hinge on the renunciation of specific activities historically deemed worldly (theater attendance, swimming with members of the opposite sex, etc.) but simply that there be renunciation of something. In other words, the objects of renunciation are less important than the fact of renunciation. Significantly, not only are the number of traditional prohibitions dwindling, but they are not being replaced by others.

The culmination of this process is seen in the shifting presuppositions about the nature of the self. The traditional conception was a social-psychological precondition for an intense commitment both to success in vocation and to the building of moral discipline and fortitude. It undergirded, even made possible, the other core elements of inner-worldly asceticism. These traditional conceptions though have given way to a relatively novel conception, one that implicitly venerates the self. The meaning of this for inner-worldly asceticism is plain. At a purely practical level, how is self-denial or self-mastery for the purpose of developing moral character possible when that which is to be denied or mastered is under almost constant examination? How is the renunciation of the self possible if it is being "improved," or is being developed to its "full potential," or is needing stimulation by "new experiences"? At a more philosophical level, the Evangelical preoccupation with the self and with human subjectivity has brought about a profound cultural contradiction. Formal Evangelical theology, of course, still maintains the view that the self and human nature are inherently sinful. Man, indeed, is separated from God by this fact. The implicit message behind this new orientation, however, belies this pessimistic view. However benign the intentions, however qualified by the grammar of their faith, the extraordinary attention given to matters of the self by Evangelicals softens the meaning and the implications of any traditional notions of the self's inherent depravity. The meaning of the self, of human nature, becomes ambiguous. It becomes both good (worthy of esteem, of improvement, of fulfillment, etc.) and bad (a source of human rebellion against God). While in one sense this contradiction has always existed, it can be reasonably maintained that the positive assumptions have been accentuated to a historically unprecedented level in the contemporary Evangelical world view. To the degree that the meaning of human nature is revised in this way, the infrastructure of traditional Protestantism is undermined.

It should not be forgotten that the life-ethic of asceticism was originally born out of religious conviction and devotion and not the reverse. This being so, it would be reasonable to assume that varying gradations of religious orthodoxy would still account for some variation among Evangelicals in their attitudes toward work, morality, and the self: namely, that the more intensely orthodox the Evangelical is, the more self-denying he or she will be. This is, in fact, the case: the more orthodox and dogmatic do tend to be more vocationally and morally ascetic in their orientation.[22]

There are those among the younger generation who do, indeed, remain fairly strongly committed to traditional ideals of work and morality, and they are characterized by more than a high degree of theological orthodoxy. They also tended to be affiliated with the smaller, more sectarian denominations of the Holiness-Pentecostal tradition in conservative Protestantism. Finally there is just a slightly greater tendency for them to be from lower-middle-class and working-class families (with less educational achievement). But again these differences are statistically different but not substantially different. In the main, the demographic variations make only marginal differences in the degree to which Evangelicals have abandoned the old ethic.[23]

In a word, the Protestant legacy of austerity and ascetic self-denial is virtually obsolete in the larger Evangelical culture and is nearly extinct for a large percentage of the coming generation of Evangelicals. The caricatures of Evangelicalism as the last bastion of the traditional norms of discipline and hard work for their own sake, self-sacrifice, and moral asceticism are largely inaccurate. Far from being untouched by the cultural trends of the post–World War II decades, *the coming generation of Evangelicals, in their own distinct way, have come to participate fully in them.*

But there is more one can say, for implied in the decline of traditional asceticism is the adoption of a new set of obligations, a new structure of norms. In this, the coming generation can be distinguished by degree. If there are those who are unreflectively committed to the traditional norms of vocational and moral asceticism, there are also those who seem particularly committed to this new, implicit set of obligations. In contrast to their counterparts, although they reside within the boundaries of theological orthodoxy, they are less traditional on some doctrinal points and exhibit a measure of uncertainty about others. They are also better represented in the nonsectarian denominational churches of the Reformational-Confessional and Anabaptist traditions. They are a little more likely to be from urban areas and from better educated families whose chief wage-earner is either a professional, a technician, or even a minister. In the middle, between extremes, however, are the majority, who share a more innovative orientation toward work and moral discipline yet are more moderate. For these, the new rules are less of a cause.

For the majority, then (and this would hold for the larger Evangelical population), commitment to success in the public sphere is overshadowed to varying degrees by a commitment to an increasing quality of life in the private sphere. Strong and meaningful personal relationships and a creative and expressive style of living are of paramount concern. Correspondingly, in the place of moral certainty is a concommitant measure of moral ambiguity. There is no indication, however, that the latter is accompanied by a romanticized longing for previous moral commitments. To the contrary, all indications point to a demand for a high degree of tolerance for a diversity of life-styles. Indeed, the majority (58%, collegian; 50%, seminarian) agreed "that people should be free to *live* the way they want even if it is very different from the way I live." Finally, self-fulfillment is no longer a natural by-product of a life committed to higher ideals but rather is a goal, pursued rationally and with calculation as an end in itself. The quest for emotional, psychological, and social maturity, therefore, becomes normative. Self-expression and self-realization compete with self-sacrifice as a guiding life-ethic.

As if to prophesy of things to come, one Evangelical writing in 1948 in a popular Evangelical magazine called *His* spoke of "soft Christians"— soft because they are "self-indulgent" and "undisciplined." "Oh, they are probably Christians. They don't seem wicked; they are not committing open sin; they are satisfactorily orthodox; they are mildly active in the work of Christ. . . . But they are soft, flabby. They lack discipline, hardness, and fiber."[24] Specifying what constitutes indulgence, the author noted the desire of "pleasant food and drink," for "easy chairs and easy riding cars," for "physical sensation," and "sex satisfaction" (including "petting, necking, and smooching"), as well as the desire to be "satisfied with our achievements" and "to be popular."[25] It is clear, then, that Evangelicals generally and the coming generation particularly have adopted patterns which even a generation ago (not to mention a century ago) would have been considered improper if not scandalous. What had been a cause for judgment is presently (for most Evangelicals) entirely uncontroversial or else celebrated as part of the Christian experience. In this, they are set off from a tradition that had, in one way or another, long characterized Protestantism.

Historical research has shown that the archetypal Protestant of generations past, albeit shrouded in myth, was not without his benevolent, compassionate, and forbearing side. At bottom though, he was a rather grim character, obdurate in maintaining the legitimacy of harsh standards for life and work. His duty as a Christian demanded nothing less. This character though is, in the main, gone. His contemporary descendant is one who, instead, "works out his salvation" not in his vocation but in the private sphere of family, personal friends, and intersubjectivity, who has either forgotten, repudiated, or "outgrown" traditional definitions of worldliness, and who has made a moral and spiritual virtue of self-understanding and self-expression. The broader significance of this remains to be seen.

# Family: Toward Androgyny

Helen V. L. Stehlin, coauthor

The relationship between religion and family in most if not all religious traditions is so intimate and complex that the two are virtually inseparable. In the main, family provides the most rudimentary context in which religious faith is expressed in day-to-day living. It also forms the single most important institutional setting for passing the traditions on to successive generations. Religion, on the other hand, provides a cohesive moral order into which children are socialized and within which the network of human relationships takes on ultimate significance. Christianity, of course, is no exception to this. As is well known, the family and its structure of relationships have, from the beginning, carried theological significance. This is seen, for example, in the relationship between bridegroom and bride as a metaphor of Christ and the Church or the relationship between father and son as a metaphor for understanding an aspect of the Trinity. In this sense, the family has long occupied hallowed ground in the Christian imagination.

That the family is important within Evangelical Christianity, then, comes as no surprise. It occupies a central place in the Christian life and world view. What is curious, however, is that the significance of the family has achieved dimensions perhaps never before seen. Transcending the concrete and taken-for-granted reality (the medium in which ordinary people live their lives) the family has in recent times become a symbol to Evangelicals, a symbol of social stability and traditional moral virtue. And as a symbol it is commonly reduced to a slogan. The so-called traditional family has generated tremendous passion, and its survival in the modern world has become perhaps the highest priority on the Evangelical social agenda.

The programs given to the articulation of what the Christian family should be and to the defense of this "traditional family" are almost numberless. There are, for example, films such as "Focus on the Family"

(Word, Incorporated), "Maximum Marriage" (Merit Media), "Marriage Enrichment" (New Day Productions), "Strike the Original Match" (New Liberty Films), "The Family Gone Wild" (New Liberty Films), "Family Life Film Series" (Christian Leadership), "Crisis in the Homes" (Worldwide Pictures), "The Family—God's Pattern for Living Series" (Moody Institute of Science), "Love and Marriage" (Malaga Cove Pictures), and "Six Keys to Marital Happiness" (Malaga Cove Pictures). There are seminars and workshops such as Family Life Seminars, James Dobson's workbook/cassette series "Thirty Critical Problems Facing the American Family," and Bill Gothard's Institute in Basic Youth Conflict (over 1.3 million people have participated in seminars conducted by this institute since 1964, when it was founded). There is the publishing industry as well. As of 1982, 10 percent of all mass-market and trade books published by Evangelical publishing houses (a multimillion dollar industry) dealt with some aspect of the family, from child rearing and parenting to proper sex roles to emotional and sexual compatibility to the ethics of divorce and remarriage. There is hardly any family topic that has not been dealt with in this literature.[1] There are also political organizations. The Moral Majority, the Coalition for Better Television, Christian Family Renewal, United Families of America, Pro-Family Forum, Pro-Family United, Family Protection Lobby, National Pro-Family Coalition, Family America, and Christian Action Council all have a stated or implied objective of buttressing the "traditional family" and upholding traditional values and mores. This, of course, entails opposition (in varying degrees) to the Equal Rights Amendment, abortion legislation, and gay and lesbian rights. But it also suggests fairly cohesive support for such legislative initiatives as the Family Protection Act, the purpose of which is "to preserve the integrity of the American family, to foster and protect the viability of American family life by emphasizing family responsibilities in education, tax assistance, religion, and other areas related to the family."[2]

It is difficult, then, to exaggerate the significance of the "traditional family" to Evangelicals. It is viewed as the bedrock of the American way of life—its social, cultural, and political institutions. Perceived as being weakened by post–World War II social and political developments, its defense has become an Evangelical passion. It is its cause célèbre.

The politicization of the family on the part of Evangelicals is not entirely without historical precedent. In the late nineteenth century several groups of Evangelical hue concerned with the welfare of the family emerged. Organizations such as the National League for the Protection of the Family (1896), Mothers' Congress (1896), the White Cross Society (1883), and the women's movement generally gained surprising visibility and power in their attempts to shield family life from the evils of industrialization and urbanization.[3] The difference between past and present is, first of all, one of volume. There are simply more groups on the present scene, and this is evidence of a larger constituency concerned about the family. In different terms, there is a greater popular sense of crisis about the traditional family in the modern world. This means that the traditional family and its survival in contemporary America have become problematic for large numbers of Evangelicals. For example, in a survey of faculty at Evangelical colleges, over two-thirds agreed that "the traditional family is in a state of crisis." Evangelical theologians, as another survey showed, felt much the same way.[4]

It is not specific, individual families (e.g., the Witherspoons next door) that are in mind here. In some ways, they are entirely irrelevant. It is, rather, the family as an *ideal* (a generic phenomenon) that has become problematized. This presupposes the elevation of the family to unprecedented levels of symbolic importance. Indeed, one commentator noted, "the family—next to God—is the most important and influential agent on earth."[5] It is, then, a symbolic reality which is seen as being in a state of crisis. Yet it is the family as a symbolic reality which is romanticized as well. In the Evangelical case, that ideal is the traditional family, on the surface, a fairly opaque amalgam of ideas about family structure and family life in an earlier and more genteel time. But when the mists of nostalgia burn away, what really is meant by the "traditional family"? In the broader historical context of the American (and European) past, can this ideal be fairly described as "traditional"? And how do the present and coming generations of Evangelicals fit into this picture?

The first task is to explore what Evangelicals mean by the traditional family. To the degree that the family has become problematized, there has arisen a coterie of "experts" to address these problems. As is well known, this has been true for both the Evangelical and non-Evangelical worlds, and for the former as with the latter, their number is quite large. Thus, in portraying the traditional family (which is taken as Judeo-Christian in essence) there is no better source than the writings and pronouncements of these specialists. They define for Evangelicalism the symbolic reality of what is taken to be the traditional family.

## THE TRADITIONAL FAMILY: MYTHIC QUALITIES

"The family belongs to God. He created it. He determined its inner structure. He appointed for it its purpose and goal . . . to bring glory and honor to God."[6] Though ties with the extended family are legitimate and encouraged, the family in mind here is nuclear (husband, wife, and children), with fairly well-defined roles and structures of authority for all members. These naturally are viewed as essential for the fulfillment of God's plan for the family. The general pattern is familiar. The husband holds the primary responsibility of providing materially and spiritually for the family: "the burden of caring for the support of the family lies upon the man."[7] It is assumed that he will be the chief if not sole breadwinner. As spiritual leader, he is "overseeing his family in order that they might reflect the image of God properly, . . . raising his children to love and follow the Lord, . . . being totally responsible to God for his wife and family."[8] In day-to-day life, the husband has the "final say" though he is to honor and respect his wife's opinions. He is warned not to abuse this position of power because his authority derives from "divine order and not natural superiority." He should rather seek to maintain "the same self-sacrificial manner as that of Christ toward the Church." One author summarized it this way: "God said it! It is your duty to 'take charge'—to maintain a home atmosphere where your wife and children have no question of who is watching out for them. You are responsible for the mood and direction of your household."[9]

In raising the children, the father's role is to be the disciplinarian, with disciplinary power delegated to the wife in his absence. Beyond this he is encouraged to spend "quality" time with his children. Against the pattern of paternal absenteeism, a specialist exhorted: "Is Dad necessary? You bet he is! He is part of a God-designed team and his teamwork is essential to the personal growth of his children."[10] Others concur as well. "It is a perverted altar which sacrifices a man's relationship with his wife and kids for the sake of the job or ministry." Fathers should "devote a generous parcel of undivided attention to the kids."[11]

Within the biblical line of authority, the wife takes on the role of "helpmeet"—companion and helper to her husband. She acknowledges her husband's position of leadership and authority and responds accordingly with love, respect, and submission. While the husband and wife are viewed as equals in terms of ultimate worth, they are still considered to be endowed with different aptitudes and responsibilities. Most if not all place the wife's principal responsibility in the home, serving the needs of her husband and children, transforming the home into a "haven, . . . a place of God's peace and warmth and love."[12] She is a homemaker in the fullest sense of the word, accountable to her husband and ultimately to God for her performance in this role.

A wife's primary responsibility is to give of herself, her time and her energy to her husband, children and home.[13]

What is the key to success for a married woman? First it is constantly seeking God's perspective on life. Secondly it is modeling a personal plan for utilizing herself and serving her husband, children and home. At last it is allowing God to meet her needs through her husband, children and opportunities found through the home.[14]

The home is potentially the greatest place for women to be fulfilled.[15]

A family is a blending of people for whom a career of making a shelter in a time of storm is worth a lifetime.[16]

As mother, her role naturally involves more than bearing offspring to continue the family name. Motherhood for her is a "challenging career"—a woman's "unique and most obvious role."[17] One family counselor noted that the

> maternal role is more than just one component in the pattern of complementary roles. It is the crucial pivot—the foundation—upon which both family and society revolve. How women fill that role determines the potential happiness and fulfillment of all of us.[18]

Mothers are then encouraged to stay home with their children, especially during their formative, preschool years. According to another specialist, motherhood is a "full-time job during the child's first five years." "What activity could be more important than shaping human lives during their impressionable and plastic years?"[19] "Traditional motherhood" also implies that she will place the needs of her children as well as her husband above her own.

> If you choose to be a mother, you temporarily, at least agree to lay aside some of your other involvements, recognizing that bringing children into the world obligates you for their best possible care. The woman who cannot face making her personal interests secondary to the concerns of a family should not have children.[20]

As important as children are, parents are also encouraged to adopt an antipermissive approach to childrearing. James Dobson's *Dare to Discipline* (over one million copies sold as of 1984) is perhaps the most representative of this. The advice is clear:

Identify the rules well in advance; let there be no doubt about what is and is not acceptable behavior; when the child cold-bloodedly chooses to challenge those known boundaries in a haughty manner, give him good reason to regret it; at all times, demonstrate love and affection and kindness and understanding.[21]

Most experts endorse spanking as a legitimate if not essential means of punishing disobedience in children as part of the disciplinary process. One advocate noted:

Parents will never have a clear-cut approach to the discipline of their children until they accept the rod as God's appointed means of discipline.[22]

The impression would be mistaken if it is of a callous instrumentalism in childrearing. To the contrary, parents are urged to try to understand their children's behavior for, as Dobson points out, "the art of good parenthood revolves around the intepretations of meaning behind behavior."[23] Therefore, parents are advised to

take time to reason with your child. Never allow your child to talk back, but take advantage of every opportunity to point out to your child the good and bad of certain things.[24]

Still another counselor wrote: "Helping our children build a healthy picture of themselves is the key to successful parenthood."[25]

The family, in this view has an organic simplicity and natural cohesion to it. But it is further idealized in terms of its place and function in the larger world. The family is to be a refuge and a shelter from the harsh and intemperate forces of the modern world. It is a place of security and solace. There is even a self-conscious quality about this, as several experts have expressed:

Only through the family can we hope to achieve security, a sense of well-being and belonging.[26]

In such times as these . . . the Christian home should be a holy refuge. A place of peace. An enclave of loving authority and Godly grievances and truth.[27]

Our earthly family should be the ones to whom we want to run, cry, telephone, telegraph—when we feel overwhelmed by fail-

ure! An earthly family is meant to be a shelter, a solid, depend-
able "ear" that will hear and understand, as well as a place to
which to run.[28]

[The home is] an island of serenity and support and understanding in a hectic, plastic, often avaricious world. A Christian oasis
far from the maddening throng and godless currents and
pressures.[29]

For it's in our homes that we are needed, it's to our families that
we are important. For the home is the last bastion against
depersonalization and dehumanization.[30]

It goes so far that for many of these experts, a spiritually strong and
loving family is ultimately the basis for a strong and healthy nation.
"Weak families beget weak societies." The following illustrate that
theme:

The family is that basic institution of society which undergirds
all else. . . . If the family fails then all the other institutions of
society will fail.[31]

The hope of America today is strong Christian families. Determine to make your family a fortress of spiritual and moral
strength against the shifting tides of moral change.[32]

America is in trouble today because the home is in trouble.[33]

If we are to rebuild our nation we must first strengthen our
homes and make sure they are Christ-centered. Husbands and
wives must assume the full responsibilities of Christian parents
so that children may walk in the ways of the Lord.[34]

Given this perspective, it would only follow that individuals, organizations, political movements, and social trends oriented away from this
model (such as feminism and homosexuality) would be viewed as threatening and even pernicious. Such developments would not only be untraditional and un-American, they would literally be anti-Christian as well.
The traditional family, so defined, must be protected and supported at all
costs.

Though to some the question will be rhetorical, it still deserves
asking: In what sense is this model of family life traditional? Is this the
Judeo-Christian ideal handed down from generations past? To those
familiar with social history, it is clear that this model of the family is

historically specific—unique to a certain historical period and to certain sociological structures. For those unfamiliar with social history, it would be instructive to elaborate upon where this ideal originated by reviewing broad themes in the social history of the family in the past several centuries. But a caveat first. A comprehensive review and analysis of this social transformation would be not only impossible within the confines of this chapter but inappropriate for our purposes. This review masks no such pretense. The interest here is only to chart the broad contours of these changes in order to illustrate the historical and sociological nature of the family idealized in contemporary Evangelical culture. In making this sketch, the focus will be on the quality of relationships in the family and not the structure of relationships. Indeed, there is evidence that the nuclear family structure has been the continuous and enduring family structure since the fourteenth century (Laslett 1972, 1977). The principal changes then have been cultural. It is the *meaning* of family and the meaning of roles within the family that have undergone the greatest change.

AN EXCURSUS
THE "TRADITIONAL FAMILY": REFLECTIONS ON SOCIAL HISTORY
One of the most important functions of the family in the twentieth century is the satisfaction of the emotional needs of its members.[35] "Feelings" play a prominent role at all points of the family life cycle: in uniting couples, in rearing children, in binding families together. Yet the emotional factor has not always figured so prominently. It was nearly foreign to family dynamics in centuries past. In all social strata from the late Middle Ages to the eighteenth century (though by this point, only in the lower classes) in a culture that was overtly "Christian" in name if not in practice, family life was conducted with little if any emotionalism and sentimentality. The most important function of the family was survival from day to day. Connected, of course, was the concern with transmitting property and lineage from one generation to the next. In this light, success of the family could be defined only in terms of having adequate food, shelter, and protection and not in terms of the degree to which husbands and wives and parents and children were "relating" well. Above all, family was defined as a common economic enterprise (Shorter 1975; Aries 1962).

From day to day, life was lived in public with the home being little more than an open dwelling shared by servants, friends, clients, guests, and the like. Privacy was virtually nonexistent. Accordingly, marriages were open to public scrutiny. Typically arranged by parents, they tended to lack much romantic affection, especially among the peasants, who were preoccupied with the austere demands of everyday life.

A strong form of patriarchal rule also typified the preindustrial family type, requiring total submission from children and wife. Children in the Middle Ages viewed their father with such fear and respect and were taught to behave with such formality and awe that the familiarity often experienced in the twentieth century would have been unimaginable (Queen and Habenstein 1967, 238; Aries 1962, pt. 3). Accordingly roles and tasks for family members were sharply distinguished.

Childhood was not considered a distinct and separate period of life. Adolescents of the Middle Ages were viewed as little adults. As Philippe Aries noted, "as soon as the child could live without the constant solicitude of his mother, his nanny, or his cradle-rocker, he belonged to adult society" (1962, 128). No distinction was made between the young and old in work or in play, aptly symbolized by the fact that children and adults wore similar dress. Infants were distinct from adults, of course, yet they were typically regarded with a measure of indifference. This was so for three reasons. In part it was due to the fact that mothers were forced by material circumstances and community attitudes to subordinate infant welfare to the economic demands of daily existence. There was simply very little time for playful tenderness. More importantly, it was a function of a high rate of infant mortality. For rich as for poor a large proportion of infants (estimates of one in three) died in the first three years of life. Still more (approximately one in two) did not live to maturity (Banks 1981, chap. 9). It simply was too much to expect parents to allow maternal and paternal affections to grow and to invest energy in the child's future given the likelihood that the child would not live to see that future. Still a third reason was that infants, for all practical purposes, did not really warrant human status. Though perhaps overstating his point, social historian Edward Shorter speaks to this: "Barely possessing souls of their own, they came at the will of God, departed at His behest, and in their brief mortal sojourn deserved little adult sympathy or compassion" (1977, 169). Thus, it was not uncommon for children who died in infancy to be buried in the garden or next to the house in the same way that people of later centuries buried domestic dogs or cats (Aries 1962, 39). Naturally mothers rarely thought to concern themselves with the development and happiness of their young children.

Life was a struggle for all family members. Children were brutalized as much by the daily routines of life as by outbursts of parental rage—beatings, sexual abuse, and abandonment were not at all uncommon. This was so even as late as the eighteenth and early nineteenth centuries for the popular classes. In rural France, for example, there was virtually a universal practice of leaving infants alone for long periods of time "stewing in their own excrement," sometimes "attacked and eaten by the barnyard hogs" (Shorter 1977, 170–71). It appears that maternal indifference was not only characteristic of the rural families where women worked in the fields; the lower-class workers in the early industrial period treated their young children in a similar manner. Yet economic necessity by itself did not account for this maternal indifference, for mothers who stayed with their children during the day tended to display a similar attitude. Children who survived infancy during this period did not remain long with their parents. It was common practice among privileged and unprivileged alike to have their children apprenticed at an early age (Queen and Habenstein 1967, 239). All in all, family life was tremendously austere, providing little space for emotional expression.

Changes did take place, however, though they were not universal in scope. Initially they found expression in the aristocratic classes of six-teenth-and seventeeth-century Europe. There was a change in the way the nobility and upper-class families viewed their children. Infants and children came to be distinguished from adults and came to assume a greater moral worth. As Aries comments, "a new concept of childhood had appeared, in which the child, on account of his sweetness, simplicity and drollery, became a source of amusement and relaxation for the adult" (1962, 129). This attitude (expressed by mothers as well as nannies) was a significant departure from that of the medieval family. As such it did not go unchallenged. Wrote Montaigne in the seventeenth century: "I cannot abide that passion for carressing new-born children, which have neither mental activities nor recognizable bodily shape by which to make themselves lovable, and I have never willingly suffered them to be fed in my presence" (quoted in Aries 1962, 130). While maternal indifference was giving way to affection and sentimentality in the upper classes, by the end of the seventeenth century and early eighteenth century, "coddling" was beginning to be practiced in the lower classes as well.

Accompanying the sentimentalization of childhood and adolescence was the view that children were not just "charming toys" but "fragile creatures of God who needed to be both safeguarded and reformed." Other moralists of the period were then concerned with the behavior of the child and ways to understand and correct it. (Thus by the seventeenth century, texts on the subject of child psychology emerged.) This had implications for the education of children. Previously a matter of apprenticeship, education increasingly became institutionalized in the school. Aside from a desire on the part of pedagogues to isolate children from the "negative influences of the adult world," the schools served the parents' relatively new interest in "watch[ing] more closely over their children, stay[ing] nearer to them, and avoid[ing] abandoning them even temporarily to the care of another family" (Aries 1962, 369). Thus the family as well as the school isolated the child from adult society.

Clearly a new significance was being placed on the upper-class child. Unlike his medieval predecessor, he became increasingly regarded as an indispensible element of everyday life, and his parents worried about his education, his career, his future. The seventeenth-century child of privilege, though still not the center of the family, had gained a significance not previously known.

Another important trend just beginning to take hold among the upper classes of Europe had to do with household space. There was a direct correlation between privacy and social position. Rooms were becoming larger and more partitioned, allowing men and women of privilege to lead sexual and emotional lives that would not be monitored by outsiders. But once again, the emergence of "privacy" was class-based. The lower classes in Europe during this same time period continued to conduct family life very much in public (Aries 1962, 405; Shorter 1977, 39–40).

In America at this time, there was no real equivalent to the landed aristocracy in Europe. American culture was, in fact, fairly well insulated from many of the cultural changes taking place across the Atlantic. The predominant cultural form taking shape in the new colonies was that of Puritan New England, which evinced its own orientation toward family life.

Like middle-class, lower-class, and peasant families in Europe, the Puritan family experienced little privacy in day-to-day living. Rooms in households served multiple purposes and were not set aside for specific functions. Families also continued to be open to the obtrusive world of servants, friends, clients, boarders, and other people's children. The presence of strangers was a normal part of family life. In spite of this public and seemingly cacophonous quality of family life, a clear structure of authority prevailed. Husbands were superior to their wives, and parents were superior to their children. The place of women in this arrangement was distinct. Women, it was maintained, were made "ultimately for God, but immediately for man" (Morgan 1966, 20). In seventeenth-century New England it was unquestionably held that a woman's place was in the home. She was expected to "keep at home, educate the children, and keep and improve what is got by the industry of the man."[36] Her place was to "guid[e] the house" and not "guid[e] the husband." As Edmund Morgan notes: "The proper conduct of a wife was submission to her husband's instructions and commands. He was her superior and she owed him an obedience founded on reverence. He stood before her in the place of God; he exercised the authority of God over her and he furnished her with the fruits of the earth that God had provided" (1966, 44–45).

In terms of a basis for family order, sentiment and affection were still fairly sparse features of Puritan life, though more evident than in the past. The Puritans believed that God commanded husbands and wives to be kind and loving toward each other. Yet this spousal love was not without limits, for to value anything too greatly was to upset the order of creation and descend to idolatry. Accordingly, Puritan marriage typically resulted neither from falling in love nor from parental arrangement (though parental influence was formidable) but from a rational decision to enter a married state. This was followed by the calculated choice of a suitable spouse.

Sentimentality was also a sparse feature of Puritan childrearing practices. Puritan children were often raised within other families even when there was no educational purpose behind it. It was believed that by bringing children up in other people's homes, children would learn better manners. However, while their own children were in their care, Puritan parents saw discipline and instruction as among their chief responsibilities. Underlying this orientation was the Calvinistic conviction that children were vessels of sin. Therefore, they required continual correction and chastisement (including sound beatings) in order to make them human beings—indeed, in order to save their souls. As Cotton Mather quipped, "Better whipt, than Damn'd." Indeed, these themes were so prominent that some modern-day commentators have described Puritan family government as "authoritarian" and "rigorously repressive" (Greven 1977, 32). Puritan parents held complete control and power within the family, and thus, the subjugation "of the child's will by the exertion of systematic efforts on the part of the parents was justified by the conviction that parental power and authority were beyond question within the confines of the household" (Greven 1977, 99). Children were expected to look toward God and their parents with love and fear; obedience and submission were the only acceptable responses for children.

The many different economic and political changes associated with the emergence of industrial capitalism (such as urbanization, the separation of work from the home [of public from private], and the development of surplus wealth for individuals and nations) are complex to be sure. It is clear that they had profound effects on family life—in particular, in accelerating and intensifying themes of privacy, individual autonomy, and even sentimentality. The tendencies in family life emerging among the upper classes in the sixteenth and seventeenth centuries had begun to filter downward in the social structure in the eighteenth century such that by the nineteenth century, they had become diffused and firmly institutionalized in what is known as the bourgeois (middle and upper middle class, industrial) family (Aries 1962, 404; Lasch 1977, 4). This was true both in Europe and in America.

For one, the bourgeois family became separated in many ways from the larger community in which it was embedded. This meant, on the one hand, that the community exercised less control over courtship, marriage, and family relations and had fewer sanctioning capabilities in the face of the violation of social and familial norms. Accordingly, the family became increasingly isolated from the bustle of public activity, segregated from strangers, outsiders, and basically all nonfamily members. This *privatization* process had important consequences for the inner dynamics of family life as well. This period and this social stratum witnessed an emotional revolution (after a fashion). For example, romantic love and intimacy played an increasing (and increasingly legitimate) role in the courtship process and in the sustenance of marriage. No longer instrumental and largely affectionless as in previous centuries, husbands and wives came to value the relationship for the companionship it provided. Yet romantic love was not equalitarian either. It was interpreted in terms of the authority structure of the family. For men, it therefore meant protectiveness; for women, it meant service and chaste submission.

Children came to hold a central place and therefore a new status in the family. As fewer youths were needed to help with agricultural work, factory work, or infant care, middle-class children gradually became viewed not as objects of utility but as beings of sentimental worth (Hareven 1977, 67). A child soon became irreplaceable; his death an irreparable loss. Never before had children been treated with such considerateness and solicitude. Emerging, then, was a new conviction that childhood was a time of innocence and purity, a period of life not yet contaminated by the vulgarities of the modern industrialized world. Even so, Calvinistic notions continued to inspire parents to drive their children on to moral excellence. The nurturing of children became a parental and societal priority. The ethic of improvement predominated. Parents were to do the best they could for their children (with a proper education and good job prospects for their sons and careful grooming of daughters as desirable candidates for marriage), and children were then to improve upon their parents in terms of status and material comfort. The net effect of these cultural changes was a prolongation of the period considered proper to childhood and adolescence.

Perhaps the single most important cultural development surrounding the family had to do with its legitimating ideology, its place in society. In the face of a competitive world of commerce and industry and the loneliness and alienating circumstances of the modern city, the family and the home came to be viewed as a place of peace, a refuge, and a "haven in a heartless world" (Jeffrey 1972; Laslett 1973; Lasch 1977). Here the tension and stress of work would be abolished, the vulgarity of the public realm would be excluded, and true standards of taste would be preserved. As one Victorian commentator put it, "when the father returns home [from work] . . . it ought to be a scene of order, harmony and comfort."[37] The utopian qualities of the notion of family and home as Edenic retreat cannot be overemphasized. The perfection of society was attainable largely through the perfection of the home. This in large part was the impulse behind the domestic science movement and other reform movements of the late nineteenth century (Calder 1977; Pivar 1973).

Naturally, husbands and wives continued to have distinct roles and operate in distinct spheres of authority. The man's first duty continued to be to provide a good living for his wife and children. The husband's role in this new model altered little from his role in the past. By virtue of having to leave home in order to work, he was necessarily removed from the routines of everyday life. Thus, his authority became more abstract and symbolic. Still, his influence in the affairs of the family remained virtually uncontestable. Family hierarchy remained resolutely patriarchal though not always or necessarily tyrannical. For example, it appears that he became more sentimentally attached to his children (especially now to his daughters) than in the past. Overall, however, the image of the bourgeois father and husband continued to be one of autocratic dominance, paternal severity, and moral and religious rigidity.

The woman's authority remained under that of her husband and her sphere of responsibility became the details of domestic life. But within this sphere, the meaning of her role changed dramatically. It was now understood that the burden of familial perfectibility fell upon her shoulders. She would be the architect of the Edenic retreat. Women as "angels of consolation" were to minister to their husbands, exhausted by the demands of the public sphere, to repair the spiritual damage inflicted by the market, and to shelter their children from the corrupting influence of the modern city (Lasch 1977, 168). It was the last which took on special prominence. As the household ceased to be the center of production, the wife was able to devote enormous amounts of time and energy to raising her children, who were no longer viewed as little adults but rather persons of vulnerability and impressionability who required a warm, protected, and prolonged period of nurture. Increasingly, violence was replaced with persuasion as a means of familial control. The home in this scheme would be an orderly, secure place where children could be indoctrinated with the proper values before being sent forth to make their way in a rapidly changing world (Lasch 1977, 5-6). By the middle of the nineteenth century, motherhood had emerged as a full-time vocation and it was exalted in the culture accordingly (Hareven 1977, 69). "Good mothering," an invention of the period, had become the moral standard for all women of standing, the significance of which was the reform and perfection of the entire social order.

The cultural history of the family since the nineteenth century has evolved in predictable fashion. The main features of the bourgeois pattern of family life spread to all classes of Western society. Lower-class but upwardly mobile women, in fact, came to regard the attainment of this family arrangement as the height of liberation and fullfillment. But in the post–World War II era, the family underwent what can only be described as a further intensification and radicalization of the tendencies predominant in the bourgeois family model. Hyperindividuation and hypersentimentalization became particularly prominent (Berger and Berger 1983, chap. 5).

The former entails an increasing emphasis on the individual over against *every* collective entity. Ironically it was the bourgeois family that had provided the context out of which modern individuation could occur. But up to this point individuation meant placing individual needs and interests over those of the state and, more practically, over those of the local community. Hyperindividuation takes this process one step further such that the concerns and interests of the individual have priority even over the family itself. The rise of contemporary feminism takes on meaning in this regard. The *individual* woman (her rights, her needs, her occupational and political interests) is now emphasized over against every social context in which she finds herself. In the context of the family, her identity and rights are redefined independently of her spouse's authority (previously absolute); her identity and rights are defined independently of the culturally defined needs of her children (previously all-encompassing). This can even extend to a priority of her independence over that of a fetus/unborn child—in this case, a right to control her own body.

Hypersentimentalization entails a propensity to reorder family priorities such that emotional considerations are elevated to a level equal to or above other immediate considerations—community concerns, the honor and integrity of the family name, and even the material well-being of the family. This clearly constitutes an extension of the propensities already evident in the nineteenth century. In childrearing, it is seen in the tendency to impute high moral value to the emotional stability, psychological development, and happiness of the child. (The inclination to define all corporal punishment as child abuse is important in this regard as is the concern of parents and professionals with the mental health and emotional development of children.) In courtship and marriage, it is seen in the singular role of romantic love and intimacy in the selection of a mate and in the foundation of a long-term commitment. But hypersentimentalization is especially noticeable in the redefinition of patriarchal authority—the role of men in the household. For women sentimentality had already achieved a high level of expression in the nineteenth-century definitions of motherhood and homemaker. Not so in the nineteenth-century definitions of husbanding and fatherhood. A strong patriarchal form of authority prevailed at this time (and for centuries before). As father and as husband, his authority was, for all practical purposes, an unquestioned reality. This was so in Evangelical homes and non-Evangelical homes alike. Yet, it is this paternalistic dominance which has been qualified if not completely redefined.

Together hyperindividuation and hypersentimentalization have, among other things, fostered a radical cultural and political disposition toward androgyny. The pressure to affirm the equality if not sameness of men and women in all spheres is compellingly strong. Role distinctions are downplayed. Familial responsibilities (including the responsibility of care for small children and domestic chores) are no longer to be the wife's alone but are to be distributed more evenly between husband and wife. Husbands no longer dominate the role of providing economically for the family but now share that responsibility with their wives. In this effort, women are no longer restricted to occupations long held to be feminine but are free and legally protected to pursue career paths traditionally dominated by men. The picture is familiar and hardly needs elaboration. Still it is worth noting that androgynization (for lack of a better word) is an affair of the middle and upper-middle classes. It is not yet widely diffused in the rest of the population—hierarchical distinctions being particularly prevalent in the working classes.

## THE TRADITIONAL FAMILY RECONSIDERED

If the historical perspective outlined thus far is correct, then two things should be plain. The first is that there has been enough variability in family structure and relations in the last several centuries in the (predominantly Christian) West that it is not entirely clear what the traditional family is. One could make a plausible case, however, that the traditional model really is a strong patriarchal model (repressive by contemporary standards) where both husbands and wives are engaged in economically productive (not just consumptive) labor, where the marital relationship is largely unromantic and instrumental, where parents are generally indifferent to the emotional, psychological, and sometimes physical needs of their children, and where the boundaries between home and the world of work and public concourse are thin or nonexistent. Certainly these features have characterized family life for a longer period in Western history than they have not.

The second point to be made is that when contemporary Evangelicals (preachers, spokesmen, family experts, lobbyists, and politicians) speak of the Christian family, the traditional family, or traditional family values, they are really referring to the prototypical nineteenth-century bourgeois family. Its structure of relationships (nuclear), its quality of relationships (the place of intimacy and sentiment), and even its place and function in the modern world (family as utopian retreat) are all idealized in similar ways. The language is even the same.

The association of the traditional and Christian family with the bourgeois family is even explicit (though undoubtedly unconscious). For example, family specialist James Dobson speaks lamentingly of overcommitted parents who drop their children off at day-care centers, "leaving little time for traditional parenting activities."[38] Day-care centers, he maintains, are no substitute for the traditional family concept. In a message to husbands of Christian homemakers he writes: "It is high time you realized your wives are under attack today! Everything they have been taught from earliest childhood is being subjected to ridicule and scorn. Hardly a day passes when the traditional values of the Judeo-Christian heritage are not blatantly mocked and undermined."[39] Among these "traditional" values being attacked, Dobson asserts, is the idea that motherhood is a "worthwhile investment" of a woman's time. "All of these deeply ingrained values, which many of your wives are trying desperately to sustain, are continually exposed to the wrath of hell itself. The Western media—radio, television and the press—are working relentlessly to shred the last vestiges of Christian tradition. And your wives who believe in that spiritual heritage are virtually hanging by their thumbs."[40] This association of traditional with bourgeois constitutes the implicit assumption of virtually all Evangelical family specialists.[41]

The Evangelical ideology surrounding the family is puzzling for what it claims to be and what it really is. The ideal Christian family is, in fact, novel inasmuch as it is related to the process of national development itself: structurally, a precondition and product of modernity; culturally, a reflection of its symbolic realities. In this perspective, its claims to traditionality are only understandable in light of more recent trends in the Western family. What are those trends? Perhaps the most important reality of family life at present is a pervasive ambiguity about what the family is and what the roles of family members should be. There is simply no clear and taken-for-granted consensus about what the family ought to be. But this cultural ambiguity is not contentless. Discernible within this ethos is an implicit repudiation of "traditional" bourgeois family values. It reasons like this. We may not know precisely what the family should be but we know what it is not: it is not hierarchical, it is not rigid in its role assignments, and so on. In this rejection of bourgeois formalism then is also an emerging consensus about what it should be—vague for most but for many others it is patent. Indeed, it takes on social and political relevance as a "progressive" agenda of norms and values which, as we have noted, maintains that authority in the family should be egalitarian and role distinctions should be abolished in favor of an androgynous arrangement. In this view, progressive definitions of family life are only extensions of those leanings toward individuation which made the modern bourgeois family unique; precisely what contemporary Evangelicals celebrate as traditional and "Christian." They represent the bourgeois impulse but are taken to a higher level of public expression. Caught in this situation is a generation of Evangelicals who in part symbolize where (empirically) Evangelicalism is and where (more speculatively) Evangelicalism may be going. Where does the coming generation fit in this larger context?

## TOWARD ANDROGYNY

It would be impossible to explore in depth the attitudes of this younger cohort of Evangelicals on every dimension of family life. Although, many of these attitudes are interesting and suggestive, they are ultimately tangential to our principal concern—which is the ways in which the coming generation of Evangelicals relates to both the ideals of the Christian family publicly advocated by those who supposedly represent them and to "postmodern" or "postbourgeois" family patterns developing in the broader culture.

### Husbands and Fathers

Men and their place in the family have received little public attention in the past century. It is in part due to the fact that successive waves of feminist activism since the mid–nineteenth century have eclipsed discussion over the place of men in their families. The focus on women meant,

**Table 10**

Attitudes toward the Role of Men in the Family according to Campus Setting

| | Evangelical College | | | Evangelical Seminary | | | Public University |
|---|---|---|---|---|---|---|---|
| | Men (N = 811) (%) | Women (N = 1,161) (%) | Total (N = 1,972) (%) | Men (N = 684) (%) | Women (N = 156) (%) | Total (N = 840) (%) | Total (N = 426) (%) |
| Agree that the husband has the "final say" in the family's decision making | 57 | 58 | 58 | 64 | 55 | 62 | 12 |
| Agree that the husband is primarily responsible for the spiritual well-being of the family | 64 | 58 | 61 | 81 | 53 | 76 | 11 |
| Agree that the father is primarily responsible for disciplining children | 34 | 18 | 25 | 30 | 10 | 26 | 9 |
| Disagree that sensitive and gentle men are less appealing than men who have the more traditional male characteristics | a | a | a | 67 | 80 | 70 | a |

NOTE: Chi-square for all of these figures is significant at .000.
a Question not asked.

in large part, an indifference to the role of men. Perhaps more fundamentally, it has simply been assumed that his role and place have changed very little. On the surface the assumption was not misplaced. Men have continued to play the role of chief provider and have continued to assume predominant authority in the family. This, of course, does not mean that there has not been any change. To the contrary, there has been a demonstrable softening of paternalistic authority. But to what extent has this blurring of the role distinctions between men and women taken hold within Evangelicalism?

Table 10 provides initial insight. The gap between the Evangelical and public university students is wide regarding the role of men in the household. The majority of Evangelical students (collegians, 58%; seminarians, 62%) did agree that "the husband has the 'final say' in the family's decision making" compared with only a minority (12%) of the public university students. Importantly, roughly one-fourth (collegians, 27%; seminarians, 22%) of the Evangelicals *disagreed* with that statement. The same is true regarding the husband's authority over the spiritual aspects of the family. Again in contrast to the public university students, the majority (collegians, 61%; seminarians, 76%) accepted the notion that "the husband is primarily responsible for the spiritual well-being of the family." A minority, however, dissented (collegians, 26%; seminarians, 15%). An attitudinal gap also exists over a third dimension of paternal responsibility: child discipline. Only one in four of the Evangelical students agreed that the father is primarily responsible for disciplining children (roughly 60% disagreed). Now it is obvious that compared with public university students, Evangelicals give a hearty endorsement to paternal authority, but the division over these issues within Evangelical quarters is significant too. Significant minorities (and in one case the majority) are either unsure or disagree with the traditional formulations about the male role. It is significant as well (for what it portends) that women are even less likely than men to endorse traditional formulations. This is particularly true among seminary women.

Even the image of masculine instrumentalism, an image which certainly underlay traditional paternal authority (and may be requisite to it), is curiously undervalued by the coming generation. For example, among seminarians only 6 percent agreed that "sensitive and gentle men are less appealing than men who have the more traditional male characteristics." A full 70 percent disagreed, and when comparing men and women, women (80%) were significantly more likely to disagree with this statement than men (67%). While suggestive of the kind of sentimentalization of the male role discussed earlier, it should be kept in mind this is not unique to the younger cohort but is even advocated by the family specialists. The advice is prolific:

> If American families are to survive the incredible stress and dangers they now face, it will be because husbands and fathers provide loving leadership in their homes, *placing their wives and children at the highest level on their system of priorities*. (italics added)[42]

> Parents should strive with all their power to make the home the center of the child's happiness, and of pleasant recollections for his whole life.[43]

> It is of great importance [for fathers] to keep in touch with the feelings of their children . . . [and to give them much] love and affection.[44]

> A father must every day relax a while from his work, in order to serve God in his children.[45]

> [Fathers,]what are some positive ways to develop your child? 1. Listen to him. . . . 2. Accept him as a person. . . . 3. Praise him. . . . 4. Spend quality time with him. (This is probably the best way a dad can show his child that he loves him.) . . . 5. Give him meaningful responsibility. . . . 6. Instruct him.[46]

An unusual kind of doublespeak is taking place. On the one hand, the man is encouraged to assert a forceful leadership in all matters pertaining to the organization and development of the family. This would include matters of spiritual maturation, child discipline, family responsibilities, and the myriad decisions any family has to make. He is to command respect and ultimately the willful submission of his wife and children. He is, after all, ultimately responsible for keeping his household in order. On the other hand, he is encouraged to cultivate the emotional development of his children and open and expressive emotional bonds of intimacy with both his children and his wife. The upshot is this: though the husband and father has ultimate authority, that authority is qualified by an emphasis on sentiment. To maintain final authority and carry out the form of strong leadership normative for centuries past, a clear difference in status from other members of the family was required. Patriarchy, in other words, required the husband to maintain social distance from the rest of the family. That social distance though is significantly reduced if not eliminated altogether by the normative expectation of sensitivity and intimacy. In this sense his authority becomes purely theoretical and abstract. Paternal authority is little authority at all.

### Wives and Mothers

The domestication of bourgeois forms of paternal authority is not an isolated phenomenon but occurs in concert with other cultural changes. It is, in a sense, a parallel development to the century-long effort to define womanhood and to bolster her status in society. At the end of the nineteenth century, feminists were among the leading advocates of the bourgeois family.[47] Theirs was a crusade to elevate the status of women by advocating that women champion the household in a serious, even academic fashion. Domestic science would be a science of "right living"; its mastery, the vocation of every conscientious homemaker. It should be recalled that the germ theory of disease, only recently discovered and popularized, gave credence to the claims of domestic science that proper homemaking was a moral responsibility of the highest order—a way of protecting one's family and the public at large from the menace of germ-caused disease. Thus, the neglect of housecleaning was tantamount to child abuse. Positing housework as a science was, again, an attempt to elevate the status of women—to dignify the tasks and her role.

More recently, of course, feminism, still involved in the crusade to increase the status of women, has repudiated bourgeois familism for being a symbol of sexual oppression. Liberation and fulfillment are only legitimately found outside the private sphere of the home and family and in the public sphere of career. The norms surrounding women's work have reversed themselves in a generation. That women work is not new. Neither is it new that women work outside the home. While it is true that the number of women in the work force has increased in recent decades, the real novelty is the *cultural meaning* of women at work. What had been a source of fulfillment and moral aspiration is more recently defined as intellectually hollow and ethically vacuous. But all of this is well known. It would also seem true though, if the Evangelical specialists are to be believed, that Evangelicalism has not been willing to assent to these newer cultural realities. Their passion has been to preserve the domestic sphere as the rightful place of women. Their opposition to the Equal Rights Amendment lends credibility to these claims. But is this true? Where do Evangelicals and the coming generation position themselves on the changing definitions of womanhood?[48]

Table 11 sheds some light on the problem. Nearly all of the Evangelicals (85%) agreed that "a woman can live a full and happy life without marrying." This by itself would be unremarkable except that in 1957, 80

**Table 11**

Attitudes toward the Role of Women in the Family according to Campus Setting

| | Evangelical College | | | Evangelical Seminary | | | Public University |
| --- | --- | --- | --- | --- | --- | --- | --- |
| | Men (N = 811) (%) | Women (N = 1,161) (%) | Total (N = 1,972) (%) | Men (N = 684) (%) | Women (N = 156) (%) | Total (N = 840) (%) | Total (N = 426) (%) |
| Agree that a woman can live a full and happy life without marrying | a | a | 85[b] | 86 | 89 | 86 | a |
| Disagree that married women who do not want at least one child are being selfish | a | a | 81[b] | 55 | 72 | 58 | a |
| Agree that a woman should put her husband and children ahead of her career | 69 | 74 | 72 | 76 | 72 | 75 | 24 |
| Agree that though it is not always possible, it is best if the wife stays at home and the husband works to support the family | 39 | 30 | 34 | 56 | 38 | 53 | 7 |
| Disagree that a married woman should not work if she has a husband capable of supporting her | 58 | 72 | 64 | 48 | 72 | 52 | 86 |
| Disagree that assertive and self-reliant women are less appealing than passive and dependent women | a | a | a | 44 | 65 | 48 | a |

NOTE: Chi-square for all of these figures is significant at .000 level.
[a] Question not asked.
[b] EAP minisurvey.

percent of the American population had the *opposite* opinion (Yankelo-vich 1981, 93).[49] By 1978 that figure dropped to 25 percent. Traditional formulations defined womanhood as complete only if the woman was married. Her identity would be incomplete without a husband to pro-vide for her economically, emotionally, and sexually. The same sentiment held for married women who were childless. She was "barren" and by definition "incomplete as a woman" because she had not had the experi-ence of childbirth and nurturing. Evangelist Billy Sunday in the early part of the twentieth century even said that a "woman so selfish as to dislike having children is in effect a criminal" (McLaughlin 1955, 139). But attitudes about this have changed as well such that now 59 percent of the general population disagreed with the statement that "married women who do not want at least one child are being selfish" (Yankelo-vich 1981). Among the younger cohort of Evangelical collegians, the figure was notably higher—81 percent. (Seminarians were roughly on par with the general population.) Singleness as a life-style option for women has then become increasingly legitimate not only for the larger population of Americans but for Evangelicals as well. Evangelical women are particularly committed to its legitimacy.

This pattern is suggestive for the definition of womanhood in the context of marriage as well. For example, roughly three out of four of the Evangelicals (compared to only one of four in the public university) agreed that "a woman should put her husband and children ahead of her career." (Evangelical students, incidently, reflected the opinion of the general population of Americans, 77 percent of whom agreed with this statement [Yankelovich 1981]). As conservative as this sounds, it is qualified by the fact that almost as many insisted, as one coed did, that "a man should also put his wife and children ahead of *his* career too."[50] This unwillingness to designate the domestic sphere as the exclusive realm of women is further suggested by the fact that a minority of the collegians (34%) and seminary women (38%) (and a slight majority, 56% of seminary men) agreed that "though it is not always possible, it is best if the wife stays at home and the husband works to support the family." Their posture is again very conservative compared with their peers in the public university, but this traditionalist posture is still a minority view. This was confirmed by responses to a stronger wording of the issue. Though less uniformly than students at the public university, a majority (collegians, 64%; seminarians, 52%) disagreed that "a married women should not work if she has a husband capable of supporting her." Evangelical women (72%) were much more uniform in their rejection of this notion than men. So too the image of women as passive and subordinate was roundly rejected. More seminarians disagreed (48%)

than agreed (17%) that "assertive and self-reliant women are less appealing than passive and dependent women." Once more, the seminarian women were especially dissonant: 65 percent disagreed: among these, 24 percent disagreed strongly.

The abandonment of bourgeois norms surrounding the role of women in the family is further suggested by the cohort differences seen in table 12. In a national survey conducted in 1977, Evangelicals were only slightly more likely than non-Evangelicals to agree that "it is more important for a wife to help her husband's career than to have one herself."[51] Yet among Evangelicals themselves, there was a dramatic difference between the younger and older cohorts—the younger were much less likely to agree. This general pattern was repeated in still another question on the same topic. A majority of Evangelicals and non-Evangelicals agreed that "it is much better for everyone involved if the man is the achiever outside of the home and the woman takes care of the house and family."[52] Once again, however, younger Evangelicals were notably less likely than older Evangelicals to accept this. So too, one-third (33%) of the younger Evangelicals agreed that "women should take care of running their homes and leave running the country

Table 12
Attitudes toward the Role of Women in the Family
among Evangelicals: Cohort Differences

|  | Younger Cohort (18–35 yr.) (N = 174) (%) | Older Cohort (36 yrs. and older) (N = 275) (%) |
|---|---|---|
| Agree that it is more important for a wife to help her husband's career than to have one herself | 41 | 73 |
| Agree that it is much better for everyone involved if the man is the achiever outside the home and the woman takes care of the house and family | 52 | 81 |
| Agree that women should take care of running their home and leave the running of the country up to men | 33 | 57 |
| Approve of a married woman earning money in business or industry even if she has a husband capable of supporting her | 73 | 56 |
| Believe that it is all right for a woman to refuse to have children even against the desires of her husband to have children | 71 | 58 |
| Disagree that most men are better suited emotionally for politics than are most women | 51 | 35 |

SOURCE: National Opinion Research Center, General Social Survey, 1977.
NOTE: Chi-square is significant at the .05 level.

up to men," compared with over half (57%) of the older cohort. And the belief that women are not as emotionally stable as men was rejected by a significantly greater number of younger Evangelicals than older Evangelicals as suggested by the fact that over half (51%) of the former disagreed that "most men are better suited emotionally for politics than are most women," compared with roughly one-third (35%) of the latter. In all of these cases, the relationship held true even when holding educational levels constant.

To the extent that bourgeois familism implies a commitment to a distinct and subordinate role for women within the private sphere, there is, then, compelling reason to question the commitment of the coming generation of Evangelicals to it. Yet one should not pass by too quickly the fact that they are far more likely to be committed to this view of womanhood than are their counterparts in the public university. Given this comparison Evangelicals are stoutly conservative. Still the majority of these Evangelicals are not committed to strictly bourgeois formulations of womanhood. What is more, among the younger, women (to whom these definitions refer) are notably less committed than men.

Evangelicals do fall along the stretch of the continuum on the role of women, and even among Evangelicals, this has a great deal to do with one's position on women's political issues. Table 13 compares attitudes toward the role of women in the family with such issues as the Equal Rights Amendment, abortion legislation, and the ordination of women in the ministry.[53] Among Evangelical college women the differences between the most conservative (traditional) and most liberal (contemporary) are moderately strong on all three issues but are strongest on the issues of abortion and the ERA. Attitudes toward the legitimate role of women in the family, then, do have political and policy consequences. They have consequences for church policy as well—concerning the leadership role of women in the church. This was not only true for college women but for the male collegians and the seminarians (both men and women). In fact the relationship between opinions on the woman's role and opinions on these public policy issues among college men and the seminarians was generally stronger.[54]

Having said this, it is only fair to say that for most of the younger cohort, the commitment to a more androgynous definition of womanhood (and the rejection of bourgeois forms) is, by and large, neither ideological nor political but unreflective. This is revealed, for example, in the serious questioning on the part of ordinary Evangelicals about biblical norms requiring the submission of women, particularly in the home but also in the church. An indication of the lessening plausibility of traditional notions of wifely submission is seen in table 12. When asked,

**Table 13**

Stance on Women's Issues according to View of the Role of Women
(College Women Only)

| | Traditional | | Role of Women[a]<br>Moderate | | Contemporary | | |
| | 1<br>(N = 43)<br>(%) | 2<br>(N = 107)<br>(%) | 3<br>(N = 274)<br>(%) | 4<br>(N = 187)<br>(%) | 5<br>(N = 57)<br>(%) | Range<br>between<br>Extremes<br>(%) | Gamma |
|---|---|---|---|---|---|---|---|
| Favor the Equal<br>Rights Amendment | 7 | 11 | 26 | 43 | 58 | 51 | −.47 |
| Favor the ordination<br>of women | 21 | 26 | 33 | 51 | 68 | 47 | −.25 |
| Oppose a ban on all<br>abortions | 10 | 17 | 29 | 50 | 72 | 62 | −.49 |

NOTE: Chi-square for all of these figures is significant at .000 level.
[a]Alpha coefficient = .72.

"If the husband in a family wants children but the wife decides that she does not want children, is it all right for the wife to refuse to have any children?" the majority of Evangelicals agreed that it was all right. Yet again the younger cohort agreed even more uniformly than the older cohort.

The questioning over the problem of submission has even evolved into a public debate. The problem is how to provide alternate meanings to biblical passages describing the normative structure of relationships between men and women/husbands and wives that have always been taken to be direct, unambiguous, and without need of reinterpretation. These are passages commanding wives to "submit [themselves] to [their] husbands," describing husbands as "ruling over wives," or as being the "head of the woman,"and describing women as the "weaker vessel" (see Eph. 5 and 1 Tim. 2"). The inference of sexual subordination and inferiority is hardly concealed. What makes these passages especially "difficult" (as one Evangelical feminist euphemistically put it) is the Evangelical commitment to biblical literalism and inerrancy. Without that commitment, such "problem verses" present little problem at all. They can easily be ignored or relativized by claiming that these Scriptures simply reflect the cultural setting of the writer and not transcendent truths. The problem, again, in light of their belief in the final authority of Scripture and twenty centuries of "unenlightened" Christian practice, is to redefine the reality of the message—to discover what is "really" meant by these statements.

Popular Evangelical literature has, since the mid-1950s, suggested three fairly distinct strategies.[55] The first was more prevalent up to the mid-1960s. It began by acknowledging that cultural changes are occurring widely but ended with the conviction that biblical norms, as unpopular as they may be, need to be reaffirmed. Even as late as 1969, one author wrote that the Apostle Paul "does not appeal to the cultural norm as the basis of his command to the Christian woman to submit to male leadership" but "to timeless spiritual principles."[56] Wives should find their fulfillment as helpers to their husbands because "God created Eve to be Adam's helper." "God did not create woman as a second Adam, . . . free to determine her destiny apart from [him]." Men have social and spiritual priority in the family and in the church "because of the priority of man's creation. 'Adam was first formed, then Eve.'" Moreover, Eve was the first to sin.[57] As helper she should recognize her responsibilities in the home. As another writer explained, "it is as mothers, wives and homemakers that [women] make their unique contribution to humanity."[58]

Since that time a slight shift in orientation occurred. Many Evangelicals came to express sympathy with the feminist critique by thoroughly rejecting any suggestions that submission implies inferiority or that headship implies superiority. One author labeled such notions "insidious."⁵⁹ To be sure, the sins of sexual oppression need to be opposed. The distinctions in roles and responsibilities are nevertheless biblically inspired and deserve to be taken seriously regardless of the "sinful distortions" that can occur. The husband has no right to "bully his wife," to "exercise tyranny" over his family, to be "rigidly authoritarian," to give into "aggressive domination" and "dictatorship" in the administration of the household. Rather he is "to be the fountainhead of love in the home. This is a love which nourishes, cherishes and protects his wife."⁶⁰ The emphasis on the requirement of the husband to love his wife (defined as follows: to be "sensitive to her emotional needs," "to be patient with," to show "eager and solicitous concern for her happiness," and to consider her "opinions as seriously as he regards his own") is so prominent that the relationship remains hierarchical in principle only. This becomes especially clear when lay and professional experts affirm the authority of the husband but simultaneously describe wives as "equal partners," "total companions," "friends," "joint heirs," "true comrades," and the like. By redefining the husband's authority as an administrative technicality, the marriage relationship as a functional equality, and her nature as "weaker vessel" in exclusively physiological terms, Evangelicals have been able to maintain the integrity of their commitment to biblical literalism while at the same time making the submission of women much less intellectually and emotionally objectionable. We are thus assured that subjection of this kind is "not at all demeaning."

The third strategy for addressing biblically inferred status inequalities between men and women/husbands and wives is the one put forward by Evangelical feminists. Because of its novelty and its break with traditional formulations, its presentation has necessarily been more systematic. The strategy though is not terribly complicated. As with its secular counterpart, the goal is total equality between sexes. It proceeds on the one hand from the conviction that conventional views of Christian family life are "bogged down with historical encrustations."⁶¹ Some maintain that through the centuries, these Pauline passages were misinterpreted by the church. Still others go so far as to argue that Paul's teachings were based upon "erroneous rabbinical exegesis" which misunderstood the created order described in Genesis, chapter 2. Paul's teachings, then, are simply "human statements that should not be followed." At the same time, this perspective proceeds from a genuine emotional revulsion of the image of mindless domesticity in submission to brute authority—what one young woman described as the "submissive, bootlicking wife." Status inequality between men and women is morally objectionable and contrary to a sense of godly justice.

From this perspective, the problem is that notions of subordination and submission of the woman intrinsically imply inequality and inferiority, and this is contrary to the more prominent New Testament themes of justice and equality among all of God's people. To be more specific, the problems with traditional approaches to the subject stem in large part from faulty biblical exegesis. The task for Evangelical feminist theology is to "correct mistranslations and misinterpretations." One Evangelical feminist put it this way: "*Properly interpreted* [italics added], the text of Scripture is not inimical to women. . . . It is up to Christian feminists to call a halt to [the] inequitable handling of the Holy Word."[62] Proper interpretation, in this case, functions to delegitimate traditional formulations and to legitimate androgynous ones. To be specific, the end result of this reality construction is a belief that the Bible is really not teaching a hierarchical arrangement at all but rather a *mutual submission* of male and female under the headship of Jesus Christ. The rationale was summarized eloquently as follows:

> When Paul says that the husband is the "head" of the wife clearly he did not mean the husband was the decision maker for the wife . . . Instead, he is using the metaphor of headship in two ways. First, Paul uses it to reinforce organic oneness and mutuality, since the head and the body need each other equally much. . . . no one way subordination can be intended. The second meaning of headship is "source." The church could not come into being until Christ became its source (head) by giving his divine prerogatives up for her. The husband is told to follow this model, giving up his social prerogatives as "owner" of his wife to become instead the servant of his wife.[63]

From this perspective the prerequisite of wifely submission is balanced by the submission of husbands to wives.

The feminist contingent within Evangelicalism is a small though vocal minority. Within the coming generation of Evangelicals the number of strongly committed and politically oriented feminists is about 9 percent among college women and 7 percent among seminary women. These are accompanied by roughly 7 percent (college) and 3 percent (seminary) of like-minded men.[64] The Evangelical feminist movement has been noticeable since the early 1970s and active since 1974. Since that time an Evangelical feminist journal, *Daughters of Sarah* came into being(3,400 paid subscribers), and over eighty books have been published (among them, *All Were Meant to Be* (Word, 1974), *Women, Men and the Bible*

(Abingdon, 1977), *Man as Male and Female* (Eerdman's, 1975), *Women Be Free* (Zondervan, 1977), *Equal Marriage* (Abingdon, 1976), and *The Apostle Paul and Women in the Church* (Regal, 1977).[65]

Though only a minority has accepted the rigors of feminist ideology, feminist sensibilities are, nevertheless, ingrained within substantial sectors of Evangelicalism and particularly within its coming generation. The propensity toward androgynous role definitions, then, is formidable. But there is yet another dimension of family life to be considered before any conclusions can be drawn: the realm of parents and children.

### Parents and Children

As with other dimensions of the private sphere, parenting has become politicized. Debate centers around its relative autonomy from the state and the rights of the state (in the form of agencies) to intervene in the family on behalf of children (the implication being that certain types of parenting and parental practices are unacceptable or inadequate). The "rights of children" are often pitted against the "rights of parents" and vice versa. Child abuse and other health-related issues as well as the educational prerogatives of parents have been among the more visible areas of concern and debate (in and out of the courts). Though parenting in itself as a public issue has not been nearly as politicized as women's rights, it is still an important issue and an especially important one for Evangelicalism.

So as not to lose the logic of the argument, it is necessary to restrict our focus of inquiry to what it suggests about the decline of so-called traditional forms of parenting; conversely, the extent of androgynization in the Evangelical world. Predictably, the image of ideal parenting is one in which moral discipline is highly developed in a context where parents act out clearly definable roles and, therefore, socialize their children into distinct gender identities. The obverse—moral permissiveness encouraged by parents who share equally the responsibilities for the care and nurture of children and, by this, encourage the development of both "masculine" and "feminine" characteristics in their children—is a perversion of the social order. Again it is appropriate to ask the empirical question, where do Evangelicals stand on this topic?

As has already been seen, only a moderately sized minority agreed that the father is primarily responsible for disciplining children. This does not mean, however, that Evangelicals are opposed to discipline. Indeed, less than 10 percent of the Evangelical students agreed that "spanking, as a form of parental punishment, has a tendency to produce violent behavior in children" (table 14). Public university students, on the other hand,

**Table 14**

Attitudes toward Parenting according to Campus Setting

| | Evangelical College | | | Evangelical Seminary | | | Public University |
| --- | --- | --- | --- | --- | --- | --- | --- |
| | Men (N = 811) (%) | Women (N = 1,161) (%) | Total (N = 1,972) (%) | Men (N = 684) (%) | Women (N = 156) (%) | Total (N = 840) (%) | Total (N = 426) (%) |
| Agree that spanking, as a form of parental punishment, has a tendency to produce violent behavior in children | 7 | 9 | 8 | 5 | 6 | 5 | 21 |
| Agree that strict, "old-fashioned" upbringing is still the best way to raise children | 30 | 30 | 30 | 38 | 35 | 37 | 12 |
| Agree that both father and mother have the responsibility to care for small children | 98 | 97 | 98 | 99 | 98 | 99 | 97 |

NOTE: Chi-square for all of these figures is significant at .000 level.

were twice as likely (21%) to hold this opinion. Firm moral discipline, then, would appear to be a priority in childrearing; corporal punishment does not at all present an objectionable means of developing it. Yet it would also appear that Evangelicals are not of the opinion that a high sense of moral sensitivity should be cultivated by more austere (even traditional) methods. Predictably, the public university students were even less likely than Evangelical students to maintain this view; however, only 30 percent of the Evangelical collegians and 37 percent of the seminarians agreed that "strict, 'old-fashioned' upbringing is still the best way to raise children." It may be appropriate to justify the word "only" in this case. First, for a group that is alleged to be among the principal defenders of traditional familism, it is somewhat surprising that the majority would be unsympathetic to an image of traditional parenting. Secondly, when this question was posed (in 1979) to the general population of Americans, a slight majority (51%) agreed with it (Yankelovich 1981, 89). At least among the younger cohort, Evangelicals were then significantly less likely than other Americans (of all ages) to have this orientation.

All of this is suggestive of a general style of parenting. Conservatives have argued that to deprive small children of undivided maternal attention in the first few years of life as a result of the mother's employment is to unnecessarily increase the likelihood that they will not develop emotionally, psychologically, and morally. Mothers need to stay at home with their infants and toddlers. As has been seen, the moral mandate among Evangelical experts is strong. In fact there would appear to be little gap at all between their opinion and the opinion of most Americans. In 1977, a majority (nearly seven out of ten) agreed with this notion, that "a preschool child is likely to suffer if his or her mother works."[66] Evangelicals were no different (no more conservative) than all others in this regard. Interestingly though, the Evangelicals were not all of one mind. When comparing younger Evangelicals with older Evangelicals, there was a substantial difference. Less than one-half of the younger cohort agreed with this, compared with three-fourths of the older cohort (see table 15). A similar pattern (though not quite so dramatic) was apparent when the public was asked about this issue from an opposite perspective. Roughly half of all Americans (49%) agreed that "a working mother can establish just as warm and secure a relationship with her children as a mother who does not work."[67] Again there was little difference between Evangelical and non-Evangelical opinion on this point, yet between younger and older Evangelicals, the younger were notably *more* likely to agree. In a word, maternal objections to women working in the public sphere (i.e., taking on a more androgynous

**Table 15**

Attitudes toward Motherhood among Evangelicals: Cohort Differences

|  | Younger Cohort (18–35 yr.) (N = 174) (%) | Older Cohort (36 yrs. and older) (N = 275) (%) |
| --- | --- | --- |
| Agree that a preschool child is likely to suffer if his or her mother works | 48 | 76 |
| Agree that a working mother can establish just as warm and secure a relationship with her children as a mother who does not work | 56 | 40 |

SOURCE: National Opinion Research Center, General Social Survey, 1977.
NOTE: Chi-square is significant at the .05 level.

role) are not nearly as credible to younger Evangelicals as older Evangelicals. Among these younger Evangelicals, care for young children is not the exclusive or necessarily principal responsibility of the mother. This is seen, for example, in the fact that there is unanimous consent among all Evangelical collegians, seminarians, and public university students that "*both* father and mother have the responsibility to care for small children (see table 14). This, in itself, is not remarkable except that when the question was posed to a general sample of Americans in 1970, only one-third agreed, and in 1980 just over one-half (51%) agreed (Yankelovich 1981, 94). In short, the opinion of the younger contingent of Evangelicals marks a dramatic departure from the traditional parenting ideals of their older counterparts.

The unevenness of commitment to traditional forms of parenting on the part of these Evangelicals is noteworthy. It is in part a reflection of the ambivalence specialists have concerning the socialization of children into distinct gender identities. In Evangelical literature published up to the mid-1970s, the dominant themes in the advice experts gave to their readers was that parents should foster well-defined sexual role expectations in their children. The assumption, naturally, was that more differentiated males and females than just genitalia. There are also intrinsic differences in emotional and psychological discipline. For example, "boys have a stronger aggressive drive than girls." They also have a "greater natural tendency toward leadership." Moreover, men are far more likely to "tackle life in a rational head-first way" whereas for the female the "emotional" and "intuitive predominate in her approach to life."[68] From this perspective it is only logical that any cultural disposition toward androgynous gender roles would be unwelcome. Consider, for example, the commentary of two family specialists:

> This blurring of mother-father roles can have harmful effects on children. Because many fathers now wash dishes, bathe the baby, and perform other traditional female tasks, their sons often don't know what it means to be a man. If mother and father do the same chores, a child doesn't have a clear father or mother image. No wonder so many boys and girls are mixed up about their roles in later life.[69]

> The main reason fathers should spend quantities of time with their sons and mothers with their daughters during preschool years is that these are the years in which sexual identities become solidified. Children need a parent of the same sex to identify with and to model themselves after. Today it's hard to tell a boy from a girl, and that's not right. Boys should dress like boys and girls like girls, and that applies to their hair styles too.[70]

For this reason, fathers are encouraged to build strong intimate bonds with their sons and mothers the same with their daughters so that proper sexual identities can be cultivated.

Yet even in this literature, the experts concede that "no chores are exclusively masculine or feminine" and that women "can handle most of men's jobs, and do them well."[71] They also concede that it is important that parents develop the girl's ability to compete in the world just as they should develop the boy's ability to express emotion. Charles Swindoll, for example, observes: "A show of emotion—is that effeminate? I'll be frank with you, it is a sign of a great man."[72]

Since the mid-1970s, however, some family counselors and specialists in Evangelicalism have come out boldly in favor of a more androgynous approach to childrearing. For example, *The Encyclopedia of Christian Parenting* (1982) approves of fathers and sons shopping, vacuuming, washing clothes, cooking, setting the table, and washing dishes."[73] One woman explained it this way: "Contrary to what I had heard all of my life, the six months at home [with a newborn baby] taught me that *a woman's place is where she chooses to be.* [italics in original] That may be in the home, and then it may not be. This also applies to men."[74] The key conceptual difference, we are told, is between sexual identity (physiological and God-given) and sexual roles (sociological and therefore relative). Children, then, "should *not* be forced into a specific sexual role," because they will otherwise not acquire independence—an "independence that is achieved by mastering the skills of both sexual roles."[75] Still another reason for not forcing children into sexual roles is that "some boys are born with gifts and skills that are more suited to the feminine role, while some girls are born with gifts and skills that are more suited to the masculine role. Forcing sexual roles onto these children inhibits them from achieving their full potential"[76] Predictably the advice given to Christian parents is to "model equality in your home," "provide non-sexist records and books for him to hear and read," "allow boys to have dolls and girls to have trucks," and summarily, "encourage your child to become his or her own person, regardless of whether or not it fits into his sexual role."[77]

The significance of all of this is plain. First, it represents a distinct and historically unique pluralization in the formal ideology of parenting on the part of conservative Protestants. Within this, though, is an official legitimation for social processes already occurring widely within Evangelicalism. Perhaps more importantly though, to the degree that this orientation is taken seriously and adopted by Evangelicals, androgyny will be culturally and sociologically reproduced in the subculture. The impulse toward androgyny in the culture becomes institutionalized as part of the taken-for-granted reality of the next generation.

## Summary

Earlier it was noted that perhaps the most pervasive reality concerning the family (within and outside Evangelicalism) was that the normative expectations that surround it are in a state of flux. At one level this is expressed in a tentativeness in stating what it should be. This is confirmed by the fact that nearly half of all students were unsure of their views on at least one aspect of the role of men and women in the family. When asked about what the Bible taught concerning the role of women and of men in the family, many admitted that the Bible "was not always very clear about such matters" and that it "could be confusing sometimes." As one seminarian confessed, "there is a lot of room for interpretation." The breadth of interpretation appears to have expanded in the past generation.

Because of this breadth, there is inevitably wide diversity of opinion. That diversity is summarized in the indexes presented in table 16.[78] Several things deserve highlighting. The first is that most Evangelical students are neither strongly traditional (bourgeois) nor strongly contemporary (androgynous) in their views of roles within the family. On average only about one in ten of the collegians and seminarians would be likely to endorse, enthusiastically, the model of the family advocated by Evangelical spokesmen. Another one-fourth to one-third would be sym-

Table 16
General Attitudes toward the Role of Men and Women
in the Household according to Campus Setting

| | | College | | Seminary | |
|---|---|---|---|---|---|
| | | Role of Women[a] (N = 1,036) (%) | Role of Men[b] (N = 1,277) (%) | Role of Women[a] (N = 394) (%) | Role of Men[b] (N = 544) (%) |
| Traditional | 1. | 7 | 10 | 16 | 11 |
| | 2. | 19 | 30 | 28 | 36 |
| Moderate | 3. | 41 | 36 | 39 | 35 |
| | 4. | 25 | 16 | 14 | 13 |
| Contemporary | 5. | 8 | 9 | 4 | 5 |

[a]Alpha coefficient (measuring reliability) is .72.
[b]Alpha coefficient is .72.

pathetic with that model, but this still leaves less than half of the coming generation holding to the ideal of traditional bourgeois familism. At the other end of the continuum, there is another 10 percent who vigorously repudiate that model in favor of a vision of the family where there are no essential role distinctions between husband and wife and where there is equality of status and authority. A minority of 13–25 percent are sympathetic with this orientation. Themes of androgynization are indeed prevalent within Evangelicalism and particularly within the younger cohort.

Yet the diversity is more subtle than this. Table 16 confirms what had already been discernible, namely, that Evangelical students tend to be more *traditional* in their view of men in the household while more *liberal* in their attitudes toward the role of women. In different words, they are more likely to be willing to advocate a more "masculine" gender identity for women but less likely to concede a more "feminine" gender identity for men. This pattern was more prominent among collegians than seminarians but still noticeable among the latter.

But what accounts for this diversity? One of the more important factors is the degree of orthodoxy one holds to: those more intensely orthodox are significantly more prone to accept "traditional" role definitions in the family, just as the less intensely orthodox are significantly more prone to accept androgynous ones.[79] Among seminarians, commitment to more traditional ideals is also more likely to be held by those who are married and have children than by those who are married without children or those who remain unmarried.[80] This might suggest that when single students eventually get married, their views of the family may change. In any case, this pattern is offset in part by the number of years they have been training in seminary—a longer duration in seminary (whether married or unmarried) mitigates the appeal or plausibility of traditional familism.[81] A final factor explaining some of the diversity is the gender factor. Though women can be found along the continuum as well as men, women are consistently more liberal than men in their views of the man's and woman's roles in the family. Seminary women on the whole tend to be slightly more liberal than women collegians. This might have been expected among non-Evangelical women and, more generally, nonreligious women, but it is somewhat surprising to find it is the case in Evangelicalism. Even among lay and (aspiring) professional Evangelical women, there is the perception that androgynous role definitions are in their collective interest as women. Given the fact that among Evangelicals, women are in the majority and that the number of professionally trained Evangelical women has been growing, this could portend a more widespread abandonment of traditional family arrangements in preference to an egalitarian model.

## THE EVANGELICAL FAMILY BESIEGED

The relationship between Evangelicalism and the family is laced with irony. The ideal family celebrated by Evangelicals (especially its ministers and specialists) is claimed to be both traditional and biblical. This is the family of the Judeo-Christian heritage—an ideal inspired by the divine; its qualities, timeless. Yet perhaps the only transhistorical aspect to this ideal is that it involves a fundamental relationship between a man, a woman, and their children. The participants of this relationship have remained the same. Maybe the only other quality which comes close to transcending the vagaries of historical change in the past two millennia has been its hierarchical nature. An intractable form of patriarchy has characterized family organization for virtually all of this time. But the similarities between this ideal family and whatever else preceded it stops there. The ideal Christian family currently celebrated is decidedly bourgeois in its sociocultural ethos, its quality of relationships, and its definitions of family roles. It is, then, largely foreign to Christianity before the modern age. But in a very real sense, the ideal Christian family is not even bourgeois. It is a hypersentimentalized variant of that model. As such it would be more accurate to label this model *neobourgeois*. That this model is historically unique there is little doubt. Whether or not it is the biblical and the divinely intended model, as many Evangelicals have claimed, is another matter. It may be; it may not be. If it is, then it has taken nearly twenty centuries of Christian experience to realize. But there is more to the relationship between Evangelicalism and the family.

To the extent that hypersentimentalization is advocated in theory and adopted in practice, bourgeois patriarchal authority is undercut. Such authority, then, comes to exist in name (or in principle) only. Add to this the fact that large sectors of the Evangelical population (particularly within the younger cohort) no longer accept the legitimacy of traditional (bourgeois) role assignments, and one is left with a normative pattern of family life that is very untraditional indeed. In brief, *the Evangelical family specialists (including many ministers) advocate and defend a model of the family that is said to be traditional but in fact has no real historical precedent* in Christendom or anywhere else) *in the name of a constituency that has largely abandoned it in favor of an androgynous/quasi-androgynous model.*

The existence of family specialists and advocates of the family necessitates further reflection about their role in family life. Public advocates of the "traditional" family in Evangelicalism, whether lay, clergy, or professional, are not somehow unique in the cultural landscape in America. They merely represent the Evangelical component of a larger group of social pathologists who have, for over a century, made the family a social cause. Both defended and criticized, the family has in this time emerged as a major industry. It was only a matter of time before Evangelicals joined in making their own unique contributions. As we have seen, they have joined in and done so in force.

What Christopher Lasch (1977), Brigitte Berger (Berger and Berger 1983) and others have described for the secular movement holds for the Evangelical side as well. "Helping professionals" of the family have monopolized the knowledge necessary to generate marital satisfaction, to socialize the young, and to bring about productive coexistence in the family. Through the massive enterprises of film, mass-market and trade books, seminars, workshops, church-sponsored educational programs, and counseling sessions, this knowledge and experience are given back to couples, parents, and entire families. The mere existence of these professionals and their cognitive wares has generated a "need" for their use. The implicit message has been and continues to be that couples, parents, and families are incompetent to run their lives in the private sphere and that commonsense knowledge is not good enough. Students themselves (in personal interviews) admitted to being "somewhat naive" or "somewhat ignorant" about family matters. The intervention of these specialists into the family, thus, creates a sense of inadequacy, as though the family cannot function without their expert advice. With a sense of inadequacy comes a sense of dependency on that knowledge. Indeed, all of the students said that as they approach marriage and childrearing, they would consult expert opinion, if not for specific advice, then, as one seminarian put it, "as a point of conversation for us—a launching point for us to talk about certain issues." Oftentimes, though, that knowledge is either so general and opaque or so technically mystifying that it is impossible to appropriate it, leaving families even more "abject in their dependency upon expert opinion" (Lasch, 1977, 18).

Though it is undoubtedly true that Evangelicals do feel inadequacy and thus dependency upon the experts, at this point, it is not altogether clear how effective these advocates are or will be in salvaging the traditional family, not only in America at large but within Evangelicalism itself. If the disposition of the coming generation of Evangelicals provides any indication, then they will likely have little effect at all.

# Politics: Civility Extolled

A fourth dimension of the contemporary Evangelical experience revolves around a political axis. Though by no means a part of the theological/cultural orthodoxy of conservative Protestantism, a particular constellation of political values and ideology has, nevertheless, become part of its legacy in the twentieth century. As such the political dimension of contemporary Evangelical experience has important indirect consequences for the nature and future of Evangelicalism in North America.

The nature of this constellation of political values is well known. Indeed, the association between Protestant orthodoxy and political conservatism is perhaps the most reliable and enduring of all commonplaces concerning this subject, and not without good reason. For generations it has openly and patriotically celebrated a certain idealized vision of the American identity and experience, almost a myth, encompassing an interpretation of what America is all about: its history, its present, its calling in the world. The relationship is more compelling than this for its own sense of history and historical identity are deeply linked to that myth. It views itself has having helped to create and sustain all that is good in America: its traditions of moral virtue; its ethic of hard work, commitment, and individual achievement; and its political and economic institutions. Conservative Protestantism has, then, helped to define America. It is part of the myth itself. It is not surprising, therefore, that conservative Protestantism would define its political interests as the conservative defense of all that constitutes the American ideal. In so doing, it fosters and protects its own interests as a religious people.

Whether or not this myth about America has any basis in reality is unimportant. Their political values and their justifications are, in themselves, interesting and certainly not alarming—that is, except for the fact that certain other features have come to characterize the political orientation of conservative Protestantism in the public imagination. The first is the image that they are monolithically and persistently conservative in their politics. In this they constitute a potentially important if not decisive political force. The second and more alarming to many is the image that they carry their political views to extreme if not fanatical proportions. Their religious orthodoxy crudely translates into a concomitant political orthodoxy—intolerant of cultural and political pluralism when that pluralism threatens to undermine their own political and cultural hegemony. Because they are so disposed, they are capable of harsh and intolerant political backlash when they sense their collective survival (or America's) is at stake. Though they would likely define their motives and agenda as always being in the American interest, the political extremism of conservative Protestantism is viewed as expressing an ultranationalism only part of the time. At other times it emerges as an overzealous effort to buttress or defend a certain narrowly defined way of life understood to be Christian and/or American.

The public image of conservative Protestantism as a bastion of unwavering conservatism and fanatical intolerance of cultural diversity is neither a total fabrication nor a caricature unrelated to historical reality. It is, in fact, born out of the unique experience of conservative Protestantism with the changing cultural and political currents of America in the twentieth century. The image, then, is accurate in many ways. Having said this it is important to press on. Generalities do not suffice. When looking at the conservative Protestant experience in the twentieth century, one can quickly see that there have been three principal waves of Evangelical political activism. Each one has contributed in particular ways to the image of conservative Protestantism as an extremist conservative political phenomenon. In this chapter I will cover what to some may be familiar historical territory, but in doing so, it will be possible to begin to explore the sources of this image and, in turn, to assess its accuracy. I will then explore the ways in which these themes are expressed in the coming generation of Evangelicals.

## THREE WAVES OF EVANGELICAL POLITICAL ACTIVISM
### Wave One: The 1920s

The first wave of conservative Protestant activism occurred in the first quarter of the twentieth century but crested in the 1920s. It was shaped by three relatively distinct issues: antievolutionism, Prohibition, and anti-Catholicism. The last first.

By the second decade of this century, anti-Catholicism was a fairly diffuse cultural attitude having specific political consequences. It was also a posture not unique to conservative Protestants but one characterizing all of Protestantism to varying degrees. The American Protestant antagonism toward Catholicism was rooted, in large part, in the general anti-immigration sentiment of the nineteenth century. Mass immigrations by East European Jews and ethnic (Irish and Italian) Catholics from the 1830s and on introduced a certain degree of economic and political displacement and, ipso facto, instability. This was particularly true in the urban areas of the Northeast. Perhaps more important was the cultural diversity brought about by their arrival: the introduction of "un-Protestant" and therefore "un-American" values and sentiments into a nearly homogeneously Protestant religious and cultural milieu.

A variety of groups and movements, principally based in a rural and working-class Evangelical Protestant populace, emerged which explicitly or implicitly had as their guiding purpose the suppression of Catholic influence and interests. The American Alliance (1876), the National Christian Association (1868), the American (Anti-Masonic) Party (1874), and the American Protective Association (1887) were among the more prominent groups to emerge at this time (Lipset and Raab 1970). There were also many other lower-status patriotic organizations which lent their support to this campaign (Lipset and Raab 1970, 83). All shared the basic nativistic conviction that the Pope and the Roman Catholic church were engaged in a clandestine conspiracy to subvert, indeed overturn, American institutions and the Christian (read Protestant) system in favor of a Papist regime. There was also the suspicion that Catholic elements provided an institutional network necessary for the growth of socialism. These groups, as historical research shows, were somewhat effective. They were especially effective in keeping Catholic politicians out of office, particularly at the local level.

Anti-Catholic sentiment grew through the turn of the century and through World War I simultaneously with the continued mass immigrations of the Irish, Italians, Germans, and East Europeans. The war both heightened and lessened these prejudices. It intensified the anti-Catholic and anti-Semitic sentiment by heightening suspicions of all foreign (un-American) influences (Lipset and Raab 1970, 103). Yet the war also intensified industrialization and urbanization and the cultural values associated with these developments. Thus, it had the latent effect of mitigating xenophobic propensities in the populace. The ultimate decline in anti-Catholicism was ironically brought about by the victory of the nativist campaign: first, the passage of strong immigration legislation in 1924 restricting the flow of immigrants to annual quotas and, secondly, the defeat of Catholic (Democrat), Al Smith in the 1928 presidential election. Anti-roman prejudice did persist after this period, of course, but no longer was it embraced in a national political movement.

Like the anti-Catholic crusade, the Temperance movement had deep roots in the nineteenth century and had the institutional and popular support of the wider Protestant establishment. It was in direct ways a consequence of the religious revivals of the 1820s and 1830s and the perfectionist impulse that followed. Temperance, of course, was predicated on the belief that the consumption of alcoholic beverages was a primary source of social and moral decline in society. It was a chief characteristic of worldliness, and a stable Christian civilization could not be adequately ensured without its citizenry protecting itself from this evil. As one Victorian preacher put it, "Of all the evils that have cursed mankind, crushed woman's heart, sent youth to destruction, driven virtue to the haunts of shame and paved the pathway to hell, there is nothing that can compare with the evil of intoxicating drink" (Hammel 1908, 4).

Through the nineteenth century a variety of temperance initiatives were sponsored and legislated at the state and local level. This was largely due to the efforts of such organizations as the Prohibition Party (1869), the Women's Christian Temperance Union (1874), and the Anti-Saloon League (1906) (Gusfield 1963). The drive for national prohibition, however, did not emerge in force until the early twentieth century. Indeed, through the first two decades it was the only issue upon which Fundamentalist and liberal organizations (themselves deeply ensconced in the Fundamentalist-Modernist controversy) could agree. Yet it was not only an organizational initiative. It is true that many Fundamentalist and liberal Protestants were indifferent to the subject; however, there were sizable numbers in both factions who believed that the future of Christian civilization depended upon the success of the Temperance movement. By the end of 1919, prohibition laws were already in effect in thirty-three states. Thus, the National Prohibition Act (or the Volstead Act) and the Eighteenth Amendment to the Constitution making Prohibition federal law were easily ratified in that year.

The problems that Prohibition created are well known: the illegal manufacturing and sale of liquor were widespread. Discontent with this legislation quickly surfaced even among those who had been its major supporters. By the end of the 1920s, the Fundamentalists were essentially alone in their attempts to maintain the legitimacy of the Temperance movement and Prohibition. Accordingly, Prohibition increasingly acquired a misbegotten and crankous quality. Thirteen years after it had been ratified, Prohibition was repealed. Though short-lived, Prohibition symbolized the power of Protestant groups to mobilize enough support to realize their interests in a national public policy.

The third and most notorious effort was to ban the teaching of evolution in the public schools. Unlike the other two efforts this one was almost exclusively a Fundamentalist initiative though some Roman Catholics also supported it (Marsden 1980, 170, n. 28). Darwinism was the symbol of the gaining predominance of secular, scientific rationality in American culture and in the churches. To then allow, at the policy level, equal time for an alternative explanation for the origin of man was to give it scientific credibility and official legitimacy it did not deserve. It was a godless explanation, and like socialism, it represented a formidable atheistic threat to "Christian America." As one Fundamentalist put it, "It eliminates the idea of a personal God and with that goes all authority in government, all law and order" (Marsden 1980, 209; who takes the quotation from an editorial in the *Moody Monthly*, 1923). Christianity and evolution were incompatible. Thus, to allow its presentation in the public schools was tantamount to advocating atheism.

The issue was politicized for Fundamentalists particularly from World War I on when it became associated with saving American civilization from German modernistic theologies and philosophies (which were believed, because of their implicit materialism, to have "laid the foundation for the bloodiest war in history" Marsden 1980, 169). Indeed, antievolutionism became sensationalized in a way none of the other issues of the day did. One of the reasons is that William Jennings Bryan (leader of the Democratic party until 1912 and Woodrow Wilson's Secretary of State until 1915) made the cause his own.

The Fundamentalists of the day were remarkably successful too. Between 1921 and 1929, thirty-seven antievolution measures were introduced in twenty state legislatures. In nine of these states various antievolution laws were approved (Furniss 1954, 42-70). One of those states was Tennessee, also the site for one of the most celebrated trials of the century. The American Civil Liberties Union sought out and found a public school teacher willing to defy Tennessee's antievolution laws by teaching evolution in the classroom.[1] Representing John Scopes, the teacher, and the ACLU in the resulting legal dispute was the very prominent attorney Clarence Darrow. For the state of Tennessee and the Fundamentalists was Bryan. Yet two trials really took place: a legal trial and, more importantly, a trial for public opinion. As is well known, Bryan and the Fundamentalists won the former (though the decision was later reversed on a technicality); Darrow indisputably won the latter. In the technical sense though, the conservative Protestants were successful. At least temporarily (and despite the turn of public opinion against them) their political aspirations were realized.

Apart from these three issues, Fundamentalists were not especially politicized (Carter 1968; Wenger 1973). (Years before, the Sabbatarian movement, whose goal was the legal protection of the Sabbath, had lapsed.) They were generally conservative and Republican, but some Fundamentalists could in fact be found on most sides of most issues. Protestantism, after all (whether liberal or conservative), had never produced a systematic body of political theory nor had such an exercise ever been attempted. The impulse for these political initiatives seemed to emerge more from the effort to retain the vague though long held hope for an America that was Christian and under the sovereignty of God (as Protestants understood him). That hope (which to some was the promise and calling of America) was being abandoned. In light of this, these three issues constituted a means to preserve it. At least in the short run, as we have seen, they were successful. The cost, however, was their own standing in the public mind. From this point on, conservative Protestants became objects of derision for their anti-intellectualism, their bigotry, and their "narrow-minded moralism" (Marsden 1980, 189). Their efforts, as H. L. Mencken put it, were the "stupid and anti-social crazes of inferior men" (1924, 28, 29). Their leaders were all suspected of gross charlatanism (an image popularized by the 1927 publication of Sinclair Lewis's *Elmer Gantry*. Even as early as the 1920s, Fundamentalists were believed to have the objective of a political takeover—the result being that the best in American culture would be "suppressed or banned" thus leading America "toward the pall of the Dark Age" (Shipley 1927).[2]

## Wave Two: The 1950s

Before World War I, widespread nationalistic sentiment was not especially strong (Marsden 1980, 207). Americans were patriotic, but that patriotism did not extend to inordinate suspicion of (or paranoia toward) any threats to traditional American values and institutions. This pattern, however, reversed after the war. With the successful Bolshevik revolution in Russia in 1917, most Americans became aware of the growing dimensions of an international socialism. It was easy for all to see that bolshevism could constitute a genuine danger to the free industrialized world. Nationalistic and patriotic loyalties grew accordingly in the populace, but no where did they develop more quickly and intensely than they did among conservative Protestants. By the mid-1920s many highly visible Fundamentalist leaders were speaking out against the spread of an atheistic communism. Through the 1930s and 1940s "native fascism" in conjunction with a virulent anti-semitism gained prominence, particularly through the efforts of William Dudley Pelley, Gerald

B. Winrod, and Gerald L. K. Smith. All three were extremists—marginal even to conservative Protestantism. Nevertheless Winrod's and Smith's personal roots in Fundamentalism betrayed a certain ideological and religious affinity between Protestant Fundamentalism and the popular base of the broader movement.[3] By the 1950s this sentiment had culminated in the second major wave of political activism: the unqualified participation on the part of certain sectors of conservative Protestantism in the campaign against alleged communist infiltration into the United States and her government.[4]

Conventional wisdom would have it that the "Red Scare"of the 1950s was a national catastrophe entirely without grounding, an event based upon a willful fiction. At one level this is true; at another it is not. For one, following the Second World War Americans witnessed a successive pattern of Communist initiatives globally: the Berlin blockade of 1948, the Communist takeover in China in 1949, and the outbreak of the Korean conflict in 1950. These very nonfictional events loomed large and clear in the minds of most Americans at that time. They created a common anxiety in the nation as a whole. It was in this environment that the more dubious undertakings of Wisconsin Senator Joseph McCarthy and the House Committee on Un-American Activities emerged.

As several commentators have noted, it was not the reality of international politics that formed the focus of McCarthyite antipathy during the 1950s. It was, rather, communism as ideology—more accurately it was communism as the predominant symbol of evil in the world, particularly as this "insidious force" threatened to undermine, internally, the strength of American institutions and values (Lipset and Raab 1970, 234). It was this which generated the political hysteria of the period and led to the public interrogations and trials of suspected Communists.

For all of the attention the anti-Communist campaign received, it was a phenomenon which even at its height had the active support of only a minority of the American population. And within this, the support was mixed. Overall, it came from the less-educated, lower-status, and working-class (including farming) population. They were also disproportionately Republican in party preference. Notably, some of the strongest support came from a substantial portion of working-class Catholics.[5] Yet given this demographic characteristic it is also not surprising that this population included a significant portion of conservative Protestants. Most of these could be found within the Baptist and Independent Fundamentalist churches though a sizable number of Lutherans and Presbyterians were found in these ranks as well. Together, they were a block of public opinion in general allegiance with a "moralistic, monistic, conspiracy-style anti-Communism" (Lipset and Raab, 1970, 228–35).

Institutionally, the majority of conservative Protestant denominations and organizations were publicly neutral toward McCarthyism and the anti-Communist movement. There were exceptions to this rule, however, and groups existed who accepted and promulgated the Communist-conspiracy ideology unreservedly. Among the more prominent were the American Council of Christian Churches (under the leadership of the Reverend Carl McIntire), Christian Crusade (under the leadership of Billy James Hargis), and Church League of America (under the leadership of Edgar C. Bundy).[6] All identified communism with Satan and the Antichrist; all maintained the belief that a Communist conspiracy was behind virtually every crisis and problem in the United States. With a proven aptitude for attracting media attention, their contribution to the general hysteria was not insignificant. Indeed, in the early 1950s, McCarthy himself described them as a "militant anti-Communist Protestant group usefully serving the interests of America and God" (Gaspar 1963, 63). Yet most of their energies were channeled into the effort to root out Communists and their fellow travelers from the Protestant establishment itself—a subplot in a larger drama (Gaspar 1963, 64).

Among those singled out for criticism were the Federal Council of Churches (and later the National Council of Churches), the National Religion and Labor Foundation, the Fellowship of Reconciliation, and a large number of liberal Protestant churchmen.[7] It is true that virtually all of these were critics of capitalism (some calling it un-Christian because it was based on "selfish competition") and proponents to varying degrees of economic redistribution and collectivization. Yet none was ever proven to be actively aligned with the Communist party. However, a formal alliance was beside the point as far as their critics were concerned. Their adversary posture toward capitalism was enough to qualify them as being either pro-Communist, pro-Communist sympathizers, or unwitting dupes of the Communists whose every activity aided and abetted the socialist program. Their resolutions, their relief work, and even their Sunday School literature were believed to promote communism. Communist influence was further seen in the 1952 publication of the Revised Standard Version of the Bible, called an effort to "destroy the historic faith" (Roy 1960, 229). Largely due to the pressure of public opinion generated by these groups, the House Committee on Un-American Activities did, in fact, make G. Bromiley Oxnam, a Methodist bishop and prominent leader in the National Council of Churches, the subject of a public inquiry in July 1953. Nothing ever came of the inquiry or the many other investigations into religious organizations and clergy (Protestant, Catholic, and Jewish), but these widely publicized events proved tremendously embarrassing for these mainstream religious groups. It also symbolized the kind of political leverage that the more sectarian Protestants could wield at that time.

The exoneration of Oxnam, the National Council of Churches, and other clergymen, a Senate reprimand of McCarthy, and the eventual collapse of McCarthyism in 1954 discredited all anti-Communist groups, not least the Evangelical/Fundamentalist ones. Throughout the controversy and subsequent to it, these groups and their leaders were effectively accused of "Red-baiting" and of being fascist. These accusations came not only from the secular news media and mainline religious denominations but from centrist Fundamentalists/Evangelicals too. Public opinion was never strongly in their favor and soon it was decidely against them.[8] Public humiliation, however, was not enough to substantially reduce the drive of these groups or their leaders. Through the late 1950s and early 1960s they continued to advocate a conspiratorial, anti-Communist ideology and as such became allied with other radical rightist groups, the John Birch Society in particular. They became more and more eccentric and discredited in the public imagination.

The events of the 1950s and the participation of conservative Protestantism in them alerted the academy and the broader liberal culture to certain propensities within the conservative Protestant subculture. Social scientists came to uncover other latent prejudices. Through the early and mid-1960s, racist and anti-Semitic attitudes were found to be disproportionately represented among conservative Protestants (Selsnick and Steinberg 1969; Glock and Stark 1965, 1966). Thus, there were objects of bigotry and intolerance besides alleged Communists in the United States. Yet because these objects of intolerance (blacks and Jews) were more tangible than Communists, these prejudices were considered to be of more practical danger. Ironically, through the 1950s and 1960s theologically conservative Protestants were almost uniformly politically quietistic. As a population they were shown to be far less inclined toward political participation of any kind than any other religious subgroup in America.[9] They further maintained these expectations for their clergy. This suggests that though a general anti-Communist attitude was common enough among conservative Protestants through this period, the bold political forays of such groups as the American Council of Christian Churches, Christian Crusade, and the Church League of America were somewhat anomalous within the subculture as a whole. It also suggests that for conservative Protestants, racial, ethnic, and ideological hostilities (against blacks, Jews, and Communists, respectively) remained latent and untranslated into public activism.

## Wave Three: The 1980s

The third wave of conservative Protestant political activism was almost exclusively oriented toward stemming the tide of moral decline in American culture. It is not as though this theme was novel to conservative Protestantism. The Sabbatarian movement, the Temperance movement, and abolitionism, for example, all had a strong moral dimension to them. They opposed, on moral grounds, the Supreme Court decisions against prayer and Bible reading in schools in 1962 and 1963. And as has been seen from chapter 3, they have also long disparaged moral laxness of any kind: sexual immorality, the use of alcohol and narcotics, and even too much preoccupation with worldly amusements. Yet to this point, their disapproval of moral problems such as these was evidenced only by an unpoliticized cultural discontent. The one major exception was Prohibition. In the early 1980s though, "moral decline" became the focus of an entire movement. Unlike Prohibition, which was a single-issue phenomenon, this wave had as its dominant ideological focus the moral decline of the entire cultural system in America. An important dimension of this was their opposition to the pervasive "amoral" ideology of secular humanism that was supplanting traditional values and to a cultural elite of "secular humanists" who in pursuit of their own interests accelerated this moral decline. A diffused cultural discontent, then, became congealed into a full-fledged political movement.

Coming to the fore as its self-proclaimed leadership were such organizations as the Moral Majority (founded in 1979), Christian Voice (founded in 1979), and Religious Roundtable (founded in 1980). All were committed to lobbying Congress on moral issues and to mobilizing the conservative Protestant constituency as a political force. According to self-reports, by 1981 active support for these groups ranged from 150,000 to 4 million laymen and 37,000 to 70,000 clergy. They also claimed (and some evidence supports this) to have registered 2 to 4 million voters for the 1980 and 1984 elections, most of whom supported conservative Republican candidates. These figures are debatable, but it is clear that however many *active* supporters there were, these political themes resonated within a larger and more diverse Evangelical population.[10]

The core of their platform was the adoption of a conservative posture toward such issues as abortion, the role of women, homosexuality, and school prayer. Though their support among Evangelicals was not unanimous, a significantly larger percentage of Evangelicals than non-Evangelicals held conservative positions on these issues. For example, in one national survey conducted in August 1980, Evangelicals were found to favor policy requiring prayer in school by a margin of 81 percent; only 54 percent of all non-Evangelicals did so. Likewise only 15 percent of all Evangelicals favored policy allowing homosexuals to teach in public schools, whereas 31 percent of all non-Evangelicals did so. Fifty-three percent favored the Equal Rights Amendment, as opposed to 66 percent of their non-Evangelical counterparts. Finally, 41 percent of the Evangelicals and 29 percent of the non-evangelicals favored a ban on abortion.[11] This pattern was corroborated in a survey of supporters/nonsupporters of the Moral Majority in an urban area in the Bible Belt, the Dallas–Fort Worth metropolitan area. Though the overall level of political conservatism was much higher here than in the national survey, the differences in attitudes were roughly the same (Shupe and Stacey 1983). Other studies also concurred.

These moral/public policy issues (and to this list, one could add the various conflicts of value in public schools) constituted the core of their agenda in this third wave. Beyond these core issues, however, studies in the early 1980s also showed that as in the past, Evangelicals as a whole were generally as conservative if not more conservative than the rest of the American population on the range of political issues.[12] Yet it is also important to note that in all cases, conservative Protestants were anything but a homogeneous political force. Among themselves they were divided.

The political *focus* of conservative Protestant activism in this third wave was qualitatively different from anything preceding it in this century, but its *complexion* was markedly different too. To be precise, where the broader conservative Protestant population showed little inclination to translate its political and cultural prejudices into actual political activism in the 1950s and 1960s, by the 1980s this situation had reversed, and Evangelicals were, among religious groups, the most likely to become politically involved. What is more, religious institutions and clergy were accorded a legitimate political role by their constituency which they previously did not have. For example, in 1978, 62 percent of all Evangelicals believed that religious organizations should "persuade senators and representatives to enact legislation that they would like to see become law"; only 41 percent of all non-Evangelicals held this view. Likewise, 58 percent of all Evangelicals agreed that "it is important for religious organizations to make public statements about what they feel to be the will of God on political and economic matters"; only 40 percent of all non-Evangelicals agreed with this.[13] Public activism of this sort was not unusual at this time. This, of course, is best seen in the activities of the aforementioned interdenominational, parachurch organizations (e.g.,

Moral Majority, which by 1986 had become the Liberty Federation). It is also seen in the growth of conservative religious lobbies. While there was only one Evangelical lobbying effort in existence at midcentury, by 1982 there were twenty-seven and most of these had emerged since 1971.[14] Finally it is seen in the presidential aspirations of the television evangelist, Pat Robertson.

It remains to be seen how successful or unsuccessful they will be. Their standing through the late 1970s and early 1980s was mixed. Efforts in 1984 to change federal law to allow voluntary prayer of some sort in public schools failed though legislation was passed which ensured the rights of religious groups to use these public facilities as any other group or organization might. The efforts to pass gay rights and women's rights legislation were successfully blocked in the early 1980s, but Evangelicals were only one of a large number of constituencies with whom these proposals were unpopular. Legislative efforts to require the teaching of scientific creationism along with evolution in the public schools have been focused at the state level and here success has been marginal. Arkansas initially passed legislation of this sort, but it was struck down in 1982 by a federal district court. Similar battles were waged in Louisiana, Mississippi, and Georgia. The success of Evangelicals, conservative Catholics, and others in changing the abortion laws was also mixed. Congress passed the Hyde Amendment in 1976 prohibiting the use of public funds to pay for abortions, and in 1978 the Supreme Court declared this to be constitutional. Yet pro-life groups have failed to achieve their ultimate objective of having an amendment passed outlawing all abortion. Finally, though Evangelicals have had some influence in local elections, they had no decisive impact in the 1980 or 1984 congressional elections and only marginal influence in the presidential elections even though the vast majority of Evangelicals voted for Ronald Reagan in these elections (Lipset and Raab 1981).[15] In the end, Evangelicals may achieve a certain success-through-failure (Lipset and Raab 1970). That is, they may ultimately fail in their particular policy initiatives, but simply having pursued them so aggressively, they may succeed in changing the shape and complexion of American politics.

The actual political power they wielded was, in many respects, irrelevant, however. Simply the fact that they were creating media attention over these issues and claimed to be able to mobilize support was enough to stimulate hostile dissent. In this case it came mostly from the ranks of the liberal establishment—the media, the academy, the arts, and the mainline religious denominations. Groups such as the American Civil Liberties Union, the National Organization for Women, the National Abortion Rights Legal Action Committee (NARAL), the

National Education Association, People for the American Way, Moral Alternatives in Politics, Americans for Common Sense, the National Council of Churches, and a variety of other local and state groups were loosely mobilized against this new Evangelical political phenomenon.[16] Millions of dollars were spent in mass-mailings, media blitzing, and editorializing against this "new political menace." Their complaint was multifaceted and, to be expected, it went beyond a fundamental disagreement about political opinion. For one, this new "Christian Right" was accused of maliciously manipulating public opinion by co-opting so-called traditional values (such as "family," "life," "patriotism," and the "flag") to further their own political ends. In this case, their ends were that of "discrediting" and "scapegoating all who disagreed with them," particularly secular humanists. By operating in this way, conservative Protestants were further accused of creating a political atmosphere of "irrational fear," "intimidation," "paranoia," and "hysteria." Underlying the political passions of conservative Protestants was the drive of a moral and religious absolutism derived from their anti-intellectualist and biblicist culture. As such they were accused of being militantly intolerant of religious and moral diversity. The most disquieting consequence, it was maintained, was obvious. These groups threatened to do harm to the Bill of Rights and the American tradition of democratic pluralism. Their agenda was implicitly totalitarian.

Whether or not these accusations were true, they did correspond to and contribute to a general image of conservative Protestantism. The effect has been consistent and cumulative. Throughout this century, largely in reaction to their periodic surges of political activism, conservative Protestantism has been viewed as a hyperreactive, ultraconservative political group that is, by virtue of its religious convictions, bigoted and intolerant, absolutist and fanatical. From the 1920s, when the association between Fundamentalism and bigotry and intolerance first emerged, through the "Brown Scare" of the 1930s and 1940s (when it was thought that "native fascism" was on the rise), down to the 1980s, conservative Protestants have consistently been regarded as the largest segment of "potential fascists" in the United States (Ribuffo 1983, chap. 5). The parallels between the waves of activism have not been lost on their critics either. As a commentator in the 1980s put it, "only the faces of the demagogues and the object of their suspicions have changed" (Hunter 1983b, 155). Two other brief observations can be made about this backlash. The first is that it has consistently been most vocal in the same sector of society, that is, in a liberal echelon of cultural elites, particularly centered in the media and in the universities. The second is that with each wave of activism, the backlash has intensified. Though hardly comparable to the groups they opposed, the reaction was never more well organized and more widespread than it was in the 1980s. After all, groups such as the People for the American Way, Moral Alternatives in Politics, and Americans for Common Sense came into being as an attempt to countermobilize against the Christian Right. Previously, the reaction typically came episodically from the editorial offices of newspapers and from offended academics.

But what can be said about the accuracy of this image? What can be said about the character of conservative Protestant politics from their century-long experience? First off, the political agenda of conservative Protestantism has been consistently preservationist, with the goals of preserving the cultural and political hegemony of white Protestantism, preserving American institutions (especially government and the churches) from the threat of communism, and preserving the traditional (Judeo-Christian) moral and familial virtues from the menace of secular humanism. In this way they have adopted the conservative platform. This is not to say that they have been uniformly conservative. Evidence shows fairly clearly that this is not the case. They have always been somewhat divided among themselves on the various issues of concern; this appears to have been particularly true in the 1980s. To the degree that the preservationist impulse has been a theme, it has been preservationism of a particular sort. Namely, it has always had a strong populist appeal. Beyond populism though it seems to consistently establish itself as antielitist. The scientific and cultural elite are perceived to be the carriers of their nemeses, be it evolutionism, communism, or secular humanism. This should not necessarily be interpreted as an antieducational, antiscientific, or antitechnological bias. Even a superficial awareness of the Evangelical adaptations to modern education and technology in this century is enough to displace that notion. They simply have wanted education, science, and technology on their own terms. Again, their antielitism has expressed itself less as anti-intellectualism and more as a distrust of intellectuals themselves. Intellectuals and their secular adaptations of science and education have been seen as unnecessarily and perniciously undermining traditional definitions of truth and virtue.

Conservative Protestantism has also cultivated a heritage of political and cultural intolerance. At different times, they have maintained a posture of prejudice and intolerance toward Catholics, Jews, blacks, and political leftists and liberals. This posture, of course, has been linked with their preservationist sentiments, but in reality, this has been far less ominous than might be supposed. For one, though it is true that conservative Protestants on the whole have been more intolerant than other religious bodies, these prejudices have typically remained suppressed if not completely latent. Rarely if ever have they been translated into open and violent political activism. Never have they been translated into acts of political militarism. Secondly, political extremism, when it does surface, is virtually always a marginal phenomenon, even within conservative Protestantism. Extremists are a fairly small, though vocal, minority. This was less so in the 1920s, but it was particularly true in the 1950s and appears to be the case in the 1980s as well. In other words, though always a marginal phenomenon, it appears that extremist politization has decreased somewhat through this century insofar as the extremists are fewer in number.

All of this provides a backdrop to the present inquiry. The coming generation of Evangelicalism is, of course, emerging within the third wave of conservative Protestant political activism. How do these themes express themselves within the coming generation? How do the views of this generation compare with the legacy of this century and with the views of an older generation presently holding political sway. By attempting to grapple with these questions, it will be possible to explore more carefully the nature and character of this third wave of conservative Protestant political activism.

## THE POLITICS OF THE COMING GENERATION

### Political Orientations: Conservatism Considered

While it is impossible to probe in great depth the attitudes of the coming generation on every issue that has concerned Evangelicals in the past, it is possible to determine their general political temperament and, beyond that, the specific contours of their political orientation. At first glance it is striking how similar the coming generation is to other generations of conservative Protestants: a very large percentage of both collegiate and seminary populations (40%–48%) identify themselves as being conservative—the majority of these being conservative Republicans (see table 17). However, a similar proportion of students identify themselves as politically moderate. The moderates are fairly evenly distributed among Democratic and Independent party lines though many are also Republicans. Finally, there is a small though significant minority (collegians, 12%; seminarians, 9%) who identify themselves as politically liberal (most describing themselves as liberal Democrats). At least in the way Evangelicals perceive themselves politically, here as with previous generations the pattern is uneven.

This diversity is clarified by their responses to a variety of public policy issues and proposals (see table 18). On crime and punishment issues, they do not distinguish themselves significantly from their public university counterparts. Though the seminarians tended to be slightly more

**Table 17**

Party Preference and Political Self-identification according to Campus Setting (In Percentages)

| | Evangelical College Students | | | | Evangelical Seminary Students | | | |
|---|---|---|---|---|---|---|---|---|
| | Republican (N = 963) | Democrat (N = 282) | Independent (N = 634) | Total | Republican (N = 367) | Democrat (N = 181) | Independent (N = 259) | Total |
| Very liberal | — | 3 | 1 | 1 | — | 3 | — | 1 |
| Liberal | 4 | 26 | 13 | 11 | 1 | 24 | 6 | 8 |
| Moderate | 39 | 54 | 62 | 49 | 29 | 54 | 58 | 44 |
| Conservative | 55 | 18 | 23 | 38 | 65 | 18 | 34 | 45 |
| Very conservative | 2 | 1 | 1 | 2 | 5 | 1 | 2 | 3 |
| Total | 51 | 15 | 34 | 100 | 46 | 22 | 32 | 100 |

NOTE: — = less than 1%.

**Table 18**
Views of Various Public Policy Issues and Proposals
according to Campus Setting

| | Evangel. College Students (N = 1,980) | Evangel. Seminary Students (N = 847) | Public Univ. Students (N = 426) |
|---|---|---|---|
| | Percentage Favoring | | |
| **Crime and punishment** | | | |
| Registration of all firearms | 76 | 67 | 78 |
| The death penalty for all persons convicted of murder | 47 | 59 | 49 |
| **Social welfare** | | | |
| Government social programs as a way to deal with social problems | 54 | 44 | 64 |
| **Women and Family** | | | |
| The Equal Rights Amendment | 25 | 25 | 66 |
| A ban on all abortions | 55 | 67 | 10 |
| **Education** | | | |
| Requiring prayer in schools | 27 | 31 | 5 |
| Requiring *only* the creation theory of the origin of the world be taught in public schools | 11 | 8 | 4 |
| Requiring *equal time* for the creation theory and the evolution theory of origin of man as taught in public schools | 83 | 84 | 59 |
| Busing to achieve social integration in the public schools | 22 | 23 | 24 |
| Allowing homosexuals to teach in public schools | 18 | 18 | 57 |

conservative than everyone else, roughly three-fourths of the college populations favored a policy requiring the registration of all firearms, and approximately half of each group favored the death penalty for all persons convicted of murder. Similarly, concerning government-sponsored social welfare, Evangelicals did not distinguish themselves; roughly half of the collegians (54%) and seminarians (44%) favored "government social programs as a way to deal with social problems." A slightly greater percentage of the students at the public university (64%) maintained this posture.[17]

Educational issues evoked a peculiar set of responses. Evangelical students, for example, were far more likely than the non-Evangelical students to favor policy "requiring prayer in schools," yet less than one-third of the former supported this policy. They were also only marginally more in favor of "requiring *only* the creation theory of the origin of the world be taught in public schools." On this issue, only one

**Table 18** (cont.)

|  | Evangel. College Students (N = 1,980) | Evangel. Seminary Students (N = 847) | Public Univ. Students (N = 426) |
|---|---|---|---|
| Energy and defense | Percentage Favoring | | |
| Increased spending for defense | 27 | 26 | 13 |
| Registration for the draft | 43[a] | 68 | — |
| More nuclear power plants as a means of gaining national energy independence | 33 | 35 | 18 |
| A "freeze" on the construction and deployment of nuclear weapons | 69[a] | — | — |
| Political economy | Percentage Agreeing | | |
| The private business system in the U.S. works better than any other system yet devised for advanced industrial societies | 45[a] | 42 | — |
| Economic growth is a better way to improve the lot of the poor than redistributing existing wealth | 35[a] | 58 | — |
| The U.S. would be better off if it moved toward socialism | 14[a] | 9 | — |
| Foreign affairs | | | |
| It is important that the U.S. at least maintain a "balance of power" with the Soviet Union | 63 | 69 | 70 |
| America should do everything it can to support Israel | 47 | 39 | 21 |

NOTE: — = less than 1%.
[a]EAP minisurvey.

out of ten Evangelicals agreed with the 1920s antievolution policy position. Ironically, in the 1920s, it was the evolutionists who were striving for the legal right to have evolution considered a competitive theory on the origin of the world. Yet by the 1980s, the situation had reversed. The creationists now wanted to be given "equal time" for a biblical explanation to this question. This opinion was actually shared by the majority of respondents from both Evangelical and public university settings, though a substantially larger majority of Evangelical collegians and seminarians (83%) than public university students (59%) endorsed this idea. Finally there is the issue of "busing" children to school districts other than the ones in which they live for the purpose of achieving racial integration. Predictably this was not strongly favored by any of the groups.

Energy and defense issues also evoked an unpredictable set of responses. Though twice as many Evangelical students as public university students favored a policy of increased defense spending, they constituted only 27 percent of their group. Though Evangelicals were divided on the issue of draft registration (collegians, 43%; seminarians, 68%), a majority (nearly 69%) favored a "freeze" on the construction and deployment of nuclear weapons. This pacifistic tendency is not weak. Though 17 percent were unsure, 20 percent of the seminarians believed that it was rarely if every wrong to "withhold that percentage of [their] tax which would be used for national defense purposes." Likewise almost twice as many Evangelical collegians and seminarians as public university students endorsed policy encouraging the construction of "more nuclear power plants as a means of gaining national energy independence," yet only about one-third of the former (collegians, 33%; seminarians, 35%) favored this proposal.

So far it is clear that this cohort of Evangelicals remains relatively conservative when compared with students attending the public university. Nonetheless, on six of the eleven issues reviewed thus far (gun registration, school prayer, creationism exclusively in the public schools, increased defense spending, nuclear power, and the "freeze"), the *majority* of Evangelicals position themselves firmly on the *liberal side*. On three others (the death penalty, social welfare, and draft registration), the Evangelicals are split fairly evenly among themselves and are not dramatically different from non-Evangelicals in their opinions. On still two others (busing and requiring equal time for the creation and evolution accounts of the world's origin to be taught in public schools), the majority of Evangelicals are positioned on the conservative side of the issue, but so are the majority of public university students. Interestingly, on most of these issues, the coming generation is more liberal than the general population.[18] This is especially true on the issue of gun control, defense, and nuclear power.

There are, however, three remaining issues upon which the majority of Evangelical students are firmly conservative and yet stand in stark opposition to the opinion of their counterparts in the public university. Notably, these are precisely the issues singled out by the organizations of the Christian Right: abortion, the rights of women, and homosexuality. On the first of these, over half of the collegians and two-thirds of the seminarians favored a ban on all abortions, compared with only 10 percent in the public university. Their relative conservatism is highlighted by the fact that only 41 percent of the general population of Evangelicals favored this policy. Likewise, only 25 percent of the Evangelical cohort favored the passage of the Equal Rights Amendment to the Constitution, compared with two-thirds in the public university.

This, as will be recalled, is dramatically more conservative than even the larger Evangelical population, 53 percent of whom supported the ERA. Finally, only 18 percent of the collegians and seminarians (roughly the same as the rest of the Evangelical population: 15%) favored policy allowing homosexuals to teach in public schools, whereas 57 percent of the public university students favored this. School prayer, of course, is the last issue. As has been seen (table 18), Evangelical students are five or six times more likely to favor a required school prayer, yet still only a minority of them favored this. It is quite plausible that had the question been rephrased to say "'allowing' prayer in schools," the majority of Evangelical students would have favored it as well; however, the same precise wording was used in the 1980 Gallup survey in which 81 percent of all Evangelicals were found to support this policy.

Why these three or four issues have so captured Evangelical opinion (and particularly the ERA and abortion issues for the younger cohort) will be addressed later. For now, two other categories of issues remain to be explored: political economy and foreign affairs (table 18). Given the caricature of conservative Protestants being staunch defenders of free-enterprise capitalism, it is somewhat surprising that less than half of the coming generation agreed with the statement that "the private business system in the U.S. works better than any other system yet devised for advanced industrial societies" when nearly 80 percent of the American population as a whole agreed with this.[19] This corresponds to the fact that only 35 percent of the Evangelical collegians and 58 percent of the seminarians agreed that "economic growth is a better way to improve the lot of the poor than redistributing existing wealth." (45% of the college population and 34% of the seminarians *disagreed* with this statement.) The majority of Evangelicals then do not enthusiastically endorse capitalism, but neither do they endorse socialism. Though there was a minority who agreed (collegians, 14%; seminarians, 9%) and a sizable percentage who were unsure (collegians, 34%; seminarians, 26%), better than half of the collegians (51%) and seminarians (65%) disagreed with the statement that "the U.S. would be better off if it moved toward socialism."

On two very important issues of international scope, the presumed Evangelical opinion is also exaggerated insofar as the younger cohort is concerned. Roughly two-thirds of the Evangelicals surveyed (collegians, 63%; seminarians, 69%) agreed that "it is important that the United States at least maintain a 'balance of power' with the Soviet Union." Interestingly, this was just *under* the percentage of those in the public university holding this opinion. On the political significance of Israel, approximately twice the percentage of Evangelicals as non-Evangelicals agreed that "America should do everything it can to support Israel." Nonetheless, they constituted less than half of the coming generation (collegians, 47% seminarians, 39%). This hardly fits the image of a religious group unanimously and fervently committed (for religious reasons) to a well-being of the state of Israel.

### Conservatives, Moderates, and Liberals

Perhaps the most striking feature of this review is the lack of unanimity among Evangelicals on the range of issues. It is a diversity that has been seen to exist within the larger Evangelical population. One way of more closely examining this is to create a composite index derived from attitudes toward a series of public policy proposals.[20] The result is very intriguing for what it tells us about the distribution and intensity of political perspectives not only within the younger cohort of Evangelicals but within Evangelicalism generally.

From table 19, it is clear that the variation seen thus far is not random but, in fact, falls along the length of the political continuum. Yet the distribution is far from even. As one would expect, the greatest portion is conservative. A substantial percentage of these would be classified as very conservative: 7 percent of the collegians and 14 percent of the seminarians. These, by and large, are those whose political convictions are very clear; they fundamentally oppose social (governmental) welfare, passage of the Equal Rights Amendment, and allowing homosexuals to teach in public schools, and strongly favor legislation banning all abortions, increasing defense spending, and increasing the use of nuclear energy. The remainder are more moderately conservative but squarely conservative all the same. Another fairly large percentage are politically moderate

Table 19
Political Orientation according to Campus Setting (In Percentages)

|  | Evangelical College Students ($N$ = 1,980) | Evangelical Seminary Students ($N$ = 847) |
|---|---|---|
| Very liberal | 5 | 6 |
| Liberal | 25 | 20 |
| Moderate | 34 | 29 |
| Conservative | 29 | 31 |
| Very conservative | 7 | 14 |

NOTE: Alpha coefficient = .59 college; .68 seminary.

(uncommitted to any particular political philosphy), and thus, as a group they take the conservative position on some issues, the liberal position on other issues, and on still others are undecided. Beyond this, there is a minority among the coming generation that are decidedly liberal in their political ideology. Roughly 5 percent are radically liberal, even left wing. Given the conservative heritage of American Evangelicalism, it is this minority of liberals/radicals that is the most intriguing dimension of the Evangelical political landscape. In contrast to the conservative agenda, they strongly endorse government-sponsored social welfare, the Equal Rights Amendment, the occupational rights of homosexuals, and federally enforced racial integration in the schools. Moreover, many of them are either undecided on the abortion question or they support the legal apparatus that would allow women to make their own choice.

Political ideology, of course, extends beyond opinion on these domestic policy issues. The internal consistency of these political orientations is seen in table 20, where the political position (from table 19) of seminarians was held against their opinions on various issues.[21] The differences in opinion between the very liberal and very conservative are dramatic indeed for such issues as the promises of socialism, the utility of free-enterprise capitalism, American support for Israel, the United States military competition with the Soviet Union, draft registration, abortion legislation, tax breaks for parents who send their children to private religious schools, and even the ordination of women in the ministry. A similar pattern was evident among Evangelical collegians.[22]

But from where do these ideological differences derive? In part they stem from differences in the backgrounds of these Evangelicals.[23] For example, those on the liberal to radical Left are more likely to have grown up in the larger metropolitan areas of the Rocky Mountain and Pacific states. They are also more likely to have come from either working-class (blue collar) or upper-middle-class (technical professional) backgrounds. Perhaps their most important characteristics were religious and familial in nature: they were more likely to have come from the denominational churches of the Reformational-Confessional tradition, and more importantly, they were more likely to be weaker in their commitment to early twentieth-century definitions of orthodoxy. Most importantly, they believed in an ideal of the family that was egalitarian and androgynous. Those on the conservative to extreme conservative side were more likely to have come from the suburban areas of the Midwest and the South. They were also more likely to be from either farming or upper-middle-class (business executive) family backgrounds. On the religious side, conservatives tended to draw more from the moderately sectarian churches (neither highly denominational nor highly sectarian)

**Table 20**

Stance on Various Political Issues according to Political Position (Seminary Only)

| | Political Position[a] | | | | | Range between Extremes (%) | Gamma |
|---|---|---|---|---|---|---|---|
| | Very Liberal (N = 47) (%) | Liberal (N = 166) (%) | Moderate (N = 239) (%) | Conservative (N = 253) (%) | Very conservative (N = 110) (%) | | |
| | Percentage Agreeing | | | | | | |
| The U.S. would be better off if it moved toward socialism | 28 | 16 | 8 | 6 | 2 | 26 | .52 |
| The private business system in the U.S. works better than any other system yet devised for advanced industrial societies | 23 | 48 | 56 | 62 | 86 | 63 | −.33 |
| America should do everything it can to support Israel | 11 | 19 | 31 | 55 | 64 | 53 | −.41 |
| It is important that the U.S. at least maintain a "balance of power" with the Soviet Union | 41 | 51 | 66 | 79 | 96 | 55 | −.51 |
| | Percentage Favoring | | | | | | |
| Registration for the draft | 40 | 44 | 62 | 82 | 97 | 57 | −.51 |
| A ban on all abortions | 49 | 51 | 64 | 77 | 84 | 35 | −.37 |
| Tax breaks for parents who send their children to private religious schools | 38 | 42 | 50 | 58 | 71 | 33 | −.23 |
| The ordination of women in the ministry | 96 | 74 | 50 | 34 | 25 | 71 | .42 |

NOTE: Chi-square for all of these figures is significant at the .000 level.

[a] Alpha coefficient = .58.

of the Baptist tradition. Not least, they were much more prone to be highly orthodox in their beliefs and have a strong traditionalist orientation toward the family.

Ideological differences among Evangelicals also derive from varying assumptions about the religious origins and character of America as well as from perceptions of perceived threats to its existence. (see table 21).[24] For example, roughly two-thirds of this younger cohort of Evangelicals (collegians, 64%; seminarians, 63%) believed that "America was founded on Christian principles." Even so, there are wide differences of opinion on this matter when comparing liberals with conservatives: a range of 39 percent. The strongly conservative were much more likely to believe that American government and morality historically emerged from theistic principles. They would, therefore, interpret the conservative agenda as preserving what remains of a Christian civilization. While this logical connection is implicit for many if not most of these Evangelicals, it has, in fact, been formalized by many ministers and popular spokesmen.[25]

The strongly liberal on the other hand were far less likely to hold such "naive assumptions." The conservative agenda, to the degree that it is based in this belief, is therefore unfounded and illegitimate. There are two fairly distinct rationales. The first is that since America was never "Christian" to begin with, there is nothing to preserve. The second is that American culture was Christian, but Christian in a progressive and "prophetic" fashion. In either case, a progressive political agenda is what is called for in order to establish or reestablish Christian ideals in society. This is precisely the perspective of *Sojourners, The Other Side, Radix,* and their constituencies (see Hunter 1981).

Curiously, though a majority believed that America was founded upon Christian principles, only a minority(collegian, 20%; seminarian, 13%) maintained that "America was still a Christian nation"—an opinion no more likely to be held by liberals than by moderates or conservatives. This sense of betrayal—America abandoning its founding vision— would, in part, account for the apparent intensity of the conservative reaction in the 1980s. But for the conservative it is not simply that American society is slowly drifting from its moral and religious moorings. It is also being pulled away from those moorings by antagonistic ideological currents and by a minority who promulgate that ideology. By and large, it is not communism that poses a threat anymore, though a fairly substantial minority of the coming generation (collegian, 29%; seminarian, 38%) agreed that "communism is still a serious threat within our country." Predictably, a more imposing force is that opaque ideological presence, secular humanism. Though there are strong differences

**Table 21**

Political Theology and Attitudes toward Threats to America according to Political Position
(College Only)

| | Political Position[a] (percentage agreeing) | | | | | | |
|---|---|---|---|---|---|---|---|
| | Very Liberal ($N = 94$) | Liberal ($N = 483$) | Moderate ($N = 159$) | Conservative ($N = 549$) | Very Conservative ($N = 142$) | Range between Extremes | Gamma |
| Political theology | | | | | | | |
| America was founded upon Christian principles | 32 | 60 | 65 | 70 | 71 | 39 | −.21 |
| America is still a Christian nation | 14 | 20 | 19 | 21 | 28 | 14 | −.13 |
| Threats to America | | | | | | | |
| Communism is still a serious threat within our country | 5 | 20 | 29 | 39 | 38 | 33 | −.26 |
| Secular humanism has greatly eroded the moral fiber of our society | 43 | 67 | 80 | 82 | 84 | 41 | −.29 |
| The major universities in our country today are controlled by secular humanists | 40 | 55 | 62 | 66 | 67 | 27 | −.20 |

NOTE: Chi-square for all of these figures is significant at .000 level.
[a]Alpha coefficient = .59.

among the politically liberal and conservative on this issue (41% difference among collegians and 72% difference among seminarians), a majority of the Evangelical college students (76%) and seminarians (85%) agreed that "secular humanism has greatly eroded the moral fiber of our society." What is more, the majority believed that secular humanists control the information- and culture-producing sectors of the economy—the universities, public schools, media of mass communications, and the like.[26] Secular humanism and secular humanists then, for younger and older Evangelicals alike, are phenomena to be reckoned with at the political level. In this way, the coming generation fully shares Evangelicalism's century-long animus against the secular cultural elite. This sentiment is particularly strong for the seminarians.[27]

All of this, however, stands in sharp contrast to the perspective of the politically liberal. For them, communism poses virtually no threat, secular humanism poses only a marginal threat, and secular humanists are not perceived to significantly control the universities or any other sector of the "knowledge industry." But how is one to account for this anomaly? More will be said later, but for now a few observations can be made. The mainstream Evangelical perception that the information sector and the public sector generally are heavily influenced by secular humanists and secular humanism is not entirely without empirical merit. There is ample evidence that cultural or knowledge elites who dominate these sectors are disproportionately irreligious (secular) and disproportionately Left-liberal in their political ideology as compared with the general population.[28] Though not sharing their secular assumptions, the Evangelical Left does fully share their political values and positions. As documented elsewhere, their ideological alliance with this "new class" of cultural elites is fairly unreflective (Hunter 1980). They are unlikely partners pursuing common political (and even class) interests. If this is true, then it is highly unlikely that the Evangelical Left would be critical of its secular counterpart. Indeed, the evidence fully confirms this.

### Mobilization and Intolerance: Extremism Considered

Far from monolithically conservative, Evangelicals are divided among themselves on most if not all issues. But they are divided in surprisingly predictable ways—according to fairly cohesive political ideologies. Right-conservative, moderate, and Left-liberal factions all exist in varying proportions. At this point, what remains as the most distinctive political feature is their strong concern with the issues of abortion, school prayer, homosexuality, and the ERA. Given this background, what is the likelihood of Evangelicals and the coming generation, particularly, engaging in well-organized political action in pursuit of these special interests? What is their potential for mobilizing opinion against the moral decline of contemporary society?

One indication is the kind of legitimacy they give to religious organizations engaging in political affairs. When asked if they thought religious organizations should or should not try to persuade senators and representatives to enact legislation they would like to see become law, in stark contrast to their counterparts in the public university (37% of whom said that they should), both the collegians and the seminarians almost uniformly agreed that they should (see table 22).[29] It is significant that they were also far more likely to endorse this idea than the general population of Evangelicals. The identical pattern was evident in the responses to queries about the relative importance of religious organizations making public statements about what they feel to be the will of God in ethical and moral matters, spiritual and religious matters, and political and economic matters. Among Evangelicals, the degree of legitimacy accorded to religious organizations engaged in these activities declines the further removed the organization is from the religious realm. Nonetheless, the majority still endorses those rights. Again, the younger cohort accords as much if not more legitimacy than the broader (and older) Evangelical population. This attitude is also curiously uniform among the coming generation. Though the more intensely orthodox tend to be slightly more activistic than the less orthodox, Evangelicals of

**Table 22**

Campus Setting and View of the Political Role of Religious Organizations
(In Percentages)

|  | Evangel. College Students (N = 1,980) | Evangel. Seminary Students (N = 847) | Public Univ. Students (N = 426) | General Pop. of Evangel.[a] (N = 347) |
|---|---|---|---|---|
| Religious organizations persuading lawmakers: |  |  |  |  |
| They should | 88 | 91 | 37 | 62 |
| They should not | 12 | 9 | 63 | 38 |
| It is important for religious organizations to make public statements on: |  |  |  |  |
| Spiritual and religious matters | 87 | 93 | 65 | 92 |
| Ethical and moral matters | 82 | 90 | 47 | 88 |
| Political and economic matters | 63 | 67 | 27 | 58 |

[a]1978/1979 Gallup/*Christianity Today* survey, reported in Hunter 1983a.

all political convictions, social class, and demographic backgrounds equally accept the political rights of religious groups and organizations.[30]

It is not as though Evangelicals are politicized and non-Evangelicals are not. This would be misleading. For example, nearly nine of ten (86%) public university students claimed it was rarely or never wrong to take part in political protests, whereas roughly seven of ten Evangelical students made this claim (collegians, 72%; seminarians, 74%). The issue then is the *kind* of politization. In this instance it is the legitimacy or the right of religious people and the religious organizations presumably representing them to pursue their particular group interests through public and political channels. Evangelicals, as one religious group, very enthusiastically maintain this, while non-Evangelicals do not. This is further reflected in the issue of boycotting the products of corporations who sponsor television shows in which there is "morally objectionable content." Once again, the majority of Evangelicals (collegians, 50%; seminarians, 70%) favored this kind of political action, while only one in five (21%) of the public university students favored it. The norms surrounding the role of religion and religious organizations in the public sphere have altered significantly within Evangelicalism since the 1950s, and this participation in the public sphere shows no sign of lessening. The political realm in their view is not off-limits. In principle, in any case, Evangelicals place high expectations upon the churches and parachurch organizations to advocate and defend in the public realm those positions regarded as being in their interest.

To this point, it would seem as though the worst fears of the liberal elite are justified. Though the majority of Evangelicals stand firmly on the liberal side of many issues and though they are divided on many others, overall they remain markedly more conservative than their secular counterparts. In sharp contrast to non-Evangelicals, they also strongly endorse their political rights as a religious group. It would seem that certain preconditions for extremist political activity are largely met, at least for a substantial sector of the Evangelical population. Yet what has not been seriously considered to this point, but what may be the single most important issue, is the issue of intolerance. It is only logical that for extremist political action to be a plausible course, there must be a further precondition: namely, that there be a zealous intolerance of those who have different beliefs and life-styles and a willingness to impose one's own particular orientation upon all those who do not share it. In this light, do Evangelicals pose a threat to American traditions of democratic tolerance as many commentators claim? Are they disposed to legislating a fundamentalist agenda of social and moral principles? Or are

**Table 23**
Tolerance for the Rights of Various Types of People
(Percentage Believing the Listed Groups Should Be Allowed to Speak Publicly)

| | General Population | | Evangelicals | | Evangelicals with high educational attainment[a] | |
| --- | --- | --- | --- | --- | --- | --- |
| | Non-Evangelicals (N = 1,036) | Evangelicals (N = 415) | Younger Cohort (18–35) (N = 166) | Older Cohort (36 and older) (N = 249) | Younger Cohort (N = 48) | Older Cohort (N = 40) |
| An atheist (against religion and the churches) | 71 | 51 | 66 | 41 | 85 | 68 |
| A racist (on the genetic inferiority of blacks) | 65 | 49 | 56 | 44 | 73* | 58* |
| A communist | 65 | 40 | 49 | 33 | 77 | 55 |
| A militarist (on doing away with elections and letting the military run the country) | 61 | 42 | 54 | 34 | 75 | 55 |
| A homosexual | 74 | 51 | 62 | 43 | 79* | 64* |

SOURCE: National Opinion Research Center, General Social Survey, 1982.

NOTE: Chi-square is significant at the .05 level except for those figures marked with an asterisk.

[a]High educational attainment = at least one year of college or university training.

there limits to their political passions? Just how tolerant of political, cultural, and social pluralism are they?

Two questions are really being asked. One refers to the predisposition to "impose" a Christian (Evangelical) world view on American society. The other refers to their actual capability of amassing the necessary support to do it. Both are empirical questions, but it will be the first that will be explored, for the latter in large measure depends on the former.

It has been noted that since the 1950s most commentators on Evangelicalism (academic, editorial, or otherwise) have simply assumed that to be strongly conservative is to be intolerantly conservative. Thus whether Evangelicals were capable or not of imposing their political agenda against the will of the majority, they were certainly predisposed toward doing so. Their own commitment to certain political, moral, and social values, then, eclipsed any commitment to pluralism and democratic tolerance. Yet with little reflection it is clear that these issues are analytically separable. Passionate conservative sentiment may, in fact, preclude tolerance, but the relationship can vary considerably by degree. Public opinion surveys provide insight into these issues.

Table 23 illustrates tolerance of the rights of people whose "ideas are often considered bad or dangerous" (atheists, racists, communists, militarists, and homosexuals) among three different groups of people: Evangelicals and non-Evangelicals, younger and older Evangelicals, and younger and older Evangelicals who are highly educated (having had no less than one year of a college education). The differences are striking. As a whole Evangelicals are significantly less tolerant of the public expression of marginal political opinion than are non-Evangelicals, with the largest divergences between the two existing over the rights of communists and homosexuals. Yet Evangelicals are not made of one cloth in this regard. A sense of generational change is implied in the differences between the younger and older cohorts within Evangelicalism. The younger cohort as a whole is not quite as tolerant as the general population, but it is notably *more* tolerant than its older counterpart. Finally, the educational background of Evangelicals makes a substantial difference in how tolerant they are as well. Those with at least some exposure to higher education are far more tolerant than those without it, and the younger among these are significantly more tolerant (nearly unanimously so) than the older. The bedrock of social and political intolerance appears then to have come a long way toward breaking up. Nowhere is this process occurring more rapidly than among the coming generation.[31]

Tolerance of religious, moral, and political diversity on the part of Evangelicals and non-Evangelicals is further illustrated in table 24.[32]

**Table 24**
Religious, Moral, and Political Tolerance according to Campus Setting
(In Percentages)

|  | Evangelical College Students (N = 1,980) | Evangelical Seminary Students (N = 847) | Public University Students (N = 426) |
|---|---|---|---|
| Highly tolerant | 26 | 16 | 66 |
| Tolerant | 53 | 53 | 31 |
| Moderate | 19 | 26 | 3 |
| Intolerant | 3 | 5 | — |
| Highly intolerant | — | — | — |

NOTE: Alpha coefficient (measuring index reliability) = .55 (college and seminary). — = less than 1%.

Two important and related patterns immediately suggest themselves from this table. The first is that only a very small number (3%–5%) are in principle even moderately intolerant of such pluralism. The majority of Evangelical students, like the public university students, are firmly committed to principles of tolerance and civility. This is true for the very conservative and the very liberal alike. The second is that while committed to these ideals, they are not nearly as "enthusiastic" in their commitment as is the cohort of public university students. For example, 66 percent of the students from the public university measured highly tolerant, compared with 26 percent of the Evangelical collegians and 16 percent of the seminarians.[33]

Both patterns are important but in light of prevailing cultural images about conservative Protestantism, it is the former which should be emphasized—only a very small percentage is flatly intolerant of cultural and political diversity. (Most of these, incidently, are very conservative in their political orientation.)[34] Those who equivocated did so because they wanted to be assured that individual freedoms did not extend to the point of causing physical harm to others. With that condition met, the moderately tolerant quickly agreed with the notion that people should be able to believe as they wish or live in any way that they choose even if it is very different from their own manner of living.[35] As one sophomore explained:

Certainly people should be able to live as they please. I think that that is the way God intended the humans to be: to have the freedom to walk with God or not walk with God; to be sinful or not to be sinful; to think their own thoughts; to have their own beliefs; to live any way they choose even if it is very different from the way I live. I think those are rights or freedoms that God has given all people.

Since only a small number expressed strong intolerance, only a small number would likely be predisposed to imposing their particular values as normative for the society as a whole. This was further implied in the seminarian response when asked if they would "support a constitutional amendment to make Christianity the official religion of the United States." The overwhelming majority (87%) said that they would not, though a minority (13%) responded that they would.[36]

The unwillingness to legislate their particular cultural orientation is also suggested by the fact that the majority (collegian, 76%; seminarian, 57%) were either neutral toward or disapproved of the goals and the methods for achieving the goals of the most prominent organization of the Christian Right, the Moral Majority.[37] Most further believed that the Moral Majority is politically ineffectual, that it will lose influence in the years to come, and that it overall *harms the cause of religion in America.*[38] Whatever else one may say, evidence strongly suggests that the objectives and political strategies of the Moral Majority have generated significant backlash within the coming generation of Evangelicals. Not surprisingly this backlash extends to the larger population of Evangelicals in America too.[39] This is so in spite of the real ideological affinity that exists between the organization and its presumed constituency. The reason for this is precisely because the Moral Majority and its allies are perceived by Evangelicals themselves as exceeding the limits of political decorum by attempting to impose their will upon an unwilling majority. (Some even described their political techniques as unethical.) The feeling was ubiquitous:

The Moral Majority is overly legalistic about life-style issues. It is trying to force people into its idea of what a "nation under God" should be. This, to me, is not what Christianity is all about. (male, first-year master of arts candidate in marriage and family ministries, Baptist)

I generally disapprove of the Moral Majority, both its goals and methods. I think that they mix a lot of unbiblical things in with their Christianity. School prayer, for example. I personally do not mind the idea of public prayers in schools but there are a lot of non-Christians out there and they should not have to have prayer imposed upon them. It seems as though they want to remake the American legal system after the book of Deuteronomy. (male, senior, Bible major, Episcopalian)

You just can't slap on morality from the outside. You can't force people to be good. The whole premise of the Moral Majority is haywire. (female, second-year Master of biblical studies candidate, Independent Baptist)

A final indication of an unwillingness to "impose" particular political and cultural values is made by the seminarians' professors. Evangelical theologians almost uniformly (more than their liberal counterparts) held that it was inappropriate to use the pulpit to urge parishioners to vote for or against specific candidates.[40]

At this point it would appear as though the political designs of Evangelicals and particularly the coming generation do have formidable, self-imposed limits. In this there is a peculiar anticlimax. To be specific, a substantial portion of Evangelicals are conservative or very conservative with a specific political agenda; they are almost uniformly committed to their rights as religious people to engage in political action to realize their plan; yet they are decidedly reluctant to carry out their plan at other people's expense. Tolerance prevails.

The image of political extremism then would seem a grossly exaggerated characterization of contemporary Evangelicalism and its coming generation. If it has any truth, it does so with regard to a small minority—two to three percent of the coming generation.[41] This is a population of individuals who are simultaneously very politically conservative, highly committed to political activism on the part of religious organizations, and, in principle, exceptionally intolerant of religious, moral, or political diversity. One seminarian who fit this description justified his views this way:

Christians do carry a responsibility of turning our culture around. Not that it is possible but at least we should try. And who not? We know that our beliefs are ultimately right; we also know that [a Christian] life-style and morality are ultimately right. Therefore we should have the confidence to believe that it would serve [the interests of] the general population by having it constitute our culture. (male, second-year master of biblical exposition candidate, Methodist)

As might be expected, these extremists tend to be from the most sectarian religious backgrounds and are among the most literalistic and orthodox in their theological beliefs.[42] They also tend to be more representative among the seminarians or aspiring religious professionals. In summary, "fanaticism" after a fashon *is* discernible among a minority of Evangelicals and slightly more so among aspiring religious professionals than their lay counterparts. In light of what has been reviewed here, it is highly doubtful that these elites would be credible to or could mobilize anything but a small number of lay followers. Yet one should not be naive either. Marginal groups such as these (if carefully mobilized) can effect severe political consequences. In the Evangelical case, however, it is improbable that extremist political action could proceed very far without a serious backlash, not just from a secular cultural elite but from the vast majority of Evangelicals themselves. This was illustrated by the students themselves. When asked if they could imagine any circumstance in which they would support violent activity on the part of Christian groups in an attempt to achieve certain moral or political ends, invariably they replied as one coed (English major) did. "I think such actions would be totally wrong. It would be the biggest mistake they could make. It's just not a Christian solution." Could they themselves ever engage in an act of violence even if they felt God's name and purpose were defamed? Another student's reply was also typical.

> No, I just don't think that that is something that would come from the Holy Spirit. My outcry might be vocal, verbal, or it could take shape in other forms of political protest, but it would never be violent. (male, third-year master of divinity candidate, Assemblies of God)

Political extremism would indeed not likely proceed very far. Such a policy would be discredited from the outset by precisely those who would be its natural constituency.

It bears repeating, with these exceptions, that it would appear as though Evangelicals generally and the coming generation particularly, despite their relative conservatism and their commitment to the principles of political activism, are firmly committed to the liberal traditions of social and political tolerance. Their religious exclusivism then has not translated into a social and political exclusivism. In this light, the possibility of broadly based, countervailing, political extremism on the part of conservative Protestantism is highly unlikely for not only is Evangelical public opinion sharply divided on most issues but most Evangelicals are no longer even predisposed toward "Christianizing" American society. Evangelical opinion *is* fairly cohesively mobilized on the issues of abortion, the Equal Rights Amendment, homosexual rights, and school prayer, yet there is no evidence suggesting that Evangelicals would operate outside normal democratic channels. This is so even among the small number who could fairly be labeled extremists. To the contrary, inasmuch as they interpret their own religious heritage as part of American political experience, violent and/or undemocratic activism is doubtful indeed. It would be un-American; it would be un-Evangelical.[43]

EVANGELICALS AND THE ETHIC OF POLITICAL CIVILITY

Through the coming generation it has been possible to explore more completely the complexities of the relationship between Evangelicalism and politics in contemporary America. The continuities with previous generations within Evangelicalism are considerable. The most obvious, of course, is the conservative impulse. Another is the antielitist impulse. Though less prominent than the former, the latter (a dark suspicion of secular, cultural elites) does continue to the present as a fairly deep-rooted, populace sentiment. Still another theme concerns the role of the leadership of Evangelicalism. From the early part of the twentieth century, these political movements have, with but a few exceptions, been inspired and sustained by conservative Protestantism's elite (e.g., clergy, evangelists, theologians, and church leaders). This was true in the 1920s, 1950s, and 1980s. It is also true for the coming generation. The seminarians are consistently more conservative on the issues of the day, more suspicious of communism and secular humanism, more uniformly politicized, more likely to support the Moral Majority, and more prone to intolerance than their lay counterparts in the college setting. Whether they are more "enlightened" about the social and political realities of the day than their public is not an issue that can be judged here. It *is* plain, however, that they would have more to gain—a greater vested interest—from a successful realization of the Evangelical political objectives. Power and privilege would follow.

Despite continuities, there are important differences in the contemporary political surge of Evangelicalism; differences that are especially prominent in the coming generation. The most obvious difference is the substantive focus of the movement: the moral decline of American culture. As we have seen, Evangelicals have chosen to counter this perceived trend on several fronts: the women's issue (ERA), the abortion issue, the homosexual issue, and in some ways, the school prayer issue. Again, it is appropriate to ask why is it that these issues so effectively mobilize Evangelical opinion? The matter is open to speculation. One possible clue, however, is that each of these issues is directly related to sexuality and the family. In other words, moral decline is perceived to be embodied in the changing definitions of gender roles, in the changing assumptions about prenatal life, in the greater militance and visibility of deviant sex role models, and in the sanction against public spirituality (namely, prayer for children). For Evangelicals and many other highly religious groups, sexuality and the family have long been regarded as quasi-sacred, off-limits to public manipulation, and exempt from secularization. Protestants long ago conceded control over the affairs of state and economy, education, and other institutional areas, but the family, sexuality, and the private sphere generally—the well-spring of moral discipline in society—have remained heavily under their influence. *The private sphere, and the family in particular, may prove to be the final battleground in conservative Protestantism's century-long battle with modernity.*

The texture of their political orientation has altered as well. From all indications, Evangelicals are at least as divided if not more divided on issues than in previous generations. Fully developed political divisions covering the entire ideological spectrum exist in their subculture. What is more, though the Evangelicals as a whole remain more conservative relative to non-Evangelicals, the coming generation is significantly *more liberal* than their forebears. The political mean, in other words, has shifted leftward on the ideological continuum.

Perhaps the most important difference is the apparent increase in levels of tolerance. Clearly Evangelicals are not as exuberant as non-Evangelicals in their support of religious, moral, and political diversity, and even the younger cohort has its extremists. Nonetheless, it is fair to say that in principle they strongly defend the right of others to believe and to live as they wish. This extends to the realm of political ideology as well. For example, only a fraction (collegians, 6%; seminarians, 3%) agreed that "people who hold political ideas which are un-American should be kept from voicing their opinions." The overwhelming majority (collegians, 76%; seminarians, 90%) disagreed and most, strongly. In some respects, they are paragons of democratic tolerance. But why? To begin to answer this, it is necessary to make a brief theoretical digression.

## The Ethic of Civility

At least two major innovations have taken place in the political culture of advanced industrial societies—innovations which have special consequences for the relationship between religion and politics. The first has to do with the "proper" place of religion in a "civil society." American political theory and practice has for over two centuries forbidden the establishment of a national state church. Even so it is also well known that within these legal restrictions, religious leaders, organizations, and lobbies played an active and powerful role in the political affairs of American society through the beginning of the twentieth century. For a variety of reasons (having to do with the institutional specialization that accompanies modernization in its advanced stages), the separation of church and state has come to be, by and large, the *isolation* of religion from politics. Recent interpretations of the "establishment clause" in the Constitution reflect this structural change: religion is segregated from political affairs and this is viewed as the way it should be (i.e., the way the framers and ratifiers of the Constitution "intended it to be").[44]

The second innovation in the political culture centers around the issue of tolerance. The civil society, in theory, is a tolerant and democratic society. In this situation one may, in principle, hold any political ideology or religious theology one wishes however "offensive" or distasteful it may be to other sectors of the population. In spite of any ideological diversity and any attendant hostilities, the civil society remains intact as long as all parties agree to abide by the procedural norms of tolerance of opposing views, respect for civil liberties, and nonviolent, legally proscribed political action and dissent (Dahl 1956; Griffith, Plamanatz, and Pennock 1956; Prothro and Grigg 1966; Lawrence 1976). In theory, citizens are required neither to agree nor to passively comply with the opposition's initiatives. Sharp disagreement and ideological countermobilization are expected in a healthy democratic environment. Once again, the only requirement is a toleration of the opposition's existence and a defense of their right to make known their cause and complaint.

The innovation in the political ethos of toleration entails an inversion—tolerance turned inside out, as it were. Not only are individuals required to be *tolerant of others*; individuals must also be *tolerable to others*. This can be described as the ethic of civility (Cuddihy 1978). This ethic is an ethic of gentility and studied moderation. It speaks of a code of social discourse whereby religious beliefs and political convictions are to be expressed discretely and tactfully and in most cases, privately. Convictions are to be tempered by "good taste" and sensibility. It is an ethic which pleads "no offense." The greatest breach of these norms is belligerence and divisiveness; the greatest atrocity is to be offensive and thus intolerable. These two innovations are not unrelated. Together they impose profound limitations upon the functioning and expression of religious institutions and ideologies. They vastly restrict the area of legitimate movement of religion. For a religion to attempt to reclaim authority for itself in the public sphere is a coarse and tactless act of incivility—a breach which could only evoke strong moral sanctions.

From this perspective it becomes clear that the hostilities engendered by the third wave of activism centered around the fact that the "new Christian Right" has violated the moral strictures of civility by crossing over the barriers separating public and private spheres and attempting to retain, through political means, traditional moral standards. With the relatively forceful reintroduction of conservative Protestant symbols into the public realm, political decorum was besmirched. In this case it is important to emphasize that this transgression does not involve questions of legal propriety (e.g., the Moral Majority has broken no laws); it involves the cultural definitions of political decorum for religious organizations and movements.

The curious thing (and most important point) is that Evangelicals themselves have embraced this moral code of civility. One undergraduate in referring to the Moral Majority stated this clearly:

> I like [the Moral Majority's] platform but I don't think that they should go about pressuring people the way they do. If they want to say that they are against abortion, for example, they should just make their opinions known. They don't have to go into towns and have massive demonstrations picketing clinics. They should just be strong in their beliefs. It's not as though they should not try to win support for their positions. They should. They just should not pressure people all of the time like Jerry Falwell does. They shouldn't have direct conflicts with their opposition either. (male, sophomore, history major, nondenominational)

Other students concurred. Evangelicals themselves are acutely sensitive to this breach of norms. They reject it, they are embarrassed by it, and what is more, most resent, as Evangelicals, being associated with an organization as "pugnacious" and "incivil" as the Moral Majority. It is fair to assume that Evangelical political organizations since the 1950s have not been capable of mobilizing a larger segment of the Evangelical population mostly because Evangelicals as a whole have adopted this ethic of civility.

This brings us back to the original issue of this chapter: the image of conservative Protestantism as the embodiment in various degrees of a radically conservative political extremism. The basic characterization has remained fairly constant throughout the course of this century. Dissent against Evangelical political surges, however, has grown in volume and in fervor. As mentioned earlier, the political backlash created by the third wave of conservative Protestant political activism within the secular cultural elite was never stronger or better organized than it was in the

1980s. This is so in spite of the fact that the nature of conservative Protestant politics has altered in some important ways. Ideologically they are increasingly divided and, in many ways, increasingly liberal. And though in principle they agree that religious organizations have the right to take political action, they are embarrassed when these groups actually do. Their own sense of civility will not allow them to risk the moral offense of acting politically in the public realm. One final reality is demographic. As a percentage of the population, Evangelicals are shrinking in size. They are more of a minority than they were in the 1920s, which is one very good reason why Fundamentalists were successful then but are not now. In other words, hostilities based upon an image of monolithic and extremist conservatism have intensified all the while the real potential of Evangelicals to effect political change has dwindled. The image has remained just as strong even though it resembles reality less and less.

It is clear that those who have formed the most strident opposition to Evangelical political initiatives have overinterpreted the phenomenon. The political extremism of a minority has been projected upon the whole population of conservative Protestants. The radicalism of these elites has been assumed to characterize their constituencies (e.g., all Evangelicals must be as passionately anti-Communist, "paranoid," "anti-intellectual," "bigoted," and the like as the Reverends Billy Sunday, Carl McIntire, or Jerry Falwell). If it is true that liberal commentators have overinterpreted the magnitude of this phenomenon (inflated the nature, size, and importance of the Christian Right), then in so doing they have unwittingly contributed to the invention of precisely that which they fear and oppose so much—a *bête noire* (that is largely imaginary). In this sense, fanaticism is more perceived than real.

Preconceptions do die hard. If the coming generation of Evangelicals provides any indication, the images of conservative Protestant politics will continue to resemble the realities less and less. This will have critically important consequences for the future of the conservative Protestant world.

# Part Three

# Evangelicalism and the Modern World Order

# Modernity and the Reconstruction of Tradition

The caricature of Evangelicalism as an inert fortification of antique cultural traditions is certainly wrong. Even a superficial examination will reveal that an unsettled quality pervades the Evangelical world. But it is much more than this. When seen on its own terms, movement and fluctuation, restlessness, fluster, and even turbulence are all apparent. The cultural traditions which have distinguished the Evangelical heritage are visibly shifting. Though these broad changes are now discernible, their meaning is not. The most pressing question then is how to interpret these changes in a broader context. What significance do the alterations in the Evangelical approach to politics, their attitudes toward the family, their morality and life ethic, and their theological vision have? To answer this question, it is first necessary to explore further what Evangelicalism means in sociological terms.

## THE RECONSTRUCTION OF TRADITIONS

Among other things a society, any society, is a moral order. It is comprised of a complex structure of social definitions, or norms. These norms have, at root, a metaphysical character: they define reality—what is real and what is illusory or fictional. They also define what is right and wrong, correct and incorrect, appropriate and inappropriate, and good and evil in society. Very simply, they define the proper way people should think, behave, and relate to others in everyday life. The moral order then is comprised of *symbolic boundaries*. These act as rules and guidelines by which ordinary people make sense out of their personal lives. They also establish predictable patterns of relationship and social exchange in the larger community and society. Though there is invariably disagreement, tension, and even conflict over these symbolic boundaries, overall the moral order of society remains a highly organized and cohesive reality. Without these boundaries individual and collective existence would become intolerably disjointed. It is, as the social anthropologist Mary Douglas put it, part of our human condition to long for hard lines and clear concepts (Douglas 1966, 162). Thus, threats to the stability of the moral order (through various kinds of moral deviation, for example) typically provoke serious social reactions. This is so whether these threats come from outside the society or are generated internally. Society (or sectors of it) becomes mobilized both to neutralize the threat and to restore the inviolable quality of these moral and cognitive boundaries.

Evangelicalism represents a relatively cohesive moral order. Yet in contemporary America it exists as an enclave within a larger pluralistic society—a world within a world. All the same, a heritage and a cultural ethos have come to distinguish Evangelicalism, imparting it with its own unique and autonomous identity. The symbolic boundaries distinguishing Evangelicalism and the Evangelical tradition are certainly complex, but at the center is its theology. Ultimate truth is defined by a particular religious conception of God, of mankind, of salvation, and the like. Given its centrality, it would only be natural to expect that these theological commitments would spill over into the pragmatic realities of everyday life for those who believe. Thus, conservative Protestantism has been distinguished by a certain unique view of work, by its own definitions of personal morality, by particular attitudes about the place and significance of the self, and by a certain broad conception of Christian family life (including particular definitions of manhood, womanhood, and parenthood). From this has derived a certain style of political presence. Naturally the texture of this world has been rough and uneven, lacking completeness and uniformity. Nevertheless in ideal terms Evangelicalism has existed as a fairly cohesive world. Its theological, moral and ethical, familial, and political symbols have defined a more or less distinct cultural heritage as well as the practical coordinates within which ordinary Evangelicals live their lives.

Nothing reviewed to this point is either new or especially startling. Indeed the foregoing could have been descriptive of any religious tradition. Yet there is something which further distinguishes Evangelicalism and that is that Evangelicalism is an *orthodoxy*. Orthodoxy implicitly and explicitly claims to embody ultimate and final truth. In this case, truth does not unfold but has already been revealed. The truth of an orthodoxy, then, is a truth that is pure and transcendent because it remains faithful to the original vision and creeds of its founders. Ideally, it is a truth and a reality which remains unchanged and unadulterated by the vagaries of history. To frame this in sociological terms, orthodoxies are unique because of the *special significance* bestowed upon the symbolic boundaries which constitute the tradition. These boundaries are regarded as timeless. They are not supposed to change. Thus the duty of the faithful is to ensure that the boundaries remain intact—pure and undefiled. The claim of the orthodox, then, is that they alone are the keepers of the tradition; they alone are the protectors of the true faith. Their stake in keeping the tradition sound and unqualified is high because their very identity and purpose as religious people (both collectively and individually) are bound to that mission. To stray from this task is to lose faith and to lose the hope of salvation. For the orthodox, the symbolic boundaries mean everything.

The empirical question facing any orthodoxy (and not just conservative Protestantism) is how successful has it been in keeping the traditions. From the sixteenth century to the end of the nineteenth century conservative Protestantism had been relatively successful. Having said this, several qualifications are in order. The first is that some fluidity is intrinsic to all social reality. There is no such thing as a static religious or moral tradition. Some change then has always been a feature of conservative Protestantism. Secondly, to speak of Protestant orthodoxy as being relatively successful at maintaining its traditions is not to imply that those traditions have been religiously or sociologically monolithic. Far from it. Conservative Protestantism has from its beginning been a complex mosaic of traditions and subtraditions. Through the twentieth century Protestants have bitterly fought among themselves over points of doctrine or over matters of religious or moral practice. The mosaic itself, then, is in part a consequence of precisely these kinds of schisms and infighting over what the symbolic boundaries of faith and practice should be. Nevertheless *within* the traditions making up this mosaic, conservative Protestants had, at least until the end of the nineteenth century, expressed a high degree of certitude about who they were as religious people and what was acceptable and unacceptable with regard to religious doctrine, moral habit, familial practice, and political disposition. *Within* the traditions the symbolic boundaries of faith and practice remained relatively clear. Though there were exceptions, churches, sects, movements, and the like were fairly successful at maintaining continuity with the past and protecting the purity of the moral order from that which they understood would profane it. Thus, when the symbolic boundaries of the tradition were internally threatened (e.g., within the moral order itself, by unrepentant sinners, backsliders, heretics and dissenters, and the half-hearted), social and religious rituals were invoked which would reinforce those boundaries. In this case, for example, backsliders would be brought back into the fold or would be utterly and finally rejected, say through excommunication. Either way the sanctity of the tradition was maintained. When, on the other hand, the symbolic boundaries were threatened by external realities (such as by pagan or by heterodox beliefs and practices), social and religious rituals would be invoked which would intensify the solidarity and the commitment of the faithful. Once again though, the tradition and the symbolic boundaries defining the tradition remained intact.

In the twentieth century conservative Protestantism has had a marked proclivity toward ecumenism. The doctrinal points which had once spawned division and rivalry have become progressively less important. Denominational differences have been increasingly eclipsed by the more pressing demands of collective mission and survival. In fact the overwhelming majority of Evangelical collegians and seminarians felt that denominational distinctions were insignificant except for allowing, as one student put it, "different kinds of people to enjoy different styles of worship." An emphasis in Evangelicalism since the beginning of the twentieth century then has been on beliefs and values which are shared in common. This, for example, explains the remarkable success of the nondenominational parachurch agencies and organizations in conservative Protestantism. The common thread which attempts to unite various conservative Protestant groups and denominations on the contemporary scene is the common thread that technically united the myriad (even fractionated) groups before the twentieth century: namely, restorationism. This is the commitment to return to an earlier, simpler, more authentic, and therefore more apostolic form of Christianity. This, of course, is what defines conservative Protestantism generally as an orthodoxy.

Even at this level, the broad traditions of restorationist Christianity maintained remarkable continuity. This is not to say that there were not changes in the meaning and practice of faith. The history of Protestant faith has always been dynamic and fluid. Yet most of these changes were subtle and, from generation to generation, largely imperceptible. But even when ecclesiastical and doctrinal changes were recognizable and politically divisive, they typically took place in local or regional contexts, in a particular institutional or denominational setting, and rarely if ever did they involve a universal threat to the entire symbolic universe. Given this important qualification a general continuity emerges as the dominant theme between the Reformation and the turn of the twentieth century. At this point, however, this continuity was met by challenges of a more global and fundamental nature. These threats to the integrity of the moral order were so massive and imposing that traditional means of self-preservation were rendered utterly obsolete and useless. The threat, of course, was embodied in the unique social and cultural configurations of modern society, and it took form both as internal contamination (liberal Christianity and the Social Gospel) and as external contamination (scientific rationality, sociocultural pluralism, and the like). The efforts to preserve the sanctity of the symbolic boundaries of orthodoxy are well known: antimodernism, antievolution, anti-Catholicism, Biblical "chauvinism," and so on.

In the face of this unprecedented assault, however, the traditions of conservative Protestantism did not remain wholly untarnished. To defend the traditions, they needed to be restated and clarified. In this effort, the traditions were articulated in a relatively novel way. The most important change was the radicalization and simplification of the traditions. Even so, this redefinition did not signal a fundamental departure from the past. Though in many ways a caricature of its nineteenth-century confidence, still the "purity" of the moral order was essentially maintained. The *social* costs of this defense were enormous, however. Through it all orthodox Protestantism suffered the loss of cultural prestige in American society as well as numerical support. But for most conservative Protestants, the cost was irrelevant: the traditions of orthodoxy, at least in their own minds, had been preserved.

The history of conservative Protestantism in the twentieth century is both complicated and fascinating. The terms of the relationship between conservative Protestantism and the modern world order have not altered. The assault of modern secular institutions on the plausibility of religious world views has been unrelenting, and Evangelicalism has remained a cognitive minority struggling to maintain the hermetic integrity of its traditions. Until midcentury the antagonisms this generated were intense and unmitigated. After midcentury, however, the tensions gradually yet substantially subsided. Something happened. The general terms of this encounter had not changed, yet the relationship between the two cultural systems had. For some reason the relationship was now fundamentally different from that which preceded it in the first half of the twentieth century. What happened?

At one level, what we have seen in our review of Evangelical popular theology and our review of the Evangelical approach to work, morality, the self, and the family is that the symbolic boundaries defining Protestant orthodoxy (both theological and cultural) in America have eroded. This means different things. On the one hand, normative boundaries which had previously been clear and conspicuous are now opaque and indistinct. Both among the general population of Evangelicals and among the coming generation (though particularly among the latter) there are various and increasing degrees of vagueness about traditionally defined reality, a vagueness that did not previously exist to this extent.

There has emerged a greater lack of consensus on what the Bible teaches about "basic" points of doctrine (such as the authority of Scripture, the Devil, the origins of the world, Christ's return), about what the Christian family should be, or about the nature of the self and its relevance to Christian living. There is no collective agreement on many of these "essential" matters. While some dimensions of the moral order have become opaque, others are altogether obsolete. They no longer have significance or credibility. The clearest and most important example of this is the sizable inventory of activities long considered to be sinful. For most religious orthodoxies, purity of the moral order is based upon an ethic of rejection. Yet in contemporary Evangelicalism, the legacy of austerity and ascetic denial has become antiquated—subject to indifference or derisive humor. Most traditional moral prohibitions (embodying this ethic of rejection) do not even capture the attention of most believers, much less carry the authority they once carried. And as was noted earlier, there are no new prohibitions replacing the older ones. To repeat, the cultural infrastructure of orthodox Protestantism for many who claim to be orthodox is visibly weakening, eroding from the inside out. To the degree that this is true the traditions lose continuity with the past and Evangelicals lose continuity with what they have long understood to be their historical identity.

Having said this, it is important to press on for it would be superficial simply to conclude that Evangelicalism is just becoming more liberal. Much more is involved than the erosion of the symbolic boundaries of conservative Protestantism. Beyond this the traditions are being redefined. The most important aspect of this is in the realm of theology. It is significant, for example, that all of those who publicly advocate modifications in Evangelical theology adamantly defend their right to be called Evangelicals or Fundamentalists. They vigorously defend their claim to the orthodox heritage. Their claim, I contend, should be taken seriously. If that is so, is it correct to say that the criteria for Protestant orthodoxy are changing? Clearly this is not the case. The Bible and the finality of Jesus Christ as the only savior of sinners, among other doctrines, retain the highest priority in Evangelical theology for all Evangelicals. Without such an orientation they would, in fact, cease to be Evangelicals. The criteria for orthodoxy, then, are not changing. What is happening, however, is an *alteration in the cultural meaning of orthodoxy and, accordingly, an alteration in the cultural meaning of specific criteria of orthodoxy*. In each case there is a broadening of the meaning of some of Evangelicalism's fundamental religious symbols. The meaning of such doctrines as the inerrancy/infallibility of Scripture, the justification through Christ alone, and the nature and purpose of the Christian mission has become more inclusive. They mean *more* than they did even a generation or two ago. The cognitive boundaries of theological orthodoxy, once narrowly construed, become variously widened. Insofar as this is true, theological orthodoxy is reinterpreted; the tradition is redefined. Orthodoxy, then, comes to mean something novel.

Orthodoxy, as has been noted, is not just a theological matter. It is a cultural matter as well. Thus what is descriptive of theological orthodoxy also holds true for the cultural orthodoxy of conservative Protestantism. When, for example, Evangelical Christians who drink alcohol, smoke cigarettes, play cards for entertainment, or use alternative child care so that both parents can pursue a career claim that they are just as "Christian" in their behavior as those who are more circumspect behaviorally, their claim should be taken seriously. In this perspective the cultural ambiguity surrounding contemporary definitions of worldliness and worldly behavior or of the Christian family represents a broadening of the limits of acceptability. The cultural orthodoxy of conservative Protestantism includes a widening diversity of life-style behaviors. This can be put more descriptively.

One convention popular in post–World War II Evangelicalism for dealing with the "gray areas" of Christian life (areas not explicitly prohibited by the Scriptures, such as drinking and smoking) was to say that these matters fell into the realm of "Christian liberty." If Christians could engage in a particular activity in good conscience, then it would be morally acceptable. Still Christians were exhorted "not to be a stumbling block to one's brother or sister" by engaging in this activity (that is, to be offensive or to present a temptation). At the same time, they were exhorted to conduct their lives in a way that would "strengthen their testimony to the unsaved." In either case the effect was the same—moral conformity to the traditions. Not only have these devices for conformity become progressively less plausible, but more importantly, the "realm of Christian liberty" has been expanded. Moreover, intolerance for those who choose to exercise their Christian liberty is vulnerable to the accusation of illegitimate (and "un-Christian") use of moral judgment. Again, what all of this signifies is the broadening of the meaning of proper Christian living.

To this point the argument has been twofold: at one level the traditions defining conservative Protestantism are eroding; at another level orthodoxy itself (broadly construed) is being redefined. In fact the two processes are intimately related. The cultural dynamics are gradual and imperceptible enough to those involved that the process of erosion is legitimated by the process of redefinition.

Curiously, contemporary Evangelicals perceive a whirl of cultural change going on in American society. What is more, most of them do not like it. For example when students were asked about the moral climate in the United States, the sentiment was virtually universal.

> Morally, our society is getting worse and worse, and frankly, the whole thing scares me. (female, sophomore, mathematics major, Methodist)

> The moral climate in America is slowly degenerating. Homosexuality is a symbol of this but so is the materialism so prevalent today. (female, senior, literature major, Conservative Baptist)

> The country is definitely going down the tubes. . . . I do think Christians are getting stronger in their faith and non-Christians just keep going in the wrong direction. Yet, if the negative morals of the non-Christian keep going the way they have, eventually their moral beliefs will overtake those of Christians because there are so many more of them. (male, sophomore, history major, nondenominational)

Their indignation about this is strong enough that they feel it is a Christian responsibility to try to stop it. Thus they feel it is legitimate for religious groups to be politically engaged with these moral issues. Evangelical students, it will be recalled, are highly politicized in their belief that moral trends in the dominant culture need to be countered.

The first irony is that while they are opposed to many of these cultural trends, the code of political civility is so deeply ingrained that they are ethically constrained *not* to mobilize publicly (and even politically) against them. The social demands of tolerance and tolerability essentially neutralize their ability to counteract. This is particularly true among those strata of Evangelicals who are highly educated and upwardly mobile. The second and deeper irony is that Evangelicalism participates in precisely the same cultural changes that it decries in the larger society. In other words the declining plausibility and utility of traditional cultural norms in post–World War II America (what Yankelovich [1981] has called the shift from the "old rules" to the "new rules" and what most Evangelicals call "moral decline") parallel the erosion of traditional definitions of orthodoxy in conservative Protestantism. The processes are the same, though logically, the changes in the larger culture far outpace the changes in conservative Protestantism. What is more, these changes are occurring at different rates within the subculture. Thus, in general, the extent of this participation appears to be greatest within the churchlike denominations of the Reformational-Confessional tradition and weakest in the sectarian denominations of the Baptist and Holiness-Pentecostal traditions. It also appears to be greater for women than for men. Finally, and perhaps most importantly, participation in these cultural processes appears to be substantially greater among the coming generation of young, highly educated, and culturally sophisticated Evangelicals—Evangelicals who are coming of age and maturity in the middle of these historical developments. Their access to higher education invites further speculation about the role of education in the maintenance or decline of the moral order of Protestant orthodoxy.

## THE ROLE OF EDUCATION

Theoretically and ideally, higher education plays an important role in the maintenance of the moral order of orthodox Protestantism. When under the auspices of devoted believers, it has the purpose of galvanizing the commitment of its future leaders (whether lay or professional) and a sizable portion of its rank and file membership. It has the potential of making the faithful better equipped to handle the challenges of defending the faith from error and of extending the influence and witness of the faith in the larger world. As the Westminster Seminary handbook put it, its mission is "the formation of men . . . who shall truly believe, and cordially love, and therefore endeavor to propagate and defend [the Gospel], in its genuineness, simplicity and fullness. . . ."[1] The Gordon-Conwell handbook noted similarly that "the times in which we live demand Christian workers who have an unshakeable conviction of the authority and trustworthiness of Scripture, a sure grasp of the responsibilities of ministry, and a firm sense of calling to be God's servants in the world." Thus, Gordon-Conwell is committed to the "formation and education of men and women in this theological perspective."[2] This general orientation defines the mission of "Christian" higher education but not just in the contemporary world but in the past as well.

### Historical Patterns

Historically, higher education in the United States, from the founding of Harvard in the Puritan period (1636) to roughly the mid–nineteenth century, was established and operated within a Christian theological and moral universe. Colleges and universities were founded as Christian (read sectarian denominational) institutions with an agenda of creating a literate laity and an erudite clergy all of whom would be model citizens of the new world and, later, the new republic. From the late eighteenth century to the middle of the nineteenth century when the new republic was expanding rapidly westward, Protestant denominations and clergymen carried this vision with them, founding and operating dozens of small colleges along the way. By 1860 there were approximately two hundred of these. Most were small (six to eight faculty members with fifty to a hundred students), had rapid turnover in faculty, and were plagued by poor financing. Their existence was highly precarious, as illustrated by the fact that only 20 percent of the colleges founded before the Civil War survived (Hofstadter 1970, 271; Jencks and Riesman 1969). In spite of these problems, their educational philosophy was secure and unequivocal: to propagate knowledge and to prepare upright leadership within a Christian society. The focus, then, was not so much on advanced scientific development or on the creative expansion of scholarship but rather on moral development, civic responsibility, and social integration (Hofstadter 1970, 272). By contemporary standards higher education was intellectually lax. Research was insignificant to these institutions. Professors devoted their energy to disciplining minds (through daily recitation and drilling and having students recapitulate and summarize lessons) and disciplining the moral lives of students outside the classroom. Moral philosophy, as several scholars have noted, was often the culmination of the college curriculum (Noll 1979, 7). It was a cross-disciplinary perspective grounded in Scottish commonsense realism and the "static categories" of Baconian (inductivist) science (Noll 1979, 7). The purpose of the academic science and discipline of moral philosophy was to confirm the traditional Protestant cosmology: the existence of God and his relationship with the world and with humankind. It would thus prove a useful bulwark against atheistic skepticism and a sound apologetic for democratic republicanism and social morality.

Higher education in the latter half of the nineteenth century, however, underwent a profound, even revolutionary transformation. The old-style college was scarcely recognizable in the new. Perhaps the most obvious change was its numerical and institutional expansion. In the half-century leading up to the Civil War, there had been a steady decline in the number of men of college age attending college: from 1 in 1,513 in 1826 to 1 in 1,689 in 1855, to 1 in 1,927 in 1869. Yet between 1870 and 1900, the number of college students jumped nearly fivefold: from 52,000 to 238,000. Graduate enrollments were almost a total creation of the period, growing from 198 students in 1871 to 9,370 in 1910 (Hofstadter 1970, 275). The number of faculty increased accordingly, as illustrated by the case of Harvard: in 1869 it had sixty faculty; in 1909 it had six hundred. One of the chief reasons these institutions grew was a change in the college's financial benefactors. Private industrialists, private donors, and the federal government (through the Morrill Act of 1862 establishing land-grant universities) replaced the numerous, comparatively poor Protestant denominations in this responsibility. Millions of acres of land and hundreds of millions of dollars were made available or donated outright to the establishment or expansion of colleges or universities between 1870 and 1920—a staggering phenomenon when considering the fact that in the early 1800s, Harvard was the envy of all colleges because of its ten thousand dollar annual grant from the Massachusetts legislature. A change in the financial backing of these institutions eventually resulted in a change in their control and administration. Prominent businessmen replaced ministers and denominational bureaucrats as trustees, and educationally credentialed laymen replaced clergymen as college presidents and high-level administrators.

The focus of education also changed. Perhaps the most concrete measure of this was the shift in the role of the professor. Where previously, orthodoxy (in the correct denomination) had been a major test of an academic's eligibility for a college position, the emphasis was now almost exclusively on the academic's competence and his credentials. The new academic abandoned the role of mental and moral disciplinarian in favor of intellectual experimentation and creativity and professionalization. Increasingly, then, American higher education came to follow the German model, which emphasized self-directed, specialized, and advanced scholarship in a milieu where there would be total intellectual freedom from curricular limitations and from doctrinal directives. It is important to note that this model of university life served very well the interests of the new benefactors of the universities. For example, millionaire industrialists of the period (John D. Rockefeller, Cornelius Vanderbilt, Johns Hopkins, Leland Stanford, James Duke, and others) invested large sums of money in universities in part because of the practical advantages higher education afforded capitalism and the great industrial enterprise.

There were other and, from the perspective of this chapter, more important changes in education as well. With curricular diversification and specialization came the separation of the study of religion and theology from the other academic disciplines. The integration of religious faith with academic study, one of the goals of moral philosophy, became obsolete. The perspective of moral philosophy collapsed under the imposing reality of a new, philosophically naturalistic science. Darwinism became the symbol of the new science not just for what it said about biology but for what it implied about the scientific method. Instead of prejudging the validity or utility of certain facts on the basis of traditional philosophical assumptions or of forcing empirical reality into the clearly defined interpretive framework of the past, a scientist could now (and should if he were a true scientist) allow empirical data to lead where they would, even if those data undermined the conventions and truths of the past. Typically, any resistance to this new model of intellectual inquiry on the part of conservative clergy still active in academic life served only to discredit them and the traditional model of higher education. "Science," as one scholar has noted, "once the handmaiden of morality, [was now] an ally of agnosticism" (Noll, 1979, 12).

The result of this transformation was the radical and abrupt secularization of higher education. It was now cut off from its deep roots in a Christian symbolic universe. The last major impetus for secularization came in the early part of the twentieth century when the Carnegie Foundation established retirement allowances (in what is now the TIAA/CREF) for professors teaching in private, *nonsectarian* colleges. Many of these, founded as traditional Christian colleges, renounced their sectarian heritage in order to take advantage of this financial windfall (Hofstadter 1970, 279).

Several of the older colleges retained their denominational attachments in the face of this transformation. But it is also clear that the abandonment of the founding vision of conservative Protestantism by many institutions of higher learning generated a defensive backlash on the part of what remained of conservative Protestantism. New institutes and colleges were founded to carry on in the tradition being abandoned by others. The list is not exhaustive, yet of the seventy liberal arts colleges which (as of 1985) constitute the Christian College Coalition, 4 percent had been founded before 1850, 61 percent had been founded between 1850 and 1909, and 13 percent had been founded between 1910 and 1930. (Seven of the nine colleges surveyed in the Evangelical Academy Project were founded before 1910.[3]) Within these institutions, the Christian traditions have remained relatively insulated. The trustees for these schools are deeply committed Evangelicals; some are clergymen. A signed statement of faith is still required of faculty and administrators, and at most of these colleges, a statement of faith is required on the part of students. These institutions are also committed by charter to the integration of Christian faith and the academic disciplines of learning. Within a larger secular society, these institutions labor to keep the heritage of conservative Protestantism intact and to extend its sphere of influence in the larger world.

There is, of course, irony in the history of Christian higher education in the United States. Institutions which began as systematic efforts to defend the faith have evolved into structures which oppose if not systematically undermine it. Christian higher education turned on itself. Instead of defending the moral order of orthodox Protestantism, it evolved into a structure and a process which have aggressively sought to enfeeble the moral order. What deepens the irony is that there is evidence suggesting that Christian higher education as it is currently institutionalized is evolving in a similar pattern. In other words, the institutions which were founded as a defensive reaction to the encroachment of secularization in higher education are evolving into institutions which are unwittingly at odds with their founding vision.

To illustrate, one could consider the evolution of the behavioral standards for students at these colleges. What has happened at Wheaton College, Gordon College, and Westmont College is typical of most of the colleges in this subculture. From the time of their founding to the mid-1960s, the college rules unapologetically prohibited "profaning the Sabbath," "profane or obscene language or behavior," playing billiards, playing cards and gambling, using intoxicating liquors or tobacco, theater and movie attendance, and any form of dancing—both *on- and off-campus*. Since that time, though especially since the late 1960s, all three colleges, with little variation, have abandoned all of these prohibitions but alcohol, tobacco, and drug usage, gambling, and social dancing. Movies are even shown on campus. What is more, those prohibitions which are maintained now generally pertain to behavior on-campus. Off-campus, these standards are encouraged but not enforced. Perhaps most important is the self-conscious and almost apologetic way in which these behavioral standards are understood and presented. As the 1979–1980 Westmont College catalog put it, "we do not want to be a college known for what our students cannot do."

But this is merely an illustration. The broader historical development to which it alludes is further suggested by the historical parallels between Christian higher education in the nineteenth century and Christian higher education at the present. The parallels are not perfect, of course, but they are striking all the same. As was mentioned earlier, many of these colleges began as Bible institutes. Providing direction and leadership (as the college president or as administrators) more often than not were prominent clergymen. Appropriately, all required adherence to a statement of faith on the part of faculty and administrators. From a distance, the situation has not changed considerably. Viewed more closely, however, one can see that subtle but important changes have taken place. For example, while many began as Bible colleges or institutes, the majority eventually diversified their curricula into a liberal arts design with religious studies or Biblical studies being just one of many areas of inquiry. So too among the colleges which have adopted the liberal arts educational model, professional educators capable of running the institution as a business have replaced clergymen as the principal executives. What is more, in order to enhance their stature, these schools have become increasingly professionalized, aggressively competing for faculty and administrators who are highly credentialed. Typically this means a Ph.D. or its equivalent from a secular university (the more prestigious the better). Doctrinal orthodoxy is still important but it is not enough in itself. Professionalization has also carried over into the role of faculty. Although these colleges remain predominantly teaching institutions, they have also placed a greater emphasis upon independent scholarly and scientific research and publication. Productivity in scholarship has (since the mid-1970s) become increasingly important in making decisions about faculty appointments, tenure, and promotion.[4] There is some variation among colleges on this, of course, but most of the academic deans at these colleges are actively encouraging greater scholarly publication (and the experimentation, creativity, and critical reflection that this implies) through concrete institutional incentives. Many of the faculty perceive this institutional shift as well.[5] Not insignificantly, a remarkable number have responded positively. Within nine of the colleges in the Christian College Consortium, for example, 53 percent of the faculty had published at least one refereed article in a scholarly journal, and 41 percent had published more than one; roughly 17 percent had published a scholarly book, and about 7 percent of these had published more than one; nearly 40 percent had been elected or appointed to an editorial board or professional society. Importantly, older faculty (fifty-eight and older) showed the lowest scholarly output, while junior professors had already achieved a level of productivity close to that of middle-aged associate and full professors.[6]

Admittedly these developments are far from conclusive, yet neither are they merely random. Cumulatively they are significant. They imply a growing institutional rationalization and progressivity much like that which occurred in higher education generally a century before.

There is an important difference between Christian higher education at the end of the twentieth century and that of the mid–nineteenth century though: the former never conceived of itself as being in the mainstream of higher education. They have prided themselves in their Christian (and thus minority) distinctiveness—a distinctiveness that has largely been based upon explicit doctrinal and behavioral standards. Though these standards have had conservationist influence, these standards may only impede the process of erosion rather than stop it altogether.

There is still another aspect of Christian higher education which may be at odds with the goals it strives to achieve. This is something which appears to be instrinsic to the process of higher education itself.

## Inner Dynamics

The question is not macrosociological but microsociological. It is no longer what happens to the institutions of Christian education but what happens to the moral order of orthodox Protestantism as embodied in the world view of Evangelicals as it encounters the educational process. Social scientific research since the late 1950s supported the belief that education secularizes (e.g., Campbell and Magill 1968; Hoge 1976; Hunsberger 1978; Stark 1963; Zelan 1968). Somehow, exposure to the realm of higher education weakened the grip of religious conviction over a person's life. Thus whatever religious beliefs and practices an individual carried in with him at the start of his educational sojourn would have been either seriously compromised or abandoned altogether by the time he was ready to graduate. Minimally holding on to the religion of his adolescence would have proven difficult if not impossible.

No one factor accounts for this. There are undoubtedly several factors which contribute. Among the more obvious, however, would be the nature of the activity itself. After all, any training in a foreign language invites some acquaintance with the logic of "higher criticism"; any course in a laboratory science encourages the practice of suspending judgment until results are in; and any exposure to the humanities or the social sciences develops the ability of looking at oneself and one's social world objectively and critically. Academic discipline fosters—indeed it provides the very tools for—independent and critical reflection. A second factor would be exposure to faculty—individuals whose critical reasoning is presumably well developed. The professoriate, as survey research has shown, is one of the most secularized groups of workers, and they, as objects of authority and of emulation, undoubtedly have an important influence on students. A third factor is the social environment of higher education. It is often the very first social world many students inhabit that is entirely detached from the cognitive and moral coordinates of their childhood, and it invariably plays a part in weakening the credibility of adolescent religiosity. There are, undoubtedly, other factors as well. On the surface, one would imagine the Evangelical campus as being different. It is a protected environment since faculty, administration, and virtually every student actively profess faith, and student culture offers many opportunities for Christian ministry. But even in the insulated setting of an Evangelical campus it is fair to ask whether these dynamics are at work. Public or private higher education does have a pronounced effect of loosening the grip of traditional religious and cultural attachments. But does Evangelical higher education have this effect too?

The evidence is not dramatic but it is consistent. The traditional religious and cultural orthodoxy of conservative Protestantism is weakening. The cumulative message from table 25 is that the educational process *is* a contributing factor.[7] Instead of buttressing the traditions in the lives of its adherents, it undermines them. The process is uneven yet it is still unilateral, affecting the various dimensions of the Evangelical cultural system. The figures, drawn as they are from one-time-only data, do not allow an absolute interpretation on the matter. They are highly suggestive though. Thus, inferring from freshmen through senior comparisons, there is a consistent decline in adherence to various aspects of the Evangelical world view. Theological orthodoxy reveals some attrition (an overall decline of 14% among those who score high in theological orthodoxy). Among those who score high in vocational and moral asceticism there is also a drop-off from freshman to senior year: 13 percent in the first case; 21 percent in the second. So too with traditional familism. Among those who hold strongly to a traditional view of the man's role and of the woman's role in the family, there is a sizable decline from first to last years, but it is particularly sharp with regard to the role of women. The political conservatism associated with the legacy of

**Table 25**

Percentage Scoring High on Various Indexes of the Evangelical World View according to Class Standing

| Index | Freshmen (N = 553) | Sopho- mores (N = 496) | Juniors (N = 461) | Seniors (N = 463) | Difference between First and Last |
|---|---|---|---|---|---|
| Religious orthodoxy | 56 | 51 | 49 | 42 | -14 |
| Work ethic | | | | | |
| Vocational asceticism | 23 | 19 | 12 | 10 | -13 |
| Moral asceticism | 44 | 39 | 33 | 23 | -21 |
| Traditional familism | | | | | |
| Men | 45 | 43 | 42 | 30 | -15 |
| Women | 34 | 30 | 24 | 14 | -20 |
| Political orientation | | | | | |
| Conservatism | 40 | 37 | 32 | 33 | -7 |
| Tolerance | 74 | 77 | 80 | 83 | +9 |

NOTE: All figures are statistically significant at the .000 level except those for Tolerance, which are significant at the .09 level.

conservative Protestantism in the twentieth century is also influenced by this process. Political conservatism also loses ground from freshman (40%) to senior year (33%). Finally, social, moral, and political tolerance increases (by 9%) from freshman to senior year. As students go through higher education, they come to perceive, tolerate, and perhaps even appreciate ambiguity and complexity in the social world. This perception seems to simultaneously weaken conviction and resolve in their own world view. One student reflected on his beliefs since coming to college in this way:

In high school, I was something of a Christian legalist. For example, I would argue that the Bible is literally and absolutely true and one shouldn't try to change it. Like the story of creation—I used to believe that it occurred in six twenty-four hour days. But college encouraged me to question and evaluate my beliefs, and as a result, they have changed since I've been here. I have become less dogmatic in my beliefs—almost antiabsolutist. I hope I haven't become weaker in my faith by questioning it. I guess I am now more apt to acknowledge that I don't know a lot of things. (male, sophomore, elementary education major, Bible Church)

Another responded:

Since I've been here [at college], I have had to question a lot of things I always thought were true. I don't think my faith is weaker now, but it is just a little different than it used to be. (female, freshman, English major, Mennonite)

Education, even Evangelical education, weakens the tenacity with which Evangelicals hold on to traditional cultural codes.

What is it about Evangelical higher education that has this effect? Three factors have already been mentioned: the nature of the activity itself, faculty, and the social environment of the campus. The first factor is education. While it is arguable that the educational process itself has some effects, the curriculum accounts for some of the differences. Selfselection by students in various majors undoubtedly contributes to this. Yet attrition is still more likely to occur among students who major in the social sciences and, to a lesser extent, the humanities, while students who major in the natural sciences, business, or religious studies are less prone to these kinds of world view changes.

A second factor is the influence of the faculty. As objects of authority and emulation, they would undoubtedly have an important effect on shaping the world view of students. The question is what kind of effect? Faculty who are deeply committed to the religious and cultural traditions of a faith would likely impede the corrosive effects of higher education; faculty who are less committed to these traditions would likely encourage these effects.

A survey of faculty opinion on many of the same issues that college students and seminarians were asked about was conducted to acquire a sense of where the faculty stood relative to the traditions (see table 26). On theological issues, faculty are even more divided than their students.

Table 26
Dimensions of the Evangelical World View
College Student and College Faculty Comparisons

|  | Evangelical College Students (N = 1,980) | Evangelical College Faculty (N = 447) |
|---|---|---|
|  | Percentage Agreeing | |
| Theology | | |
| "The Bible . . . is not always to be taken literally in its statements concerning matters of science, historical reporting, etc." | 50 | 65 |
| "The only hope for heaven is through faith in Jesus Christ *except* for those who have not heard of Jesus Christ" | 32 | 44 |
|  | Percentage Scoring High | |
| Work ethic | | |
| Moral asceticism[a] | 35 | 30 |
| Traditional familism | | |
| Men[a] | 40 | 19 |
| Women[a] | 26 | 16 |
|  | Percentage Favoring | |
| Political orientation | | |
| The Equal Rights Amendment | 25 | 47 |
| A ban on all abortions | 55 | 45 |
| Requiring prayer in schools | 27 | 10 |
| Allowing homosexuals to teach in public schools | 18 | 22 |
| Nuclear freeze | 69 | 67 |
| Increased defense spending | 27 | 12 |
| Busing to achieve racial integration in the public schools | 22 | 27 |

[a]Cumulative index.

For example, where half of the college students believed that the Bible was unerring on all matters except for statements concerning matters of historical or scientific reporting (item 2 of table 3), there were 65 percent of the faculty who held this view. Where one-third of the collegians and seminarians held a historically qualified view of salvation (that the only hope for heaven is through faith in Jesus Christ except for those who have not heard of Jesus Christ), nearly half of the faculty held this view. This pattern also held for matters of moral discipline. On the range of "moral" issues, faculty were more willing to see moral ambiguity and less willing to maintain that these behaviors were morally wrong all of the time: drinking alcohol (collegians, 17%; faculty, 9%), smoking cigarettes (collegians, 51%; faculty, 46%), smoking marijuana (collegians 70%; faculty, 64%), casual petting (collegians, 23%; faculty, 13%), heavy petting (collegians, 45%; faculty, 40%), premarital sexual relations (collegians, 89%; faculty, 76%), homosexual relations (collegians, 94%; faculty, 84%), extramarital sexual relations (collegians, 97%; faculty, 90%), watching an X-rated movie (collegians, 69%; faculty, 39%), and watching an R-rated movie (collegians, 7%; faculty, 8%). Predictably, faculty were also more liberal in their attitudes surrounding traditional familism. This was true for the various issues concerning the role of men: e.g. (*percentage agreeing*) the husband as having principal responsibility for the family's spiritual well-being (collegians, 61%; faculty, 45%), the husband having the final say (collegians, 58%; faculty, 30%), the father as the primary disciplinarian (collegians, 25%; faculty, 11%). It was also true concerning the role of women: e.g. (*percentage agreeing*) a woman should put her husband and children ahead of her career (collegians, 72%; faculty, 45%), (*percentage disagreeing*) a married woman should not work if she has a husband capable of supporting her (collegians, 64%; faculty, 73%). Faculty were just as liberal as collegians concerning the issues of parenting: e.g. (*percentage agreeing*) the virtues of "old-fashioned" upbringing (both at 30%) and the importance of father and mother both taking care of small children (both at 96%–98%). Finally, this pattern was seen in the realm of political values. Faculty took more liberal positions than students on most public policy issues; see table 26.

In short, faculty overall are even less committed to the theological and cultural traditions of the Evangelical heritage than their students. It is difficult to imagine this fact *not* having a profound effect on the world view of students. Not surprisingly it is faculty in the social sciences and the humanities who are more disaffected from the traditions than faculty in the arts (including the performing arts), natural sciences, and business curricula.

Importantly, many faculty see this as a professional objective. One faculty member in the social sciences expressed it this way:

> Who wants to preserve [religious] dogmatism and [moral] parochialism . . . ? Not me—and not most of my colleagues. We want salient evangelical faith, but since when must this type of religious commitment also include a firm commitment to male-centered households and all the rest of that nasty stuff? What [some] may call "contamination" or "erosion," I call a "success." Maybe Jerry Falwell thinks what we're doing is "counter-productive" but most of us who teach here . . . do not.[8]

There is then, among many faculty, a sense that true and vital Christianity depends upon a debunking of many of the traditions of conservative Protestantism. Their task, in part, is one of liberation. This opinion may or may not be true. It need only be pointed out that what one generation calls correct faith and correct Christian living, another generation may call "dogmatism" and "parochialism."

The third factor to be discussed is that of social environment.[9] Colleges and universities are not alike in the kind of environment they create. This is true even within Evangelicalism. One way in which they differ socially is in the degree to which the college community is protected or insulated from anything which would threaten the symbolic integrity of that community. For example, the public university would offer no protection to a believer, while Evangelical colleges could vary in degree. In the Evangelical Academy Project, six of the colleges qualified as highly insulated; three qualified as moderately insulated (Hammond and Hunter 1984, 226–27). The question is then how well do these different contexts compare in their ability to maintain the traditional world view of conservative Protestantism in the lives of their students?

One might suppose that the more highly insulated campus would be far better able to accomplish its mission of protecting orthodoxy than the moderately insulated or, especially, the noninsulated settings, and that the secular campus would present a nearly impossible situation for the Evangelical intent on being true to his faith. Yet evidence suggests precisely the opposite. Among those who are most orthodox in their theological commitments, the traditions cohere less or are less consolidated as the campus setting gets more insulated (see table 27). The average correlation (gamma) of various aspects of the Evangelical cultural system is .29 in the high-insularity setting, .34 in the moderate-insularity setting, and .40 in the low-insularity (public university) setting. In other words, the more intent Evangelical higher education is on

### Table 27
Correlations between the Index of Evangelical Orthodoxy
and Five Other Indexes of Evangelical World View
in Three Insularity Settings

| Index | High Insularity (N = 1,308) | Moderate Insularity (N = 638) | Low Insularity[a] (N = 262) |
|---|---|---|---|
| Piety | +.23 | +.31 | +.59 |
| Work ethic | | | |
| Moral asceticism | +.33 | +.39 | +.49 |
| Traditional familism | | | |
| Men | +.33 | +.34 | +.34 |
| Women | +.33 | +.30 | +.39 |
| Political orientation | | | |
| Intolerance | −.24 | −.39 | −.25 |
| Average (gamma) Correlation | +.29 | +.34 | +.40 |

[a]Protestant only.

preserving the integrity of its traditions, the less successful it is. Minimally, it does not distinguish itself in its task. Other studies conclude similarly. Among Protestant colleges, the more serious a commitment to the task of higher education, the more prevalent the liberalization and secularization tendencies.[10]

Why this pattern exists is open to speculation. In the case of the moderately or highly insulated campus, there is no ever-present external threat to the student's view of the world. The student's sphere of discourse is protected from significant disruptions. Such social environments are perceived as safe, and thus, one's defensive posture can be relaxed; in community with others of the same view, it is possible to take one's world for granted. In the present case, students attending these colleges were highly defensive about their faith before attending. Indeed, 40 percent of all Evangelical students studying at Evangelical colleges claimed as one of the three most important reasons for attending their college that "where my faith might have been threatened in a secular school, I believed that my college would strengthen my faith." Notably, 50 percent of all freshmen selected this as a reason, while only 33 percent of all seniors "remembers" this as being a reason. The setting of the Evangelical college, we can infer, does allow for a relaxation of "cognitive defenses." Yet it is in the safety of this setting that the erosive effects of education can take place. In this case, the threat is not external and visible but internal and, by and large, unperceived.

In the (low insularity) public university setting, religious students are continually reminded of the vulnerability of their beliefs. The threat to the plausibility of their beliefs is external and communicated. Thus mere recognition of the minority status of their convictions relative to competing perspectives appears to foster a "fortress mentality" among the strongly committed. In this situation the believer's identity as a believer is accentuated and reinforced; his world view is annealed. The Evangelical in this context becomes even "more" Evangelical (see Berger 1963, 79, for an elaboration of this point).

One could speculate further about this but to do so would be to stray too far afield from the concerns of this chapter. Some closure is necessary. At one level one can simply view the historical and institutional dynamics of Christian higher education as a mere reflection of broader changes in the Christian community. These changes, then, are a consequence of other sociological and historical factors. While this is undoubtedly true to some extent, it is probably more accurate to say that Christian higher education is involved in a dialectical process—not only an effect but a cause of these changes as well. At this level we can see the multiple ironies of Christian higher education. On the one hand, Christian higher education historically evolved into precisely the opposite of what it was supposed to be, that is, into bastions of secularity if not anti-Christian sentiment. Contemporary Christian higher education, on the other hand, produces the unintended consequences of being counterproductive to its own objectives, that is, it produces individual Christians who are either less certain of their attachments to the traditions of their faith or altogether disaffected from them. Education, to the degree that it is not indoctrination, weakens the tenacity with which Evangelicals hold on to their world view. In sum, Evangelical education creates its own contaminating effects. And the more Christian higher education professionalizes and bureaucratizes (that is, the more it models itself institutionally after secular higher education), the more likely this process will intensify. Not only would this include the more "progressive" institutions of the Christian College Coalition but also such bastions of separatist pride as Liberty University or Bob Jones University.[11] If the latter have not evolved as far as the former, it may be, in part, a consequence of different models of education: the latter "indoctrinating" in a context that is less "professionalized."

## THE ROLE OF ELITES

Higher education is only one important factor that bears upon the fate of orthodoxy. Another factor is the status and role of elites. The elites of a religious tradition (clergy, priests, prophets, religious administrators, and the like) do play an important role in the maintenance of their traditions. They provide the official interpretations of the traditions and in so doing define reality for ordinary believers, that is, what is correct belief and practice and what is not. In the case of an orthodoxy, they function additionally as the custodians of the traditions. Theirs is the formal task of maintaining and defending the integrity of the moral order, of making sure that the symbolic boundaries defining orthodoxy are not breached (by immorality, sin, deviant beliefs, or any other form of cultural pollution). Not all religious or cultural elites are the same, however. They can differ according to their vocational relationship to the orthodoxy they serve. Perhaps the most important distinction is between intellectual and prophetic elites. The former are distinguished by their responsibility for the elaboration of the deeper meanings of the truths they espouse. The traditions are not always self-evident, and neither are they always coherent. Their task then is to rationally explain and clarify the nature and meaning of the traditions. The prophetic elite are also "experts" after a fashion and can claim authority in the community. Their main responsibility, by contrast, is to encourage the weak-hearted, to upbraid the shallow-minded, and to exhort all believers to a deeper commitment to the traditions. The simple fact is that people are prone to forgetfulness. The task of the prophetic elite is one of reminding. The difference between kinds of elites, naturally, is somewhat artificial. Some intellectual elites perform a prophetic role, while some prophetic elites perform an elaborative role. At least within the religious realm, they possess or have historically possessed, extraordinary power and prestige. This, of course, pertains to all religious orthodoxies but not least to conservative Protestantism.

The irony posed by elites is their inclination to alter the traditions for which they stand.[12] For some, this inclination is expressed as a deliberate iconoclasm. Their role is not properly performed if there is not some tension between the prevailing values of the larger society and their own. For most others, however, this inclination is unwitting and unintended. In the case of intellectual elites, merely the act of rearticulating, elaborating, and/or developing further the truths of the traditions entails some degree of rejection or modification of that system. For prophetic elites, particularly those on the defensive, the alterations come through the reduction of faith to a simplified list of creeds. It is the radical simplification of orthodoxy which alters the quality and texture of the traditions.

It goes without saying that these tensions have been prominent in Evangelicalism. Given the challenge of modernity in the twentieth century, the traditions could not be trusted to perpetuate themselves. As a result both intellectual and prophetic elites have played a particularly important role in the life of conservative Protestantism.

Prophetic elites (clergy, evangelists, ideologues, etc.) in conservative Protestantism have been the most visible. The attempts to publicly defend itself against theological modernism, evolutionism, and scientism in the early part of this century, against ecumenism in the middle part of the century, and against moral/familial pluralism in the latter part of the century have all resulted in the reduction of organic cultural traditions to creedal propositions on everything from proper theology to proper relations with the non-Evangelical world to proper family relationships. Intellectual elites (theologians, college/seminary faculty, writers, and the like) have been less visible but no less influential. The efforts to provide an intellectually plausible and respectable defense of the faith by Evangelical theologians in the late 1940s and early 1950s focused on the authority of Scriptures. While all agreed that the Bible was the final authority in matters of faith and practice, Evangelical theologians disagreed over what that actually meant. Advanced biblical scholarship even led many to reject as untenable earlier understandings of inerrancy as well as literalism as the normative approach to biblical understanding. This theological debate and others are only one area in which intellectual elites have become involved. Their role in defining the family and the self, as we have seen, has led to similar ambiguities and attenuations in their cultural heritage.

As subtle and imprecise as these cultural redefinitions may be, they are significant for the future of orthodox Protestantism all the same. Prophetic or intellectual, their net effect on the traditions has been the same. The traditions are transformed.

In some respects their practical effect on the traditions is unimportant. The real significance is what their activity represents. In a word, whether defending the traditions or elaborating upon their meaning, the mere flurry or activity on the part of elites is symptomatic of a cultural tradition in disarray—unsure of what it is, of where it has been, and of where it is going.

## Is Orthodoxy Possible?

In one sense orthodoxy is a subjective matter. If a group of persons collectively believe their religious beliefs to be orthodox, then they are orthodox (at least to themselves). Outside observers interested in learning more about such a group would be well-advised to take these claims seriously. Whether or not the claim is true by some objective standard is beside the point. The claim itself says much about the ones making the claim. To view orthodoxy as a subjective matter, however, is to radically relativize the phenomenon. Such an approach then has limited utility. However, orthodoxy can also be viewed as an objective phenomenon. It can be seen as a cultural system defined by clearly articulated symbolic boundaries. It bears repeating that although orthodoxy, as a cultural system, has as its centerpiece a theological complex it goes beyond that to include a range of auxiliary cultural beliefs—say, concerning the family, work, morality, the political system, etc. What distinguishes orthodoxy as a cultural system is that it represents a "consensus through time." More than this, it represents a consensus based upon the ancient rules and precepts derived from divine revelation. Its authority and its legitimacy derive from an unfaltering continuity with truth as originally revealed—its primitive and purest expression. Is orthodoxy, so defined, conceivable in the face of social and historical change? And in particular, is it conceivable in the modern world order?

Orthodoxy may be an objective system of rules, principles, codes, assumptions, and the like but it still must be internalized in the minds and emotions of real people. Objective "reality" must be appropriated into subjective consciousness. For this reason alone, orthodoxy could never be truly static and unchanging. But there are other reasons as well. Faulty collective memory, stupidity, negligence, and other facts of human nature would invariably bring about some changes. The resistance of successive generations to the authority of their elders would also create some pressure to change. Shifts in the power structure of society, movements to break away from the traditions, and movements to improve the traditions would necessarily create certain adjustments as well. There are undoubtedly other factors. The point is that modification, even if minor, is the inevitable fate of all traditional beliefs. It is simply in the nature of social reality for orthodoxy to be eroded or redefined to some degree over time.

Yet throughout church history believers have assumed that orthodoxy could be maintained and sustained over time. By the determined efforts of the faithful, the traditions could be securely passed down from generation to generation. If this is so, it has not been without struggle. The history of churches, of denominations, and of the Church can be traced by the efforts of the faithful to rout out, by even the most violent means, heresy, sin, and anything else which would contaminate the true inherited faith. The boundaries of the community had to be maintained at all costs. This goes far toward explaining the slaughter of thousands of Anabaptists and anti-Trinitarians by Lutherans in the sixteenth century, the purges of Huguenots in France, the forced exile of Socinians from

Italy, the persecutions and massacre of Erasmians in Spain, and the inquisition and subsequent execution of any suspected of heresy by the Catholic church in the same century. Excommunication, schism, and ostracism for the following four centuries were only the more moderate means of dealing with those who broke with the traditions. Truth and the future of orthodoxy (variously defined) were at stake.

These conflicts were, by and large, conflicts over secondary doctrinal issues (which are, from a modern perspective, the "superstructure" of the Christian faith): transubstantiation in the sacrament of the eucharist, the authority of the church hierarchy, the method of baptism, the nature of the church government, trinitarianism, etc. This is not to say that these issues were insignificant or epiphenomenal, only that most of them do not and did not define the heart of Christianity. The symbolic infrastructure of the Christian faith—God's existence, the nature and mission of Jesus Christ, the need for salvation, Biblical authority, and the literal truthfulness of Biblical stories, etc.—was rarely called into question by ordinary people or fought over by ecclesiastical structures. When it was, the defense was successful.

Thus through all of this, it was inevitable that orthodoxy would be modified and reconstituted to some degree. Yet in the main, the fundamental assumptions of Christianity and most of the superstructure remained firmly intact. The traditions remained securely institutionalized. Most of the modifications that have taken shape have been subtle, imperceptible, and minor, having more to do with the superstructure than the infrastructure of orthodoxy.

The situation in which Evangelicalism presently finds itself is altogether unique. This is to say that there is something unique about the social, historical, and cultural context of the modern world order. Social scientists have written at length about the structural and cultural distinctives of contemporary society.[13] It is clear that philosophical (or scientific) and "functional" rationality, intensive sociocultural pluralism, the bureaucratization of public life, the subjectivization of private life, and other features of the modern world have imposed extraordinary constraints on religious institutions and belief systems. Though often exaggerated and sensationalized beyond proportion, it is still fair to say that in their cumulative effect, these constraints are unprecedented as well.

From this perspective, the history of Evangelicalism in the twentieth century is the history of an orthodoxy struggling as perhaps it never before has to maintain continuity with the past, to stay true to its heritage. Its ultimate success or failure is not readily determinable or perhaps ever determinable. This much is clear, however: conservative Protestantism has changed in significant ways since the beginning of the century and, from all appearances, it is continuing to change. Indeed, not only are the sociohistorical conditions Evangelicalism finds itself in unique but its response to those conditions is unique and unprecedented as well. Many of conservative Protestantism's fundamental assumptions have begun to lose plausibility within the subculture itself.[14] In the early 1920s the president of the World's Christian Fundamentals Association described the modernist movement in liberal Protestantism as employing "that weasel method of sucking the meaning out of words, and then presenting the empty shells in an attempt to palm them off as giving the Christian faith a new and another interpretation" (quoted in Lippmann 1929, 30–31). In the early part of the century, this was indeed the conscious policy of many theologians, clergy, and lay leaders in many of the large mainstream denominations. Fundamentalism, of course, was a protest against these redefinitions and attenuations. In the following half-century or more, conservative Protestantism continued its protest by institutionalizing it in an expansive network of organizations and structures. Succeeding in its institution-building efforts, conservative Protestants gained a sense of self-confidence about their place in the larger American culture and a sense of security about the future of orthodoxy. Such assurances may have been premature, for what was conscious policy on the part of the modernists in the early part of the twentieth century has become the unconscious and unintended reality of Evangelicalism and the Evangelical life-world in the latter part of the century. Though Evangelicalism has not gone as far as the modernists in Protestantism, the process is identical.

Though these changes may level off, the process is likely to continue, for the simple reason that the symbolic boundaries of Protestant orthodoxy are not being maintained or reinforced. To be sure, there is good reason to believe that conservative Protestantism may be *incapable* of adequately reinforcing these boundaries. This is so for three important reasons. The first has to do with the "ethic of civility." As seen in chapter 5, Evangelicals generally and the coming generation particularly have adopted to various degrees an ethical code of political civility. This compels them not only to be *tolerant of others'* beliefs, opinions, and life-styles, but more importantly to be *tolerable to others*. The critical dogma is not to offend but to be genteel and civil in social relations. While their adoption of this ethic expresses itself politically, it expresses itself as a religious style as well (Hunter 1983a, chap. 6). In this latter sense, it entails a deemphasis of Evangelicalism's more offensive aspects, such as accusations of heresy, sin, immorality, and paganism, and themes of judgment, divine wrath, damnation, and hell. Anything that hints of moral or religious absolutism and intolerance is underplayed. Indeed there is enormous social pressure to adapt to this code of civility. As one national opinion survey showed, the predominant image of conservative Protestantism is still negative. They are very often viewed as "overly strict on moral issues," "closed minded," "intolerant of others' religious views," and "fanatical about their own beliefs" and are believed to place "too harsh an emphasis on guilt, sin or judgement" and to be "too rigid and simplistic."[15] This kind of characterization cannot help but create tremendous social constraints to be less strict, less fanatical, more open-minded, and so on.

In short, to reinforce the traditional symbolic boundaries of orthodox Protestantism would require Evangelicals to operate defiantly against these social and cultural constraints. They would have to publicly invoke and rigorously apply the "harsher" and more "offensive" symbols of their faith. In practical terms this would mean publicly labeling some people sinners, heretics, or infidels; all, though, in danger of God's judgment and eternal punishment. To do so would undoubtedly generate untoward consequences. They would risk offending and alienating not only non-Evangelicals (those they hope to win over to the faith) but their own following as well. The Evangelical backlash against the "religious Right" in the 1980s has been a potent image of this. Given this situation, there are few who would be willing to consistently violate the moral code of civility. To do so would jeopardize their social and even spiritual standing in the community.

The second reason can only be inferred, but the logic and the evidence are compelling. It is that an increasing number of Evangelicals no longer really believe in the sanctity of these symbolic boundaries. A deep, compulsive, organic faith in the eternal and transcendent verities that emerge out of a quiet, taken-for-granted certainty is disappearing (Lippmann 1929, 32).[16] It is not as though these Evangelicals no longer believe in God, his authority, or the authority of Scriptures, or the divine sanction of the traditions. It is that they have difficulty believing in these things simply and literally, the way a person would say that his neighbor exists. Once the belief that the central facts (carried by the traditions and taught by churches) are facts in the most literal and absolute sense is weakened, traditional religion begins to disintegrate. The most important case in point is the place of Scriptures. When it is allowed, as it is increasingly so in Evangelicalism, to interpret the Bible subjectivistically and to see portions of the Scripture as symbolic or nonbinding, the Scriptures are divested of their authority to compel obedience. They may still inspire but they are substantially disarmed. The same is true for codes of behavior and belief traditionally held to be biblically inspired. When these lose a sense of divine origin or divine sanction, or when they are seen as having a human and temporal origin, the believer's conviction is enfeebled.

The modern world order, then, not only creates conditions which constrain modifications in the belief system of orthodoxy but also undermines the disposition of the orthodox to believe unequivocally. As Walter Lippmann expressed it, the "acids of modernity" dissolve their very feeling of quiet certainty. The most telling evidence of this is found in the attempt to defend the traditions. "Faith is not a formula which is agreed to if the weight of evidence favors it. It is a posture of one's whole being which predisposes him to assimilate not merely believe his creed. . . . Arguments are for the unbelievers and the wavering;" they are for those who are losing their primordial attachments (Lippmann 1929, 60). When opinion motivates the believer and not conviction born out of total certainty, any effort to revitalize the boundaries of a moral community will be difficult. In light of this, it is not surprising to note that while Evangelicals roundly recognize change in their own quarters and, in many instances, disapprove of that change, they themselves feel little urgency to defend the boundaries from further erosion. Thus, for example, less than one-third (30%) of all faculty at Evangelical colleges felt that a defense of the inerrancy/infallibility of the Bible was "essential" to the preservation of Christian orthodoxy in the contemporary world.[17] More to the point, though, in the interview setting, most seminarians expressed a deep uneasiness with the idea of church discipline for members who consciously and deliberately violate the religious and moral boundaries of the church community (i.e., confrontation with church leadership, public repudiation, disfellowship, etc.).[18]

The third reason Evangelicalism may not be capable of reinforcing the boundaries is the simplest of all. It is that there is no longer any abiding consensus as to what many of the boundaries are. This is so among ordinary laymen and clergy, but it appears to be particularly true for the coming generation. From all indications the pluralism of opinion over theological, moral, familial, and political issues in Evangelicalism (already wide-ranging) is expanding and not coalescing into a new consensus.

All of this contrasts sharply with the experience of earlier generations of conservative Protestants. For them, maintenance of the symbolic boundaries making up the traditions of orthodox Protestantism was possible because they rarely were constrained by social decorum or fear of offending the deviant, because there was a high degree of consensus on what constituted the moral order, and because they knew with the certainty of the sun's rising that the traditions were from God.

Mary Douglas has written that purity of the moral order is pursued by rejection. Elsewhere she notes that change, ambiguity, and compromise have always been the enemies of purity (1966, 161). For an orthodoxy to remain hermetic it must be highly "pollution conscious" and be capable of rejecting that pollution when the moral order is breached. Is orthodoxy possible? The answer from the perspective of the social sciences can only be partial. If it means carrying on the "faith of one's fathers"—faith and practice as one's religious forebears understood it to be and in the settled certitude that they enjoyed—no, not for an increasing number of American conservative Protestants. This should in no way imply that in some ultimate sense every change conservative Protestantism has undergone in the twentieth century represents a fatal compromise from the truths it has traditionally espoused—a further movement down the "slippery slope" of religious apostasy. No such normative judgment is being made (nor could be made from a social scientific perspective). Neither should this imply that the religious experience of Evangelicals is somehow illegitimate or inauthentic. To the contrary, the continued resilience of conservative Protestantism in the face of the difficult circumstances it finds itself in bespeaks a profound religious vitality. Their claim to the defense of orthodoxy, then, should be taken seriously. At the same time, however, it should be clear that this orthodoxy resembles less and less what earlier generations understood it to be.

# Evangelicalism in the Modern World Order

To this point, the cultural developments within American Evangelicalism have been considered only in terms of their meaning for the organization and practice of Protestant orthodoxy (broadly defined). Yet beyond the structural and functional significance of these developments is their global significance. Protestantism is, after all, a world religion, and like any world religion, it has had a profound effect on political, economic, and cultural history in whatever region it has been established. It is only reasonable to imagine that any developments in the cultural complexion of Protestantism would affect its position and role in the larger world. In a world-historical perspective then, what is one to make of the conservative Protestant legacy in the modern world order? More to the point, how does one make sense of the Evangelical experience in this century?

## THE DECLINE OF CULTURAL HEGEMONY

The historical linkages between contemporary Evangelicalism and the restorationist challenge to Western Christianity are clear. However well it maintains the purity of the Reformational vision, it is certainly a prominent inheritor of that legacy. But that legacy was originally more than theological or even cultural. It was sociological as well insofar as the Protestant movement had considerable import in the development of Western civilization. Of course, some go so far as to argue that industrial capitalism was spawned by the Protestant movement; that the modern world order could not have developed as it did without the moral fervor of Protestant faith. This argument deserves some elaboration.

The notion that the Protestant sects (particularly in the Reformational-Confessional tradition) played a role in the development of modern capitalism has been an idea debated intensely for nearly a century.

Max Weber, of course, was the principal and original source of this hypothesis. His argument was simple: a popular variant of Reformational theology provided the psychological impetus for a highly rationalized, commercial, and entrepreneurial capitalism. The reason why this form of capitalism developed in Western Europe and not in China, India, the Middle East, or Latin America was precisely because the cultural preconditions suitable for the acceptance of this religious and economic ethic (e.g., vocational discipline, productivity, frugality) were established in the former region to an extent unknown in the latter.

The critics of this argument, needless to say, have been many.[1] Some have taken issue with Weber's contention that Protestant theology was unique in its influence upon economic activity (Tawney 1938). Its casual role, many argue, was more complicated than Weber realized or articulated. What is more, many argue that Weber's formulation of Protestant theology was facile. He neither recognized the subtle changes it had undergone between the sixteenth and eighteenth century nor realized the fact that the Catholic tradition also had a well-developed notion of "vocational calling" (Robertson 1933; Sammuelson 1961). Others maintain that rationalized capitalism developed first not in the sixteenth century in the aftermath of the Reformation but in the High Middle Ages (Collins 1983) or even during the Renaissance (Cohen 1980) and not among Protestants but among Jews (Sombart 1915) or among Catholics (Fanfani 1955; Cohen 1980; Robertson 1933). Still other critics maintain that Weber's argument for the rise of capitalism has been misunderstood by those who have sought to criticize it. Weber has himself, it is argued, advocated a broader, more institutional theory of the origins of capitalism in which the psychological factor provided by Protestantism plays only a small part (Collins 1980).

This intellectual debate is one of the most famous in the modern history of social science; it remains an important one to the present. Even so, to pursue it much further would be to stray too far afield from present concerns. One need not accept the details of the argument to accept the basic and profound association between Protestantism and modern capitalism (an association which, incidentally, even the strongest critics of the Weberian hypothesis accept). Ascetic Protestantism may have been historically and intrinsically necessary to the rise of rational capitalism, or the historical association may have been "accidental." The Protestant ethic may have originally spawned the modern economic enterprise, or it may have merely intensified and extended capitalistic tendencies already present. Whatever position one takes on these issues, it does not obscure the central reality that Protestantism became identified to a large extent with the forces favorable to the expansion of commercial capitalism

(Wallerstein 1974, 151–56). Those countries that became and remained Protestant industrialized, while those countries that remained Catholic did not. Indeed, those parts of Europe where the Counter-Reformation succeeded in the sixteenth century were also those that "re-agrarianized."[2] Even the classes of merchants in Catholic countries in this period were very often Protestants and not just Jews. Thus, by the middle of the seventeenth century, a Protestant northwestern Europe came to dominate western European economic expansion. Though different countries in this region of the continent came to the fore at different times, the Protestant powers generally maintained economic and political hegemony through the nineteenth century. It comes as little surprise then that Protestants dominated economic expansion in North America as well. The Puritan ethos of hard work, sobriety, frugality, and restraint was institutionalized in the family—the predominant form of social organization in the United States up to the early decades of the twentieth century (Bell 1976). The family and churches of small-town America, therefore, provided an effective stimulus and legitimation for economic growth, first in an agrarian/mercantile/artisan economy and later in a budding industrial and commercial economy.

Whether by accident or by design, then, Protestantism has been a significant factor in the shaping of the modern world order. This is part of its portentous legacy. It is also a role that has distinguished Protestant-ism from the other world religions. No other world religion is associated with the modern world system more than it.

The association of Reformational Christianity with the economic and technological forces which gave rise to the modern world system is only one sense in which Protestantism can be thought of as having cultural hegemony. In America especially, its hegemony was far more extensive. For one, the population of America from the colonial period to the middle of the nineteenth century was almost uniformly Protestant. At the time of the first census in 1790 Catholics constituted approximately 1 percent of the American population; Jews an even smaller number (Handy 1953, 8–20). While most did not have formal membership in a denomination, the overwhelming majority of Americans were Protes-tant either in background or in conviction (Hudson 1961, 4). The cultural hegemony of classical Evangelical Protestantism in America is also suggested by the political authority of churches in the years prior to the founding of the Republic and by the religious and moral authority of denominations in the years following the founding of the Republic. It is largely because of the close association between Protestantism and the religious and moral goals of the Republic that the majority of Protes-tants, even as late as the mid–nineteenth century, were willing to entrust the state with the responsibility of educating children. Protestants of all denominations were "confident that education would be 'religious' still. The sects identified their common beliefs with those of the nation, their mission with America's mission" (Smith 1967, 687).

Related to all of this is the religious and moral meaning of America; its mythic identity. It is here, in the vision of a Christian America, of a righteous empire, that the cultural hegemony of Protestantism was perhaps most firmly rooted.[3] Protestant activity for more than three centuries derived both inspiration and direction from this vision. There was unity on this in spite of real doctrinal and liturgical differences.

Thus for Protestants themselves, particularly in the eighteenth and nineteenth centuries, their cultural dominance and their role in the expansion of the modern world order were not at all coincidental. At one level these were viewed as the logical expression of the superiority of true religion. As one nineteenth-century Baptist leader put it, Christianity "is the highest and purest form of religion in the world, and contains the highest and purest conception of man and society."[4] Because of this, Protestants believed that they were the "vanguard of true progress." Another nineteenth-century Evangelical put the matter even more bluntly: "Our many-sided modern civilization, with its immense superiority over that of the heathen and ancient times, is the effect of Christianity" (Handy 1971, 120). Others concurred. "By the intellectual, moral, commercial, and political blessings—in a word, by the civilization which God has given and is still giving to those nations which have adopted Christianity—He has indicated His approval; it is evident that He intends that these Christian nations shall have the predominant and moulding influence in the world at this state of its development. The real reason why Christian nations are predominant is because they, more than others, have discovered and loved and lived the truth, the eternal principles on which God created this world" (Handy 1971, 123).

The advance of modern civilization also corresponded to most Protestants' view of *divine* history. "Progress" had, in other words, eschatological significance. Between the American Revolution and the Civil War the prevailing view of the Last Days among Americans was postmillennialism, a view positing Christ's return after a millennium of spiritual advance and global evangelization. Postmillennialists of the eighteenth and nineteenth centuries believed that the moral and spiritual ground was being cleared in their own day for the event to take place. The millennium was imminent and thus it was the responsibility of all Christians to work in their own vocation toward this end. In this light, the "advance of civilization" was anything but accidental. The decline of Catholic and Islamic powers in the world order, the extraordinary success of foreign missions in the colonial expansion of the Protestant countries, and the advance of science, technology, and industry within Protestant countries themselves were empirical proof of Biblical promises (Marsden 1980, 49–53). Their optimism, then, was amply justified. Indeed, the ascending power of the United States in the world order through the nineteenth century merely confirmed what many American Protestants openly suspected—that America, as a Christian matron, would assume a position of leadership in the unfolding of the eschaton.

Though the United States did achieve a dominant position in the world order by the early decades of the twentieth century, the promise of the millennium failed. First in Europe and then in the United States, the Protestant cultural system lost its specific influence in society. To the degree that it continued to be associated with the dominant powers of the social order, it did so only in a diffused way—as an opaque religion of the Republic. In this form it did continue to legitimate market exchange, industrial/corporate development, and colonial expansion. Nonetheless, as a specific concrete and religious orientation it rapidly became less and less important to the *pragmatic* realities of incentive and duty in the workplace. Protestantism's own claim on the fortunes of the modern world order remained high but its real influence became nominal, and its practical effect (despite its boasting) was little at all.

Another way of putting this is to say that the modern world order achieved real and practical *autonomy* from a cultural system that had favored if not borne significant responsibility for its development. All of this is well beyond argument. The curious reality is that the cultural system of an Evangelical Protestantism retained its status as a *public ideology* in America right through the end of the nineteenth century. Its grip on the public imagination of America was tenacious to an extent unknown in Great Britain or anywhere else on the Continent. In America, in other words, the cultural system of Evangelical theology maintained a certain hegemony in the sphere of public and official discourse. Its theology, while taken personally seriously by only a minority in America at this time, still carried the weight of cultural respectability. The same can be said for its definitions of moral propriety, familial relations and responsibility, and individual subjectivity (the place and significance of the self). *The significance of the twentieth century for American Evangelical Christianity is the deterioration of this cultural hegemony in America.* The modern world has *extended* and finalized its autonomy from the cultural system which originally shaped much of its character.

The collapse of the cultural hegemony of pre-twentieth-century Protestantism has taken place in two principal stages. The "first disestablishment" took place in the last decade of the nineteenth century and the first two and a half decades of the twentieth century, and was primarily concerned with the theological facet of the cultural system. The events have been mentioned already and are, indeed, well known. The issues of the nature of Scripture, the origin of the world, the validity of biblical miracles, and the primacy of spiritual salvation were the symbolic terrain upon which this first disestablishment took place. The impetus for change was first external. The gaining prominence of European scholarship, competing secular philosophies, indigenous pluralism resulting from mass immigrations, and the material and spiritual malaise of industrial life together provided a challenge at every level to the credibility and workability of orthodox belief in the modern milieu. The impetus, though, was also internal. Ecumenism and the deemphasis of doctrinal truth, the advocacy of the Social Gospel, higher biblical criticism, and the so-called new theology of the modernist movement in Protestantism defied at every level the internal consistency and viability of established truths and church practices. Not surprisingly, these challenges to conservative Protestant hegemony generated tremendous resistance. The "first wave" of political activism (described in chap. 5) was the spontaneous attempt to prevent, impede, or even postpone what eventually became an inevitable decline. The symbolic end to this first disestablishment was the Scopes trial of 1925. From this point on, the theological vision of traditional Protestantism would no longer have de facto prominence in the American culture. It would be one among several others. Indeed, its fate was more dire than this. From this point on, this theological vision would be an object of ridicule, derision, and contempt. It had lost credibility and respect as a public ideology.

Though the theological dimension of the Evangelical world view had been displaced, the moral and familial dimensions remained sustantially institutionalized in the lives of most ordinary Americans. From the 1920s to the 1960s, most Americans, whether they were conservative Protestants or not, continued to believe in the legitimacy of nineteenth-century definitions of moral and familial propriety (e.g., premarital chastity, modesty of adornment, heterosexuality, marital fidelity, moral discipline). Now it is not as though Protestants could claim this moral system as exclusively their own. Protestantism did not invent it. The other religious traditions in the Judeo-Christian orbit could also identify with it. Still, insofar as this moral and familial system was forged out of centuries of Protestant experience and domination, it developed in American society as a whole with a distinctly Protestant quality. It retained that quality into the twentieth century.

The second disestablishment has involved the decline of the moral and familial facets of the traditional Protestant world view. The trend had started certainly as early as the late nineteenth century, but it was not until the 1960s that it gained momentum. Here again, the events have already been reviewed. In this case, the issues of sexuality (homosexuality versus heterosexuality), authority in the family, role definitions in the family, the definitions of the beginning of human life, the ideological uses of public education, and the like have provided the symbolic terrain upon which this disestablishment has taken place. The major impetus here is also external. The wide experimentation in life-styles (from open marriages to homosexual marriages to cohabitation outside marriage), in drugs, and in religious experience (from human potential cults to Eastern mysticism) provided an *indigenous* challenge; the Equal Rights Amendment, the Gay Rights initiative, and changes in abortion and school prayer laws provided a *formal* challenge. Yet except for the activities of the Evangelical Left, there has been no serious formal internal challenge. Even so, the external challenges were formidable enough, for once again they fostered significant backlash within conservative Protestant quarters. The "third wave" of Evangelical political activism then has been the effort to stem the tide of further decline.

This second stage in the hegemonic decline of traditional Protestantism in contemporary America is essentially an accomplished reality. There has not yet been a symbolic end to it—there may never be one. It is even conceivable, if not probable, that conservative Protestants and their alliance with conservative Catholics and Jews may be able to win back some of the symbolic territory already lost (i.e., through continued resistance to the ERA and through modifications of abortion laws). Such success might ultimately be futile though, for two reasons. The first is suggested by the precedent set in the 1920s. Conservatives, after all, did succeed in passing Prohibition. They also "won" the Scopes trial. Yet, as has already been noted, both were eventually reversed. It is plausible then that successes on the contemporary scene may lead to similar reversals. The second reason is that the rejection of traditional moral and familial patterns has already become well institutionalized in the lives of the vast majority of Americans, as public opinion surveys have shown. Ironically, from what has been reviewed here (particularly in chaps. 3 and 4), this rejection has also been substantially institutionalized within a sizable part of Evangelicalism. Except on the issues of abortion, homosexuality, and perhaps the ERA, Evangelicals themselves have adjusted comfortably to the decline in hegemony of traditional moralism and familism.

From this point on, the moral/familial vision familiar to conservative Protestantism becomes one of several possibilities. Moral pluralism (within certain limits) takes its place alongside religious pluralism in America, and with it comes the final dissolution of the long-established dominance of the traditional Protestant moral order. The process has not been slow and gradual but lurching and episodic, with some generations seeing more dramatic change than others. Neither has it been peaceful but almost always antagonistic; often generating deep rifts in the class, status, and ideological structure of American life. But what does the decline in Protestant hegemony mean? Does this reality have any broader significance?

### TRANSITION IN THE WORLD ORDER

The process is hardly isolated from the push and pull of change in economic, political, and cultural realms. To be sure, the decline of Protestant hegemony accompanies a major shift in the structure and cultural ethos of the contemporary world order. It is, in some respects, dialectically related, that is, both in part a cause and an effect of these changes.

Commonly (though inadequately) referred to as a shift from modern to postmodern society, the changes entail a certain intensification of rationalistic principles and tendencies dominant in the West through World War II. In the *economic* sphere, this intensification is seen at several levels: the widening internal dependence upon technological innovation for corporate survival and growth, the displacement of traditional manufacturing skills through technological obsolescence, the increasing amount of economic activity oriented toward the production and distribution of technology and technological services, and the expanding proportion of national wealth and international trade revolving around advanced technology.[5] At the *organizational* and *political* level, it is evidenced by the growing portion of the population whose occupations depend upon the development of this sector of the economy (Gouldner 1979; Bruce-Briggs 1979; Kristol 1979; Brint 1982). They participate in this sector of public life by virtue of their formal claim upon specialized knowledge and technical capabilities. The credentialing of these skills, of course, is only possible through their access to higher education. Yet by virtue of their access to higher education and middle- to high-status occupations, they constitute an elite/quasi elite with at least the potential, if not the actual capability, for common political action (Kirkpatrick 1979; Gouldner 1978a, b). At the *cultural* level (the most important level for the purposes of the present discussion), this extension is seen in the development of a new code of moral authority and legitimacy—one based upon technical competence and technical capacity.[6] In brief, it is an intensely secular cultural orientation which de-legitimates any moral authority based upon tradition, personality, or status. Moral authority, rather, is defined by and based upon the technical competence, empirical adequacy, and linguistic precision of the positions taken. Thus, moral options in human activity (decisions about life-plan, care for the aged and infirm, family size and organization, etc.) are increasingly shaped by the values implicit in technical rationality (cost-effectiveness, efficiency, etc.). The adequacy of social relationships and definitions of self-worth are also increasingly measured by this new moral code. So too do the major public institutions of modern life, from economic planning to energy policy to political organization, increasingly seek legitimacy from this new moral system.

The idea that the ideological basis of the modern world order is in transition to a cultural order such as described here is hardly novel. Though characterized in a wide variety of ways, it has been a theme of social criticism and social theory at least since the 1930s.[7] Many discussions about the extent to which the modern world order has progressed in this transition, however, are wildly exaggerated if not extremely distorted. A new cultural epoch has not been established as many would argue. It is likely that it will never fully be established. *The collapse of the cultural hegemony of traditional Protestantism merely represents the end of an early stage in a cultural transformation that points in this direction.*

At one level the changes now taking place within conservative Protestantism represent various ways of coping with this transformation in the world order. But how? Periods of transformation such as this are very often characterized by religious ferment.[8] Sectarian movements, for example, generally emerge within sectors of the population whose access to power and privilege in society is waning. Prominent among such phenomena are backlash movements arising in response to emerging social and cultural changes. Movements of accommodation are also highly visible at these times; sometimes overt and deliberate in cause and at other times unwitting, but in either case they represent an adaptation to the emerging cultural ethos. When movements of accommodation occur, they are generally among groups whose fortunes are increasing. However, both accommodationism and sectarian resistance are means of carving out a place in an emerging world order.

The cultural dynamics taking place within Evangelicalism defy simple categorization. Contemporary Evangelicalism contains both sectarian backlash and accommodationist tendencies concurrently: it vigorously resists many aspects of the transformation and actively enjoins others.

To the extent that contemporary Evangelicalism adopts an ideology of accommodation (deliberately or unwittingly), it is kept from being entirely displaced by this shift. It eases the tensions that necessarily exist because of the growing incongruities in world views. In practical terms, it allows conservative Protestants to participate in the broader institutions of society with a minimum of cognitive dissonance. Without that accommodation, the social dislocations would be so severe that their only practical option as a community would be withdrawal and isolation.

To the extent that it forms a sectarian response, it serves more than its own adherents. Indeed, it operates in the interest of a broader yet more diffuse world view—all of those who are displaced by this cultural and structural realignment in the world order. The explicit efforts of the general interest groups (such as the Moral Majority, Christian Voice, Religious Roundtable), antiabortion groups (such as Christian Action Council, Family America, and Prayers for Life), anti-ERA groups (such as Life Action Ministries, Concerned Women of America, and the National Pro-Family Coalition), and morality in television groups (such as the Coalition for Better Television, Clean Up TV Campaign, and the National Federation for Decency) to form linkages with conservative Catholics, Orthodox and Conservative Jews, and secular conservatives are significant in this regard. Together they are able to pool both the material and the moral resources to sustain them in the face of the broader realignment. To the degree that Evangelicalism forms a sectarian response it generates a backlash in the form of countermovements. Groups such as People for the American Way, the American Civil Liberties Union, the National Organization for Women, Americans for Common Sense, the National Abortion Rights Action League, merely represent a broader coalition of people who are carriers of the new moral code. Naturally their interests are served by the structural and cultural realignments in the world order. It is not at all surprising, then, that the image of conservative Protestantism as an extremist, bigoted, and dangerous movement has been cultivated in this sector of the population since the 1920s. This image is cultivated here not only because it is sincerely believed to be true but also for the strategic advantage it affords them.[9] It is a discrediting image and if its proponents are taken seriously by the American public, they will have gone far toward neutralizing the sectarian response of cultural conservativism in America.

Once again, contemporary Evangelicalism contains both sectarian and accommodationist tendencies. There is extraordinary pressure to resist these transformations because they have too much at stake to simply give in. Likewise there is extraordinary pressure to accommodate because, again, they have too much at stake to simply withdraw into an isolated cultural ghetto. Therefore, ideological tension between these two polar responses remains deeply rooted in the world of contemporary Evangelicalism. It is inherent to the faith as it is now lived and experienced.

## "Crisis" In The World Order

Change and transition in the contemporary world order can be viewed from a very different angle from the one pursued thus far. The starting point is the assessment of the quality of human experience in the context of these changes. From this perspective, many have argued that the last half of the twentieth century has posed a crisis of a sort for Western society. Theories of crisis are, indeed, abundant in intellectual circles, perhaps too abundant to be taken seriously. Yet if a transformation is under way, then it would necessarily present severe disruptions in the fabric of everyday life for ordinary people. It may then be appropriate to speak of crisis. At least the hypothesis of a cultural "malaise" should be approached seriously, if not always cautiously.

There are, however, many different perspectives on what constitutes the crisis of contemporary culture. Some emphasize the shift in the *locus of authority* in modern life to an oppressive form of scientific and technological rationality.[10] Because technology operates according to its own logic and its own rules, it is increasingly autonomous from human values and, therefore, increasingly unharnessable by those who have created it. There is, then, a totalitarian quality about technological rationality for it creates a milieu which is progressively one-dimensional—a social order without alternatives and without opposition. Thus it not only fosters a cultural aridity—a world without magic, ritual, rite, or surprise—but it also threatens the very core of human freedom—individual and collective self-determination. Others emphasize a shift in the *quality of human relationships*. Clearly a technologically induced economic growth generates enormous wealth and material comfort (particularly under capitalism), yet it also tends to "distort" human values, redefining what is valuable and worthwhile.[11] For one, rather than seek meaning and personal fulfillment in deep interpersonal bonds, these things are sought in an obsessive and competitive materialism. Indeed, community progressively disintegrates into a mass of semiautonomous individuals who relate to each other not as unique persons but as objective and manipulable possessions. Thus they relate to others not in a milieu of trust and human bondedness but in one of fear and loneliness. Still others emphasize the shift in the nature of *personality and consciousness* in contemporary civilization. At one level this is seen as the reflection of the rationality of public life in the personality; consciousness becomes "bureaucratized" and "technologized." At another level it is seen as an expanding fixation with the self and the complexities of human subjectivity (i.e., narcissism, hedonism, subjectivism, expressive individualism).[12] While the two are related, the latter is especially distinct. Largely a result of changes in the private sphere of family, personal friendships, and personal meaning,[13] it is expressed in the popular culture as the search for identity or the problem of meaning or even the quest for authenticity. The emergence of a large meaning/identity industry in the latter half of the twentieth century is merely an artifact of the new "problems of subjectivity" many modern individuals face.[14]

What virtually all of these perspectives hold in common is that technical rationality is directly or indirectly tied into this cultural malaise. In some respects it is almost irrelevant whether any of these arguments are exactly true. The point is that even if empirical reality only marginally corresponds to these descriptions of crisis, contemporary civilization still faces a serious predicament.

The question then becomes, What is the solution to the dilemma? On this the academic community is divided. Some contend that nothing at all can be done to alter either the direction of the modern world order or the complexion of experience in it.[15] Others are less pessimistic. Some of these argue that the solution is, at heart, structural.[16] If one can change the fundamental economic and political structures and organizations of contemporary society, one can improve the quality of human experience. Economic redistribution, political and organizational decentralization, and corporate and community cooperation are the chief means of bringing this about. There are those, however, who insist that the answer is mainly cultural.[17] For them, the only decisive way to regain control over technological civilization and to restore depth and quality to individual and corporate life is to encourage a renewal of human values. Structural changes, such as those just mentioned, will only happen when based upon this "more fundamental" transformation. For the present purposes, it is the last which is the most interesting, not because it is any more plausible than the others but because it ultimately leads back to an understanding of the place and role of conservative Protestantism in the modern world order.

The hypothesis that a renewal of value can alter the course and complexion of the modern world order is a compelling one and deserves attention not only for its intrinsic merit but for the fact that it has been taken up by some of the more prominent intellectuals in social science and social criticism. Amitai Etzioni, for example, argues that what is necessary is a renewed sense of commitment to community needs and collective concerns ("mutuality"), a deepened sense of civility ("tolerance"), an inner discipline, and the development of high standards for work and social relationships (particularly in the schools) (Etzioni, 1984, pt. 1). Most others go beyond this secular prescription to argue that the source of this renewal must be religious in nature. For example, as Daniel Bell wrote in the late 1970s:

We stand, I believe, with a clearing ahead of us. The exhaustion of Modernism, the aridity of Communist life, the tedium of unrestrained self and the meaninglessness of the monolithic political chants all indicate that a long era is coming to a close.

What will come out of that clearing, I do not wholly know but since I believe that the existential questions of culture are inescapable I feel that some new efforts to regain a sense of the sacred point to the direction in which our culture . . . will move. (1977, 449)

Peter Berger has added to this by noting that in the present situation

the revitalization of the religious community is an even deeper imperative [than the revitalization of the American political community] for it points beyond America and, indeed, beyond history. (1979b, 77)

Similarly, Robert Nisbet has speculated that the future may hold either a "continuing erosion of political values and commitments" or else an "enlargement of the religious, of the sacred, in the realm of human devotion and loyalty." For him the stakes are high for it is only in a "deep and wide sense of the *sacred* [that we] are likely to regain the vital conditions of progress itself" (1980, 357). Finally, there is the view of Soviet exile Alexsandr Solzhenitsyn. Though not a social scientist, his perspective is rhetorically compatible with the others.

If the world has not approached its end, it has reached a major watershed in history equal in importance to the turn from the Middle Ages to the Renaissance. It will demand from us a spiritual blaze; we shall have to rise to a new height of vision, to a new level of life, where our physical nature will not be crushed, as in the Middle Ages, but even more importantly, our spiritual being will not be trampled upon, as in the Modern Era.[18]

Not surprisingly, some argue that conservative Protestantism may be a source of this cultural renewal. Nisbet, for example, suggests that eruptions of Fundamentalism and Pentecostalism (in Catholicism and Protestantism) may foreshadow the beginnings of a religious transformation, "another full-blown 'awakening,' even a major religious reformation" (1980, 356). Others have concurred. Indeed one argument maintains that the current Charismatic movement and mainline Evangelical movement contain the seeds of a "second Protestant Reformation" (Rifkin 1979). The Charismatic movement, with its emphasis on spiritual gifts, extrahuman powers, and the like, it is argued, has begun to replace science, technique, and reason with supernatural powers as the critical reference points for interpreting daily life. The protagonists of this view further contend that if "this unconscious challenge to the modern world view continues to intensify, it could provide the kind of liberating force that could topple the prevailing ethos and provide a bridge to the next age of history" (Rifkin 1979, xi). The mainline Evangelical movement, on the other hand, has begun to provide a theological complement to this by redefining its traditional "doctrine of creation." Instead of understanding their responsibility to have "dominion over the earth" as a license to exploit nature, Evangelicals are coming to view it as an ethic of conservation, preservation, and stewardship of God's creation. Together the Charismatic and Evangelical wings of conservative Christianity are "beginning to establish a radically new theological prescription for a non-growth, steady-state ecological future" in a postexpansionist period in Western history (Rifkin 1979, 255).

Again bracketing the question of whether cultural revitalization could effect changes in the world order, is it possible that Evangelicalism could be a source of this general renewal? If so, could the Evangelical movement (as a cultural/political force) play an independent role in the shaping of the modern world order?

To ask Evangelicals themselves is to get a mixed reply. On the positive side, roughly two-thirds of the coming generation (collegians, 60%; seminarians, 70%) believe that a "Third Great Awakening" in America is likely to occur within the next several decades. In all fairness, one must admit that anything is possible. Sociocultural conditions could become favorable to such an occurrence. One would even have to concede the possibility that extraempirical dynamics could be at play.

Yet if a revival did take place, Evangelicalism would first have to come to terms with its present and long-standing ambivalence toward the modern world. It will also have had to reconcile its exclusive claims to moral and religious truth with an intensifying sociocultural pluralism progressively institutionalized in the legal, political, and cultural areas of modern life. It is significant to note in this regard that the first two awakenings in American history took place in a political and cultural context that was Protestant in form if not in substance. There was a compatibility, in other words, between the political and legal structure of American society at that time and the religious revitalization of the awakenings. A Third Great Awakening would not have that advantage.

There are other factors to consider as well. As ecumenical as conservative Protestants have been in the post–World War II period, the denominational structure embodying Evangelicalism is still divided among a very large number of denominations, many of which maintain deep antagonisms toward the others. Evangelicals, of course, can also be found scattered among and loyal to both mainstream Protestant denominations and even Catholic parishes. Thus, Evangelicalism would need to reconcile itself to these internal and structural tensions.

If a revival were to take place and have broad effects on the culture, conservative Protestantism would also have to come to terms with its uneven regional distribution. In other words, a religion whose character is largely defined by southern and midwestern conservative populism would have to make inroads within a dominant culture whose character is largely defined by a northeastern and western liberal elitism and quasi elitism. This is related to the tensions of class division. The social and political interests of many of conservative Protestantism's intellectual and prophetic elite are quite compatible with those of the larger secular intellectual and cultural elite and, therefore, quite incompatible with those they claim to represent. Conservative Protestantism must also reconcile itself to the secular knowledge class.

These problems, in fact, may be implicitly recognized, for all Evangelicals are not very optimistic either about revival or about the likelihood that conservative Protestantism can be a source of cultural revitalization. In a national survey of theologians, for example, 62 pecent of the Evangelicals felt that the influence of religion was staying the same (which they universally perceived as "too low") or declining.[20] Liberal Protestant and Catholic theologians felt the same way. In light of everything else just reviewed, this pessimism may be justified.

The structural constraints it faces are plainly threatening. But those aside, its own internal cultural dynamics may provide enough evidence to wonder about its potential for broader cultural revitalization. For if contemporary cultural analysis is to be taken at all seriously, that is that Western civilization has become "impoverished," then conservative Protestantism participates to various degrees in that impoverishment. If the institutions of American society have become "decadent" (to use Peter Berger's term), or "hollowed-out," American Evangelicalism participates in that decadence. This is not to say that this faith is not deeply meaningful and personally vibrant. It unquestionably is for millions of Americans. Nor is it to suggest that this faith takes form as an insignificant cultural/political force. It is only to say that Evangelicalism participates in the same cultural processes that are at work in the larger contemporary world order. The level is different and the pace is different but the process (whether or not one calls it impoverishment or decadence) is the same. If current tendencies and trends continue, the likelihood that conservative Protestantism will be a prominent and autonomous source of cultural renewal in contemporary society is not very high.

# Evangelicalism in America's Third Century

Now that we have some sense of the changes American Evangelicalism has undergone in recent decades and of the significance of these developments both for its own identity and continuity as a cultural system and for its stature and role in the modern world, we can direct our attention toward speculation on its future. One can only be amazed by the resilience of Protestant orthodoxy in its long encounter with the modern world order. It certainly has fared better than most scholars or educated laymen ever imagined. Even so, nearly everything reviewed thus far could provide reasonable grounds for pessimism. Does Protestant orthodoxy have a future in the modern world order and if so, what kind of future? What are its prospects as it moves toward the third century of the American Republic?

## GROWTH, DECLINE, DIVISION

In the early 1970s, the future of conservative Protestantism was the topic of a good deal of speculation. The evidence of the period seemed to indicate that there was substantial and consistent growth within the conservative churches, while the liberal, or mainline, Protestant churches were declining. This translated in the public imagination as a simplification: religious and spiritual revival was occurring in the conservative churches, and spiritual decay had overtaken the mainline churches. Church membership statistics showed these trends as well as national public opinion data (Hoge and Roozen 1979; Gallup Opinion Index 1977; Jacquet 1981; Roof 1982). But what could account for these patterns? The dominant hypothesis that emerged from the period was put forward and popularized by Dean Kelley in his book *Why Conservative Churches Are Growing* (1972).

Kelley's argument was both simple and compelling: people are meaning-oriented beings. They require reliable moral coordinates within which to live their lives, credible explanations for the vagaries of life-experience (both the good and the bad), and assurances that their lives are ultimately significant. Nothing provides all of these things better than religion. As Kelley put it, religion is in the "business" of "explaining the meaning of life in ultimate terms" (1972, 37). It provides cognitive and normative boundaries by which people make sense of their lives. As such, it is able to generate extraordinary commitment, loyalty, and social solidarity among those who believe. As Kelley and others have noted, however, the liberal, or mainline churches from the 1960s onward were far less effective in providing these basic requirements than the conservative churches. The mainline churches did experience a widespread loss of institutional vitality and direction. They shield away from absolutist beliefs in favor of theological and moral diversity, if not relativism. Consequently, these churches were left with diminishing appeal and support; they not only experienced no growth but also sustained significant losses in membership and financial backing. The conservative churches, on the other hand, remained fairly effective in their tasks. These churches all shared certain "traits of strictness": authoritative and absolutist beliefs; social, moral, and religious conformity; exclusivism; and an unusual missionary zeal. The result was that these churches have continued to witness substantial membership growth and financial well-being.

The explanation itself—that is, the explanation for church growth and decline in contemporary America—is both logical and intriguing. It is highly plausible in light of sociological theory and is buttressed by empirical studies.[1] Yet if this argument is true, then in light of the evidence presented here, the consequences are quite arresting. To put the matter succinctly, post–World War II Evangelicalism has witnessed an erosion of precisely the symbolic boundaries that Kelley and others have argued are necessary for the growth if not maintenance of its institutions and constituencies. If the cognitive and moral boundaries of conservative Protestantism have indeed eroded, then instead of revival, we should anticipate a measure of decline within these churches in numerical support. Instead of a downward trajectory representing liberal decline and an upward trajectory representing conservative growth, the more realistic tendency would be a downward trajectory on the part of both liberal and conservative churches. This is exactly the message of figure 2.

This figure illustrates membership growth and decline in Evangelical and mainline denominations between 1940 and 1983. The data are somewhat complex. It is not as though Kelley and others who posit

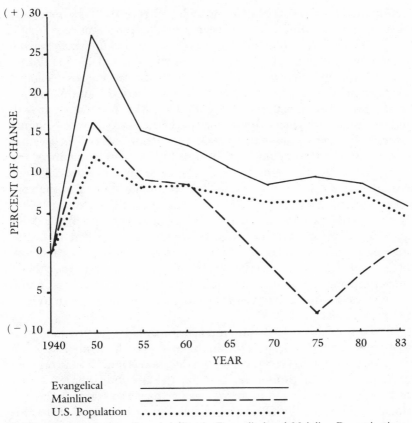

Evangelical ————————
Mainline  — — — — — — —
U.S. Population ••••••••••••••••••••••

Fig. 2. Membership growth and decline in Evangelical and Mainline Denominations (five-year moving averages).

conservative growth and liberal decline are incorrect. In terms of absolute numbers, conservative denominations *have* continued to grow, and mainline denominations, since the period 1960–1965, have declined. A substantial part of the church growth can be explained by the growth in the American population as a whole. When this demographic variable is held constant (or factored out), conservative church growth is not nearly so dramatic. But whether or not one does this, one can observe a trend in the "growth rate." Overall the average growth rate of conservative Protestant denominations has shown a fairly steady decline since the 1940s.[2] There was a slight increase in the growth rate between 1970 and 1975, but this trend reversed in the years following.

What does all of this mean? It first means that despite the discussion of a religious revival taking place in the 1970s—a revival which supposedly brought in large numbers of new believers—the revival was very slight if not nonexistent. It is true, as figure 2 shows, that the church membership growth rate did increase marginally between 1970 and 1975. It is also true that this increase was accentuated by a fairly precipitous decline in membership in mainline churches in the same period. But this in itself hardly constitutes a national revival. Besides, what real church growth did take place, evidence suggests, may have had less to do with bringing in *new* believers as it did with a certain "circulation" of "old" believers—either through the retention of geographically mobile members and offspring or else through the process of denominational "switching," changing one's denominational affiliation though staying in the conservative Protestant orbit (Bibby and Brinkerhoff 1973; Bouma 1979). In other words, while there had been some church growth in the 1970s and 1980s, the growth may have been more internal (due to demographic changes) than external (due to proselytization). The real revival of the 1970s, then, may have been more of a cultural phenomenon than a numerical phenomenon, that is, a revival of public awareness about Evangelicalism due in part to the extraordinary attention given to it by the mass media.

It is possible to extend this argument further. Earlier it was argued that higher education plays a role in the erosion of the symbolic boundaries of conservative Protestantism. If education is indeed a factor, then as educational attainment increases within the subculture, the tendencies of boundary erosion and numerical decline may also continue. Educational attainment is, in fact, rising within Evangelicalism as well as for other sectors of the American public. In 1950, for example, 2.6 million people were enrolled in higher education, in 1960 it increased to 3.6 million, and by 1970 the figure had jumped to 8.6 million, and by 1983 this figure had increased to 12.3 million.[3] This growth has not excluded Evangelicals, even though Evangelicals, as a whole, are less educationally advanced than all other religious groups (as of 1978, only 24% of all Evangelicals had at least some college education, compared with 32% among liberal Protestants, 33% among Catholics, 68% among non-Christians [mostly secular Jews], and 46% among secularists [those without religious preference]). Yet there are signs of rapid growth. Among Evangelicals, the younger are significantly more likely to attend or to have attended college than the older (in 1978 approximately 33% of the eighteen to thirty-five year age group and 38% of the thirty-six to fifty age group had attended college, whereas only 15% of the fifty-one to sixty-five age group and 13% of the sixty-six and older group had).[4] The younger are attending college at a rate roughly equivalent to the young of other religious groups. Such developments will undoubtedly have important consequences for the future of Evangelical Christianity in America.

Not surprisingly, Evangelicals have an opinion about their own future. When seminarians were asked to state their views about "the Evangelical movement in America in the next few decades," the response was mixed but very interesting. In terms of its theology and its approach to social issues, some, of course, felt that there would be little change at all over the next several decades. Some believed it would become more conservative and some felt that it would become more liberal.[5] But the majority held that Evangelicals will be increasingly divided over theological and social issues to the point that this division "may ultimately bring about a major split in the Evangelical movement."[6] The faculty at Evangelical colleges were asked the same question and an even greater majority concurred.[7]

The idea that conservative Protestantism might split into "separatist" and "moderate" camps in the way it did in the late 1940s and early 1950s is not implausible. It bears repeating, separatism and moderation are in some ways different words for sectarian divisiveness and accommodationism—both a reflection of the long-standing ambivalence about how to deal with modernity and its various transformations. It is conceivable that the internal tensions this ambivalence creates may become so intense that it does generate a division. As we have seen in the realm of formal theology, tensions have increased considerably since the 1960s. Such an idea also gains plausibility when considering the experience of two prominent conservative Protestant denominations. In 1976 the conservative Lutheran Church—Missouri Synod experienced such a divide when a conservative faction had captured denominational control and forced a number of "liberal" seminary professors to resign their positions. The result was the formation of the Association of Evangelical Lutheran Churches, a group of theologically moderate and liberal Missouri Synod churches and the so-called Seminary-in-Exile. The other denomination is the largest denomination in the conservative Protestant orbit, the Southern Baptist Convention.[8] The internal tensions have been present for many decades though it was not until the mid-1970s that they surfaced into open political infighting. The antagonism is deep, perhaps comparable only to the antagonism between modernists and fundamentalists at the turn of the century. The pattern is the same. "Conservatives" have sought to stem the tide of "liberalism" in their denomination, while "moderates" have sought to resist the efforts of political takeover and domination by the "fundamentalists." Denominational policy on inerrancy, the ordination of women in the ministry, school prayer, abortion, tobacco and alcohol consumption, and denominational centralization (on the issue of missions) constitute the symbolic territory over which conservatives and moderates conflict. As in the Missouri Synod Lutheran case, control over the denominational seminaries is particularly important to the outcome. While moderates predictably dominate the administration and faculties of Southern Baptist seminaries, conservatives actively seek to win back this beachhead by both replacing the membership of the seminaries' boards of directors and discrediting the doctrinal positions of faculty and administration through the "archiving of instances of heresy." By the 1979 annual convention, conservatives had shifted the balance of denominational control at the highest levels of administration to their side. A countermovement among moderates quickly emerged with the resolve neither to give in nor to separate. Many denominational leaders believe that the only resolution is separation. If so, it would create tremors thoughout the entire Evangelical world.

It is also conceivable that a split in the larger Evangelical house will not occur. If the sectarian and accommodationist impulses took expression according to clear theological positions or even according to clear demographic criteria (e.g., poor, rural southerners being sectarian and middle-class, urban northerners being accommodationist), then a split might be not only possible but probable. The problem is that the ambivalence between defensive reaction and accommodation is present *within* various theological camps and *within* demographic groupings. Thus, for example, there are no substantial differences between seminarians who call themselves Fundamentalists and those who call themselves Evangelicals in the realm of theology, morality, family, and politics. Nor are there vast and consistent differences of attitude and opinion according to demographic criteria. In this light, to the degree that this ambivalence is internalized, Evangelicalism may simply suffer a form of cultural paralysis where moral and religious authority become an impossibility.

Whether or not there is a split, American Evangelicalism seems to face an uncertain future, a future as ambivalent as its own present nature. It is hardly imaginable that conservative Protestantism will disappear, but what it will look like and the degree of resemblance it will have to what previous generations have taken as the true heritage of Christianity and how large it will be demographically are all unknown. While no one can predict with any certainty, the prospects are not all bright.

It is highly significant that many conservative Protestants in North America have already given up hope for an "authentic Christian experience and witness" in the West. Instead there is a progressive conviction that these things can be found only in the struggling Christian communities of the developing countries. This theme is particularly prominent in the liberal and radical (Left) circles of Evangelicalism in their persistent criticism that American (Evangelical) Christianity has become decadent, idolatrous, and materialistic.[9] Yet it also has currency in the mainstream. Billy Graham, for example, observed that "It may be that the center of spiritual gravity in the world is shifting from the West to the East."[10] Another Evangelical leader has argued that "the Third World [has become] the cutting edge of the Christian Church."[11] Still others have argued that the United States constitutes "a mission field for Third World Christians."[12] This theme also came up in discussions with seminarians. One seminarian, training to be a missionary, expressed it this way:

> I would really love to see revival here in America, but personally I think it will happen elsewhere. I think it is going to happen in a Third World country. I think God is going to raise up his church elsewhere. It's already happening in Africa and in Latin America. That is where I think the future of the church lies. In fact, that is where I would like to go. (male, third-year master of divinity candidate, Assemblies of God)

His perspective was typical of the opinion of many among the coming generation of Evangelicals. The Third World represents the hope of true Christianity; his personal goal, to be a part of the realization of that hope.

Needless to say, such a notion would have been unthinkable in the late nineteenth century. These regions represented anything but a hope. As already indicated, it was widely accepted that misery prevailed in these countries because they had not become Christianized. Their economic, social, and moral backwardness was proof of their spiritual backwardness. Even those who converted and formed the indigenous Christian community were considered a measure inferior to the extent that they were not cast in the mold of Western Christianity. The hope of the millennium again was in the West; its brightest symbol was America itself.

The ideological shift then has been dramatic, but what is one to make of it? At one level the change from the West to the Third World as the symbol of this eschatological hope marks a displaced utopianism.[13] "Third World Christianity" in this light represents a compensation for the millennium that never occurred in Western Christianity. But a displaced utopianism also implies a certain degree of disappointment and guilt. In this case it represents disappointment and guilt over the failure of the Christian community to have realized that eschatological vision here—centuries of optimism ending in defeated expectation. Beyond this, however, the shift may represent a certain projection of genuine spiritual need. Here, though, it is the desire for a Christian community marked by "authenticity" and a faith unencumbered by ambiguity and self-doubt.

## THE LOSS OF BINDING ADDRESS

The strength of a culture is defined by how deeply it is ingrained in the consciousness of those who live within its boundaries.[14] When strongly institutionalized it is buried so deeply into the self that its meanings are understood implicitly—as a taken-for-granted certainty. There is no need or compulsion to reflect upon its significance or to ponder its mysteries. Indeed, any effort to articulate its total meaning would fail, for what is known explicitly is superficial, like an outcropping which reveals only a tip of a rock of enormous mass. Culture, when deeply institutionalized, is an inner imperative, binding people to inherited rules and guiding them in virtually every detail of their day-to-day lives. Deviation from that imperative in everyday life for most can only come at the expense of self and spirit. It is to deny a reality so plain and obvious to the senses that to do so would be to flirt with insanity. The strength of culture, then, is measured by the power of its address on people. Only when there is binding address is there the moral energy necessary to motivate men and integrate communities.

The dissolution of culture is the loss of that binding address. It begins when the societal structures can no longer communicate the ideals they embody to people in ways that are inwardly motivating or subjectively compelling. It happens in the modern age in part because the implicit meanings of culture succumb to the modern imperative of analysis, reflection, and introspection—what Philip Rieff has called the "therapeutic attitude"; what Helmut Schelsky has called "permanent reflectiveness"; what Arnold Gehlen has called "subjectivization." The predilection toward introspection and reflection both creates and is a product of a separation of the self from the institutions that give it form and substance. There is, then, a subjective detachment that is cultivated, from which one necessarily reevaluates what had previously been taken for granted. Contradictions and contrary meanings are sorted through; traditional understandings are reassessed. The tangible effect of all of this is either to render the old meanings totally irrelevant or, more typically, to redefine the old meanings in ways that make them more suitable to the times. In some ways though, the final and tangible result is unimportant. A more fundamental event has taken place. Belief has not dissolved but the feeling of serene certainty has. Truth is no longer something unconsciously assumed but is something to which one must consciously and intellectually assent. To paraphrase Rieff, all moral and religious convictions lose their force when subject to the therapeutic. Culture, in a word, loses its binding address.

From the Reformation to the late nineteenth century, conservative Protestantism maintained that binding address on most who professed its faith. The moral energy it created in its communities was extraordinary. All those who surrendered to the magnificent consistency of its inhumane doctrine (as Weber called it) understood and realized in their own lives the passion it generated. Yet for conservative Protestantism the confrontation with the modern world order (particularly from the end of the nineteenth century) has meant the slow but decisive loss of its binding address.

For conservative Protestantism as for the larger culture, this loss occurs first and perhaps deepest among the cultural elite, especially the intellectual elite (as opposed to the prophetic elite). The intellectual elite generally, by virtue of their role in the social world, intellectualize and rationalize their world before and more intensely than the rest of society. It is basic to their vocation and social position to strive for deeper meaning and broader and contextualized understanding. In the contemporary world this entails some if not total familiarity with the logic and tools of scientific and secular rationality. It also entails a certain cosmopolitan awareness if not sophistication about the larger world around them. These facts alone mean that the cultural elite (Evangelical or not) face more directly than most the realities and challenges of modernity. Yet the cultural elite of conservative Protestantism also face their own communities with the responsibility to engage and lead ordinary believers in the practical matters of faith and Christian living. They cannot help but carry over with them into this exchange the residue of modern consciousness. It is not as though the man in the street is isolated from these processes. His own experience is fundamentally shaped by modern contingencies. Cultural elites though confirm, extend, and intellectualize that experience. Thus in the process of receiving moral leadership, the man in the street gets more than he may have bargained for.

This is the significance of the coming generation of Evangelicals. To the extent that the younger cohort of Evangelicals represents the lay and professional leadership in conservative Protestantism in the next generation, it will play an important role in defining the image and the reality of Evangelicalism generally. In light of their strategic place and role in the

Evangelical world, they may indeed be a harbinger of things to come, a bellwether for the future of conservative Protestantism as a whole.

For the moment, the place of cultural elites explains some of the diversity in the Evangelical world. It also provides some clues as to the future shape of this movement. Yet even now, the predilection to reflect, subjectivize, evaluate, and choose is not only a compulsion that a minority of elites experience, it is institutionalized as an ethical demand for all whose social experience is encompassed by modernity. The sense of subjective detachment it creates is progressively the norm of human experience in the modern world.

There is a curious consequence to this. When the binding address of a faith is weakened, it becomes virtually impossible to be too exclusively attached to an ideal or too passionate about a cause. Such a condition, in other words, fosters a "sensibility" and a "civility" in the affairs of one's life. It forces one to "play it safe." The significance of this as it pertains to conservative Protestantism is best seen when reflecting on its past. The binding address of early Protestantism cultivated a fanatical devotion and adherence to faith and an incivility and intolerance toward any deviation, practical or theological. "Knowing the truth" with calm and absolute certainty is in itself (according to contemporary standards) a brazen act of anti-intellectuality, arrogance, incivility, narrow-mindedness, and extremism. Yet these things were intrinsic to the life of the believer. The historical irony is that those cultural expressions that were symptomatic of early Protestantism's moral energy and vitality are precisely those cultural expressions which, on the present scene, are despised by non-Evangelicals and are a source of embarrassment to Evangelicals themselves, particularly the coming generation. Overcommitment and moral zeal have, in the main, been displaced by sensibility and civility.

On the surface this would seem to give solace to Fundamentalists and others for whom sectarian incivility in the pursuit of a cause is not troublesome. Their offense to cultural or political decorum, though, is not automatically a sign of its vitality nor is it a sign that they are more committed to the preservation of truth. The first irony of sectarian reaction has already been touched on: any attempt to defend the traditions ultimately ends in a redefinition of those traditions. The truths of a religious tradition are distorted by the simplification, reduction, and exaggeration that inevitably take place. But there is another irony which is more closely related to the present concerns. Under contemporary conditions such public agitation is generally not made by those moved by the quiet assurance of the moral rightness of their cause. To the contrary, such reaction very often proceeds from an underlying uncertainty about the fate and resilience of the beliefs they espouse. If they were fundamentally convinced that Protestant orthodoxy had a future in the modern world order, there would seem to be less urgency to launch a defensive assault on it. As Walter Lippmann put it (referring to the fundamentalist response of the 1920s), if they were "utterly sure they [were] right, they would exhibit some of that composure which the truly devout display. . . . But because their whole field of consciousness is trembling with uncertainties, they are in a state of fret and fuss; and their preaching is frousy, like the seductions of an old coquette" (Lippmann 1929, 61).

Unwitting accommodation and sectarian defensiveness, then, are both signs that the traditions and creeds they live for are being transformed. Perhaps more fundamentally, they are also prominent symptoms of the loss of binding address.

In closing, the story of conservative Protestantism in America is in some ways the story of the pilgrim in John Bunyan's epic allegory. In his journey from the City of Destruction to the Celestial City, Bunyan's pilgrim stumbles into innumerable difficulties and temptations—from the Slough of Despond to Doubting Castle; from the Town of Vanity to the Valley of Humiliation; from Hill Difficulty to the Valley of the Shadow of Death. This is not to mention his encounters with such unsavory figures as Mr. Wordly Wiseman, Mistrust, Timorous, Pliable, and the like. Yet what our pilgrim (Evangelicalism) endures and Bunyan's does not is a long and sustained season in the Labyrinths of Modernity. Not only does he emerge a little dizzy and confused, but out of the experience our traveler is transformed. The pilgrim becomes a tourist. Though still headed toward the Celestial Country, he is now traveling with less conviction, less confidence about his path, and is perhaps more vulnerable to the worldly distractions encountered by Bunyan's pilgrim.

# Epilogue
# Orthodoxy in the Modern
# World Order: In Search of
# a Paradigm

The issue of orthodoxy in the modern world generates several questions. Two that immediately come to mind are (1) why be interested in orthodoxy to begin with? and (2) what do other orthodoxies encountering the modern world order share in common with the Protestant case? The first question is not difficult to answer. One need only recall that "orthodoxy"(or, as some would prefer, religious extremism) is the historical rule and not the exception. Because of the association of orthodoxies with religion, myth, and the transcendent (and/or the supernatural) they would, from all appearances, be more at odds with the modern world order and have more to lose from a sustained encounter with these structural forces. The study of orthodoxy, therefore, would seem to be capable of revealing many important precedents and lessons for other forms of religion confronting contemporary social change.

The answer to the second question, however, is more complicated. The question may need to be framed in a different way. As I mentioned at the beginning of this book, the proposition has been advanced that Protestantism is the world religion that has confronted the modern world longer and more intensely than any other religion. If this is true for Protestantism generally, then it must also be true for Protestant orthodoxy relative to other forms of orthodoxy. The question that follows is simply this: might the Evangelical experience be paradigmatic for all other orthodoxies confronting the modern world order?

The question and the proposition underlying it are reminiscent of the old modernization arguments that took economic and political developments in Western Europe and North America as paradigmatic for national development generally in the world. It is a credit to contemporary scholarship that these arguments have been shown false. Likewise, one could anticipate that any argument positing that the orthodox Protestant experience is generalizable to the experience of other forms of religious orthodoxy would also fall short. The question is, then, largely rhetorical. Still it is an idea worth considering if for no other reason than it allows one to look for points of similarity and difference. Indeed, among the notable weaknesses in the sociology of religion is its lack of comparative perspective. The need for such work is clear. Having said that I should emphasize that this epilogue is not interested in providing an in-depth and systematic comparison of all orthodoxies in the contemporary world. (It is, after all, just an epilogue!) At best, this is a cursory comparative exploration. Its purpose is twofold. For one, comparative analysis, even if tentative, will add perspective and proportion to the kinds of insights gained on American Evangelicalism. Beyond this, the comparative treatment of orthodoxy will also be suggestive of new and potentially fruitful directions in the theoretical quest to understand religion in the modern world.

It is worth emphasizing it would be impossible within the confines of this epilogue to examine a comprehensive list of all orthodoxies (monotheistic or polytheistic) at different stages of the national development (more advanced or less advanced) or to even treat a few cases exhaustively. It is possible, however, to embark upon a tentative exploration of a vastly limited number of cases. The four that will be pursued here are Catholicism, Judaism, Islam, and Buddhism—four global religions. The concern with the first two, however, is with their experience in advanced societies and, particularly, the contemporary American context. The third will be considered in its place of greatest cultural strength, the Middle East. The last will be considered in the context of the most advanced region of East Asia, Japan. It goes without saying that evidence for the four cases varies considerably. For this reason alone, the following can only be suggestive. Regardless, if the orthodox Protestant case alerts the observer to anything in the following, it would be the profound ambivalence of orthodoxy in the contemporary world. Orthodoxy neither declines nor flourishes in this situation (at least decline and growth are not the most prominent characteristics) but it is transformed all the same. And it is transformed by the tensions inherent in the requirement to accommodate and to resist the structural and cultural constraints of the modern world order. It is to these tensions and to this transformation that the present inquiry looks in each of the following four cases.


## CATHOLICISM AND ORTHODOXY

The Roman Catholic church has undergone such profound changes that a summary is impossible without oversimplification. The most obvious changes over the long term have been changes in its role in the changing world order. From the time when it forged an alliance with the state more than a millennium and half ago to the sixteenth century, its role alternated between being the ideological legitimator of the state and being the actual infrastructure of the state itself. The pope often functioned as the religious equivalent of the emperor; he had control over separate territory, an army, serfs to work the land, and power even to depose secular rulers. The authority of the church in both religious and secular matters, therefore, ranged considerably. On the one hand, its influence was defined by a basic reliance upon traditional beliefs and sentiments deeply rooted in the laity. Beyond that, of course, was a legal-bureaucratic power, based upon a highly developed code of administrative rules and procedures. (Under feudalism, for example, Roman law and administrative procedures served as a model for the development of canon law as well as the church's administrative organization.) In its treatment of infidels, heretics, and schismatics, its authority often extended well beyond these forms to the point of despotic and authoritarian rule. It could be as coercive and as oppressive as the state largely because there was little restraint capable of being imposed on the church, either by popular will or by competing secular authority.

The collapse of the Roman Catholic hegemony began with and was in many ways concomitant with the collapse of medieval society. From the sixteenth to the eighteenth century, the church found itself progressively alienated from an expanding bourgeoisie and from regional monarchs interested in building nation-states. With its own interests tied to a feudal order, the church remained a conservative force. Yet it became increasingly difficult to maintain its hegemony over the masses either through its own raw coercion or through alliances with the state. What authority it did maintain, it maintained through the proliferation and use of disciplined religious orders loyal to Rome, through the co-optation of lay revitalization movements, through the increasing centralization of church authority and law, and through the negotiation of agreements (concordats) with secular political leaders for the regulation of church affairs. It also maintained certain institutional and ideological authority through the education of the young in its expansive control over schools and universities and through the care of the infirm and dispossessed in its monopoly over hospitals and charitable organizations. Yet by the nineteenth and twentieth centuries, even these means failed. It lost the monopoly over educational and welfare institutions, and concordats were nullified or ignored by changing secular authority. What hegemony remained in Europe remained indirectly as a result of an indigenous lay adherence to the authority of the church and through the incorporation of militant lay organizations and congresses (such as Le Sillon, Action

Française, and Action Catholique de la Jeunesse Française in France; Societa della Gioventu Cattolica, the Federation of Catholic Men, and the Italian Federation of Catholic University Students in Italy; and similar organizations in Belgium, Germany, and Ireland) (Vaillancourt 1980).

More recent changes in Roman Catholicism have less to do with its role in the world order as they do with the internal structure and ideology of the church. Since the end of the Second Vatican Council in 1965, enormous changes have taken place. Liturgical and devotional practices which had been institutionalized for many centuries were abandoned. For example, the introduction of the vernacular into the mass began in 1964, and a complete new rite was mandated in 1970. Sentimental and popular "paraliturgies" also disappeared: obligatory abstinence from meat on Fridays ended in 1966, the Lenten discipline of fast and abstinence was dramatically modified and weakened, and long-standing forms of confession were replaced by new forms (Hennesey 1981). An authority structure which had stood since the Counter-Reformation was also fundamentally challenged and changed through the impulse of laicization outside the church hierarchy (symbolized, for example, in the Third World Congress for the Lay Apostolate), demo-cratization within the hierarchy (symbolized in the many national con-ferences of Catholic bishops and the international biennial meeting of the Synod of Bishops), and the cultural redefinition of priest and bishop as servant (Vaillancourt 1980; Varacalli 1983). Profound ideological changes occurred as well. The endorsement of the Ecumenical Move-ment (the Decree on Ecumenism) and the support of religious pluralism and religious toleration (the Declaration of Religious Liberty) in the mid-1960s ended, in principle, roughly sixteen hundred years of church dogma concerning other Christian and non-Christian religious tradi-tions (Hennesey 1981, 311). The "Constantinian" era was over. Impor-tantly, these structural, religious, and ideological changes were roundly endorsed by the Catholic laity, especially in the United States. As public opinion surveys showed, the post–Vatican II church, or "new church," was approved of by a majority. Only a small number of Catholics at the time wanted to return to "the old ways" (Greeley, McCready, and McCourt 1976, 29).

Institutional disaffection in the post–Vatican II period on the part of the American laity is another important trend. Though Catholic support for parochial schools has remained high, both enrollments and numbers of schools have declined significantly from the mid-1960s to the 1980s. Enrollments fell from 5.5 million in 1965 to just above 3 million in 1982. The number of grade schools and high schools declined from

13,290 to 9,432 in the same period.[1] Interestingly the ratio of religious instructors to lay instructors was three to one in 1960 but by 1982 this had reversed—for every three lay teachers there is now only one religious teacher.[2] Likewise the number of Catholic colleges and universities declined from 309 in 1965 to 239 in 1980 (Hennesey 1981, 323). Mass attendance and confessions have also declined from the 1960s to the 1980s, as well as the number of Catholic seminarians (Greeley, McCready, and McCourt 1976). Much of this disaffection had already taken place by the mid-1970s. Thus while between 1975 and 1985 some stabilization had taken place, the Roman Catholic church in the United States had not recovered its losses.

The disaffection of American Catholics from their faith has not only been institutional but it has been personal as well. Here is where the problem of orthodoxy surfaces. The term *orthodoxy* does not apply easily to Catholics. There is no group within the church or subdivision of Catholic experience that calls itself orthodox. Orthodoxy is, in large part, what the church hierarchy defines it to be. If the church hierarchy changes those definitions, orthodoxy changes. For the laity, then, orthodoxy would be defined as loyalty to church teaching on religious, spiritual, and moral matters. The institutional definitions of orthodoxy and orthopraxy have changed, but where do the Catholic laity stand? As defined by Catholic experience, how and in what ways has there been a lay disaffection from orthodoxy?

On the surface one might conclude that there is little disaffection from the church at all—ecclesiastical leadership, from the parish priest to the regional bishop, is still held in high regard by the laity (Greeley, McCready, and McCourt 1976, 34). It would be a mistake, though, to stop there. Favor does not necessarily translate into deep respect. In 1963, 70 percent of all Catholics thought it was "certainly true" that Jesus had turned over the leadership of his church to Peter and the popes. Within a decade that proportion fell to 42 percent. In a 1974 survey of Catholics, only one-third thought that it was "certainly true" that the pope was infallible when he speaks on matters of faith and morals (Greeley, McCready, and McCourt 1976, 32). Other measures are less direct. The percentage of Catholics who would be pleased to have a son become a priest or a daughter become a nun has declined since the 1960s, and sympathy for priests who leave the priesthood remains high (Greeley, McCready, and McCourt 1976, 34). What is more, the number of Catholics believing it is important for Catholics to marry only those of their own faith is less than half of what it was in the early 1960s. In short (as other researchers have pointed out), Catholics remain committed to the church but do not see the church as important for their personal lives; they remain loyal to church authority, yet they are not as certain about the legitimacy of that authority.

This posture toward the church also reflects a posture toward church teaching on religious and moral matters. Tenets that were considered central to Catholic faith are no longer as plausible as they once were to many Catholics (Hoge 1981). This disaffection carries over to church teaching on moral matters as well. In spite of the papal encyclical *Humanae Vitae* (1968) banning artificial birth control, roughly 90 percent of all sexually active American Catholic women in 1982 had used contraception methods unapproved by the church (Sciolino 1984, 40). And though abortion is defined as one of the seven sins punishable by automatic excommunication, 72 percent of all Catholic women would consider abortion under certain circumstances, according to a 1984 survey. While divorce is not considered sinful, remarriage after divorce is. Yet the percentage of Catholics approving of the practice has increased dramatically since the early 1960s. Indeed this is seen in practice. In order for Catholics to legitimately remarry, they must have their previous marriage annulled by the church. In 1967, 700 annulments were granted in the United States, but by 1980 that number had grown to 40,000—83 percent of the annulments granted world-wide (Sciolino 1984, 101). Tolerance of sexual relations before marriage has increased dramatically as well as tolerance of practicing homosexuality.

Curiously this overall defection is not universally condemned by Catholic elites. Indeed some actively encourage it. For example, in a 1982 survey of theologians, virtually all Catholic theologians (96%) condemned abortion as morally wrong. Yet only two-thirds thought it should be against the law. Over one-fourth (28%) of these theologians believed that homosexual relations were either neutral or morally acceptable, 24 percent felt the same way about premarital sexual relations, and 59 percent felt this way about remarriage after divorce.[3] Even those who maintain integrity with official teaching are finding it extraordinarily difficult to reintegrate Catholics disaffected by the "moral rigidity" of the church back into the life of the church. As one priest put it, "We are trying to carry out our ministries with integrity, compassion, and faithfulness to the church's teachings, but in this restrictive atmosphere, it's sometimes not all that easy" (Sciolino 1984, 70).

It is clear from the Protestant case that the modern world order does not merely extract compromise. It can and does evoke its own backlash. Religious revitalization is one important form of backlash. Catholicism itself has not been immune to precisely this form of revitalization. The

Catholic charismatic movement, which began in the late 1960s and peaked around 1978, still numbers more than a half million Catholics (McGuire 1982; Paloma 1982). The movement can be seen in part as an "orthodoxification" within Catholicism; Catholic charismatics are on the conservative side of virtually all moral and religious issues. Orthodoxification in this case has not necessarily meant any new and heightened loyalty to church authority. It does represent an intensified loyalty to ritual truths for which that authority stands. In this sense the renewal may represent "protestantization" as much as it does "orthodoxification." For example, Catholic charismatics maintain a literal reading of Scripture on the historical Pentecost, on the immediacy of God's presence and influence in everyday life for ordinary believers, in the realities of miracles (such as divine healings, exorcisms, prophesies, speaking in tongues), and a literal millenarianism. Experientially they recognize the need for personal conversion (for being saved) and the "baptism in the Holy Spirit" (McGuire 1982, chap. 2). Ritually, they acknowledge the need for confession and absolution. All of these elements are implicit if not explicit in the catechism by which they were taught, but they are amplified and made explicit in their experience. Overall, current Catholic revitalization in the United States has many commonalities with the larger Pentecostal phenomenon and is, indeed, structurally interrelated with it. Even so, the term *protestantization* may go too far, for Catholic charismatics view themselves not as Catholic Evangelicals but as "renewed Catholics," renewed in the "true traditions" of their Catholic faith. In this, the revitalization of Catholicism takes on a uniquely modern quality.

When considering Catholicism as a North American phenomenon, Catholic revitalization here is a small though visible development. Thus far it has had very limited influence both on church structure (except to encourage democratization) and on ritual participation by the wider Catholic community. It is significant in itself, but it has not (yet) altered the fundamental experience of Catholic orthodoxy in the modern world order.

## ORTHODOX JUDAISM

More like Protestantism than Catholicism, Judaism does have a distinct orthodox wing. Also like Protestantism, Orthodox Judaism did not emerge as a distinct "denomination" until the nineteenth century. This is not to say that there were no divisions within Judaism before this time. Indeed vast differences existed along ethnic and religious lines (e.g., the Ashkenazic Jews and the Sephardic Jews of Europe, not to mention Bene

Israel and the Cochin Jews of India, and Jews of southwestern and eastern Asia). What they all shared in common, however, was a deep commitment to classical orthodoxy. Thus traditional Judaism in Europe was an orthodox Judaism, and therefore, the faith the earliest Jewish settlers brought with them to America was also an orthodoxy.

But what of the place of classical Western Judaism in the modern world order? In brief, its legacy is mixed (Sharot 1976; Baron 1967). At one level, as an ethnic and religious minority, it could never begin to compete for political or cultural hegemony at any time. Indeed in early modern Europe, the social and political contexts within which Jewish communities were found varied considerably and changed often. In some situations, Jews were openly tolerated and to some degree integrated in the larger society. In other situations, they suffered tremendous persecution: forced expulsion from cities, forced conversion, and even open and violent oppression. Most commonly, however, they simply endured forced segregation into semiautonomous ethnic ghettos. At another level, though, they played an important role in the emerging world economy. By the late feudal period, Jews had evolved from a people with a wide variety of occupations to a predominantly mercantile and commercial people heavily involved in money trade. Indeed they came to dominate international trade between eastern and western Europe at this time. But their fortunes, both in terms of legal status and economic role, soon declined. Even though slowly displaced by Protestants over the next several centuries, their economic role continued, and thus they contributed to the development of commercial capitalism. All of this is simply to say that the stake of Western Judaism in the modern world order was mixed. Their own fate as a religious people was never exclusively identified with the growth of the modern world order as it was for Protestantism, and yet their varying fortunes have never been unrelated.

At a numerical and institutional level (as opposed to the political and economic levels), the survival of orthodoxy in the contemporary world is another story. The "denominationalizing" of Judaism both in Europe and in America into Orthodox, Conservative, and Reform communities also occurred in the nineteenth century, and like Protestantism it was a distinct response to the challenge of modernity. The Reform Jews were the most accommodationist.[4] They aggressively sought to emancipate Judaism from the ethnic and religious isolation and separation that had long characterized it. Thus they moved away from "excessive ritualism," from theological tenets which were no longer considered viable, and from overt expressions of Jewish nationalism. In this they sought to make the theology and ritual of Judaism more compatible with the intellectual, cultural, and political realities in the post-Enlightenment period. Perhaps its chief impetus though was its desire to broaden the ethical and spiritual vision of Judaism and to share its ethical idealism with all of mankind. Conservative Judaism did not emerge in the United States until the 1880s.[5] It took shape within the Reform movement but was, in fact, a backlash against many of its radical accommodationist policies. In principle they believed that Judaism had always been an evolving and an adaptable faith (and indeed they were committed to theological and ritual innovation), yet they also believed that change should take place slowly, according to biblical and talmudic principles, and always in accordance with the collective will of the Jewish people. Conservatives, in other words, were more traditional in their commitment to the teachings of the Torah and to the practice of Halakah (a body of commandments and laws), yet they could no longer claim to be orthodox. By contrast, the Orthodox Jews remained steadfast in the traditions they had inherited. They claimed to be the "true preserver and guardian" of the Jewish heritage. Out of the nineteenth-century challenge, the Reform movement gained predominance in American Jewry. The Conservative movement followed in strength, and Orthodox Jews found themselves a minority. Thus, for example, only a dozen or so out of the two hundred major congregations in the United States by 1881 remained Orthodox (Spero 1978, 84).

The first surge in the growth of American Judaism generally can be dated to the massive immigrations of Jews from Eastern Europe in the late nineteenth century. While all these denominations were invigorated by the numerical infusion, Orthodoxy benefited least. This was largely because most of these early immigrants and their descendants were more ethnically committed than religiously committed to Jewish tradition.[6] It was not until the 1940s that Orthodoxy was revitalized in this way. A substantial number of relatively militant Orthodox Jews were among the large group of pre– and post–World War II immigrants from Europe. Combined with the small but faithful American-born Orthodox, Orthodoxy surged. After the 1940s Orthodox Jews struggled and succeeded in creating a stable institutional infrastructure. At its heart were the institutions of cultural reproduction—schools. For example, immediately following World War II there were only thirty Orthodox day schools. By 1967 this figure had jumped to 330 (with an enrollment of 67,000), and by 1983 this number had increased to well over 500 with an enrollment of close to 100,000 (Bulka 1983). Not surprisingly (given the Evangelical case) the greatest growth in all Hebrew day schools has been not within the Conservative or Reform camps but in the Orthodox camp. Though perhaps the most important, this is not the only area of institutional growth. As in conservative Protestantism, a number of parallel institutions have emerged since midcentury to serve the Orthodox community: in publishing (e.g., *Jewish Life*, *Tradition*, and *Jewish Observer*), in entertainment (e.g., "Hassidic Rock and Roll"), youth groups (National Conference of Synagogue Youth, B'nai Akiva, Pirchei Agudah, B'nos Agudah, and Binos Chabad), women's organizations (Women's Branch of the Orthodox Union, Mirachi Women, N'shei Agudah, N'shai Chabad, and Emunah Women), and professional organizations (National Association of Orthodox Jewish Teachers and the Association of Orthodox Jewish Scientists), not to mention the almost universal availability of kosher food (including Chinese, French, and Italian kosher cuisine) (Bulka 1983, 7–14). Though many held the opinion around midcentury that Orthodoxy was suffering from severe decay, recent decades of institutional growth belie all such pessimistic predictions.

At present Orthodox Jews in the United States constitute roughly 350,000 people, or about 6% of the larger American Jewish population.[7] This includes the nonobservant and the residual Orthodox. What they all (at least the observant ones) hold in common is a belief in the divine inspiration of the Halakah (Jewish law) as derived from the Torah and Talmud (and explicated by the rabbinic scholars of each generation), a belief that this is uncompromisable and binding for all Jews, and a belief that all Jews should live all of life according to *mitzvot* (religious commandments contained within Halakah). The latter includes strict observance of *Shabbat* (the Sabbath), holy days and festivals, family purity rituals (use of the *mikvah*), *kashrut* (Jewish dietary regulations), attendance at a synagogue with separate sections for men and women and a structure separating them, and many other commandments pertaining to ritual purity. Yet as with Protestantism, Orthodox Judaism is anything but one seamless fabric but is, in fact, a richly diverse population. To understand that diversity is to understand at the *cultural* level Judaism's own varied response to modernity. In other words, the relationship between Judaism generally and modernity (with the Reform wing being most accommodationist and Orthodoxy being most uncompromising) has a parallel within Orthodoxy itself. There are among the Orthodox those who reject modernity in toto. These are the more sectarian Orthodox and include the world of Hassidic Orthodoxy. There are also those who find their faith enhanced when certain elements of modernity are incorporated within it—those known as the "Modern Orthodox." There is also a range that falls in between these two poles.

At one level, these differences stem from the relative degree of strictness with which Halakah is understood and observed. The more traditional and sectarian view every observation of a ritual prohibition as a manifestation of purity—the more strictly one observes these prohibitions, the more committed and authentic is one's faith. The Modern Orthodox are equally committed to Halakah yet see little spiritual significance in adopting the more stringent observances. Authentic faith from this perspective has more to do with a proper relationship with God and a proper attitude toward one's fellow human beings than it does with observance for its own sake. In this sense the Modern Orthodox are often thought to be more lax in their observance of Jewish law than their counterparts on the religious Right, though they view their approach as more "creative" and "flexible." This is reflected, for example, in the range of synagogue practice in Orthodoxy. In the more traditional synagogues, services are informally structured, even spontaneous; and in strict accordance with Halakah, no microphone is used and men and women are separated by a wall so that the women cannot be seen. At the other end of the continuum are synagogues in which microphones are used, the service is more subdued, and men and women worship together or are separated by a partition that is mainly symbolic.[8] Interpretive differences are reflected in other ritual issues as well (Liebman 1965).

The differences between traditional and Modern Orthodoxy go beyond Halakah too. They stem from fundamentally different approaches toward non-Orthodox, indeed, non-Jewish culture.[9] The traditional Orthodox, for example, will not pursue occupations that will disturb halakic observance. Thus of necessity they become employed exclusively in Orthodox institutions (as kosher butchers, ritual slaughterers, yeshiva teachers, scribes, etc.). They avoid secular education at all levels except that which can be justified for making a living. For them, knowledge of anything except the Torah is essentially useless. This attitude carries over to all dealings with the non-Orthodox. Traditional Orthodoxy repudiates Reform and Conservative doctrines and practices as deviations from true religion and thus will avoid any contact with those who represent and advocate those positions. By contrast, the Modern Orthodox will, for the sake of Jewish unity and the promotion of matters of collective concern (i.e., the preservation of Israel), cooperate with Conservative and Reform and even secular Jews as well as Gentiles. They are, in a word, more tolerant of pluralism, such that the term *apikorus* (heretic) is virtually unheard in these circles (Heilman 1982b, 195). They are willing to make compromises with ritual observance in order to pursue an occupation in the secular world and, therefore (implicitly), adopt a very different attitude toward the broader culture (e.g., secular education). The Modern Orthodox view Torah as the necessary basis of a proper religious and moral life; however, it must be rounded out by a wider understanding of created order (i.e., all truth is God's truth). Thus Modern Orthodoxy not only encourages secular learning in the arts and sciences but institutionalizes these within its own educational programs. (Some traditional Orthodox, for example, have condemned Yeshiva College, a bastion of Modern Orthodox higher learning, for possessing books in its library that were written by nonbelievers.) It is not surprising then that the Modern Orthodox also find many contemporary social issues such as political intolerance, changing sexual mores, feminism, and the women's movement all intellectually problematic. Orthodoxy, it is felt, must deal with these issues directly. (Gittelson 1984).[10]

In short, Orthodox Jews differ in the degree of separatism they develop between themselves and the non-Orthodox world. This cultivates still other tensions. The radical separatism and isolationism within the more sectarian wing of Orthodoxy allow these Jews to live within a highly integrated world, a world that is largely unproblematic. Because traditional Jewish theology sees no difference between a sacred and a secular realm, traditionalists feel they are being truer to Jewish ideals of faith and practice. The lack of separatism on the part of the Modern Orthodox, in contrast, forces them to compartmentalize their lives into Jewish and non-Jewish realms. This dualism necessarily fosters a de facto inconsistency which is not only formally incompatible with halakic principles but is personally problematic for many as well. Whether or not this dualism is sustainable over time or to the next generation, it is nonetheless a fact of their existence.

The ideological divisions within Orthodoxy both cause and are a function of social class. The Modern Orthodox are well entrenched within a highly educated, American middle class (and have experienced tremendous upward social mobility since the mid-1960s), while the social position of the traditional Orthodox remains lowest among all Jews. Social class, however, does anything but explain away the differences. Indeed many of these ideological debates within Orthodoxy stand above contemporary social structural configurations. They have been intense from the beginning of the nineteenth century and have existed in some form at least since the fourteenth century (Heilman 1982a, 1982b, 194–96; Spero 1978, 95). The crux of the issue is that these ideological differences are relevant to fewer and fewer people. This can be put in different terms.

As an orthodoxy, Orthodox Judaism has always been on guard against pressure to change the substance of its beliefs or the practice of its rituals. Compromise of any sort to the pressures of modern culture is flatly unacceptable. Notably the efforts to maintain the doctrinal and ritual integrity of Orthodoxy have been very successful. Within traditional Orthodoxy anyway, Halakah has been successfully "frozen." (Indeed, some Hassidic communities will informally compete over which can be stricter in observance.) The experience of these Jews is, for all practical purposes, identical with the religious experience of Eastern and Western European Jews of the eighteenth and early nineteenth centuries. Even the styles of clothing and adornment have not changed appreciably. Yet while Orthodoxy remains frozen in these circles, there are fewer and fewer Jews who find this faith practical or plausible. If Orthodoxy, in all of its diversity, was normative for most if not all Jews two centuries ago, now it is normative for a progressively smaller minority.

In one sense the disaffection is a generational phenomenon. The greatest part of Orthodox Judaism is made up of first-generation Americans. Similarly, most Conservative Jews are second-generation and most Reform Jews are third-generation (or more) Americans (Liebman 1983b, 107–9). There are exceptions to this rule, of course—first-generation Reform Jews and third-generation Orthodox Jews. Overall, however, the pattern holds. What is more, Orthodoxy boasts the oldest population in Judaism. Yet demographically the Jewish community in America is increasingly made up of a native American population. The immigration of foreign-born Orthodox Jews has declined rapidly. In this light it is hardly surprising that the number of Jews nationally who consider themselves Orthodox declined from 11 percent in 1970–1971 to 6 percent in 1981–1982 (Himmelfarb and Loar 1984, 150).

The disaffection with traditional Orthodoxy is a cultural phenomenon as well. Modern Orthodoxy, which numerically dominates Orthodoxy as a whole, is openly syncretistic.[11] As such, it unwittingly is engaged in a process whose outcome is a redefinition of Orthodoxy itself. Notably they have been unsuccessful at legitimating their approach to Orthodox faith to their counterparts to the Right. This is largely because they can legitimate their approach only through a philosophical logic that exists outside Jewish law proper (Liebman 1983b, 110–12). It operates without a well-articulated theological and halakic justification.[12]

As with conservative Protestantism and Catholicism, Orthodox Judaism also experienced a certain revitalization in the early to mid-1980s.[13] Most dramatically this is seen in the Baalei Teshuvah, a movement of secular and non-Orthodox Jews who have "returned" to Orthodox Judaism.[14] However small the movement may be and whatever its cultural style, it still represents something of a reversal of the demographic tendencies that haunt Orthodoxy. A second reason for optimism is that Orthodox Jews have been bearing more children than Jews of any other denomination (G. Helson 1984). There is also some reason to believe that the younger Orthodox are better able to successfully pass on their faith (without defection) to their children. Thus the high birthrate may promote some numerical growth of Orthodoxy in the future.

Though there is some reason for optimism, such optimism remains guarded. After all, the number of Baalei Teshuvah has been too small (thus far) to replace the losses of a dying generation of older Orthodox. Moreover, though birthrates may favor the Orthodox, any real numerical stability or growth is still a generation away from being realized. There remains ample reason for concern about the fate of Orthodox Judaism in the modern world order.

## ISLAM

In Islam, of course, one moves to a georeligious phenomenon (stretching from northern Africa to Indonesia, and from the Middle East to the Soviet Union and China), where economic, political, and cultural modernization (to the degree that they exist) are not indigenous but externally introduced. This in itself would fundamentally alter the nature of the encounter between religion and the modern world order, yet there are qualities, unique to Islam, which independently affect its own fate (or fates) in this encounter.

In Islam there is no distinction between orthodox and non-orthodox camps. The most one can say is that there are different orthodoxies, with Sunni, Shiite, and Sufi being the most important. These orthodoxies are not distinguished so much by belief. All Muslims believe in an all-powerful, all-knowing God; in the divine inspiration and integrity of the Koran, as revealed to the Prophet Muhammad, and the Sunna, the accepted practices and beliefs of the community of believers; in the authority of the sharia, Islamic law derived from the Koran and the Sunna; and in the spiritual importance of the "five pillars" (bearing witness, praying, alms giving, fasting, and making pilgrimage) among other ritual practices. What differences do exist have more to do with rights of succession, political theory and organization, and religious experience.[15]

Within Islam, then, there is only one truth, yet the word *orthodoxy* as applied to Islam needs some qualification. In many ways the word is entirely inappropriate for it places the emphasis on the cognitive side of faith—on correct doctrine. The theological component articulating the relationship between God and human beings is essential to Islam, clearly, yet the theological priority is not on correct doctrine but on correct behavior. The word *sunni* in Arabic is better translated "orthoprax" than "orthodox." It is not surprising then that the word *islam* means "submission" and the word *muslim* means "those who submit to the will of Allah." This priority takes concrete expression in the strict conformance to sharia, the total body of legal doctrine governing the life of a Muslim and of the Muslim community. It defines the divinely intended way man should relate to both God and other men. As in all religions, however, behavior has consequences. The spiritual consequences, of course, are eternal paradise or punishment. There are social consequences too. Disobedience, it is believed, spawns dissension and chaos in the community and in society; collective obedience can bring about nothing short of the kingdom of God on earth.

In this light, the community, or *ummah*, takes on spiritual significance. The relationship is dialectical. The spiritual fate of the individual Muslim is directly tied to the spiritual health of the community, and the historical destiny of the community depends directly on the moral righteousness of the individual Muslim. Their futures are linked.[16]

In this sense, history as well is endowed with religious meaning. There is a design to history. Through Islam, history is being redeemed; it is moving progressively toward Paradise. Though this is the collective responsibility of the people of Islam, the individual Muslim will be judged for his personal contribution toward bringing about this end. Neither the individual nor the group must deviate from the path, and it is the special responsibility of the religious leadership—religious and legal scholars (*ulama*), preachers (*mullah*), and the leaders of public prayer (*immam*)—to see that they do not.

The radical unity of all of life and belief is perhaps the important distinctive of Islam. Individual faith and practice and the institutions of the community (not least the political, educational, and familial institutions) are bound together in a sacred destiny. Any deviation at any level represents a denial of that historical redemption.

All of this is central to understanding the encounter of Islam with the modern world order. As one historian of Islam put it, "the fundamental malaise of modern Islam is a sense that something has gone wrong with Islamic history" (Smith 1957, 41). Early Islamic history, of course, was marked by tremendous success. The community of believers expanded numerically, grew in geopolitical dominance, and prospered in their cultural and religious accomplishments. In its first five centuries it established a new and vibrant civilization. It was as though Allah was confirming the truth of the Islamic vision within history itself. Yet this "classical" age eventually came to an end. The first major crisis came in the thirteenth century with the Mongol invasion and the collapse of the growing Muslim dynasty. Curiously, as disastrous as this was for Islamic civilization and the Islamic view of its own destiny, the event slowly translated into a victory for the Islamic cause. Within fifty years after the Mongol dynasty had subjugated the Islamic world, the conquerers had themselves become converted to Islam (Smith 1957, 34). The most important consequence of this was a revitalization and expansion of Arab civilization in its medieval period (Hodgson 1974, especially book 5). This allowed Muslims to reinterpret this crisis as occurring within the divine pattern of historical development. This has not been possible for Muslims in the face of the second major crisis to confront Islam: the confrontation with the modern world order. Something *has* gone awry for Islamic history, and there is a pervasive confusion over how to salvage that history and even fundamental doubt as to whether that history can be salvaged at all.

The confrontation with modernity is not an abstract phenomenon but can be discussed in terms of concrete historical events (Hodgson 1974, 274–76; Smith 1957, 58–59; Voll 1982, 87–110). It began most visibly in the seventeenth and eighteenth century with the expansion of Western capitalist economics into the Middle East, Mongol India, and the Ottoman Empire. By the end of the eighteenth century, various Western powers had established direct economic, political, and military control over much of that region and virtual hegemony over the rest of that region as a result of their deep economic, technological, and intellectual dependence on the West. This was true in Indonesia (in the case of the Dutch), Iran (in the case of the Russians), India (in the case of the British), and northern Africa and the Ottoman Empire (in the case of the French and British). Among other things, what European hegemony meant was the introduction of radical political and administrative reform and the subjugation of Islamic culture and ideals to Western traditions of rationalism, secularism, and dualism. Muslim society had indeed lost control over its collective destiny.

This situation evoked a variety of responses, but two of the most significant were adaptationism and militant conservatism. These responses have existed concurrently since the end of the eighteenth century, though each has been predominant at different times.

The adaptationist impulse in modern Islam has been seen at different levels. At one level it has simply meant political reform in the form of administrative centralization, the development of constitutional or parliamentary procedure, the formulation of a civil code, and the elaboration of a new legal and judicial system. In practical terms this meant a loss of power by the *ulama* and the obsolescence of the caliphate/sultanate. (Turkey is exemplary here.) At another level it meant the modernization of the military and of the mode of production and economic exchange. Adaptationism though always implied some form of ideological liber-

alization. These reformist ideologies express themselves as an advocacy—either to synthesize European and Islamic civilization or else
(more typically) to incorporate elements of Western experience into the
Islamic experience and, overall, to remain true to the Islamic heritage.
Common to all liberal ideologies was the belief in the need to "reopen the
gates of *ijtihad*" (interpretation)—to reinterpret the Scriptures in order
to adapt Islam to the requirements of the modern age. Since the eleventh
century the gates of *ijtihad* had been "closed" because it was believed that
all possible questions of interpretation had been answered and that no
one after this time had the spiritual or intellectual credentials to engage in
genuine *ijtihad*. But the confrontation with the modern West brought
about new contingencies the ancient *mujtahids* (or legal scholars) could
not have foreseen. With the gates open many advocated a new interpretation of the holy writings. Though the basic theological doctrines of Islam
were never directly challenged, other peripheral teachings of the Koran
were reinterpreted as largely symbolic and metaphorical in nature (Smith
1957, 66). This laid the groundwork for a new (and relativistic) view of
history and of correct living. It also allowed Islamic theology to legitimate scientific and technological rationality as wholly compatible with
the designs of Allah.[17]

Liberal reform, and thus adaptationism, formed a dominant ideological and public policy tendency in most Muslim countries from the
mid-nineteenth century to the early decades of the twentieth century. It
was in this period that major realignments in educational policy, economic development, political structure, and legal administration took
place. Yet this historical movement was short-lived. On the one hand, the
ground was never fertile enough to allow the roots of a formal adaptationist ideology and policy to grow too deeply.[18] On the other, there
were strong social and ideological movements running counter to these
currents which soon gained predominance. This was the militant and
fundamentalist reaction to Western modernity.

Protests against the internal "deterioration" of Islam and its external
encroachment by Western imperial powers were the initial reaction of
Islam in the modern age. The Wahhabi movement (Arabia), the Waliyul-
lah movement (India), the Sansusi movement (Libya), the Madhi movement (Sudan), and Sarekat Islam (Indonesia) among others were all
eighteenth- and nineteenth-century efforts to bring about purification
and revitalization in the face of these changes. (Smith 1957, 52) Fundamentalist reaction though also surfaced in the *wake* of the failure of
nineteenth-century and early-twentieth-century liberalism. Such groups
as al-Ikhwan al-Muslimun (the Muslim Brotherhood), Jund al-Rahman
(Soldiers of God), Jamaat al-Muslmun (the Muslim Group), Shabab

Mohamed (Muhammad's Youth), al-Takfir wa al-Hijra (Repentance and Holy Flight), and al-Jihad (Holy War) were just a few of the twentieth-century manifestations of the same impulse. The difference between early fundamentalism and the neofundamentalism of the twentieth century is that the former was a conservative movement grounded deeply in traditional Islamic learning in jurisprudence and theology, while the latter is more a reactionary movement for those with little traditional education (Rahman 1981, 23–35). The activists in the latter movement also tend to be young adults (twenties to thirties) from modest-income families rooted in small-town or rural areas who have migrated to the cities to pursue secular education (engineering, medicine, pharmacy, etc.) (Ibrahim 1984). The activists are, in other words, individuals who have, in their own lives, experienced serious disjunctions between the old order of Islam and the new world of secular modernity.

There is ideological variation, of course, in neo-Islamic militancy, yet the common passion of all neofundamentalist groups is to recover the classical experience of Islam (a history without deviation) and the original meaning of the Islamic message (a faith without distortion). *Ijtihad* is also an important issue for them. As a reactionary phenomenon, though, *ijtihad* has taken on a negative quality defined by an ethic of rejection—a rejection principally of indigenous Islamic liberalism and Western secular rationality.

Liberal adaptationism and fundamentalist militancy are only two of the more prominent responses of Islam to the challenges of Western modernity. One can also observe liberal and radical secularism, Islamic socialism, and moderate conservatism as still other responses. (Voll 1982, 149–347) Making simple summary even more difficult is the fact that most of these responses have been fused, to various degrees, with nationalistic and/or pan-Islamic movements and ideologies (themselves a certain response to the modern world order). The challenge of the past two and a half centuries of Western hegemony in the world order has left a deep imprint on the traditions of Islam. There is yet another way in which this is true.

As we have seen, one of the institutional innovations created by national development is the division of social life into public and private spheres. For religion this means being faced with extraordinary pressure to be relegated to the private sphere. Faith becomes a personal matter; religion adopts an individualistic style. The public spheres of government, economics, law, education, and the like are freed from the influence of religious institutions and symbols. To the extent that Western modernity has encroached upon the Islamic countries, Islam has had to face this challenge as well. All of the Islamic world has had to deal with this reality, though these tendencies have gone furthest in such countries as Turkey, Egypt, and Tunisia.

One area in which this tension is reflected is in the area of education. Education in most Muslim countries is divided between modern (national) schools and traditional (Islamic) schools. Not only do these reflect different curricula, but they reflect different and competing world views as well (Esposito 1982, 132). Yet where the pressures of privatization create the greatest tension in the case of Islam is in the area of "family law." As a body of legal doctrine, it requires the technical knowledge of legal experts and the sanctioning of the state. In its substance though, it impinges on the most personal areas of private life. Because family law bridges both public and private realms, the tensions are, indeed, great.

Accommodation in this situation has meant a separation of traditional religious and political authority from the family. Its most visible consequence has been the development of various ideologies and policies of reform surrounding family organization and women's rights.[19] The provision of legal grounds for divorce to women, the discouragement of hasty (male-initiated) divorces, the restrictions on polygamy and on child marriages, rights of inheritance for lineal descendants, the financial maintenance of divorced women, the formal encouragement of education and social participation for women, and the redefinition of "man's priority over women" are the most prominent policies being advocated.

Although the public/private dichotomization and its attendant privatization have been an important source of reform in nineteenth- and twentieth-century Islam, they have also been a source of sectarian backlash as well. Such dualism is explicitly contrary to the Islamic sense of history, identity, and destiny. Movements to create an Islamic theocratic state are simply symptomatic of the effort to do away with that dualism. The abandonment of Western costume in favor of *al-ziyy al-shari*, or lawful dress (for women), is another (Williams 1980, 71–86).

Either through accommodation or through militant reaction to the rationality and structural differentiation of the modern world order, the traditions of Islam emerge as something different from what they were before the confrontation. This is obviously the case in Islamic adaptationism but it is also true in Islamic fundamentalism. In the latter case, certain religious principles are exaggerated and given a prominence heretofore unknown in Islamic tradition such that in some cases the traditions are altered dramatically. (In contemporary Egypt, for example, veiling and *shari* take a different form than they did in traditional Egypt; Williams 1980, 76). In any event, the cultural and historical dilemma Islam has experienced in its confrontation with the modern world order has already been deep and profound. As Islam faces the future it will undoubtedly continue to know this ambivalence.


## BUDDHISM

Like Islam, Buddhism spans an enormous part of the world (including India, China, Korea, Japan, and other countries in Southeast Asia) where economic, political, and cultural modernization are not indigenous but have been imposed from the outside. As with Islam, there is a perplexing unevenness in the extent to which the modern world order has made inroads in countries in the Buddhist orbit. Yet the variation is even wider in the latter case. While Islam cannot boast of a country that is an equal economic and political competitor with the West, at least one country in the Buddhist georeligious sphere does qualify: namely, Japan. It is Japanese Buddhism that will be the focus here. The significance of the Japanese case is that it is here where the encounter between this world religion and modernity has gone furthest. In contemporary Japan, an enormous portion of the population still considers itself Buddhist (though, as will become clear, this means something very different from what it would in the West).

Buddhism (of the Mahayana tradition) was imported from India through China and Korea in the sixth century.[20] Its initial appeal was not as a popular religion but as a religion for the ruling elite of Japan. It gained acceptance among the leading families within the court and finally by the state itself and within two centuries it had come to overshadow Shinto and other expressions of Japanese folk religion. From the earliest centuries of its presence in Japan, Buddhism was not a monolithic faith but one highly varied. In the Nara period (710–784), for example, at least six philosophical schools of Buddhism were recognized by the state. It achieved further (and uniquely Japanese) elaborations in the Heian period (794–1185) (e.g., in the flourishing of the Tendai and Shingon sects) and in the Kamakura period (1185–1333) (e.g., in the expansion of the Pure Land sects, the Nicheren sect, and the Zen sects). It was only in the Kamakura period that Buddhism was translated into a popular religion. This was in large part due to its association with rituals for the dead: from funeral rituals to regular family rituals surrounding the veneration of ancestors, including the enshrinement of memorial tablets on the family Buddhist altar. In this way Buddhism evolved more toward an otherworldly faith which could ensure bliss after death and peace for departed ancestors than as a body of ethical prescriptions oriented toward the present world.

One of the most important realities for an understanding of contemporary Buddhism in the modern world is its relation to other religions. From its first introduction, Buddhism coexisted with shamanistic forms of folk religion (Shinto), religious Taoism, and Confucianism. With the exception of a few Buddhist sects (notably Jodo Shin and Nicheren) none of these maintained exclusive rights on religious truth. As such, centuries of religious pluralism existed with only infrequent incidents of antagonism and intolerance. All contributed without contradiction to a common concern for ancestor worship and the religious support of the state.

Though Buddhism coexisted with other formal and informal religions, it gained in prominence and influence in the feudal order of early Japan. With the establishment of the shogunate in the Tokugawa period (1600–1868), Buddhism for all intents and purposes became the state religion. The government, in its efforts to unify the country, gained control over all the Buddhist sects and temples, transformed priests into government functionaries, and required all families to belong to a temple and to register all births and deaths with that temple. Buddhism thus became tied to the state as an important means of legitimation and social control. Buddhism both benefited and suffered from this alliance. Institutionally, Buddhism profited from the infusion of government funds into temple maintenance and restoration. Yet much of its popular vitality as a religious faith over these two and a half centuries was lost.

The beginning of modernization in Japan is associated with the decline of Buddhism as a state religion and popular religious ideology. The Tokugawa period was conservative, resisting all forms of political and cultural change, particularly those imported from the West. With the Meiji Restoration (beginning in 1868) and the reopening of Japan to the West, Buddhism was formally disestablished and was replaced by a nationalistic form of Shinto (a so-called nonreligion) as the state cult. After a brief period of anti-Buddhist iconoclasm associated with the effort to "purify Shinto," Buddhism came to occupy much the same place it did in the Tokugawa era: mainly concerned with ancestral rites and politically subservient to the state. Traditional Buddhism essentially maintained this posture to the end of the nineteenth century. Indeed, in the twentieth century the inner vitality of traditional Buddhism continued to wane such that many scholars have felt justified in declaring Buddhist teaching and practice virtually defunct, with Buddhist temples being little more than "funeral parlors."

Thus far, the nature of Japanese Buddhism and its encounter with the modern world order have been considered only in the most general and institutional sense. The relationship has clearly been much more complex than this. At this point, though, our interest is more cultural than institutional. What has been the consequence of this encounter in terms of the substance of Buddhist faith?

The Buddhist case is particularly important because it is so distinct from Protestantism, Catholicism, Judaism, and Islam. The traditions of Buddhism show absolutely no common heritage with the other orthodoxies. There is little in the traditions of Buddhism that is even similar to the other faiths. For one, it is not a monotheistic faith but a faith which maintains (at least in the Mahayana tradition) a place for demigods called *bodhisattvas* (saints or quasi divinities who have achieved enlightenment but who postpone entering the final bliss in order to assist those living who are still struggling to achieve enlightenment).[21] Buddhism, like other Asian religions, is also "immanentist" in contrast to the "transcendentalist" nature of the other global orthodoxies. This is to say that where the others posit the locus of the sacred in an omniscient and omnipotent spiritual being, Buddhism posits the locus of the sacred in nature and in the souls of human beings both alive and dead.[22] A third distinctive is the fact that in Buddhism there is no such thing as "orthodoxy" (at least as understood in a conventional Western sense). There are, to be sure, one or two sects which attempt to propagate a "pure faith," but these are the exception and not the rule. In most traditional expressions of Buddhism there simply are no correct creedal positions, no absolute doctrinal points, and no final and exact set of ritual practices that must be followed to achieve salvation. It is for this reason that Buddhists can boast of a long heritage of toleration of other religious traditions. It is also for this reason that Buddhists can call themselves adherents of Shinto and practitioners of Confucian ethics without any sense of hypocrisy or contradiction. At least the last two of these distinctives (its immanentist character and its lack of an orthodox creedal orientation) are shared with other East Asian religions. In some ways the experience of Japanese Buddhism may be paradigmatic for the others.

Given these unique qualities, how has Buddhism as a cultural system fared in the modern world order? An appropriate starting point is the pluralism and pluralistic tolerance which, from all appearances, inheres within the religious traditions in central and eastern Asia. While Japanese Buddhism has always existed within a pluralistic situation, before the Meiji Restoration it was pluralism of a particular sort. The diversity of religious traditions was "balanced" in a relatively stable pattern.[23] The various faiths existed within certain circumscribed boundaries and were subject to specific cultural rules (the most important of these being that each contributed to the *wa*, or "harmony," of Japan). In this way Buddhism did not and could not become a monopoly. All imported faiths (including Buddhism, Confucianism, and even early "Kirishitan"

[Christianity] were simply "Japanized."[24] In this a special kind of cultural homogeneity emerged, one based upon syncretism.

Modernity has upset that traditional pluralistic balance. There have been other times in which the balance was challenged, of course. The first introduction of Christianity in the sixteenth century was such a time. When the impact of Christianity and the West became too strong, threatening to upset that balance (in the early seventeenth century), Christianity was expelled and the country was closed. The balance was restored—that is, at least until the end of the Tokugawa period. With the reopening of the country during the Meiji Restoration, the traditional pluralism was displaced by a new and unsettling form of pluralism, one incorporating alien (Western, mainly) cultural traditions. The fervent nationalism embodied in Shrine Shinto leading up to World War II inhibited, in part, the full expression of this new pluralism. Yet with the end of the war and the disestablishment of Shrine Shinto, the grounds for Japan's incorporation into the modern world order were fully established.

But what have these developments meant for the cultural system of Japanese Buddhism? A decline in classical Buddhist teaching and ritual practice in the twentieth century has already been noted, but this does not really address the question. At the cultural level there has been some change. At one level, it is seen in a certain privatization of faith. Buddhism, in contemporary Japan, has increasingly come to reflect the modern reality that faith is a matter of individual conscience and decision. Related to this is the relatively novel ethical theme, implicit in twentieth-century Buddhism, of the unique value of the "individual person" (Swyngedouw 1976). All of this is extraordinary when one remembers that Japanese Buddhism has always been, at heart, a family religion. This implies an expanding freedom from the pressures to conform to traditional community expectations. These tendencies are also reinforced by geographic and social mobility and the change from the traditional two- and three-generation household to the nuclear family.

To the degree that Buddhism as a cultural system is no longer institutionally supported by extended families, local communities, and national ideologies, it loses much of its specifically Japanese identity.[25] To this degree, traditional Buddhism in Japan has been free to "rediscover" its heritage as a "universal" religion. The ethic of "the oneness of all humanity" has been especially prominent in the classical sects of Zen and Jodo Shinshu.[26] In these sects a universal humanism has evolved; in some quarters it has been actively pursued. A "Common Buddhism," free from the constraints of any particular sect, would seek to bring enlightenment to all individuals by awakening them to their true self and their place within human history. Indeed, the ideological thrust of some of these groups has been broadly ecumenical.

Still another area of accommodation at the cultural level entails certain alterations in ancestor worship (Smith 1974; Yanagawa and Yoshiya 1978). Though the rituals still remain nominally associated with Buddhism, the explicit role of Buddhism in ancestor worship has declined. The religious quality of ancestor worship has, in short, diminished. But another way in which the meaning of these rituals has changed concerns the focus of worship. Compatible with changes in the Japanese family, there are signs that ancestor worship is experiencing a shift from a household-centered tradition to a nuclear-family-centered tradition, where even one's deceased parents are defined and venerated as ancestors (Smith 1974, 174, 220–21).

As in the other orthodoxies reviewed, Buddhism's confrontation with the modern world order has not only generated accommodation within the traditions as well as ritual decline, but has simultaneously spawned an impulse of spiritual renewal. The "new religions" of Japan are the most prominent expression of this. Indeed, the vitality of these new religions has been such that one scholar has wondered whether modernization has "contributed less to Japanese 'secularization' than to its opposite" (Eger 1980, 21).

Revitalization within Japanese religion can be traced back into the early to mid–nineteenth century; however, most of these movements did not generate large popular support until after World War II (McFarland 1967, Murakami 1980). This is true for Japanese Buddhism as well. The relationship between their emergence and later flourishing and Japan's experience in the modern world order (as discussed here) is not coincidental but is a response to modernity.[27] In any case, their growth in the postwar period has been remarkable, with up to 15 percent of the Japanese population having become affiliated with at least one of the movements (Eger 1980; 18).[28]

The largest and most active of the Buddhist movements are Reiyukai Kyodan, Rissho Koseikai, and Soka Gakkai, all three based upon the teachings of the Lotus sutra. The most prominent among these, however, is Soka Gakkai. Through the 1970s it was considered to be the fastest growing religious movement in Japan if not the entire East. But if not the largest, it has been the most politically active and powerful, with its Komeito party (or Clean Government party) being by the late 1960s the third largest political force in Japan's National Diet.

Although Soka Gakkai has an interesting story of its own, for the present purposes it simply is representative of a larger phenomenon which, at least in part, can be understood as a cultural response to modernity. Not unlike the revitalization movements in the other orthodoxies, revitalization here is not simply a reassertion of classical forms of Buddhism. There is, rather, a curious blend of the traditional and modern. Even in the new religious movements of Japan (not least those in Japanese Buddhism) a modern form of individualism is apparent (Davis 1977).[29] The voluntaristic nature of membership and recruitment is just one measure of this. And though localism and Japanese nationalism are evident in many of these movements, there is a prominent universalist quality in their cultural systems as well. Their spiritual world is principally *hitogami* (individualist/universalist) as opposed to *ujigami* (clan/territorial) in nature (Hambrick 1974; Iwao 1976). In short, in both the traditional and newer manifestations of Buddhism, the cultural meaning of Buddhist faith and practice emerges as something different from what it was before the encounter with the modern world order.

## In Search of a Paradigm

Even from this fairly superficial review it becomes clear (as anticipated) that the experience of conservative Protestantism in America is not paradigmatic for other orthodoxies facing the modern world order. At any level of specificity such a paradigm probably does not exist. One reason why it is impossible to speak of a "model" has to do with what makes up orthodoxy. Apart from the enormous differences in the substance of these faiths, the *criteria* which define orthodoxy for these religious traditions vary considerably. For Protestants it is defined principally by cognitive (belief) criteria. For Catholics it is defined largely by loyalty to church teaching; for Orthodox Jews it is defined mainly by commitment to Torah and to the community which upholds it; in Islam it is defined principally by behavioral criteria, that is, by conformance to sharia, though, of course, adherence to the teaching of Islamic tradition is also important; and finally, in Buddhism (if orthodoxy exists at all) it is defined in a plurality of ways by the various philosophical schools and sects, but mainly in devotional terms. Another reason is that their encounter with modern political and cultural history has differed so greatly: from faiths that came to be associated with the expansion of the modern world order to faiths that have known economic and political development only after they have been introduced from the outside. The stake that each of these traditions has in the modern world order, then, varies widely. For these reasons alone, specific comparisons become impossible.

Yet, one would be coarse and insensitive if one did not notice some parallels. In each case there appears to be a dialectic operating at the cultural level. The dialectic is between an accommodation to and a rejection of modernity. In some cases this interplay divides the communities of faith; in other cases both tendencies exist simultaneously within the religious and cultural system. Whether accommodation or rejection, though, the cultural order of an orthodoxy undergoes changes. As Samuel Heilman put it, the traditions of orthodoxy are "worked-through."[30] The term is borrowed from psychoanalysis and refers to a process in which an individual (ego) confronts his resistances and, in so doing, learns to accept what he formerly repressed. The individual may still act the same way he did before this process, but now his actions are the result of deliberate choice rather than habit. In the same way, those who hold to one of the various orthodoxies, if they want to repeat the patterns of life and faith of their parents, must exert a much greater effort than their parents. The contemporary world has undermined the taken-for-grantedness of the traditions. As such the traditions are *reinterpreted* to make sense of the present, and the present is made comprehensible in traditional ways. In this way, the traditions come to mean something different from what they had meant to previous generations of believers.

Of course, it is improbable that other orthodoxies facing the modern world order will be "worked-through" in the particular ways that conservative Protestantism has in twentieth-century America. Still the *process* in which orthodox Protestantism has been worked-through and the general direction this process is taking may say much about what is taking place in the other orthodoxies. In this very broad sense the Evangelical case may be paradigmatic.

In all of this is implied a somewhat new approach to the very old question about the fate of religion in the modern world. At one level it suggests that all theoretical interpretations which seek to answer this question in terms of a generic conception of religion (i.e., the "decline of religion" or the "persistence of religion") are inadequate from the start. While certain generalizations are possible (and, indeed, should be made), there are limits to what one can say summarily. This is for two reasons. One reason, of course, is that modernity means different things in different contexts. Structurally, it asserts itself differently in various national and regional contexts. And, just as important, the various indigenous cultures interpret the significance of modernity in divergent ways. The other reason comes more directly to the point: the unique characteristics of *each* belief system play an active part in determining the outcome. Religion, then, is not simply a "dependent variable" but is dialectically related as a cultural system to the structures of the modern world order—determining, in part, its own fate. The question, then, must first be answered in the context of individual cases before broader generalizations are made.[31]

Another way in which this approach departs from previous theory concerns the level of analysis. Earlier work concerned with this question viewed religion in either structural terms, behavioral terms, or in social-psychological terms. As a result the answer to the question, "what happens to religion in the modern world?" came out in three different ways depending on how one viewed religion. For those who viewed religion in structural or institutional terms, religion was declining because the power and influence of church structures in advanced societies were declining.[32] For those who viewed religion mainly in behavioristic terms, modernity seemed to have little effect on religion because public opinion surveys showed that people were going to church, praying, being married in churches, going to Bible studies, etc., just as much if not more than they used to.[33] For those who viewed religion in social-psychological terms (as a subjective state or a matter of consciousness) national development had an ambivalent effect. It eroded the plausibility of traditional religious beliefs but it did not take away the need to believe in something (Berger, 1967a).

In this book the focus of analysis has been mainly on religion as a *cultural system*—as a set of symbols, rules, codes, and reality definitions. The concern at this level of analysis is the changing meanings of certain symbols and cultural codes. One advantage to viewing religion this way is that it allows one to see, more clearly perhaps, the subtleties of shift and response—the dialectic if you will—involved in the relation between religion and the modern world order. Religion, from this vantage point, does not simply decline; nor does it merely persist as it always had. In some ways it incorporates both tendencies. Religion continues to exist but it is transformed. The traditions come to mean something different than they did for previous generations of the faithful. And how it is transformed has as much to do with the character of orthodoxy as it does with the structure of modernity in a national context. In pursuing this strategy, one does not have to sacrifice an empirically oriented research program. In fact it would seem that one would be enjoined to be even more close to the empirical realities one seeks to interpret than other strategies. The reason is plain. Though cultural meanings are objectified in empirically available artifacts, they cannot readily be conceptually reduced into third- and fourth-order abstractions (i.e., mathematical models, which are often an excuse for careful empirical research). One must remain close to the sources in order to understand the subtleties of change and response.

Clearly this is not the only way of answering the question of religion in the modern world. Any thorough treatment of the subject would, of course, need to include all levels of analysis. Still the cultural approach is an important approach that has all but been ignored in theoretical and empirical research.[34] It offers a promising perspective, not only for what more it can tell us about this relationship, but for its potential to lead intellectual debate about the subject out of its current stalemate (i.e., secularization versus persistence).

Because this approach allows one to see the interactive quality of the relationship between religion and the world-historical reality of modernity, one can see that the question of the fate of religion in the modern context will probably never be answered once and for all. There will always be new mutations, shifts, accommodations, and reactions both in religious systems and in the structures of the modern world order. On this question, the future undoubtedly holds many surprises.

# Appendix
# The Study

The principal source of data upon which this book rests comes from a research project entitled the Evangelical Academy Project (EAP). The project was initiated in the autumn of 1981, and data collection took place in the spring and autumn of 1982, the spring of 1983, and the winter of 1985. Funding for this research came from several small grants: one from the Society for the Scientific Study of Religion, one from the Lilly Endowment through the Institute for the Study of American Evangelicalism, another from Westmont College in Santa Barbara, California, and finally one in the form of a summer faculty research grant from the University of Virginia.

It will be apparent at this point that the project was, in fact, split into two major parts: a college survey and a seminary survey. In the autumn of 1982, a third survey was conducted: the college questionnaire was distributed to a sample of students attending a large public university in California. In early 1985 a fourth survey oriented toward assessing the attitudes of college faculty was conducted at the nine institutions of the college survey. A brief description of these surveys follows.

## THE COLLEGE SURVEY

Data collection for the college survey began in the early spring of 1982. Nine of the thirteen member colleges of the Christian College Consortium were invited to participate in the survey: Wheaton College (Wheaton, Illinois), Gordon College (Wenham, Massachusetts), Westmont College (Santa Barbara, California), Bethel College (St. Paul, Minnesota), Houghton College (Houghton, New York), Seattle-Pacific University (Seattle, Washington), George Fox College (Newberg, Oregon), Taylor University (Upland, Indiana), and Messiah College (Grantham, Pennsylvania). All of these institutions, as members of the Christian College Consortium, are private liberal arts colleges committed to "the ideals of Christian education," that is, "to integrating the Christian faith with the academic disciplines and with daily life for students, faculty and administrators." At all of these institutions, faculty and administrators are required to adhere to a statement of faith which includes core Evangelical Protestant doctrines.

This sample of colleges was "purposive," which is to say that the selection of colleges was deliberate and calculated. Purposive samples in the social sciences are generally considered to be not as strong as "probability samples" (e.g., random or systematic samples), where each unit of the working population has a known chance of being included or excluded in the sample before the sample is collected. The principal problem with purposive samples, of course, is that the representativeness of the sample is less certain since one cannot estimate the bias in the sampling. The purpose behind our strategy was to achieve as much representativeness as possible and at the same time acquire a certain quality in the institutions to be studied. To this end, in selecting the institutions for this study a particular rationale was followed.

To begin, the Christian College Consortium, out of which the EAP sample was drawn, is a preexisting subgroup in the realm of Evangelical higher education. A larger subgroup, the Christian College Coalition, which is made up of 70 colleges (as of January 1983), has a similar vision—the integration of Evangelical Christian faith with higher learning in the liberal arts tradition. In 1976 the coalition emerged as an outgrowth of the consortium, but in 1981 it became a separate legal and organizational entity.

It is possible to locate the EAP sample within the parameters of a larger universe at this point. According to the *Educational Directory 1981–1982*, there are 3,253 colleges and universities in the United States. Roughly 54 percent of these are private. Within this category 773 have some sort of religious affiliation; approximately 100 of these (3% of the total universe) meet the criteria of the Christian College Coalition as Evangelical liberal arts colleges or universities. The coalition presently accounts for 70 of these. The EAP sample of colleges represents roughly 13 percent of the coalition.

Purposive sampling has some limitations to be sure, yet some purposive sampling techniques are better than others. The type employed in this research was a "heterogeneous representative purposive sample" (Smith 1975, 116). This means that in selecting institutions for study, diversity was sought. The regional diversity of this universe is tapped by this sample as seen in the fact that the eastern, midwestern, and western regions of the country are each represented by these colleges (see table

A1). A broad diversity of religious tradition is also represented in this sample. Wheaton, Gordon, Westmont, and Taylor are independent of denominational affiliation—this independence being, itself, a distinct Evangelical tradition. The other colleges maintain denominational ties: Seattle-Pacific, Free Methodist; George Fox, Friends; Messiah, Brethren in Christ; Bethel, Baptist; and Houghton, Wesleyan Methodist. It should be made clear that students attending any one of these institutions do not necessarily maintain the same denominational affiliation as the institution itself. The split between denominational and nondenominational schools is seen in the larger coalition, though with a much greater percentage being denominationally affiliated 78% (see table A1).

In terms of the student population, the EAP sample of Students ($N = $ 1,980) represents 14.8 percent of the sample universe and 3 percent of the coalition student population. The proportion of men and women in the EAP sample is roughly the same as that found in the EAP sample universe and the coalition as a whole (see table A1).

In one important respect the sample of Evangelical colleges used in this study does not reflect the larger universe of Christian liberal arts education: the EAP colleges are generally "stronger" institutions than those in the broader coalition. These nine schools are more selective in

Table A1

Representativeness of the EAP Sample of Colleges

|  | EAP Sample ($N = 9$) | Christian College Coalition[a] ($N = 63$) | Sample Universe |
|---|---|---|---|
| Region |  |  |  |
| Northeast | 33.3% | 14% |  |
| Midwest | 33.3% | 46% |  |
| South | — | 20% |  |
| Rocky Mountain/Pacific | 33.3% | 20% |  |
| Affiliation |  |  |  |
| Independent | 44% | 22% |  |
| Denominational | 56% | 78% |  |
| Faculty (, 50% with Ph.D.) | 89% | 44% |  |
| Selectivity of admission |  |  |  |
| (rated "competitive" or better) | 100% | 57% |  |
| Students (total $N$) | 1,980 | 66,941 | 13,403 |
| Men | 42% | 47% | 43% |
| Women | 58% | 53% | 57% |

[a]All figures in this table are calculated on the basis of the 63 institutions listed in *A Guide to Christian Colleges: The Christian College Coalition* (Grand Rapids: Eerdman's, 1982).

their admissions policies than are the other colleges in the coalition. According to the rating of *Barrons Profile of American Colleges* (1980), all nine colleges in the EAP sample are rated "competitive" or better, whereas only 57 percent of the total number of colleges in the coalition are rated as high. The remainder of these coalition schools are in the "less competitive" or "noncompetitive" categories. Thus, it would follow that the type of student each of these nine schools attracts will, on average, be slightly better motivated than those attending the others. What is more, a significantly greater percentage of the EAP sample colleges (89%, or eight of nine) have over 50 percent of their faculty with earned doctorates, as compared to colleges in the entire coalition (44%). Finally, when a panel of experts was asked to select the fifteen most important Christian colleges in the United States, all but one of the EAP sample colleges were consistently selected for this distinction.

Heterogeneity was not the only quality desired in this sample of colleges. High academic standards were also desired and thus deliberately sought. It was reasoned that, since a significant percentage of the lay and professional leadership of the coming generation of conservative Protestants will be educated in an Evangelical liberal arts college, the strength of these particular institutions would increase the likelihood of acquiring a sample of strongly committed and highly motivated Evangelical students—ones who would provide a clear indication of the temperament of the coming generation of Evangelicals.

One final disclaimer is necessary. While the EAP sample of colleges is representative of the academically stronger Evangelical colleges in the United States, there are others that are strong and important to the Evangelical orbit that are neither included in the EAP sample nor currently affiliated with the coalition. Among these are Bob Jones University (Greensboro, South Carolina), Liberty University (Lynchburg, Virginia), and the large number of Bible colleges and institutes, such as Philadelphia College of the Bible (Philadelphia, Pennsylvania) and Moody Bible Institute (Chicago, Illinois). The limitations of time and expense prohibited their inclusion in the EAP sample, though their participation might have strengthened the sample.

With the assistance of sociologists at each of these institutions, a 20 percent stratified systematic or random sample of the student body of each college was drawn. In January and February 1982, these sociologists received a package containing questionnaires, cover letters, and reminders. The initial administration of these questionnaires took place at this time. Reminder cards were sent out to those not returning a completed questionnaire two weeks later. After an additional two weeks, another copy of the questionnaire was sent to those still not returning a questionnaire. The data collection process was closed down after another three weeks. The exception to this rule was at George Fox, where after the sample was drawn, the students were brought together in an auditorium and invited to complete the questionnaire. The total number of questionnaires initially administered was 2,750. The total number of questionnaires returned was 1,980, representing a 72 percent response rate. Apart from the special circumstances of George Fox, where a 95 percent response was achieved, the high was 74 percent at Westmont; the low was 63 percent at Gordon.

It should be noted parenthetically that some of these colleges have an admissions policy of admitting a very small percentage of non-Christian students. In this sample of college students, less that 1 percent would be classified this way. Because of the smallness of their number, they were included in all analysis.

One final note, an EAP minisurvey is referred to periodically in this book. One-fifth of the Westmont College student body ($N = 195$) were randomly sampled in May 1983 and were given a one-page questionnaire of items not included on the original questionnaire. A 52 percent response rate was achieved in this survey ($N = 102$).

## THE SEMINARY SURVEY

Data collection for the seminary survey began in mid-September 1982. Seven Evangelical seminaries participated: Fuller Theological Seminary (Pasadena, California), Conservative Baptist Theological Seminary (Denver, Colorado), Asbury Theological Seminary (Wilmore, Kentucky), Talbot Theological Seminary (Los Angeles, California), Westminster Theological Seminary (Chestnut Hill, Pennsylvania), Gordon-Conwell Theological Seminary (Hamilton, Massachusetts), and Wheaton Graduate School (Wheaton, Illinois).

Once again, a purposive sample was employed here. An organization for Evangelical seminaries similar to the Christian Coalition does not exist. Getting a sense of the larger universe of Evangelical seminary education, then, is precluded. Nonetheless, the rich diversity of region and tradition in Evangelical seminary education was tapped by this sample. Regional diversity was achieved in that three seminaries in the Rocky Mountain/Pacific regions and two seminaries each in the midwestern and eastern regions were included. Of all Protestant seminaries in the United States, 21 percent are in the Northeast, 42 percent in the Midwest, 24 percent in the South, and 13 percent in the West (see table A2). Diversity in religious tradition was also achieved. Fuller, Wheaton, Gordon-Conwell, and Talbot are independent of denomina-

**Table A2**
Representativeness of the EAP Sample of Seminaries

| | EAP Sample (N = 7) | All Protestant Seminaries[a] (N = 117) |
|---|---|---|
| Region | | |
| East | 28% | 21% |
| Midwest | 29% | 42% |
| South | — | 24% |
| West | 43% | 13% |
| Affiliation | | |
| Independent | 71.4% | 18% |
| Denominational | 28.6% | 82% |
| Students (total N) | 4,280 | 41,537 |
| % of total | 10.3% | 100% |
| Sample N | 847 | |

[a]All Protestant seminaries in the continental United States noted in the 1982 *Directory of the Association of Theological Schools*. Westminster Theological Seminary and the Wheaton Graduate School are not listed here. Figures for this table are calculated on the basis of the statistics listed in the ATS directory.

tional affiliation. Nonetheless, Gordon-Conwell has had a strong Calvinist orientation, and Talbot has had a strong dispensationalist orientation. Conservative Baptist is affiliated with the Conservative Baptist Association of America. Westminster has the strongest Calvinist tradition, it is affiliated with the Orthodox Presbyterian Church in America. Finally, Asbury, though formally independent, was affiliated with the Free Methodist Church and, to be sure, still represents perhaps the most important divinity school in the Wesleyan-Arminian theological tradition in America today.

While randomization was not pursued in this sample of seminaries, the sample's suitability was confirmed by an independent panel of experts. When surveyed about their opinions of the twelve most important Evangelical seminaries and graduate schools in the United States out of a list of over twenty-five seminaries advertising in *Christianity Today*, these seven were consistently selected. It is not argued that these seven seminaries entirely represent Evangelical seminary education in America. Many other seminaries could have been included, but owing to the constraints of time and expense, they were not. As with the college survey, it can be fairly argued that these seminaries are very highly indicative of Evangelical seminary education in America and thus do afford access to a large body of students who will provide professional leadership in the next generation.

With the assistance of the office of the Dean of Students at each of these seminaries, a 33 percent systematic sample was drawn. A pattern of questionnaire administration and follow-up identical with the one employed in the college survey was employed in the seminary survey. The initial distribution of the questionnaire took place in the last two weeks of September and the first week of October. The total number of questionnaires distributed was 1,330. The total number of questionnaires returned was 847, or a 64 percent response rate. The range was a high of 79 percent (at Asbury) and a low of 50 percent (at Talbot).

As in the college survey, a small percentage of students not committed to the Evangelical tradition are admitted to a few of the seminaries. In this sample, approximately 1 percent would have been classified in this manner. Because of their small number, they were included in the analysis.

### OTHER RESOURCES

For the purpose of having a comparative base, a number of other surveys were consistently employed. Three are particularly important to this study and deserve mentioning. In one of these (the public university sample) students at the University of California at Santa Barbara were surveyed. The selection of this university was made for reasons of convenience to the researcher and the facilities made available to him. With the help and generosity of Phillip E. Hammond and R. C. Gordon-McCutcheon, students in several religious studies classes were given the EAP college questionnaire and asked to complete it. While suggestive of the attitudes of students in public higher education in America, no attempt will be made to contend that this institution and its students are strictly representative of those attitudes. The regional uniqueness of this sample is one factor detracting from its representativeness; the sexual ration (women, 67%; men, 33%) is another factor. Still it does provide interesting comparative data and useful data when supplemented with other national surveys of student opinion.

Still another part of the Evangelical Academy Project was a survey of faculty opinion. This was conducted in January/February 1985 with the assistance of Jeffrey Schloss of Westmont College. Through the Academic Dean's office at each of the nine institutions participating in the college survey, a questionnaire was sent to all faculty. The total number of questionnaires distributed in this saturation sample was 810.

The total number of questionnaires returned was 447, representing a 55 percent response rate. The range was between 76 percent (at Bethel) and 41 percent (at Seattle-Pacific), though Seattle-Pacific was the only institution whose response rate was less than 52 percent.

The 1977 and 1982 General Social Survey of the American population produced by the National Opinion Research Center was used in this book, as were two Gallup surveys: the 1978/1979 Gallup/*Christianity Today* national survey and the 1984 Gallup/Robert H. Schuller survey. Both of these were surveys of the general American population based on a modified probability sample of a cross section of adult Americans (eighteen and older). The samples 1,553 cases were stratified by age, gender, region, and education so as to approximate the noninstitutionalized adult civilian population of the United States.

Another survey referred to in this work is the 1963 Religion and Morality Survey. This project was initiated by David Moberg at Marquette University. The data that were recoverable from this project came from only three of the institutions originally part of the study: Bethel College, Minnesota Bible College, and North Central Bible College. Part of Moberg's methodology is detailed in his article "Theological Self-Classification and Ascetic Moral Views of Students," *Review of Religious Research* 10, no. 2 (1969): 100–107.

One final survey that was referenced periodically was a 1982 survey of Christian theologians (1982 Roper Theology Faculty Survey) in the United States. The theoretical universe for the survey was conceived of as those who are involved in teaching those persons who will be professionally engaged in religion in the United States. The sample pool from which faculty members were randomly chosen came from lists including both Protestant and Catholic schools of theology in the United States and Canada. Two thousand questionnaires were administered, and after one follow-up mailing, a 57 percent response rate was attained ($N = 1,112$).

A word on another source of data is appropriate. Quantitative survey research provides just one perspective of social reality. The effort to broaden understanding of social reality needs no justification. Alternate data not only round out one's understanding of the phenomenon in question but validate impressions gained through other means. I spent nine months as a participant-observer in the role of a faculty member at Westmont College. This aided me tremendously in understanding the subtleties of meaning and change in the Evangelical world. Beyond this, though, I was able to collect qualitative data through in-depth personal interviews. A total of thirty-two formal interviews were conducted with randomly selected students at Gordon College and Wheaton College in November 1982, at Talbot Theological Seminary and Fuller Theological Seminary in February 1983, and at Gordon-Conwell Theological Seminary and Gordon College (again) in January 1985. Comments from these interviews are included thoughout the book.

# Notes

All bibliographic references cited in the author-date style can be found in the Selected Bibliography. Full bibliographic details are given in the notes for works not appearing in the Selected Bibliography.

## CHAPTER 1

1. On the nexus between Western colonial expansion and the Christian missionary movement, see Latourette (1943), vols. 2 and 3; and Wright 1943, vol. 5, chaps. 45–46; vol. 6, chap. 17; vol. 10, chap. 25.

2. These figures are compiled from Barrett 1982. Included as Evangelicals in these tabulations are Evangelicals of all racial and ethnic backgrounds, neo-Pentecostals of all racial and ethnic backgrounds, and Anglican Evangelicals and Pentecostals. For a most helpful review of this volume and the reliability of the statistics contained therein, see the review written by Rodney Stark in *Sociological Analysis* 44, no. 1 (1983): 70–73. In my opinion, the figures for 1980 may be inflated. I conclude this because most survey results from 1980 put the number of conservative Protestants at approximately 22 percent.

3. Figures mentioned here are derived from the successive volumes of *Yearbook of American and Canadian Churches* (edited by Constant H. Jacquet [Nashville: Abingdon]). See note 2 in chap. 8 for a complete breakdown of these figures. See also Carroll, Johnson, and Marty 1979 and Roof 1982 for further corroboration.

4. Figures noted here are also derived from the successive volumes of the *Yearbook of American and Canadian Churches*. See particularly the 1985 edition for the last two figures given. Churches under the Evangelical heading were Baptist General Conference; Christian and Missionary Alliance; Church of God, Anderson, Indiana; Church of the Nazarene; the Evangelical Covenant Church of America; the General Association of Regular Baptists; Lutheran Church—Missouri Synod; the Seventh Day Adventists; and the Southern Baptist Convention. Mainline churches were the American Lutheran Church, the Episcopal Church, the Lutheran Church in America, the Presbyterian Church in the

U.S.A., the United Church of Christ, and the United Methodist Church. Figures are taken from the column "Per Capita Full or Confirmed Membership."

5. Telephone interview with Paul Kienel, director of The Association of Christian Schools International, 2 October 1985.

6. These figures were derived from Hacker 1983, 233.

7. The figures concerning the Evangelical Press Association came from a telephone interview with Gary Warner of the EPA, 19 September 1985. Figures concerning the Christian Booksellers Association came from a telephone interview with Eloise Danley of the CBA, 20 September 1985.

8. Telephone interview with Scott Middleton, National Religious Broadcasters, 24 September 1985.

9. Of the college sample, 86 percent attended public school, 2 percent attended private, nonsectarian high schools, and 1 percent attended Catholic parochial schools. For the seminarians, it is much the same: 90 percent attended public high schools, while only 4 percent attended private, nonsectarian schools and 3 percent attended Catholic schools.

10. An elaboration of this typology may be found in Hunter 1983a, 7–9, and 1982, 363–72.

11. Twenty percent of the collegians and 31 percent of the seminarians claimed to be charismatic, and 14 percent of the collegians and 34 percent of the seminarians claimed to have spoken in tongues.

12. On the concept *generation* there has been much discussion in many, many disciplines. In sociology, several works are notable: Mannheim 1952, Heberle 1951, Gusfield 1957, Eisenstadt 1956. In the sociology of religion, the work of Robert Wuthnow (1976) is prominent. My usage closely follows Wuthnow's.

13. The data are systematic and highly suggestive though not entirely comprehensive. From three of the most prominent Evangelical periodicals (*Christianity Today*, *Eternity*, and *Moody Monthly*), four prominent Evangelistic outreach organizations (Campus Crusade for Christ, The Navigators, Inter-Varsity Christian Fellowship, and Youth for Christ), six large Evangelical publishing houses (Zondervan, Scripture Press, Moody Press, Gospel Light, Word Books, and Bethany Publishing Company), forty-six colleges in the Christian College Coalition, and five Evangelical relief organizations (Medical Assistance Program, World Concern, Compassion, Food for the Hungry, and Samaritan's Purse), the educational backgrounds of the top policy makers were tabulated (in the case of the colleges, it was the educational background of the college faculty). In this survey, the results were very compelling. In each area, the percentages of the total number of policy makers with at least one degree from *any* Evangelical institution were as follows: periodicals, 88 percent; outreach groups, 60 percent; publishing houses, 74 percent; college faculty, 60 percent; and relief organizations, 68 percent. In each area, the percentages of the total number of policy makers with at least one degree from one of the sixteen institutions surveyed in the Evangelical Academy Project were as follows: periodicals, 75 percent; outreach groups, 47 percent; publishing houses, 33 percent; college faculty, 19 percent; and relief organizations, 27 percent.

14. See Marvin Rintala, "Political Generations," in *International Encyclopedia of the Social Sciences*, vol. 6. The most recent and comprehensive review of the empirical literature on this subject can be found in an article by Hoge and Hoge (1984). In their study of University of Michigan alumni, the only value area in which alumni become more conservative is on the issue of free enterprise ideology. In all other areas (civil liberties, religious belief, etc.) they remain roughly the same or become even more liberal. This is further documented by the very extensive research of Astin (1977), Hyman, Wright, and Reed (1975), and Yankelovich (1981, 61).

## Chapter 2

1. The following are only a few of the sources of documentation: Ahlstrom 1972, Chiles 1965, Mathews 1977, Bruce 1974, Loveland 1980, Wyatt-Brown 1972, Issac 1982. The principal exception to this biblicism was the eighteenth-century Unitarian movement.

2. Harold Lindsell in *Battle for the Bible* (Grand Rapids: Zondervan, 1976) provides a clear definition of the doctrine of inerrancy from the Evangelical perspective.

3. In the early part of the twentieth century, this was articulated most clearly in the debates between science and the Scriptures. As Marsden (1980, 212, n. 8) notes, it was the Bible that was believed to be scientific in that it reported the facts accurately. Evolution and any other "science" incompatible with the Bible were unscientific because they were based upon hypothesis and speculation.

4. The study is reported in Stark and Glock 1968. Conservative Protestants in this case refer to Missouri-Synod Lutherans, Southern Baptists, and a miscellaneous category of smaller denominations that Stark and Glock label "Sects." At least 90 percent of those in these denominational categories chose the literalist position.

5. The institutions of the Christian College Consortium, all Evangelical seminaries, the publishing houses and magazines of conservative Protestantism, and the like maintain this distinctive belief.

6. On the theology and history of the neo-orthodox movement in Europe and America, consult G. C. Berkouwer, *A Half Century of Theology*, translated and edited by L. Smedes (Grand Rapids: Eerdmans, 1977); Horden 1959; Zahrnt 1969.

7. Illustrative of the Evangelical reaction to neo-orthodoxy are Bolich 1980; Clark 1963; Edward J. Carnell, *The Case for Orthodox Theology* (Philadelphia: Westminster Press, 1959); Henry 1976–79; Cornelius Van Til, *Karl Barth and Evangelicalism* (Philadelphia: Presbyterian and Reformed Publishing Co., 1964). More representative statements of the Evangelical view of biblical authority can be found in Rogers and McKim 1979; James Boice et al., *The Foundation of Biblical Authority*, vol. 1, International Council on Biblical Inerrancy (Grand Rapids: Zondervan, 1978); Geisler 1981.

8. I am not arguing that the six twenty-four hour day creation theory is the long-held orthodoxy on this point. Indeed, in the nineteenth century many

educated Evangelicals held to a Lamarckian or neo-Lamarckian theory of evolution. This theory was less concerned with the actual origin of the various species than it was with their survival and evolution. Absent from this perspective is the later Darwinian notion of radical natural selection. The Lamarckian theory was not incompatible with a basic theistic view of the world. My reason for singling this out is to emphasize again that late nineteenth-century and early twentieth-century Fundamentalism itself represents something of a reformulation of orthodoxy—one born out of defensive reaction. In this paticular case it was a rejection of any position that even hinted of secular evolutionary theories. Thus, as will be emphasized later, the traditions of orthodoxy that contemporary Evangelicals seem to be abandoning are not necessarily *the* standards of orthodoxy. In some cases they may be only the traditions established in the late nineteenth century.

9. The issue of the humanity of Scripture precipitated the resignation of Professor J. Ramsey Michaels from Gordon-Conwell Seminary in 1983 after twenty-five years of service. With regard to this issue, Michaels stated: "Specifically, these matters are the humanity and historicity of Jesus Christ, and the legitimacy of studying the Gospels historically. The issue is not inerrancy: we agree on that. The issue is whether or not inerrancy implies a hermeneutic" ("Letter of Resignation," 13 April 1983).

10. The source for these data is a secondary analysis of the 1982 Roper Theology Faculty Survey data. Sixty-one percent claimed to believe in the inerrancy of the Bible; 39 percent claimed not to believe in it.

11. These repercussions are perhaps most aptly measured by the response of the Evangelical Theological Society. Intense debate centered on the Gundry text and its methodology at the annual meeting of the ETS in December 1982. And though the ETS executive board unanimously affirmed Gundry's right to remain in the society (the criterion being the stated belief in the doctrine of inerrancy), conservative factions in the society under the leadership of Norman Geisler eventually prevailed in having Gundry's membership reevaluated such that by the December 1983 meeting, Gundry was asked to resign his membership. Voting tallies clearly indicated how the ETS membership was divided. For further details of these events and other reaction to the Gundry commentary, see Leslie R. Keylock, "Evangelical Scholars Remove Gundry for His Views on Matthew," *Christianity Today*, 3 February 1984, 36–38; Grant Osborne, "Professional Societies Evaluate New Evangelical Directions," *TSF Bulletin*, March–April 1983, 14–15; idem, "Evangelical Theological Society 1982 Annual Meeting," *TSF Bulletin*, March–April 1983, 15; Carson 1982.

12. See "'Evangelical': Integral to Christian Identity?—An Exchange between Donald Bloesh and Vernard Eller," *TSF Bulletin*, March–April 1983, 5–10.

13. Consider also the enormous *Word Biblical Commentary*, which employs the critical resources Evangelicals have long associated with the heretical assumptions and methods of liberalism. On this see Noll 1983.

14. These figures come from the author's analysis of the Roper Theology Faculty Survey.

15. Daniel Bell, "The New Class: A Muddled Concept," in Bruce-Briggs 1979; Lipset 1979; Podhoretz 1979.

16. From a hymn by Mary Ann Thomson, circa 1870, no. 382 in the 1933 edition of the hymnal of the Presbyterian Church in the U.S.A.

17. Chap. 10, "Of Effectual Calling," no. 4, Westminster Confession of Faith.

18. The original quotation is from Richard Baxter, a seventeenth-century Puritan, and it runs as follows: "I preach as never sure to preach again, As a dying man to dying men." This quotation was popularized by John Wesley in the eighteenth century. It is also engraved on a plaque on a wall of Wycliffe Hall Theological College in Oxford, circa 1880. My thanks to Canon Gethin Hughes of All Saints-by-the-Sea Episcopal Church, Santa Barbara, California, for this reference.

19. Institutionally, this defense is witnessed in all of the affirmations and reaffirmations of the faith from *The Fundamentals* to the charter statements of the American Council of Christian Churches and National Association of Evangelicals. It is seen at a popular level as well. In the 1924 study of Middletown, for example, 94 percent of all the high school students maintained that "Christianity is the one true religion and all people should be converted to it" (Caplow, Bahr, and Chadwick 1983, 94). This is clear too from the interviews conducted with Middletown residents reported in chap. 20 of Lynd and Lynd 1929. Cf. Moreland 1958, 135.

20. These figures were derived from a reanalysis of David Moberg's 1963 survey of Evangelical student opinion (see Appendix).

21. These figures were derived from Stark and Glock 1970, tables 10 and 13. Southern Baptist and Sects were combined to constitute the Evangelical category.

22. These figures came from a 1962 survey of Baptist (General Conference) youth ($N = 258$) who were gathered for the Conference Youth Fellowship Quadrennial meeting in New York City. Percentages were derived from the original tally sheets; "can't says" were eliminated from analysis.

23. See Clark Pinnock, "Why Is Jesus the Only Way?" *Eternity*, December 1976, 13–34.

24. Theologians Pannenberg and Cranfield have given intellectual legitimation to this, while C. S. Lewis (in his *The Last Battle* of the *Chronicles of Narnia* [New York: Macmillan, 1956) has been one of its more important popularizers.

25. Other possibilities included "You receive peace with God" (10%*, 17%**); "God commands you to believe" (2%*, 14%**); "You acquire a sense of meaning and purpose in life" (39%*, 26%**); "God has made a difference in my life" (28%*, 9%**) [*first reason, **most important reason].

26. The actual percentages were as follows. Freshmen: 14 percent*, 30 percent**; sophomores: 12 percent*, 25 percent**; juniors: 7 percent*, 23 percent**; and seniors: 6 percent*, 21 percent** [*first reason, **most important reason].

27. Only 3 percent felt that it "always is" in poor taste to emphasize hell.

28. The evidence of a vibrant "social consciousness" within Evangelicalism in the 1900–1960 period is plentiful but mostly anecdotal. For example, four major Evangelical relief organizations have been operating since the early 1950s (World Relief Commission (of the National Association of Evangelicals), World Vision, Medical Assistance Program, and Compassion). In most cases, however, social ministry was incorporated within a program of evangelism. Thus, social ministry, since it was not performed for its own sake, was rarely talked about. Many social commentators, liberal and conservative, have just assumed that Evangelicals have had very little sensitivity to social needs. Survey data from young adult members of the Baptist General Conference provide an interesting illustration. In 1962, 84 percent agreed that "our church should minister to all classes in our society"; 60 percent agreed that "there should be more of an even distribution of goods in our country"; 86 percent agreed that a "Negro would be welcome to attend and join my church"; and 68 percent agreed that "our Conference should promote racially integrated churches."

29. The possibilities were as follows: "to develop a strong local church" (12%); "to evangelize the world" (39%); "to pursue social justice" (2%); "to develop their own spiritual lives and those of their families"(39%); other (8%). Most of those choosing "other" said a combination of spiritual and social justice concerns.

30. Since Evangelicals give approximately 47% more than liberals in the first place, the actual amount each side gives to "benevolences" varies considerably. Though liberals emphasize social concerns rhetorically, it is the conservatives who are, in actual dollars, far more generous along the lines of social welfare. The figures given were derived from the 1972 and 1982 *Yearbook of American and Canadian Churches*, which list the 1970 and 1980 amounts. Those in the liberal category were the American Lutheran Church, the Lutheran Church in America, the United Church of Christ, the United Methodist Church, the Presbyterian Church in the U.S.A., and the United Presbyterian Church. Those denominations making up the conservative side were the Southern Baptist and the Baptist General Conference, the Lutheran Church—Missouri Synod, the Church of the Nazarene, the Evangelical Christian Church of America, and the Church of God, Anderson, Indiana.

31. I am indebted to Boyd Reese for providing much of this information on the Evangelical Left, including the lists of active communities.

32. There are two other periodicals which carry a readership among the Evangelical Left: *The Catholic Worker*, which had its origins in 1930s American socialism, and *Kattelagete*, a publication of the Committee of Southern Churchmen which got off the ground in the late 1950s and early 1960s.

33. Illustrative of the literature emerging at this time are the following titles: Richard Batey, *Jesus and the Poor* (New York: Harper and Row, 1972); Robert Benne and Philip Hefner, *Defining America* (Philadelphia: Fortress, 1974); Dale W. Brown, *The Christian Revolutionary* (Grand Rapids, Mich.: Eerdmans, 1971); Harold O. J. Brown, *Christianity and the Class Struggle* (New Rochelle, N.Y.: Arlington House, 1970); Larry Christenson, *Social Action: Jesus Style*

(Minneapolis: Dimension, 1976); Robert Clouse, Robert Linder, and Richard Pierard, eds., *The Cross and the Flag* (Carol Stream, Ill.: Creation House, 1972); Perry C. Cotham, *Politics, Americanism and Christianity* (Grand Rapids, Mich.: Baker, 1973); Dayton 1976; Vernard Eller, *The Simple Life: The Christian Stance toward Possessions* (Grand Rapids: Eerdmans, 1973); Authur G. Gish, *The New Left and Christian Radicalism* (Grand Rapids: Eerdmans, 1970); Henry 1974; Paul K. Jewett, *Man as Male and Female* (Grand Rapids: Eerdmans, 1975); Ada Lum, *Jesus the Radical* (Downers Grove: Inter-Varsity, 1970); Moberg 1965, 1972; Richard J. Mouw, *Political Evangelism* (Grand Rapids: Eerdmans, 1973); idem, *Politics and the Biblical Drama* (Grand Rapids: Eerdmans, 1976); Stephen V. Monsma, *The Unraveling of America* (Downers Grove: Inter-Varsity, 1974); Fred Pearson, *They Dared to Hope: Student Protest and Christian Response* (Grand Rapids: Eerdmans, 1969); Richard Pierard, *The Unequal Yoke: Evangelical Christianity and Political Conservativism* (Philadelphia: J. B. Lippincott, 1970); Quebedeaux 1974; Letha Scanzoni and Nancy Hardesty, *All Were Meant to Be—A Biblical Approach to Women's Liberation* (Waco, Tex.: Word, 1974); Ron Sider, *Rich Christians in an Age of Hunger* (Downers Grove: Inter-Varsity, 1977); Arthur Simon, *Bread for the World* (Grand Rapids: Eerdmans, 1975); Tom Skinner, *Black and Free* (Grand Rapids: Zondervan, 1970); William Stringfellow, *An Ethic for Christians and Other Aliens in a Strange Land* (Waco, Tex.: Word, 1973); Richard K. Taylor, *Economics and the Gospel* (Philadelphia: United Church Press, 1973); Jim Wallis, *Agenda for a Biblical People* (New York: Harper and Row, 1976); John Howard Yoder, *The Politics of Jesus* (Grand Rapids: Eerdmans, 1972).

34. My informant at the National Association of Evangelicals is its president, Dr. Billy Melvin. Among his more impressive credentials in grounding his expertise in this matter is the fact that he has over twenty-six years of experience with the NAE. A more scholarly source of support for the claims of increased legitimacy of social action can be found in Fowler 1982.

35. These organizations are World Concern, Food for the Hungry, Samaritan's Purse, and International Christian Aid. Notably, of the four Evangelical social relief agencies mentioned in n. 28, which have been in existence since the 1950s, three reported a surge of growth in the 1970s. The Medical Assistance Program, for instance, doubled its cash contributions between 1978 and 1983; World Vision increased its cash contributions tenfold (this according to MAP executive Guy Condon).

36. Information from the author's analysis of the 1982 Roper Theology Faculty Survey.

37. Thirty-four percent under thirty-five years; 20 percent for those thirty-five and older.

38. The question read: "Which should be the primary focus of missionary efforts overseas—(a) to bring people to a faith in Jesus, or (b) to improve the material lot of the poor." The 8 percent (table 6) were those who wrote in the margins that a choice would be impossible to make and thus circled both responses or none at all. Only one person in the thirty-five and older category gave this response.

39. This phrase was taken from a Victorian hymn, circa 1837, by Robert Edwards (no. 369, *Trinity Hymnal*, (Orthodox Presbyterian Church, 1961).

40. Robert Speer, "Foreign Missions and World-wide Evangelism," in *The Fundamentals*, edited by R. A. Torrey and A. C. Dixon (Chicago: Testimony Publishing Co., 1910), 12:235

41. Henry Frost, "What Missionary Motives Should Prevail," in ibid., p. 266.

42. See Os Guinness, "Worldly Wise or Just Worldly," *Eternity*, September 1983, 25–29; Hunter 1981.

43. To get an indication of the kind of variability in orthodoxy that exists, an orthodoxy index was constructed. For details of its construction, see Hammond and Hunter 1984, 221–38. This orthodoxy index is used repeatedly throughout this work. The one difference between the way it was used in the Hammond and Hunter piece and the way it is used here is that instead of six items being used, five were used here. The question on Jesus Christ was dropped. In its present configuration, the alpha coefficients measuring index reliability were .56 (college) and .65 (seminary).

44. When comparing seminarians who believe that "Jesus is the only way for salvation except for those who have not heard of Jesus" with those who believe that "Jesus is the only way period" on a number of items, a pattern was found to hold true. For example, the former were less likely to hold evangelism as the highest priority of the church, more likely to believe that social justice is "just as important" or "almost as important" as evangelism, and much less likely to choose missions as a career path—by two to one.

## CHAPTER 3

1. An elaboration of the notion of inner-worldly asceticism in relation to other religious orientations can be found in Max Weber's *Sociology of Religion*, (Boston: Beacon, 1964), especially chaps. 11–16. The introduction to this volume by Talcott Parsons is also lucid and helpful. For its application to the case of Protestantism and the development of industrial capitalism, see Weber 1958.

2. However, this relationship is highly controversial. Of those studies which call into question Weber's thesis that large-scale entrepreneurial activity in the sixteenth and seventeenth centuries as well as the growth of business and commerce in the nineteenth century was spawned in part by the ethical system of certain sects of Protestant Christianity, see Cohen 1980, McClelland 1961, Samuelson 1961, and Collins 1980.

3. One of the more interesting ethnographic documentations of this orientation may be found in Charles Edwin Jones, *Perfectionist Persuasion: The Holiness Movement and American Methodism, 1867–1936* (Metuchen, N.J.: Scarecrow, 1974). In Appendix 4 he cites twenty-nine biographical vignettes, or "testimonies," of people helped by Holiness "rescue homes." These were originally reported in such books as *Thrilling Stories of Those Rescued from the Cesspools of Iniquity*. Typical of these are the following.

Dicie, the sporting madam: Although Dicie had a Christian mother, she became a drunkard, cigarette fiend, and user of morphine, cocaine and other drugs. When missionaries visited her house, she allowed them to pray and gave up drugs for a time. After a relapse, she became a patient in a rescue home, where she was saved. As a result she went home to mother and later became a slum missionary herself.

Lulu L—, or from drunkenness to womanhood: An Ohio girl, Lulu was orphaned at eight. Having no formal education, she was ruined at seventeen with a promise of marriage. She then went to Cincinnati where she lived two years in open shame. A regular attendant at "public picnics, theaters," and dances, she eventually became a drunkard, public character, and manager of a house of ill-repute. After twelve years of sin, she went to Hope Cottage in Cincinnati and abandoned rum and tobacco.

Mabel and Origene: Mabel was of French-German extraction, and Origene of French-Spanish descent. Both were raised Catholic. Mabel went to school until age fourteen and left home at fifteen. Origene was educated for the priesthood, spending ten years in a convent and three years as a priest. After being put on bread and water "for speaking to women," Origene ran away and met Mabel. They tried to marry, but since the priest charged too much, they lived together without marriage. Origene became a sailor, and Mabel took to drink. A missionary found Mabel in a "barrel" house, and she went to Rest Cottage. Later, her "fiery preaching" converted Origene. Mabel was saved from rum and tobacco, Origene from tobacco. They were married by the matron at the rescue home.

4. There is evidence suggesting that the spiritual significance of vocational asceticism remained intact within Evangelical culture right through the mid-1800s. See Ian Bradley's cultural history of the Evangelical impact on the Victorians in *The Call to Seriousness* (London: Jonathan Cape, 1976), especially chap. 9, "Serious Callings."

5. In the post–World War II period, a great deal of research was conducted on the "Protestant ethic thesis." Most of it, however, was concerned with measuring the relationship between religious affiliation and actual achievement—skipping over, as it were, the social-psychological factor of ascetic orientation. This trait was simply assumed to exist for all Protestants; see Bouma 1973. One exception to this was Hammond and William's 1976 study. See also Blackwood 1979.

6. See also William McLoughlin, *Billy Graham: Revivalist in a Secular Age* (New York: Ronald Press, 1960), 80–84; Joe Barnhart, *The Billy Graham Religion* (Philadelphia: Pilgrim, 1972); Stark and Glock 1968: 52f; Caplow, Bahr, and Chadwick 1983, 262–65.

7. Vocational asceticism was not significantly stronger in the Reformational-Confessional tradition than in the other denominational traditions of Evangelicalism.

8. The index was constructed in the following manner. Students were asked

to rate a variety of "personal needs" on a scale of 1 to 10. The average (X) scores from each sample on each "need" were noted and then combined with those related to each other. The three *types* of needs were then derived in the following way: instrumental needs (need for *a*. financial security, *b*. achievement—a sense of accomplishment); affective self-fulfillment needs (need for *a*. personal freedom, *b*. purpose in life, *c*. self-fulfillment); and affective interpersonal needs (need for *a*. friendship, *b*. love and affection, *c*. marriage). The overall scores (X̄) on these types of needs for each group were as follows: instrumental needs, college—6.5, seminary—6.4, public university—7.6; affective self-fulfillment needs, college—7.7, seminary—7.8, public university—8.4; affective interpersonal needs, college—8.0, seminary—8.4, public university—8.2.

9. Quoted from W. Walsham How's sermon "The Shallow and the Worldly," in *Practical Sermons* (London: Wells Gardner, Darton and Co., 1899), 174.

10. D. L. Moody said the same thing a little more eloquently thirty-eight years earlier, in 1900: "A line should be drawn between the church and the world, and every Christian should get both feet out of the world" (quoted in Marsden 1980, 36).

11. Items 1, 2, 3, 4, 5, 6, 8, 9, and 11 (years 1951 and 1961) came from a 1961 Bethel College student and alumni survey. The senior classes of Bethel College from the years 1949, 1950, and 1951 (response rate = 78%, $N$ = 63) were surveyed as was the entire senior class and a 10 percent sample of the rest of the student body (response rate = 83%, $N$ = 125). Items 10, 12, 13, and 14 (year 1963) came from a religion and morality survey conducted in 1963 by David Moberg of students attending Bethel College, Minnesota Bible College, and North Central Bible College ($N$ = 388) (see Appendix). Data for 1982 are from the Evangelical Academy Project.

Because samples and surveys were not completely comparable, some question as to the reliability of the comparisons may arise. Yet these data are corroborated by data from the other surveys. For example, data from items 1, 2, 4, 5, 6, 8, 9, 11, and 12 are fully corroborated by the 1963 Moberg survey. The percentage of those considering those activities "always wrong" are as follows: 2 percent, studying on Sunday; 9 percent, playing pool; 56 percent, social dancing; 25 percent, folk dancing; 31 percent, seeing Hollywood movies; 72 percent, use of tobacco; 81 percent, social drinking; and 31 percent, casual petting. Data for items 4, 6, and 8 are also corroborated by the 1962 survey of Baptist Conference youth (high school and college age) attending the Conference Youth Fellowship in New York City ($N$ = 258). Here, 88 perent disagreed that social dancing is permissible for Christians; 26 percent disagreed that movie attendance is proper for Christians; and 88 percent agreed that the use of tobacco is wrong for Christians. In all of this, the overall pattern of high moral asceticism (relative to the 1982 generation of Evangelical students) for the 1960s generation is confirmed.

12. There are data corroborating some of these EAP and public university figures. In 1973, a representative sample of college youth was surveyed on a

variety of issues. The following are the frequencies of those considering a specific behavior to be morally wrong: premarital sexual relations, 22 percent; homosexual relations between consenting adults, 75 percent; extramarital sexual relations, 60 percent; cheating big companies, 50 percent. Concerning marijuana usage, only 38 percent in 1973 could easily accept prohibitions against its usage. See Yankelovich 1974, 62, 67–68.

13. This content analysis was performed by the author. While there were 69 articles between 1951 and 1965, there were 28 between 1976 and 1980 (and 22 between 1981 and 1983). There were 42 pieces on sexual permissiveness in this period, 31 on homosexuality, 24 on alcohol and its problems and consequences, 13 on drug usage, 2 on cigarettes, 3 general, and 4 miscellaneous.

14. For examples of earlier statements, see John Maxwell Adams, "Alcohol and God," *His*, December 1954, 18–22; "Editorial—The Alcohol Problem," *Christianity Today* 7 July 1958, 20–22; Clayton Wallace, "Liquor, Legality and License," ibid., 7–9; Roland Bainton, "Total Abstinence and Biblical Principles," ibid.; Emma Fall Schofield, "Will Alcohol Destroy Our Youth?" *Christianity Today*, 6 July 1959, 6–8. For examples from the later period, see David Veerman, "Preparing Your Child for a Drinking Society," *Moody Monthly*, April 1979, 59–61; Anonymous, "Letter to My Children from a Recovered Alcoholic," *Eternity*, September 1978, 32–33; "Editorial—A Sickness Too Common to Cure?" *Christianity Today*, 8 September 1981, 12–13; John Kolenburg, "Helping the Alcoholic in Your Church," *Moody Monthly*, November 1981, 10–12.

15. On the earlier period see, for example, Dwight Small, "Dating: With or Without Petting," *His*, March 1956, 23–36; idem, "The Christian View of Sex," *Eternity*, July 1955, 16–41; George Birney, "G.I. Morals: Whose Fault?" *His*, May 1956, 10–13; Howard Carson Blake, "The New Morality," *Christianity Today*, 27 March 1964, 7–8; Billy Graham, "Billy Graham on Teen-Age Immorality," *Eternity*, June 1965, 9–10. On the later period see Thomas Howard, "What about Unwed Mothers?" *Christianity Today*, 13 March 1970, 11–12; Anonymous, "The Subtlety of Sexual Sin," *Eternity*, February 1977, 27–29; Margaret Hess, "It Happens," *Moody Monthly*, March 1977, 74–76; David Mains, "Should We Live Together?" *Moody Monthly*, July–August 1979, 32–33; Jerry Evans, "Sex before Marriage: Why Should We Wait?" *His*, May 1981; Beth Hodges, "Saying No (and Knowing Why)," *His*, May, 1981, 8–9; Charles Mylander, "Adultery: Running the Red Lights," *Moody Monthly*. March 1982, 26–28.

16. For examples of earlier statements, see "Editorial: The Laws against Homosexuals," *Christianity Today*, 7 November 1969, 32; B. L. Smith, "Homosexuality in the Bible and the Law," *Christianity Today*, 18 July, 1969, 7–10; "Editorial: Homosexuality: No Longer Off Limits," *Eternity*, February 1970, 8–9; Anonymous, "Metropolitan Community Church: Deception Discovered," *Christianity Today*, 26 April 1974, 13–14, For examples from the later period, see Anonymous, "Our Son Is a Homosexual," *Moody Monthly*, January 1979, 61–62; "Editorial—Homosexuality: Biblical Guidance through a Moral

Morass," *Christianity Today*, 18 April, 1980, 12–13; Case Hoogendoorn, "Gay Rights and Wrongs," *Eternity*, June 1981, 19–43; "Editorial—Homosexuals in the Church," *Christianity Today*, 22 April 1983, 8–9.

17. There is another independent source confirming this trend: the Middletown III project. As Caplow, Bahr, and Chadwick (1983) summarized, there has been a "relaxation of the moral criteria that formerly separated saints from sinners" (p. 283). Coauthor Howard Bahr noted in conversation that even among the most conservative Protestants, "there is a willingness to work with 'sinners' rather than to weed them out"(personal conversation, 31 March 1984, Charlottesville, Virginia). For another independent source, see chap. 6 concerning the changes in the behavioral standards of colleges in the Christian College Coalition.

18. This of course is one of the underlying themes of Yankelovich's *New Rules* (1981).

19. Among others compare Yankelovich 1981; David Riesman, *The Lonely Crowd* (New Haven: Yale University Press, 1965); Orrin Clapp, *The Collective Search for Identity* (New York: Holt, Rinehart and Winston, 1969); Lasch 1978; Bell 1976.

20. From a conversation with Mr. Robert Eckland (Eastern College, St. Davids, Pennsylvania), 2 March 1984.

21. From a conversation with Dr. J. Harold Ellens, executive director of CAPS, 7 March 1984.

22. In both the college and seminary samples, indexes were created to summarize vocational asceticism and moral asceticism. The vocational asceticism index was constructed by combining responses to items 3, 4, and 5 from table 7 (neither agree nor disagree responses were excluded from analysis). With a range between 3 and 12, categories were collapsed into quintiles. The alpha coefficients measuring index reliability were .52 (college) and .45 (seminary). The moral asceticism index was constructed similarly by combining responses to items 1, 2, 3, and 9 of table 8. The alpha coefficients for this index were .74 (college) and .71 (seminary).

Both of these indexes were run against the orthodoxy index referred to in chap. 2, n. 43. In the college sample, among those who scored high in vocational asceticism and moral asceticism, the difference between those who were most orthodox and those who were least orthodox on the former was 12 percentage points; and on the latter, 55 percentage points. Gamma coefficients measuring the association between orthodoxy and vocational asceticism were .21 (college) and .28 (seminary) and between orthodoxy and moral asceticism were .35 (college) and .31 (seminary).

23. Bivariate analysis of the measures of moral and vocational asceticism with the standard range of demographic variables pointed up these tendencies initially. Stepwise multiple regression on a composite index (alpha coefficient = .63) generally confirms these patterns. The overall regression model accounted for about 27 percent of the variance. A traditionalist orientation toward the family and religious orthodoxy accounted for most of the variance. Father's

education and student's class standing also accounted for some of the variance. The higher in each, the less likely students would be to conform to the older ethic. Not surprisingly, religiosity also significantly accounts for some of the variance—the more pious holding to a more rigorous asceticism.

24. Lauren A. King, "Soft Christians," *His*, October 1948, 2.

25. Ibid., 3–4. See also editorial, "What You Sow, You'll Reap," *His*, March 1949, 12–14.

## CHAPTER 4

1. I have conducted a thematic content analysis of popular and mass-market books published by Bethany House, Inter-Varsity, Moody, Revell, Scripture Press, Word, and Zondervan listed in the August 1982 edition of the *Spring Arbor Distributors Catalogue*. See also the thematic analysis conducted in 1980 reported in Hunter 1983a, where again 10 percent of all popular Evangelical books were found to deal with marriage and family issues.

2. The Family Protection Act, bill S. 1378 of the 97th Congress 1st session, submitted to the Senate of the United States on 17 June 1981 by Senators Roger Jepsen (R-Iowa) and Paul Laxalt (R-Nevada). Among its thirty-eight proposals are parental notification before any federally funded organization provides any contraceptive device or abortion service (including counseling) to an unmarried minor; the redefinition of child abuse to exclude discipline or corporal punishment methods applied by parents or parentally authorized individuals; and prohibitions against the Legal Services Corporation using federal funds in litigation involving divorce or homosexual rights.

3. See Pivar 1973 for an account of these organizations in relation to other reform movements of the period.

4. The actual figure for the Evangelical faculty is 69 percent and is taken from the EAP faculty survey (see Appendix). The views of Evangelical theologians are derived from the author's analysis of the 1982 Roper Theology Faculty Survey. Of the Evangelical theologians surveyed, 76 percent described "family life" in the United States either as needing "major amendment" or else as "fundamentally deficient"; 53 percent of liberal Protestant theologians and 65 percent of the Catholic theologians held these views.

5. W. Peter Blitchington, *Sex Roles and the Christian Family* (Wheaton, Ill.: Tyndale House, 1980), 16.

6. Larry Christenson, *The Christian Family* (Minneapolis: Bethany Fellowship, 1970), 11.

7. Ibid., 127.

8. Don Meredith, *Becoming One* (Nashville: Thomas Nelson Publishers, n.d.), 129–30.

9. Dan Benson, *The Total Man* (Wheaton, Ill.: Tyndale, 1981), 144.

10. Ibid., 178.

11. Ibid., 179.

12. Rus Walton, *One Nation under God* (Old Tappan, N. J.: Fleming H. Revell, 1975), 99.

13. Christenson, *Christian Family*, 47.

14. Meredith, *Becoming One*, 156.

15. Ibid., 153.

16. Edith Schaeffer, *What Is a Family?* (Old Tappan, N.J.: Fleming H. Revell, 1975), 117.

17. Dorothy Pape, *In Search of God's Ideal Woman* (Downers Grove, Ill.: Inter-Varsity Press, 1976), 331.

18. Blitchington, *Sex Roles*, 95.

19. James Dobson, *Dare to Discipline* (Wheaton, Ill.: Tyndale House, 1980), 39–40.

20. Maxine Hancock, *Love, Honour and be Free* (Pickering and Inglis, 1975), 88, as quoted in Joyce Huggett, *Two into One: Relating in Christian Marriage* (Downers Grove, Ill.: Inter-Varsity Press, 1981), 68.

21. Dobson, *Dare to Discipline*, 17–18.

22. Christenson, *Christian Family*, 112.

23. Dobson, *Dare to Discipline*, 22.

24. Joe Temple, *Know Your Child* (Grand Rapids: Baker Book House, 1974), 99.

25. Kenneth Chafin, *Is There a Family in the House?* (Minneapolis: World Wide Publications, 1978), 73.

26. Blitchington, *Sex Roles*, 20.

27. Walton, *One Nation under God*, 85.

28. Schaeffer, *What Is a Family?*, 51.

29. Walton, *One Nation under God*, 99.

30. Blitchington, *Sex Roles*, 48.

31. Chafin, *Is There a Family in the House?*, 15.

32. Edward Hindson, *The Total Family* (Wheaton, Ill.: Tyndale House, 1980), 37.

33. Ibid., 27.

34. Walton, *One Nation under God*, 80–81.

35. Rather than give extensive references for every point made in this review, I list here the sources that inform it: Shorter 1975; Hareven 1977; Wrigley 1977; Aries 1962; Laslett 1973; Gordon 1975; Handwalt 1977; Walkerhowe 1975; Goode 1963; Tilly and Tilly 1980; Harris 1983.

36. John Cotton, as quoted in Morgan 1966, 42.

37. Sarah Stickney Ellis, 1843, quoted in Calder 1977, 28. Calder's book is one of the most fascinating descriptive accounts of the bourgeois family.

38. James Dobson, *Straight Talk to Men and Their Wives* (Waco, Tex.: Word Books, 1982), 78.

39. Ibid., 101.

40. Ibid., 102.

41. This equation is certainly made (albeit unwittingly) in Jerry Falwell's *Listen America*, (New York: Harper and Row, 1980); in Tim LaHaye's *The Battle for the Family* (Old Tappan: Revell, 1981); and in many other works,

including Michael Brown, *The Christian in an Age of Sexual Eclipse* (Wheaton: Tyndale, 1983): "Our culture has regarded motherhood as among the highest and most noble roles to which a woman can aspire. For centuries, the privilege of caring for children has been viewed as a fulfilling and rewarding task. . . . The mother's role has been preserved by the concept that the father would provide the necessary material support that would enable the wife to remain at home giving primary care to the children. The first responsibility of the mother was to provide day by day, hour by hour nurturance and guidance for the children, while the father was to provide the material needs as well as the cooperative and supportive collaboration in the childrearing responsibilities. . . . The traditional view of a man defined him as one who assumed sexual, moral and social responsibility as a leader and provider, as well as one who gave strength and stability. Therefore, the traditional masculine role included financial support of wife and children. Traditionally, the male would obtain gainful employment and career stability before entering into the permanent sexual relationship of marriage."

42. Dobson, *Straight Talk to Men and Their Wives*, 21.

43. Christenson, *Christian Family*, 121.

44. See Chafin, *Is There a Family in the House?*, 87, 91.

45. Christenson *Christian Family*, 123.

46. Benson, *Total Man*, 184–87.

47. Pivar 1973; and Anne Oakley, *Woman's Work: The Housewife Past and Present* (New York: Vintage Books, 1976).

48. For a historical overview tracing the growing ambiguity of the woman's role, see Bendroth 1983.

49. In this case the question read as follows: "For a woman to remain unmarried she must be 'sick,' 'neurotic,' or 'immoral.'"

50. In the margins of the questionnaires, students wrote comments such as these and were emphatic about men holding the family ascendant over job or career.

51. In the 1977 General Social Survey, 60 percent of all Evangelicals agreed with this, compared with 56 of all non-Evangelicals.

52. Seventy percent of all Evangelicals agreed with this, compared with 64 percent of all non-Evangelicals.

53. This "role of women" index was constructed by adding responses strongly agree to strongly disagree (neither agree or disagree excluded from analysis) on items 3, 4, and 5 of table 11. Alpha coefficient = .72 college; .79 seminary.

54. The average gamma coefficient was higher for these samples than for the sample of women collegians except on the abortion issue.

55. The following review dealing with the strategies for interpreting wifely submission is based upon a content analysis of articles on the subject from the periodicals *Christianity Today*, *Eternity*, and *Moody Monthly*.

56. Andre Bustanby, "Love, Honor, and Obey," *Christianity Today*, 6 June 1969, 3–4.

57. These quotes came from ibid., 3.

58. Ella May Miller, "Housework Doesn't Come Naturally," *Moody Monthly*, January 1976, 71–74.

59. Lane Adams, "Why a Woman Can't Be Like a Man," *Moody Monthly*, April 1976, 100–101.

60. Ibid., 100; see also Bruce Smith, "Till Death Do Us Part," *Christianity Today*, 16 January 1970, 5–10; Dwight Small, "Christian Married Love," *Eternity*, August 1955; Winnie Christensen, "What Is a Woman's Role?" *Moody Monthly*, June 1971, 22–35; George Sweeting, "Guidelines for a Christian Marriage," *Moody Monthly*, September 1981, 18–20; Nellie Stover, "God's Pattern for Your Marriage," *Moody Monthly*, June 1951, 649; D. G. Barnhouse, "The Bible Way to a Successful Marriage," *Eternity*, September 1960, 12–33; James Boice, "Marriage by Christ's Standard," *Eternity*, November 1970, 20–23.

61. Letha Scanzoni, "Elevate Marriage to a Partnership," *Eternity*, July 1968, 11–14; Phillip Yancey, "Marriage: Minefields on the Way to Paradise," *Christianity Today*, 18 February 1977, 24–27; George Knight, "Male and Female Related He Them," *Christianity Today*, 19 April 1976, 13–17; Letha Scanzoni, "How to Live with a Liberated Wife," *Christianity Today*, 4 June 1976, 6-9; Ruth Senter, "Dare to Be Liberated," *Moody Monthly*, November 1972, 81–85.

62. Virginia Ramey Mollenkott, "Interpreting Difficult Scriptures," *Daughters of Sarah*, March/April 1979, 16–17.

63. Virginia Mollenkott, "Dear Dusty—Response to a Letter to the Editor," *Daughters of Sarah*, September/October 1979, 17.

64. Strongly sympathetic to the cause of feminism though not quite as committed are another 25–33 percent of the student bodies.

65. Telephone conversation with Ms. Rita Finger, 16 July 1984. According to Ms. Finger, in the ten years of their existence the number of paid subscriptions to *Daughters of Sarah* has risen steadily.

66. Overall, 67 percent of the general population (1977 General Social Survey) agreed with this: 65 percent, Evangelicals; 69 percent, non-Evangelicals.

67. Forty-six percent of the Evangelicals agreed with this statement; 50 percent of all non-Evangelical respondents agreed with it.

68. See Adams, "Why a Woman Can't Be Like a Man," 101; and Blitchington, *Sex Roles and the Christian Family*, 114–15.

69. Christenson, *Christian Family*, 45.

70. Paul D. Meier, *Christian Child-rearing and Personality Development* (Grand Rapids: Baker, 1977), 139.

71. Ibid., 139.

72. Charles Swindoll, *You and Your Child* (Nashville: Thomas Nelson, 1977), 114.

73. *The Encyclopedia of Christian Parenting* (Old Tappan: Revell, 1982), "Modern Mother," p. 281.

74. Joy Wilt, *Raising Your Children toward Emotional and Spiritual Maturity* (Waco: Word, 1980), 182.

75. Ibid., 186.

76. Ibid., 186.

77. Ibid., 187.

78. The role of women index was described in n. 53 of this chapter. The role of men index was constructed similarly by combining responses (strongly agree

to strongly disagree) to items 1, 2, and 3 of table 10. The alpha coefficients were .72 (college) and .71 (seminary).

79. Cross-tabular analysis shows this, as does multivariate analysis. On the former, among those who placed highly traditional on a composite index (combining role of men and role of women indexes), called a traditional familism index (alpha coefficient = .81, college; .85, seminary), the range between high in orthodoxy and low in orthodoxy is 54 percent for the seminary (gamma coefficient = .54) and 44 percent for the college (gamma coefficient = .38). In a stepwise multiple-regression analysis, orthodoxy and political conservatism headed a list of independent variables that also included a religiosity index and gender and denominational affiliation. For the model as a whole, $r^2$ = .31.

80. Simple bivariate analysis shows that those who are married are, by a margin of 16 percent, more likely to hold traditional norms than are unmarried seminarians, and married seminarians with children are more likely than married though childless seminarians to hold these views by a margin of 34 percent.

81. Again, simple bivariate analysis shows that differences between married and unmarried and childless and childbearing couples disappear when controlling for the number of years attending seminary.

## Chapter 5

1. ACLU founder, Roger Baldwin, placed newspaper advertisements seeking school teachers willing to violate state laws prohibiting the teaching of Darwin's theory of evolution.

2. Shipley also stated that "for the first time in history, organized knowledge has come into open conflict with organized ignorance" (1927, 3–4).

3. The most comprehensive analysis of the extreme right wing of Fundamentalism during the Depression years and following is Ribuffo 1983. Among other things, Ribuffo provides compelling biographies of the most notorious leaders of the Fundamentalist Right, Pelley, Winrod, and Smith.

4. For a review of these events see Gaspar 1963; Roy 1960; Lipset and Raab 1970, chap. 6; Bell 1964; and Epstein and Forster 1967.

5. Though Protestants outnumbered Roman Catholics, the percentage of Roman Catholics supporting McCarthy was significantly greater than the percentage of Protestants (Lipset and Raab 1970, 230).

6. To this list one could also add the Christian Anti-Communist Crusade, under the leadership of Fred Schwarz.

7. Among those singled out were Reinhold Niebuhr, E. Stanley Jones, Harry Emerson Fosdick, and Henry Van Dusen (president of Union Theological Seminary in New York City).

8. Editorializing, *Eternity* editor Donald Grey Barnhouse said of Carl McIntire: "One of two things must be true. Either Carl McIntire is an honest man dedicated to a false cause . . . or, he must be branded as a man who is utterly and thoroughly dishonest. . . ." See Roy 1960, 230. Other Evangelical leaders such as Carl F. H. Henry, E. J. Carnell, Vernon Grounds, Harold Ockenga, and Bernard Ramm also spoke out vehemently against these groups.

9. Wuthnow 1983b cites more than a dozen empirical studies showing that Evangelical Protestants were the least prone to political action of any kind.

10. This was reflected in University of Michigan (Center for Political Studies) election data. Corwin Schmidt carefully worked through many of these issues in his paper, "The Mobilization of Evangelical Voters in 1980: An Initial Test of Several Hypotheses," presented at the annual meeting of the American Political Science Association, Chicago, September 1983. See also Reichley, 1986.

11. Figures are taken from George Gallup, The Gallup Poll (News Release), 8 September 1980.

12. Ibid.

13. This is a reanalysis of the 1978/1979 Gallup/*Christianity Today* survey reported in Hunter 1983a, 115. See table 22.

14. For a discussion of the growth in religious lobbies of all persuasions, see Weber 1982.

15. For the 1984 election, this has been documented by Corwin Schmidt in his work presented at the annual meeting of the Society for the Scientific Study of Religion, Savannah, Georgia, 1985. However, it is important not to obscure the fact that majorities of Evangelicals voted Republican in both the 1980 (63%) and 1984 (80%) presidential elections (see *New York Times*, 8 November 1984, A19). This is significant when considering the fact that most Evangelicals have long considered themselves Democrats. Evangelicals, then, are potentially decisive as a voting block, particularly at the presidential level. Indeed Reichley (1986) suggests that Evangelicals may develop a tribal identification with the Republican party. But the 1980 and 1984 elections were not tests of that potential.

16. On the liberal reaction generally, see Hunter 1983b, 149–63.

17. Other welfare issues were explored as well. The majority said it was rarely or never wrong to receive unemployment compensation (collegians, 73%; seminarians, 79%) and that it was rarely or never wrong to receive welfare (collegians, 69%; seminarians, 71%).

18. An August 1980 Gallup poll (reported 8 September 1980) of the general population showed that 57 percent favored the registration of firearms; 52 percent favored the death penalty for those convicted of murder; 41 percent favored more nuclear power plants; roughly 71 percent favored increased defense spending; and nearly two-thirds favored requiring prayer in school. A November 1984 Gallup survey showed that 42 percent of the general population favored increased defense spending and that 71 percent still favored the death penalty. On government-sponsored social welfare, the Evangelical collegians were roughly equivalent to the general population.

19. This figure is from a 1981 Roper study, reported in *Public Opinion*, October/November 1982, 21–24.

20. This public policy index measuring relative liberalism and conservatism was constructed by combining responses (mostly favor, 1; no opinion, 2; mostly oppose, 3) to items 2, 3, 4, 10, 11, and 13 of table 18. Responses to items 2, 11,

and 13 were recoded, of course, to keep responses in a common order. The range of 6 to 18 was then collapsed into five categories: 6, 7 = very liberal; 8, 9, 10 = liberal; 11, 12, 13 = moderate; 14, 15, 16 = conservative; 17, 18 = very conservative. The alpha coefficients measuring the statistical reliability of this index were .59 (college) and .68 (seminary). The gamma coefficients correlating this index with political self-identification (table 17) were .53 (college) and .65 (seminary).

21. Apart from the internal statistical reliability of the political values index, this table should be viewed as confirmation of the coherence of different ideological perspectives within Evangelicalism's coming generation.

22. Not all of these questions were posed to the entire college sample. This is one reason for their omission from table 20. All the same, the differences between liberals and conservatives on those questions which were comparable are striking: American support for Israel (53% difference; gamma = $-.31$), balance of power with the Soviet Union (61% difference; gamma = $-.46$), abortion legislation (31% difference; gamma = $-.16$), ordination of women (52% difference; gamma = $.21$).

23. Bivariate analysis between this public policy index and the range of demographic variables demonstrates this initially. Stepwise multiple-regression analysis with this index as the dependent variable also showed this general pattern. The model as a whole accounted for 24 percent of the variance. Religious orthodoxy and traditional familism were the most important determinants of political position. Also significant, however, were their parents' religiosity, denominational tradition (those from the Baptist tradition were more conservative), gender (men were more conservative), and region (southerners were more conservative).

24. Only college data are reported in table 21. The seminary data point to the same large differences between the very liberal and the very conservative: the Christian foundation of America (42% difference; gamma = $-.33$), America is still a Christian nation (4% difference; gamma = $.07$), the threat of communism (61% difference; gamma = $-.46$), the menace of secular humanism (37% difference; gamma = $-.44$), the power of secular humanists in the universities (34% difference; gamma = $-.43$).

25. Among the most vocal are the late Francis Schaeffer in *A Christian Manifesto* (Westchester, Ill.: Crossway Books, 1981), *How Shall We Then Live?* (Old Tappan, N. J.: Fleming H. Revell, 1976), and, with C. Everett Koop, *What Ever Happened to the Human Race?* (Old Tappan, N.J.: Fleming H. Revell, 1977); Franky Schaeffer, *Addicted to Mediocrity* (Westchester, Ill.: Crossway Books, 1981); John Whitehead, *The Second American Revolution* (Elgin, Ill.: David C. Cook, 1982); Jerry Falwell, *Listen America* (New York: Doubleday, 1980); John Price, *America at the Crossroads* (Wheaton, Ill.: Tyndale House, 1976); and Edward Rowe, *Save America* (Old Tappan, N. J.: Revell, Spire, 1976).

26. Consider also the finding of Shupe and Stacey (1983, 107) that supporters of the Moral Majority were more than twice as likely to agree that "one of the

problems in education today is that secular humanists have been allowed to determine the textbooks used in the public school system" (supporters agreeing, 80%; non-supporters agreeing, 37%).

27. Once again, when comparing samples (see n. 20), the differences were greater among seminarians and, more importantly, the correlations were greater too.

28. The Connecticut Mutual Life Insurance Company, "Report on American Values in the '80s," in-house publication, 1981, provides a convincing set of data.

29. For the sake of comparability with the published findings of the 1978/1979 Gallup/*Christianity Today* survey (in which all "no opinions" were treated as missing cases), "no opinion" was excluded from the analysis of the Evangelical Academy Project data.

30. These observations are based upon a simple bivariate analysis of a composite index made from the combination of these three variables. Factor analysis confirmed the strength of these as a composite measure of attitudes toward the public role of religion. The index was highly reliable, with an alpha coefficient of .72. See Hunter 1983a, 92, for a description of the index construction.

31. These facts are from an analysis of the 1977 and 1982 General Social Survey. Further support comes from the analysis of longitudinal data (between 1958 and 1978) using racial attitudes as an index of tolerance. See A. Wade Smith, "Cohorts, Education, and the Evolution of Tolerance," paper presented at the annual meeting of the American Sociological Association, Detroit, Michigan, 1983. Smith concludes that since 1958, intolerance has decreased and tolerance has increased in the American population as a whole but particularly in the southern region of the country, where tolerance has traditionally been weakest. There are some structural differences (for example, along the lines of education and age cohort), yet the norms of American culture have changed significantly. Notably, the greatest changes have taken place among the groups that have historically been the most intolerant (one could fairly count conservative Protestants among these).

32. Measuring tolerance is fraught with problems. As Sullivan et al. (1981) noted, measurement of support for civil liberties often varies with the type of questions being asked. While this is so, comparing Evangelical to non-Evangelical samples with the same measure in part neutralizes this potential problem. In relative terms then, I would contend that the following is a highly reliable measure of support for civil liberties. For a description of how this religious, moral, and political tolerance index was created, see Hunter 1984. The alpha coefficient measuring index reliability was .55.

33. The difference in "enthusiasm" for principles of tolerance, as I have termed it, is most accounted for by the differences in the percentage who circled "strongly agree" and those who circled "agree." For example, in the survey, religious tolerance was measured by the responses to this statement, "I believe that people should be free to *believe* what they want even if it is very different from the way I believe." Among Evangelical collegians, 25 percent responded "agree." Likewise with moral tolerance: "I believe that people should be free to *live* the

way they want even if it is very different from the way I live." Among Evangelical collegians, 16 percent responded "strongly agree" and 42 percent responded "agree"; of the public university students, 56 percent responded "strongly agree" and 36 percent responded "agree." Finally the same was true with regard to political tolerance: "People who hold political ideas which are un-American should be kept from voicing their opinion." Evangelical college: 23 percent, strongly disagree; 53 percent, disagree. Public university: 37 percent, strongly disagree; 44 percent disagree. This pattern also characterized the seminarians.

34. There was a statistically significant (though weak) relationship between political orientation and tolerance (gamma = .19 for the college and seminary samples). Predictably, the less liberal (or more conservative), the more intolerant one is likely to be. Within the college sample, the difference between very liberal and very conservative scoring at least moderately high in tolerance was 18 percentage points; for seminarians it was 25 percentage points.

35. This observation was made both from the in-depth interviews and from the innumerable comments respondents made on the questionnaires themselves.

36. The minority that responded that they would support a constitutional amendment to make Christianity the official religion of the United States are not taught this by their professors. In the 1982 Roper Theology Faculty Survey, only 3 percent of all Evangelical theologians said that they would support this; 97 percent said they would not.

37. On the *goals* of the Moral Majority, among collegians 37 percent disapproved and 39 percent "neither approved nor disapproved." Only 2 percent strongly approved and 22 percent approved. Among seminarians, 30 percent disapproved and 27 percent were neutral. Only 5 percent strongly approved and 39 percent approved. On their methods, 55 percent of the seminarians (collegians were not asked) disapproved, 26 percent were neutral, and 19 percent approved.

38. These questions were posed only to the seminarians. On the political effects of the Moral Majority, 38 percent said they were harmful and 27 percent said they were neutral. On its influence, 57 percent thought that it would lose influence and 27 percent said it would stay the same. Finally, 54 percent said it harms the cause of religion in America and 30 percent said it was neutral.

39. Surveys indicate that compared with other constituencies, Evangelicals are more likely to favor the Moral Majority. Still they are a minority of the total population of conservative Protestants. For example, according to a November 1984 Gallup survey (for the Robert H. Schuller Ministries), nearly two-thirds (64%) of all American Evangelicals were neutral or opposed to the activities of the Moral Majority (26% were opposed, while 38% were neutral). This pattern was further confirmed by the Roper Theology Faculty Survey. These data showed that Evangelical theologians are split over the efforts of the Moral Majority (53% favor; 47% oppose). A majority (62%) find them neutral or harmful in their political effects; a majority (45%) believed that they harm the cause of religion in America; and most (51%) believe that they will lose influence over the next few years.

40. This again is derived from my analysis of the Roper Theology Faculty

Survey. The differences between liberal and Evangelical theologians were slight but statistically significant; 92 percent of the Evangelicals held this view, and 88 percent of the liberals did.

41. Three-way cross-tabs were performed on these samples using the three indexes reviewed in this chapter. Each index, as previously noted in n. 20, was collapsed into five categories. The percentages were determined *not* by the most extreme categories of these indexes but by the less extreme and most extreme together. Thus, conservative and very conservative were combined, intolerant and very intolerant were combined, and highly public and moderately public (see n. 29) were combined. The measure of extremism is fairly liberal then. By this standard 2 percent of the collegians and 4 percent of the seminarians could be called extremists.

42. Once again, stepwise, multiple-regression techniques were employed to sort out the major determinants of variance. The model overall accounted for 27% percent of the variance. The most important sources of variability came from the respondents' views of the family, religious orthodoxy, gender (female), and degree of sectarianism in the church they belong to.

43. This is strongly illustrated by the responses to two statements in the 1982 Roper Theology Faculty Survey. More Evangelical theologians (92%) than liberal theologians (84%) agreed that "in the U.S. today, there can be no justification for using violence to achieve political goals." So too, more Evangelical theologians (83%) than liberal theologians (77%) disagreed that "meaningful social change cannot be achieved through traditional American politics."

44. Cord (1982) examines this ideological transformation at some length though his agenda is somewhat polemical. Grant Wacker ("Uneasy in Zion: Evangelicals in Post-Modern Society," paper delivered at the Conference on Evangelicalism and Modern America, 13–15 April 1983, Wheaton College, Wheaton, Ill.) discusses the broader changes in the cultural norms surrounding religion's role in the public sphere in terms of the custodial ideal and the plural ideal of church-state relations.

## Chapter 6

1. *Westminster Seminary Catalog*, 1981, 5.

2. *Gordon-Conwell Seminary Catalog*, 1980/1981, 9.

3. The founding dates of the EAP sample of colleges are as follows. Bethel: 1931; George Fox: 1891; Gordon: 1889; Houghton: 1883; Messiah: 1909; Seattle-Pacific: 1891; Taylor: 1846; Westmont: 1940; Wheaton: 1860.

4. This information was gathered from a telephone survey of academic deans or their offices at the nine colleges of the EAP sample conducted between November 1984 and March 1985. While there were differences in the degree to which institutional expectations placed upon faculty (particularly in the realm of research) had grown, all did agree that this was a noticeable trend. Most felt that although an active research and publishing record was not an absolutely essential factor in being given a faculty appointment or in being tenured or promoted, it

was an important factor all the same. Most of these deans projected that the institutional expectations would increase in the future. Certainly their own desire was to see more publishing done by their faculty.

5. The EAP faculty survey (see Appendix) posed the question, "For as long as you have been at your institution, would you say pressure to publish has increased, stayed the same, or decreased?" Thirty-seven percent of the total faculty indicated that it had increased. When excluding instructors and assistant professors (those who had not been at the institution very long) and considering only associate and full professors (those who had presumably been at their college for more than six years), this figure increased to 41 percent.

6. These figures are derived from the EAP faculty survey.

7. These cumulative indexes have already been reported. In all indexes, the top two categories were combined.

8. Excerpted from an unsolicited letter to the author, dated 15 October 1984.

9. This section of the chapter is an abbreviated and slightly modified version of the argument presented in Hammond and Hunter 1984.

10. Seriousness of approach to education in this case was measured by selectivity in admissions policy. The more selective in admissions, the more religious apostasy. For a review of the extensive literature on this subject see Astin 1977.

11. In a personal conversation, Edward Dobson (vice-president of Liberty University) admitted to me that students at Liberty University were "tired of legalism" and "separatism" and wanted to be more open and professional in their academic studies (9 November 1985).

12. For a theoretical discussion of this inclination, see Shils 1972.

13. For a review of some of this literature, see Hunter 1983a, chaps. 2 and 3.

14. I want to be absolutely clear about something implied to this point. The cultural traditions of conservative Protestantism have always experienced some change and fluidity. Thus, I am not holding up late nineteenth-century expressions of Protestant orthodoxy as a normative orthodoxy—the eternal standard against which all generations of conservative Protestants can be measured. What I am arguing is that continuity with the past can be measured along a relative scale. That is, there can be more or less continuity with the traditions and greater or lesser success at defending the boundaries of "classical orthodoxy." To put this concretely, I am arguing that until the end of the nineteenth century, conservative Protestants had been relatively successful at maintaining continuity with the orthodoxy they inherited. In the twentieth century and particularly in the post–World War II period, the challenges have been more difficult, and conservative Protestants have been less successful. This does not mean in any ultimate sense that contemporary Evangelicals are further from the Truth. It only means that they are, in *many* ways (and not necessarily in all ways), further from the truths that their religious forebears, particularly in the late nineteenth century, believed in. Many of the innovations of contemporary conservative Protestantism would have been considered by earlier generations of the faithful to be suspect if not apostate.

15. This survey was the November 1984 Gallup/Schuller Survey (See Appendix).

16. My indebtedness to Lippmann (1929) for this entire argument is obvious.

17. This figure is taken from the EAP faculty survey.

18. In the last interviews I conducted with seminarians, I asked respondents to imagine themselves as pastors of a congregation. Then I described a number of situations in which church discipline might be appropriate. The situations concerned matters of theology and morality in which a member of the congregation openly violates one of the norms of congregational life. For example, a single woman accidentally gets pregnant but decides not to carry the fetus to term even though she knows it will be wrong to abort the fetus. Or, a man decides after ten years of marriage that he is no longer compatible with his wife. He "knows what the Bible says about divorce" but he is committed to getting a divorce in order to marry another woman. Further, he wants to stay an active member of the church. Another example concerned an unmarried couple who discreetly yet unashamedly live together. They know what Scripture teaches about premarital sexual relations but do not want to get married and do not want to stop living together. Other examples concerned individuals who did not agree with church teaching on the authority of Scripture, who danced, who played cards, etc. In all of these situations, seminarians were asked if they would invoke some form of formal church discipline in order to rectify matters. While all expressed consternation about most of these situations (except dancing and playing cards), only one in four said that he would pursue such a course of action. The others said that they would try to dissuade them from following through with such actions or continuing such actions, but that they could not see themselves going much further than this, although they said that of course it would depend on the situation.

## CHAPTER 7

1. A comprehensive review of this debate was most recently charted by Marshall (1982). See also Green 1959, 1973.

2. Two exceptions to this were France and Belgium. While Protestants remained a minority here, these countries were distinguished from the other major Catholic powers to the south by their long-standing anticlerical and free-thinking intellectual traditions. These cultural differences along with their geographic distance from Rome fostered a political and economic autonomy from the center of Catholic experience in this and later centuries. See Wallerstein 1974, 152.

3. Winthrop Hudson concludes that as late as 1900, "few would have disputed the contention that the United States was a Protestant nation, so self-evident was the fact that its life and its culture had been shaped by three centuries of Protestant witness and influence" (1961, 128). Other sources on American religious history document this as well: Marty 1970; Ahlstrom 1972; Mead 1975.

4. Quotation excerpted from Handy 1971, 120; see also chap. 5 of that work for a very informative summary of this orientation on the part of pre-twentieth-century American Protestants.

5. This point is made by social scientists of a variety of theoretical perspectives. See, for example, Bell 1973 and Machlup 1962.

6. Wuthnow 1982 summarizes these cultural developments. Gouldner (1978a, b) discusses this in terms of the development of the "Culture of Critical Discourse," which he argues is an ideology of and about discourse.

7. Of course, this can be traced at least as far back as Weber, but in more recent history this theme has been elaborated and discussed by Oswald Spengler, *Man and Technics* (London: Allen and Unwin, 1932); Lewis Mumford, *Technics and Civilization* (New York: Harcourt, Brace and Co., 1934); idem, *The Myth of the Machine: Technics and Human Development* (New York: Harcourt Brace Jovanovich, 1967); Theodor Geiger, *Demokratie ohne Dogma* (Munich: Szczesny Verlag, 1963); Ellul 1957; Habermas 1979. More recent globalistic interpretations of this transformation can be found in Wuthnow 1983a and Wallerstein 1983. These few listings only begin to cover the theoretical literature speculating about the course and direction of modern societal transformations.

8. In this discussion I rely upon Wuthnow 1980.

9. See Hunter 1983b for a more careful examination of the ideological exchange between both interest groups and the strategies employed in discrediting each other's ideological program.

10. This argument has been propounded mainly by the Weberian camp; e.g., Ellul 1957, 1967; Zijderveld 1970. Since the mid–twentieth century, however, the Critical school of neo-Marxist thinking has also espoused this view; e.g., Herbert Marcuse, *Reason and Revolution* (Boston: Beacon, 1960); idem, *One-Dimensional Man* (Boston: Beacon, 1964); Henri Lefebre, *Everyday Life in the Modern World* (New York: Harper and Row, 1968); Adorno and Horkheimer 1972.

11. This critique has mainly been advanced by quasi-Freudian theorists of a liberal/Left political orientation; e.g., Erich Fromm, *Escape from Freedom* (New York: Holt, Rinehart and Winston, 1941); idem, *The Sane Society* (New York: Holt, Rinehart, and Winston, 1955); Philip Slater, *The Pursuit of Loneliness: American Culture at the Breaking Point* (Boston: Beacon, 1970); Jules Henry, *Culture against Man* (New York: Vintage, 1964); Bernard Rosenberg, Israel Gerver, and F. William Howton, eds., *Mass Society in Crisis: Social Problems and Social Pathology* (New York: Macmillan, 1964). Representatives of this view can also be found in Eric Josephson and Mary Josephson, eds., *Man Alone: Alienation in Modern Society* (New York: Dell, 1962).

12. No one school of social theory or social criticism has dominated this perspective. Weberian, neo-Freudian, and neo-Marxist theorists have examined this theme. See Berger, Berger, and Kellner 1973; Bell 1976; Lasch 1978, 1984; Sennett 1974.

13. Sennett (1974) contends the transformation entails the usurpation of the public sphere by the private sphere; Bell (1976) argues that the private sphere is transformed by the disjunction in the economic realm, the polity, and the cultural

sphere; Berger, Berger, and Kellner (1973) maintain that the transformation is a result of the weakening of the institutions of the private sphere.

14. For a review and analysis of social criticism between 1930 and 1985, see Hunter 1986.

15. Pessimism pervades most cultural critiques of modern society although Ellul (1957, 1967) and Marcuse (1964) may be the most pessimistic.

16. Those who maintain this position generally operate out of a radical reductionist model of social analysis. Consequently, advocates of this view lean notably toward neo-Marxist/neocritical theory.

17. It is not accidental that most who hold this view are on the conservative and neo-conservative side in social and political analysis. See Hunter 1986 for an explanation of why this is true in Peter Berger's case. For some work done from the conservative perspective, see Etzioni 1984, Nisbet 1980, and Bell 1977. See also Steinfels 1979.

18. Alexsandr Solzhenitsyn, *A World Split Apart* (New York: Harper and Row, 1978), 61.

19. These figures come from the Evangelical Academy Project.

20. These figures are derived from the author's analysis of the 1982 Theology Faculty Survey. When asked to assess the present influence of religion, 87 percent of the Evangelical theologians (nearly nine in ten) felt it was too low. Importantly, the sense of declining influence was greater among Evangelicals than among liberal Protestant and Catholic theologians. Forty-one percent of the Evangelicals felt that the influence of religion was declining, compared with 39 percent of the liberal Protestants and 34 percent of the Catholics (chi-square significance = .000).

## CHAPTER 8

1. Peter Berger's hypothesis (1967a, chap. 2) is that there is an anthropological requirement for a stable nomos. This takes expression in the form of a craving for meaning that has the force of an instinct. Mary Douglas (1966) is making the same argument when she states that human beings need sharply defined boundaries within which to live their lives.

2. These data are derived from the 1985 edition of the *Yearbook of American and Canadian Churches*, edited by Constant H. Jacquet, Jr. (Nashville: Abingdon). Denominations included under the heading Evangelical were the Assemblies of God; the Christian and Missionary Alliance; Church of God, Anderson, Indiana; Church of God, Cleveland, Tennessee; Church of the Nazarene; Evangelical Covenant Church of America; Free Methodists; Lutheran Church—Missouri Synod; Salvation Army; Seventh Day Adventists; and the Southern Baptist Convention. Mainline denominations included the American Lutheran Church; the Lutheran Church in America; the Episcopal Church; Presbyterian Church in the U.S.A.; United Church of Christ; and the United Methodist Church. The actual figures measuring growth rate were as follows: (*Evangelical*) 1940–1950, +28.4%; 1950–1955, +16.2%; 1955–1960, +13.6%; 1960–1965, +10.1%; 1965–1970, +7.5%; 1970–1975, +8.5%; 1975–1980,

+6.7; 1980–1983, +4.2%; (*mainline*) 1940–1950, +17.4%; 1950–1955, +9.1%; 1955–1960, +8.7%; 1960–1965, +2.4%; 1965–1970, −3.0%; 1970–1975, −7.8%; 1975–1980, −3.4%; 1980–1983, −1.7%; (*U.S. population*) 1940–1950, +13%; 1950–1955, +8.2%; 1955–1960, +8.2%; 1960–1965, +7%; 1965–1970, +5.3%; 1970–1975, +5%; 1975–1980, +5.1%; 1980–1983, +2.9%. Figures for the United States population are taken from various issues of U.S. Bureau of the Census, *Statistical Abstract of the United States* (Washington, D.C.: GPO). For a further discussion of church growth and decline and the many factors which influence it, see Hoge and Roozen 1979.

3. U.S. Bureau of the Census, *Statistical Abstract of the United States* Washington, D.C.: GPO, 1985.

4. These figures are taken from the author's analysis of the 1978/1979 Gallup/*Christianity Today* Survey (see Appendix). See also Hunter 1983a, chap. 4.

5. On theological issues, 7 percent believed that Evangelicalism would become more liberal; 12 percent believed that it would become more conservative; and 31 percent believed it would remain the same as it is now. On social issues, 28 percent believed Evangelicalism would become more liberal; 9 percent believed it would become more conservative; and 17 percent thought it would remain the same as it is at present.

6. Roughly 46 percent believed that there would be a split over theological issues; 43 percent believed that it would split over social issues.

7. Roughly 48 percent of the faculty believed that there would be a division over theological issues; 51 percent believed that it would split over social issues.

8. I am grateful to Walker Knight, editor of *SBC Today*, for his assistance in gathering information on the Southern Baptist Convention. Documentary evidence of the kinds of antagonisms present in the denominational hierarchy was drawn from the *SBC Today*.

9. Virtually every issue of *Sojourners* develops this theme. Other publications of the Evangelical Left also present this argument.

10. Quoted in J. Herbert Kane, "The White Man's Burden is Changing Colors," *Christianity Today* 25 (17 July 1981): 62–64.

11. Ibid., 63.

12. This is taken from an article by Costas (1977, 183–97). See also Boese 1983; and Gottfried B. Osai-Mensah, "World Revival: Will It Begin in Africa?" *Christian Life*, June 1980, 30-32.

13. For the ways in which the Third World has become a symbol of utopian hope for secular political ideologues, see Berger 1983.

14. Particularly helpful in framing this discussion was Rieff 1966.

## EPILOGUE

1. U.S. Bureau of the Census, *Statistical Abstracts of the United States* (Washington, D.C.: GPO, 1984), no. 247.

2. Ibid., no. 248.

3. This is taken from the author's analysis of the Roper Theology Faculty Survey.

4. The historical and social context out of which Reform Judaism emerged is discussed in Meyer 1978.

5. An overview of the sociology of the Conservative movement is provided by Martin 1978.

6. There is some debate about this development. My source is Liebman 1965, 21–97. See also Spero 1978, 84.

7. These figures are derived from two sources: the 1984 *Statistical Abstract of the United States* and Cohen 1983.

8. Descriptions of different kinds of services found in Orthodox synagogues can be found in Heilman 1976. His ethnography, though, mainly concerns life in the Modern Orthodox synagogue. See also Liebman 1983a, 55-56; Spero 1978, 86.

9. The historical and sociological dimensions of these differences are discussed in Heilman 1982a, b. See also Liebman 1983a, b; Heilman 1976, 16; Spero 1978, 92–96.

10. Gittelson (1984) cites recent attempts to create a feminist theology within a Modern Orthodox framework. She also references Orthodox speculation about the likelihood of women being ordained as Orthodox rabbis.

11. Heilman (1982a, b) provides the most compelling documentation for this argument.

12. Though the Modern Orthodox claim parity of legitimacy with the traditionalists, the traditionalists do not accord this same legitimacy to the Modern Orthodox (Liebman 1983b, 112).

13. Himmelfarb and Loar (1984) argue that this revitalization was largely illusory. Institutional growth and prominence, they argue, was falsely assumed to be numerical growth.

14. A very compelling analysis of this movement is Aviad 1983. Most of the "returnees" in her study were American Jews, but there were some European and Israeli Jews as well.

15. As is already well known, the major division is between Sunni and Shiite traditions. The Sunni constitute roughly 85 percent of all Muslims, and thus are the numerically dominant form of Islam. They believe that the succession of leadership in Islam passed down through the four "caliphs" who were the companions of Muhammad and that the authority of Sharia comes through the community of believers. By contrast, the Shiites (making up approximately 14 percent of the Muslim population) believe that the succession of leadership came through the blood lineage of Ali, the son-in-law/cousin of the Prophet. Unlike the Sunnis, they maintain that the *immam* holds special authority on matters of Islamic law—more than the community of believers. Sufism cuts across Shiite and Sunni tradition and is a form of otherworldly mysticism organized in religious orders or brotherhoods.

16. These reflections on community and history and their relation to Islamic faith are drawn mainly from Smith 1957, chap. 1.

17. The best discussion of Islamic liberalism available is Hourani 1962. See also Rahman 1968.

18. Wilfred Cantwell Smith expressed it this way: "We would attribute the decline of liberalism in recent Islam in significant part to the fact that such liberalism as has been achieved . . . has not yet been formulated in such a way as to envisage its dynamic truth as within the central structure of Islamic faith. This means that it has not been set forth in such a way as to be theoretically compelling to a Muslim as such; nor incorporated in practice—specifically, related to worship—in such a way as to give religious power to those intellectually persuaded" (1957, 66).

19. Esposito (1982) has provided the best documentation for the various reforms in Muslim family law, particularly as they pertain to women and women's rights. For a review of these dynamics in particular countries, see three essays in Stoddard, Cothell, and Sullivan 1981. These are "Education and Family Life in Modernizing Malaysia," by Muhammad Kamal bin Hassan; "Sudan: Education and Family," by Nafissa Ahmed el-Amin; and "Libya: The Family in Modern Islamic Society," by Elizabeth W. Fernea.

20. For a broad historical overview of Japanese religion and, particularly, Japanese Buddhism see Kitagawa 1966; Matsunaga and Matsunaga 1974; and cf. Earhart 1982.

21. In the Lotus Sutra, the term *bodhisattva* has two meanings. The first is the one mentioned in the text—demigods who, though achieving Nirvana, delay their entrance into eternal bliss to help a struggling humanity. The other, though, refers to all other true believers.

22. As Robert Bellah (1970, 119–20) argues, a transcendentalist impulse existed in some streams of Kamakura-period Buddhism. See also Foard 1980.

23. This argument has been put forth eloquently by Swyngedouw 1976, 1979. My argument here is mainly drawn from these two essays.

24. For early Christianity and the way in which it was incorporated into the reigning plurality of religious traditions, see Harrington 1980, 318–36.

25. "The freer and more personal this decision [about faith] becomes, however, the greater the possibility that the prime referent for the symbolization of religious needs will diminish the particularistic value of being religious" (Swyngedouw 1976, 303).

26. A fairly detailed explanation of these tendencies in traditional Japanese Buddhism can be found in Cooke 1974. His discussion of the F.A.S. is particularly interesting in this regard.

27. The flourishing of the new religions is certainly traceable to the radical demographic dislocations of the postwar period. Davis (1977) points out that in 1950, 70 percent of the Japanese people lived in the countryside. By 1963, this had changed completely; 70 percent now lived in cities. The loss of the war undoubtedly played a role as well in these developments, the new religions providing a renewed sense of Japanese identity.

28. This figure includes those people associated with movements outside Buddhism as well.

29. This is also seen somewhat in what Michihito et al. (1979) call the "vitalistic conception of salvation" characteristic of many of the new religious movements in Japan. See Michihito et al., 1979.

30. Heilman (1982a) was referring to Orthodox Judaism, but the notion of "working through" orthodoxy in the face of modernity would apply to all orthodoxies, indeed, all religious faiths.

31. This also suggests that theoretical interpretation that proceeds without careful interaction with empirical research will be of limited value. In my opinion this has been one of the most glaring shortcomings of theoretical work in this area.

32. The most prominent spokesmen of this perspective have been Wilson (1966) and David Martin (1978).

33. Andrew Greeley has been a prominent advocate of this perspective. See, for example, Greeley 1972. More recently Theodore Caplow and his associates concluded from the Middletown III project that religion seems to have become more, rather than less, important to the life of the community and to Middletown residents (Caplow, Bahr, and Chadwick 1983).

34. There are exceptions to this, e.g., Clifford Geertz's essay "Religion as a Cultural System" (1973). Robert Bellah's work on "symbolic realism" is also an effort at the methodological level to confront religion in this way. See his article "Christianity and Symbolic Realism" (1970b) and also his essays on religious change and evolution in *Beyond Belief* (1970a).

# Selected Bibliography

The following is a list of books, articles, dissertations, and other materials that bear most directly upon the subject of this book.

Adorno, Theodor, and Max Horkheimer
    1972    *Dialectic of Enlightenment*. New York: Herder and Herder.
Ahlstrom, Sydney
    1972    *A Religious History of the American People*. New Haven: Yale University Press.
Aries, Phillipe
    1962    *Centuries of Childhood*. New York: Vintage.
    1977    "The Family and the City." *Daedalus*, Spring, 227–35.
Astin, Alexander W.
    1977    *Four Critical Years*. San Francisco: Jossey-Bass.
Aviad, Janet O'Dea
    1983    *Return to Judaism: Religious Renewal in Israel*. Chicago: University of Chicago Press.
Banks, J. A.
    1981    *Victorian Values: Secularism and the Size of Families*. London: Routledge and Kegan Paul.
Baron, Salo W.
    1967    *A Social and Religious History of the Jews*. New York: Columbia University Press.
Barrett, Donald
    1982    *A World Christian Encyclopedia*. Nairobi: Oxford University Press.
Bell, Daniel
    1964    *The Radical Right*. New York: Doubleday.
    1973    *The Coming of Post-industrial Society*. New York: Basic Books.
    1976.    *The Cultural Contradictions of Capitalism*. New York: Basic Books.
    1977    "A Return of the Sacred?" *British Journal of Sociology* 28, no. 4:419–50.

Bellah, Robert N.
   1970a   *Beyond Belief: Essays on Religion in a Post-traditional World.*
            New York: Harper and Row.
   1970b   "Christianity and Symbolic Realism." *Journal for the Scientific
            Study of Religion* 9, no. 2:89–99.
   1976    "New Religious Consciousness and the Crisis in Modernity."
            In *The New Religious Consciousness,* edited by Charles Y.
            Glock and Robert N. Bellah. Berkeley: University of Califor-
            nia Press.

Bendroth, Margaret
   1983    "The Search for 'Women's Role' in American Evangelicalism:
            1930–1980." Paper presented at the Conference on Evangeli-
            calism and Modern America, Wheaton College, Wheaton,
            Illinois, 13–15 April.

Berger, Brigitte, and Peter Berger
   1983    *The War over the Family.* New York: Doubleday.

Berger, Peter L.
   1963    "A Market Model for the Analysis of Ecumenicity." *Social Re-
            search* 30, no. 1:79.
   1967a   *The Sacred Canopy.* New York: Doubleday.
   1967b   "A Sociological View of the Secularization of Theology,"
            *Journal for the Scientific Study of Religion* 6:3–16.
   1979a   *The Heretical Imperative.* Garden City: Doubleday.
   1979b   "Religion and the American Future." In *The Third Century,*
            edited by S. M. Lipset. Chicago: University of Chicago
            Press.
   1983    "The Third World as a Religious Idea." *Partisan Review* 50,
            no. 2:183–96.

Berger, Peter L., Brigitte Berger, and Hansfried Kellner
   1973    *The Homeless Mind.* New York: Vintage.

Bibby, Reginald, and Merlin Brinkerhoff
   1973    "The Circulation of the Saints." *Journal for the Scientific Study
            of Religion* 12:273–85.
   1983    "The Circulation of the Saints Revisited." *Journal for the Sci-
            entific Study of Religion* 22, no. 3:253–62.

Blackwood, Larry
   1979    "Social Change and Commitment in the Work Ethic." In *The
            Religious Dimension,* edited by Robert Wuthnow. New York:
            Academic.

Boese, H.
   1983    "Missions Come Full Circle." *Alliance Witness,* May, 20–26.

Bolich, Gregory
   1980    *Karl Barth and Evangelicalism.* Downers Grove, Ill.: Inter-
            Varsity.

Bouma, Gary
   1973    "Beyond Lenski: A Critical Review of Recent Protestant

Ethic Research," *Journal for the Scientific Study of Religion* 12, no. 2:141–53.

1979      "The 'Real' Reason One Conservative Church Grew." *Review of Religious Research* 20:127–37.

Brint, Steven

1982      "Stirrings of Oppositional Elite? The Social Base and Historical Trajectory of Upper White Collar Dissent in the United States, 1960–1980." Ph.D diss., Harvard University.

Bruce, Dickson, Jr.

1974      "Religion, Society, and Culture in the Old South: A Comparative View." *American Quarterly* 26 (October): 399–416.

Bruce-Briggs, B., ed.

1979      *The New Class?* New Brunswick: Transaction.

Bulka, Reuven P.

1983      "Orthodoxy Today: An Analysis of the Achievements and the Problems." In *Dimensions of Orthodox Judaism*, edited by Reuven P. Bulka. New York: KTAV Publishing House.

Calder, Jenni

1977      *The Victorian Home.* Boston: B. T. Batsford.

Campbell, Douglass F., and Dennis Magill

1968      "Religious Involvement and Intellectuality among University Students." *Sociological Analysis* 29:79–93.

Caplow, Theodore, Howard M. Bahr, and Bruce A. Chadwick

1983      *All Faithful People: Change and Continuity in Middletown's Religion.* Minneapolis: University of Minnesota Press.

Carroll, Jackson W., Douglas W. Johnson, and Martin E. Marty

1979      *Religion in America: 1950 to Present.* New York: Harper and Row.

Carson, D. A.

1982      "Gundry on Matthew: A Critical Review." *Trinity Journal*, n.s. 3:77.

Carter, Paul A.

1968      "The Fundamentalist Defense of the Faith." In *Change and Continuity in Twentieth Century America: The 1920's*, edited by John Braeman, Robert Bremner, and David Brody. Columbus, Ohio: Ohio State University Press.

Cauthen, Kenneth

1962      *The Impact of American Religious Liberalism.* New York: Harper and Row.

Chiles, Robert E.

1965      *Theological Transition in American Methodism: 1790–1935.* Nashville: Abingdon.

Clark, Gordon H.

1963      *Karl Barth's Theological Method.* Philadelphia: Presbyterian and Reformed Publishing Co.

Cohen, Jere
    1980    "Rational Capitalism in Renaissance Italy." *American Journal of Sociology* 85:1340–55.

Cohen, Steven M.
    1983    "The 1981–82 National Survey of American Jews." *American Jewish Yearbook* 83:89–110.

Collins, Randall
    1980    "Weber's Last Theory of Capitalism: A Systematization." *American Journal of Sociology* 45:925–42.
    1983    "The Weberian Revolution of the High Middle Ages." In *Crises in the World-System*, edited by Albert Bergesen. Beverly Hills: Sage.

Cooke, Gerald
    1974    "Traditional Buddhist Sects and Modernization in Japan." *Japanese Journal of Religious Studies* 1, no. 4:267–330.

Cord, Robert L.
    1982    *Separation of Church and State: Historical Fact and Current Fiction.* Fayetteville: Lambe.

Costas, Orlando E.
    1977    "The USA: A Mission Field for Third World Christians?" *Review and Expositor* 74 (September): 183–97.

Cuddihy, John Murray
    1978    *No Offense: Civil Religion and Protestant Taste.* New York: Seabury.

Dahl, Robert A.
    1956    *A Preface to Democratic Theory.* Chicago: University of Chicago Press.

Davis, Winston Bradley
    1977    *Toward Modernity: A Developmental Typology of Popular Religious Affiliations in Japan.* East Asia Papers, no. 12. Ithaca, N.Y.: Cornell University Press.

Dayton, Donald W.
    1976    *Discovering an Evangelical Heritage.* New York: Harper and Row.

Douglas, Mary
    1966    *Purity and Danger.* London: Routledge and Kegan Paul.

Dunn, James D. G.
    1983    "The Authority of Scripture according to Scripture." *Churchman* 96:2.

Earhart, Byron
    1982    *Japanese Religion: Unity and Diversity.* Belmont, Calif.: Wadsworth.

Eger, Max
    1980    "Modernization and Secularization in Japan: A Polemical Essay." *Japanese Journal of Religious Studies* 7, no. 1:7–24.

Eisenstadt, Shmuel
    1956    *From Generation to Generation: Age Groups and Social Structure*. Glencoe, Ill.: Free Press.

Ellul, Jacques
    1957    *The Technological Society*. New York: Knopf.
    1967    *The Political Illusion*. New York: Vintage

Epstein, Benjamin R., and Arnold Forster
    1967    *The Radical Right*. New York: Vintage

Esposito, John L.
    1982    *Women in Muslim Family Law*. Syracuse: Syracuse University Press.

Etzioni, Amatai
    1984    *An Immodest Agenda*. New York: McGraw-Hill.

Fanfani, Amintore
    1955    *Catholicism, Protestantism, and Capitalism*. New York: Sheed and Ward.

Foard, James H.
    1980    "In Search of a Lost Reformation; A Reconsideration of Kamakura Buddhism." *Japanese Journal of Religious Studies*. 7, no. 4:261–91.

Fowler, Robert Booth
    1982    *A New Engagement: Evangelical Political Thought, 1966–1976*. Grand Rapids: Eerdmans.

Furniss, Norman F.
    1954    *The Fundamentalist Controversy: 1918–1931*. New Haven: Yale University Press.

Gallup Opinion Index
    1977    *Religion in America*. Princeton: Princeton Religious Research Center.

Gaspar, Louis
    1963    *The Fundamentalist Movement*. Paris: Mouton and Co.

Geertz, Clifford
    1973    "Religion as a Cultural System." In *The Interpretation of Cultures*. New York: Basic Books.

Geisler, Norman
    1981    *Decide for Yourself: How History Views the Bible*. Grand Rapids: Zondervan.

Gittelson, Natalie
    1984    "American Jews Rediscover Orthodoxy." *New York Times Magazine*, September 30, 41–71.

Glock, Charles, and Rodney Stark
    1965    *Religion and Society in Tension*, Skokie, Ill.: Rand McNally.
    1966    *Christian Beliefs and Anti-Semitism*. New York: Harper and Row.

Goode, William
    1963    *World Revolution and Family Patterns*. New York: Free Press.

Gordon, Michael
    1975    *The American Family in Socio-historical Perspective.* New York: St. Martin's.

Gouldner, Alvin
    1979    *The Future of Intellectuals and the Rise of the New Class.* New York: Oxford University Press.

Greeley, Andrew
    1972    *Unsecular Man.* New York: Dell.

Greeley, Andrew, and William McCready, and Kathleen McCourt
    1976    *Catholic Schools in a Declining Church.* Kansas City: Sheed and Ward.

Green, Robert W.
    1959    *Protestantism and Capitalism: The Weber Thesis and Its Critics.* Boston: Heath.
    1973    *Protestantism, Capitalism, and Social Science.* Lexington, Mass.: Heath.

Greven, Philip
    1977    *The Protestant Temperament: Patterns of Child-Rearing, Religious Experience, and the Self in Early America.* New York: Knopf.

Griffith, Ernest S., John Plamanatz, and J. Roland Pennock
    1956    "Cultural Prerequisites to a Successfully Functioning Democracy: A Symposium." *American Political Science Review* 50 (March): 101–37.

Guelich, Robert A.
    1982    *The Sermon on the Mount.* Waco, Tex.: Word.

Gundry, Robert
    1982    *Matthew: A Commentary on His Literary and Theological Art.* Grand Rapids: Eerdmans.

Gusfield, Joseph
    1957    "The Problem of Generations in an Organizational Structure." *Social Forces* 35:323–30.
    1963    *Symbolic Crusade: Status Politics and the American Temperance Movement.* Urbana, Ill.: University of Illinois Press.

Habermas, Jurgen
    1979    *Communication and the Evolution of Societies.* Boston: Beacon.

Hacker, Andrew, ed.
    1983    *A Statistical Portrait of the American People.* New York: Vilarig.

Hambrick, Charles H.
    1974    "Tradition and Modernity in the Religious Movements in Japan." *Japanese Journal of Religious Studies* 3, nos. 2–3:217–52.

Hammel, George M.
    1908    *The Passing of the Saloon: An Authentic and Official Presention of the Anti-liquor Crusade in America.* Cincinnati: Tower.

Hammond, Philip E., and James Davison Hunter
    1984    "On Maintaining Plausibility: The World View of Evangeli-
             cal College Students." *Journal for the Scientific Study of Reli-*
             *gion* 23, no. 3:221–38.

Hammond, Phillip E., and Kirk Williams
    1976    "The Protestant Ethic Thesis: A Social-Psychological Assess-
             ment." *Social Forces* 54, no. 3:579–89.

Handwalt, Barbara
    1977    "Childrearing among the Lower Classses of Late Medieval
             England." *Journal of Interdisciplinary History* 8, no. 1:1–22.

Handy, Robert
    1953    "The Protestant Quest for a Christian America: 1830–1930."
             *Church History* 23, no. 1:8–20.

    1971    *A Christian America.* New York: Oxford University Press.

Hareven, Tamara K.
    1977    "Family Time and Historical Time." *Daedalus,* Spring, 55–
             70.

Harrington, Ann M.
    1980    "The Kakure Kirishitan and Their Place in Japan's Religious
             Tradition." *Japanese Journal of Religious Studies* 7, no. 4:318–
             36.

Harris, C. C.
    1983    *The Family and Industrial Society.* London: George Allen and
             Unwin.

Heberle, Rudolph
    1951    *Social Movements: An Introduction to Political Sociology.* New
             York: Appleton.

Heilman, Samuel C.
    1976    *Synagogue Life.* Chicago: University of Chicago Press.
    1982a   "The Many Faces of Orthodoxy." *Modern Judaism* 2, no.
             1:23–51.
    1982b   "The Many Faces of Orthodoxy, Part II." *Modern Judaism* 2,
             no. 2:171–98.

Hennesey, James
    1981    *American Catholics.* New York: Oxford University Press.

Henry, Carl F. G.
    1976–79 *God, Revelation, and Authority.* 4 vols. Waco, Tex.: Word.

Henry, Paul B.
    1974    *Politics for Evangelicals.* Valley Forge: Judson.

Himmelfarb, Harold S., and R. Michael Loar
    1984    "National Trends in Jewish Ethnicity: A Test of the Polariza-
             tion Hypothesis." *Journal for the Scientific Study of Religion*
             23, no. 2:140–54.

Hodgson, Marshall G. S.
    1974    *The Venture of Islam.* Vol. 3. Chicago: University of Chicago
             Press.

Hofstadter, Richard
    1970    "The Revolution in Higher Education." In *Paths of American Thought*, edited by Arthur M. Schlesinger, Jr., and Morton White. Boston: Houghton Mifflin.

Hoge, Dean R.
    1976    "Changes in College Students' Value Patterns in the 1950s, 1960s and 1970s." *Sociology of Education* 19:155–63.
    1981    *Converts, Dropouts, Returnees: A Study of Religious Change among Catholics.* New York: Pilgrim.

Hoge, Dean R., and Jann L. Hoge
    1984    "Period Effects and Age Effects Influencing Values of Alumni in the Decade after College." *Social Forces* 62, no. 4:941–63.

Hoge, Dean, and David Roozen, eds.
    1979    *Understanding Church Growth and Decline, 1950–1978.* New York: Pilgrim.

Horden, William
    1959    *The Case for a New Reformation Theology.* Philadelphia: Westminster.

Hourani, Albert
    1962    *Arabic Thought in the Liberal Age, 1798–1939.* London: Oxford University Press.

Hudson, Winthrop
    1961    *American Protestantism.* Chicago: University of Chicago Press.

Hunsberger, Bruce
    1978    "Religiosity of College Students: Stability and Change over Years at University." *Journal for the Scientific Study of Religion* 17:159–64.

Hunter, James Davison
    1980    "The Young Evangelicals and the New Class." *Review of Religious Research* 22, no. 2:155–69.
    1982    "Operationalizing Evangelicalism: A Review, Critique and Proposal." *Sociological Analysis* 42, no. 4:363–72.
    1983a    *American Evangelicalism: Conservative Religion and the Quandary of Modernity.* New Brunswick, N. J.: Rutgers University Press.
    1983b    "The Liberal Reaction." In *The New Christian Right: Mobilization and Legitimation*, edited by Robert Liebman and Robert Wuthnow. Hawthorne, N. Y.: Aldine.
    1984    "Religion and Political Civility: The Coming Generation of American Evangelicals." *Journal for the Scientific Study of Religion* 23, no. 4:364–80.
    1985    "Conservative Protestantism." In *The Sacred in a Secular Society*, edited by Phillip E. Hammond. Berkeley and Los Angeles: University of California Press.

1986    "The Modern Malaise: Assessing the Costs of Modernity." In *Making Sense of Modern Times: Peter L. Berger and the Vision of Interpretive Sociology*, edited by James Davison Hunter and Stephen C. Ainlay. London: Routledge and Kegan Paul.

Hutchison, William R., ed.
1968    *American Protestant Thought: The Liberal Era*. New York: Harper and Row.

Hyman, Herbert H., Charles R. Wright, and John Shelton Reed
1975    *The Enduring Effects of Education*. Chicago: University of Chicago Press.

Ibrahim, Saad Eddin
1984    "Egypt's Islamic Militancy Revisited." American University in Cairo. Unpublished manuscript.

Issac, Rys
1982    *The Transformation of Virginia: 1740–1790*. Chapel Hill: University of North Carolina Press.

Iwao, Munakata
1976    "The Ambivalent Effects of Modernization on Traditional Folk Religion of Japan." *Japanese Journal of Religious Studies* 3, nos. 2–3:99–126.

Jacquet, Constant H. ed.
1981    *Yearbook of American and Canadian Churches*. Nashville: Abingdon.

Jeffrey, Kirk
1972    "The Family as Utopian Retreat from the City: The Nineteenth Century Contribution." *Soundings* 55, no. 1:21–41.

Jencks, Christopher, and David Riesman
1969    *The Academic Revolution*. New York: Doubleday.

Kelley, Dean
1972    *Why Conservative Churches Are Growing*. New York: Harper and Row.

Kirkpatrick, Jeane
1979    "Politics and the New Class." In Bruce-Briggs 1979.

Kitagawa, Joseph M.
1966    *Religion in Japanese History*. New York: Columbia University Press.

Kristol, Irving
1979    *Two Cheers for Capitalism*, New York: Basic Books.

Lasch, Christopher
1977    *Haven in a Heartless World*. New York: Basic Books.
1978    *The Culture of Narcissism*. New York: W. W. Norton.
1984    *The Minimal Self: Psychic Survival in Troubled Times*. New York: W. W. Norton.

Laslett, Barbara
1973    "The Family as a Public and Private Institution: An Histori-

cal Perspective." *Journal of Marriage and the Family*, August, 480–94.

Laslett, Peter
    1972    *Household and Family in Past Time*. Cambridge: Cambridge University Press.
    1977    *Family Life and Illicit Love in Earlier Generations*. Cambridge: Cambridge University Press.

Latourette, K. S.
    1943    *A History of the Expansion of Christianity*. New York: Harper.

Lawrence, David
    1976    "Procedural Norms and Tolerance: A Reassessment." *American Political Science Review* 70:80–100.

Lenski, Gierhard
    1963    *The Religious Factor*. New York: Doubleday.

Liebman, Charles
    1965    "Orthodoxy in American Jewish Life." *American Jewish Yearbook* 66:21–97.
    1983a    "Orthodoxy in American Life." In *Dimensions of Orthodox Judaism*, edited by Reuven P. Bulka, 55–56. New York: KTAV Publishing House.
    1983b    "Orthodox Judaism Today." In *Dimensions of Orthodox Judaism*, edited by Reuven Bulka, 106–20. New York: KTAV Publishing House.

Lippmann, Walter
    1929    *A Preface to Morals*. New York: Macmillan.

Lipset, Seymour Martin
    1979    "The New Class and the Professoriate." In *Bruce-Briggs* 1979.

Lipset, Seymour Martin, and Earl Raab
    1970    *The Politics of Unreason*. New York: Harper and Row.
    1981    The Election and the Evangelicals." *Commentary* 71, no. 3:25–32.

Loveland, Anne C.
    1980    *Southern Evangelicals and the Social Order: 1800–1860*. Baton Rouge: Louisiana State University Press.

Lynd, Robert S., and Helen Merrell Lynd
    1929    *Middletown: A Study in American Culture*. New York: Harcourt, Brace and Co.
    1937    *Middletown in Transition*. New York: Harcourt, Brace and Co.

Machlup, Fritz
    1962    *The Production and Distribution of Knowledge in the United States*. Princeton: Princeton University Press.

Mannheim, Karl
    1952    "The Problem of Generations." In *Essays in the Sociology of Knowledge*. New York: Oxford University Press

Marcuse, Herbert
    1960    *Reason and Revolution*. Boston: Beacon.
    1964    *One-dimensional Man*. Boston: Beacon.

Marsden, George
    1980    *Fundamentalism and American Culture*. New York: Oxford University Press

Marshall, Gordon
    1982    *In Search of the Spirit of Capitalism*. New York: Columbia University Press.

Martin, Bernard
    1978    "Conservative Judaism and Reconstructionism." In *Movements and Issues in American Judaism*, edited by Bernard Martin. Westport, Conn.: Greenwood.

Martin, David
    1978    *Toward a General Theory of Secularization*. New York: Harper and Row.

Marty, Martin
    1970    *Righteous Empire*. New York: Dial.

Mathews, Donald G.
    1977    *Religion in the Old South*. Chicago: University of Chicago Press.

Matsunaga, Daigan, and Alicia Matsunaga
    1974    *Foundation of Japanese Buddhism*. Los Angeles: Buddhist Book International.

McClelland, David
    1961    *The Achieving Society*. Princeton: Van Nostrand.

McFarland, Neill H.
    1967    *The Rush Hour of the Gods: A Study of New Religions in Japan*. New York: Macmillan.

McGuire, Merideth
    1982    *Pentecostal Catholics*. Philadelphia: Temple.

McLoughlin, William
    1955    *Billy Sunday Was His Real Name*. Chicago: University of Chicago Press.
    1959    *Modern Revivalism: Charles Grandison Finney to Billy Graham*. New York: Ronald Press.

Mead, Sidney
    1975    *The Nation with the Soul of a Church*. New York: Harper and Row.

Mencken, H. L.
    1924    *Prejudices: Fourth Series*. New York: Knopf.

Meyer, Michael A.
    1978    "Reform Judaism." In *Movements and Issues in American Judaism*, edited by Bernard Martin. Westport, Conn.: Greenwood.

Michihito, Tsushima, Nishiyama Shigeru, Shimazono Susumu, and
     Shiramizu Hiroko
     1979     "The Vitalistic Conception of Salvation in Japanese New Re-
               ligions: An Aspect of Modern Religious Consciousness."
               *Japanese Journal of Religious Studies* 6, nos. 1–2 (March/June):
               139–61.
Moberg, David O.
     1965     *Inasmuch.* Grand Rapids: Eerdmans.
     1972     *The Great Reversal: Evangelicalism and Social Concern.* Phil-
               adelphia: Lippincott.
Moreland, John Kenneth
     1958     *Millways of Kent.* Chapel Hill: University of North Carolina
               Press.
Morgan, Edmund S.
     1966     *The Puritan Family.* New York: Harper and Row.
Murakami, Shigeyoshi
     1980     *Japanese Religion in the Modern Century.* Tokyo: University of
               Tokyo Press.
Nisbet, Robert
     1980     *A History of the Idea of Progress.* New York: Basic Books.
Noll, Mark
     1979     "Christian Thinking and the Rise of the American Univer-
               sity." *Christian Scholars Review* 9, no. 1:3–16.
     1983     "Evangelicals and the Study of the Bible." Paper presented at
               the Conference on Evangelicalism and Modern America,
               Wheaton College, Wheaton, Illinois, 13–15 April.
Ostling, Richard
     1982     "The New Missionary." *Time*, December 27, 52–56.
Paloma, Margaret
     1982     *The Charismatic Movement: Is There a New Pentecost?* Boston:
               Twayne.
Pivar, David J.
     1973     *Purity Crusade: Sexual Morality and Social Control, 1868–
               1900.* Westport, Conn.: Greenwood.
Podhoretz, Norman
     1979     "The Adversary Culture and the New Class." In Bruce-Briggs
               1979.
Pope, Liston
     1976     *Millhands and Preachers.* New Haven: Yale University Press.
Prothro, James, and Charles Grigg
     1966     "Fundamental Principles of Democracy." *Journal of Politics*
               22:276–94.
Quebedeaux, Richard
     1974     *The Young Evangelicals: Revolution in Orthodoxy.* New York:
               Harper and Row.

Queen, Stuart A., and Robert W. Habenstein
    1967    *The Family in Various Cultures*. New York: Lippincott.

Rahman, Fazlur
    1968    *Islam*. New York: Doubleday.
    1981    "The Roots of Islamic Neo-fundamentalism." In *Change and the Muslim World*, edited by Phillip H. Stoddard, David C. Cuthell, and Margaret W. Sullivan. Syracuse: Syracuse University Press.

Ramm, Bernard
    1983    *After Fundamentalism: The Future of Evangelical Theology*. San Francisco: Harper and Row.

Reichley, A. James
    1986    "Religion and the Future of Politics." *Political Science Quarterly* 101, 1:23–47.

Ribuffo, Leo
    1983    *The Old Christian Right: The Protestant Far Right from the Great Depression to the Cold War*. Philadelphia: Temple University Press.

Rieff, Philip
    1966    *The Triumph of the Therapeutic*. New York: Harper and Row.

Rifkin, Jeremy
    1979    *The Emerging Order*. New York: Ballantine.

Robertson, H. M.
    1933    *Aspects of the Rise of Economic Individualism: A Criticism of Max Weber and His School*. Cambridge: Cambridge University Press.

Rogers, Jack, and Donald McKim
    1979    *The Authority and Interpretation of the Bible: A Historical Approach*. New York: Harper and Row.

Roof, Wade Clark
    1982    "America's Voluntary Establishment: Mainline Religion in Transition." *Daedalus*, Winter, 165–84.

Roy, Ralph Lord
    1960    *Communism and the Churches*. New York: Harcourt, Brace and Co.

Samuelsonn, Kurt
    1961    *Religion and Economic Action*. New York: Basic.

Sandeen, Ernest
    1968    *The Origins of Fundamentalism*. New York: Fawcett.
    1970    *The Roots of Fundamentalism*. Chicago: University of Chicago Press.

Sciolino, Elaine
    1984    "American Catholics: A Time for Challenge." *New York Times Magazine*, November 4, 40–101.

Selsnick, Gertrude, and Stephen Steinberg
    1969    *The Tenacity of Prejudice*. New York: Harper and Row.

Sennett, Richard
 1974 *The Fall of Public Man*. New York: Vintage.
Sharot, Stephen
 1976 *Judaism: A Sociology*. New York: Holmes and Meier.
Shils, Edward
 1972 "The Intellectuals and the Powers: Some Perspectives for Comparative Analysis." In *The Intellectuals and the Powers*, Chicago: University of Chicago Press.
Shipley, Maynard
 1927 *War on Modern Science: A Short History of Fundamentalist Attacks on Evolution and Modernism*. New York: Knopf
Shorter, Edward
 1977 *The Making of the Modern Family*. New York: Basic Books.
Shupe, Anson, and William Stacey
 1983 "The Moral Majority Constituency." In *The New Christian Right*, edited by Robert Liebman and Robert Wuthnow. New York: Aldine.
Smith, H. W.
 1975 Strategies of Social Research, Englewood Cliffs, N.J.: Prentice-Hall.
Smith, Robert J.
 1974 *Ancestor Worship in Contemporary Japan*. Stanford: Stanford University Press.
Smith, Timothy L.
 1967 "Protestant Schooling and American Nationality, 1800–1850." *Journal of American History* 53, no. 4:679–95.
 1976 *Revivalism and Social Reform: American Protestantism on the Eve of the Civil War*. Gloucester, Mass.: Peter Smith.
Smith, Wilfred Cantwell
 1957 *Islam in Modern History*. Princeton: Princeton University Press.
Sombart, Werner
 1915 *The Quintessence of Capitalism*. New York: E. P. Dutton.
Spero, Shubert
 1978 "Orthodox Judaism." In *Movements and Issues in American Judaism*, edited by Bernard Martin. Westport, Conn.: Greenwood.
Stark, Rodney
 1963 "On the Incompatibility of Religion and Science: A Survey of American Graduate Students." *Journal for the Scientific Study of Religion* 3:3–20.
Stark, Rodney, and Charles Glock
 1968 *American Piety: The Nature of Religious Commitment*. Berkeley: University of California Press.

Steinfels, Peter
    1979    *The Neo-Conservatives*. New York: Simon and Schuster.

Stoddard, Phillip H., David C. Cuthell, and Margaret W. Sullivan, eds.
    1981    *Change and the Muslim World*. Syracuse: Syracuse University Press.

Sullivan, John, George E. Marcus, Stanley Feldman, and James E. Pierseson
    1981    "The Sources of Political Tolerance: A Multivariate Analysis." *American Political Science Review* 75:92–106.

Swyngedouw, Jan
    1976    "Secularization in a Japanese Context." *Japanese Journal of Religious Studies* 3, no. 4:283–307.
    1979    "A Few Sociological Notes on Sacredness and Japan." *Japanese Religions* 11, no.1:17–38.

Tawney, R. H.
    1938    *Religion and the Rise of Capitalism*. Harmondsworth: Penguin.

Tilly, Charles, and Louise Tilly
    1980    "Stalking the Bourgeois Family." *Social Science History* 4, no. 2:251–60.

Vaillancourt, Jean-Guy
    1980    *Papal Power: A Study of Vatican Control over Lay Catholic Elites*. Berkeley: University of California Press.

Varacalli, Joseph A.
    1983    *Toward The Establishment of Liberal Catholicism in America*. Washington: University Press of America.

Voll, John Obert
    1982    *Islam: Continuity and Change in the Modern World*. Boulder, Co.: Westview Press.

Walkerhowe, Daniel
    1975    "American Victorianism as a Culture." *American Quarterly* 27 no. 5:507–30.

Wallerstein, Immanuel
    1974    *The Modern World-System I: Capitalism, Agriculture and the Origins of the European World-Economy in the Sixteenth Century*. New York: Academic.
    1983    "Crises: The World Economy, the Movements, and the Ideologies." In *Crises in the World-System*, edited by Albert Bergesen. Beverly Hills: Sage.

Weber, Max
    1958    *The Protestant Ethic and the Spirit of Capitalism*. New York: Scribner's.

Weber, Paul J.
    1982    "Examining the Religious Lobbies." *This World* 1:97–107.

Wenger, Robert E.
    1973    "Social Thought in American Fundamentalism, 1918–1933."
            Ph.D diss. University of Nebraska

Williams, John Alden
    1980    "Veiling as a Political and Social Phenomenon." *Islam and
            Development*, edited by John L. Esposito. Syracuse: Syracuse
            University Press.

Wilson, Bryan R.
    1966    *Religion in a Secular Society.* London: C. A. Watts

Wright, Louis B.
    1943    *Religion and Empire: The Alliance between Piety and Commerce
            in English Expansion, 1558–1625, and History of the Church.*
            Chapel Hill: University of North Carolina Press.

Wrigley, Anthony E.
    1977    "Reflections on the History of the Family." *Daedalus*, Spring,
            71–85.

Wuthnow, Robert
    1976    "Recent Patterns of Secularization: A Problem of Genera-
            tions?" *American Sociological Review* 41:850–67.
    1980    "World Order and Religious Movements." In *Studies in the
            Modern World–System*, edited by Albert Bergesen. New York:
            Academic Press.
    1982    "The Moral Crisis in American Capitalism." *Harvard Business
            Review*, March–April, 76–84.
    1983a   "Cultural Crises." In *Crises in the World-System*, edited by
            Albert Bergesen. Beverly Hills: Sage.
    1983b   "The Political Rebirth of American Evangelicals." In *The
            New Christian Right: Mobilization and Legitimation*, edited by
            Robert Liebman and Robert Wuthnow. Hawthorne: Aldine.
    1987    "Religious Movements and Counter-Movements in North
            America." In *New Religious Movements and Rapid Social
            Change*, edited by James Beckford. Paris: UNESCO.

Wyatt-Brown, Bertram
    1972    "Religion and the Formation of Folk Culture: Poor Whites
            of the Old South." In *The Americanization of the Gulf Coast:
            1803–1850*, edited by Lucius F. Ellsworth, Pensacola, Fla.:
            Historic Pensacola Preservation Board.

Yanagawa, Kei'ichi, and Abe Yoshiya
    1978    "Some Observations on the Sociology of Religion in Japan."
            *Japanese Journal of Religious Studies* 5:5–27.

Yankelovich, Daniel
    1974    *The New Morality: A Profile of American Youth in the 1970s.*
            New York: McGraw-Hill.
    1981    *New Rules.* New York: Random House.

Zahrnt, Heinz
    1969    *The Question of God: Protestant Theology in the Twentieth Cen-*

*tury*, trans. R. Wilson. New York: Harcourt Brace Jovanovich.

Zelan, Joseph
    1968    "Religious Apostasy, Higher Education and Occupational Choice." *Sociology of Education* 41:370–79.

Zijderveld, Anton
    1970    *The Abstract Society*. New York: Doubleday.

# Index